The Tools of Policy Formulation

NEW HORIZONS IN PUBLIC POLICY

Series Editor: Wayne Parsons, *Professor of Public Policy, Queen Mary, University of London, UK*

This series aims to explore the major issues facing academics and practitioners working in the field of public policy at the dawn of a new millennium. It seeks to reflect on where public policy has been, in both theoretical and practical terms, and to prompt debate on where it is going. The series emphasizes the need to understand public policy in the context of international developments and global change. New Horizons in Public Policy publishes the latest research on the study of the policymaking process and public management, and presents original and critical thinking on the policy issues and problems facing modern and post-modern societies.

Titles in the series include:

Success and Failure in Public Governance
A Comparative Analysis
Edited by Mark Bovens, Paul 't Hart and B. Guy Peters

Consensus, Cooperation and Conflict
The Policy Making Process in Denmark
Henning Jørgensen

Public Policy in Knowledge-Based Economies
Foundations and Frameworks
David Rooney, Greg Hearn, Thomas Mandeville and Richard Joseph

Modernizing Civil Services
Edited by Tony Butcher and Andrew Massey

Public Policy and the New European Agendas
Edited by Fergus Carr and Andrew Massey

The Dynamics of Public Policy
Theory and Evidence
Adrian Kay

Ethics and Integrity of Governance
Perspectives Across Frontiers
Edited by Leo W.J.C. Huberts, Jeroen Maesschalck and Carole L. Jurkiewicz

Public Management in the Postmodern Era
Challenges and Prospects
Edited by John Fenwick and Janice McMillan

The Tools of Policy Formulation
Actors, Capacities, Venues and Effects
Edited by Andrew J. Jordan and John R. Turnpenny

The Tools of Policy Formulation

Actors, Capacities, Venues and Effects

Edited by

Andrew J. Jordan

Tyndall Centre for Climate Change Research, School of Environmental Sciences, University of East Anglia, UK

John R. Turnpenny

School of Politics, Philosophy, Language and Communication Studies, University of East Anglia, UK

NEW HORIZONS IN PUBLIC POLICY

Edward Elgar
PUBLISHING

Cheltenham, UK • Northampton, MA, USA

Published by
Edward Elgar Publishing Limited
The Lypiatts
15 Lansdown Road
Cheltenham
Glos GL50 2JA
UK

Edward Elgar Publishing, Inc.
William Pratt House
9 Dewey Court
Northampton
Massachusetts 01060
USA

Co-published by LIAISE

A catalogue record for this book
is available from the British Library

Library of Congress Control Number: 2014954960

This book is available electronically in the **Elgar**online
Social and Political Science subject collection
DOI 10.4337/9781783477043

ISBN 978 1 78347 703 6 (cased)
ISBN 978 1 78347 705 0 (paperback)
ISBN 978 1 78347 704 3 (eBook)

Typeset by Servis Filmsetting Ltd, Stockport, Cheshire
Printed and bound in Great Britain by T.J. International Ltd, Padstow

To
Hannah, who helped this to happen
. . . and Susan, Lauren and Ben, who provided the very best antidote to
academic writing

Contents

Figures

Tables

Contributors

Camilla Adelle is a Senior Research Fellow at the Centre for the Study of Governance Innovation within the Department of Political Sciences at the University of Pretoria, South Africa.

Giles Atkinson is Professor of Environmental Policy in the Department of Geography and Environment and Associate, Grantham Research Institute for Climate Change and Environment, London School of Economics and Political Science, UK.

Stephan Bartke is a Research Fellow at the Helmholtz Centre for Environmental Research (UFZ), Leipzig, Germany.

David Benson is a Lecturer in the Department of Politics and the Environment and Sustainability Institute (ESI), University of Exeter, UK.

Christina Boswell is Professor of Politics in the School of Social and Political Science, University of Edinburgh, UK.

Thomas Bournaris is a Lecturer in the Department of Agricultural Economics at the Aristotle University of Thessaloniki, Greece.

David Christopherson held an EPSRC Internship at the Centre for Integrated Energy Research, University of Leeds, UK.

Eefje Cuppen is Assistant Professor at Delft University of Technology, the Netherlands.

Bryan Evans is Associate Professor in the Department of Political Science, Ryerson University, Toronto, Ontario, Canada.

Colin Fleming is Research Fellow in the School of Social and Political Science, University of Edinburgh, UK.

Catherine D. Gamper is an Economist at the Public Governance and Territorial Development Directorate, OECD, Paris.

Matthijs Hisschemöller is an Associate Professor in the Institute for Environmental Studies (IVM), Vrije Universitet, University of Amsterdam, the Netherlands.

Michael Howlett is a Professor in the Department of Political Science, Simon Fraser University, Burnaby BC, Canada; Lee Kuan Yew School of Public Policy, National University of Singapore, Singapore.

Andrew J. Jordan is a Professor of Environmental Policy at the Tyndall Centre for Climate Change Research, School of Environmental Sciences, University of East Anglia, UK.

Petrus Kautto is a Senior Researcher at the Environmental Governance Studies Unit, Finnish Environment Institute and the Academy of Finland Postdoctoral Researcher.

Hanna Kuittinen is a Researcher at the Innovation Strategies Division of Tecnalia at Derio, Spain.

Lars Ege Larsen is a PhD Fellow at the Department of Planning and Development at Aalborg University, Denmark.

Markku Lehtonen is Research Fellow with the Sussex Energy Group, Science Policy Research Unit (SPRU), University of Sussex, UK and at the Groupe de Sociologie Pragmatique et Réflexive (GSPR), École Des Hautes Etudes En Sciences Sociales (EHESS), France.

Rob Maas is a Senior Scientific Advisor at the National Institute for Public Health and the Environment – RIVM – in the Netherlands.

Will McDowall is a Senior Research Associate at the UCL Energy Institute, University College London, London, UK.

Andrea Migone is Director of Research and Outreach/Directeur de la recherche et de l'information at the Institute of Public Administration of Canada/L'Institut d'administration publique du Canada.

Christina Moulogianni is a PhD candidate in the Department of Agricultural Economics at the Aristotle University of Thessaloniki, Greece.

Marta Pérez-Soba is a Senior Researcher with Team Earth Informatics at ALTERRA, part of the Environmental Science Group of the Wageningen University and Research Centre, the Netherlands.

Tim Rayner is a Senior Research Associate at the Tyndall Centre for Climate Change Research in the School of Environmental Sciences at the University of East Anglia, UK.

Eugénia Rodrigues is a Research Fellow in the School of Social and Political Science, University of Edinburgh, UK.

Sanna-Riikka Saarela is a Researcher at the Finnish Environment Institute (SYKE), Helsinki, Finland.

Graham Spinardi is a Senior Research Fellow in the School of Social and Political Science, University of Edinburgh, UK.

Barbara Sterk was a Researcher in the Plant Production Systems Group, Wageningen University, Wageningen, the Netherlands.

Seck L. Tan is a Post-Doctoral Fellow at the Lee Kuan Yew School of Public Policy, National University of Singapore, Singapore.

Peter Taylor is a Professor of Sustainable Energy Systems in the Centre for Integrated Energy Research, University of Leeds and a member of both the Energy Research Institute and the Sustainability Research Institute, University of Leeds, UK.

Catrinel Turcanu is Head of the Nuclear Science and Technology Studies Unit at the Belgian Nuclear Research Centre (SCK-CEN), Mol, Belgium.

John R. Turnpenny is a Senior Lecturer in the School of Politics, Philosophy, Language and Communication Studies, University of East Anglia, UK.

Paul Upham is a Senior University Research Fellow at the Centre for Integrated Energy Research and the Sustainability Research Institute at the University of Leeds, UK.

Martin K. van Ittersum is a Professor in the Plant Production Systems Group, Wageningen University, the Netherlands.

Sachin Warghade is an Assistant Professor, School of Habitat Studies, Tata Institute of Social Sciences, Mumbai, India.

Sabine Weiland is a Senior Research Fellow at the Environmental Policy Research Centre (FFU) at the Freie Universität Berlin, Germany.

Adam Wellstead is an Assistant Professor of Environmental and Energy Policy, Faculty of Social Sciences, Michigan Technological University, Houghton, Michigan, USA.

Steve Yearley is Professor of the Sociology of Scientific Knowledge in the School of Social and Political Science, University of Edinburgh, UK.

Preface

Policy analysts are accustomed to thinking in terms of policy tools and instruments. It is widely accepted that they have been developed for, and are used at, all stages of the policy process. But in the public policy literature, most of the debate amongst academics and practitioners has focused on only one sub-set of the main tools and instruments – those for *implementing* the policy objectives that have been decided upon. Well-known policy implementation instruments include regulations, subsidies, taxes, and voluntary agreements, to name but a few.

But another, equally extensive subset of policy tools has remained in the analytical shadows and thus somewhat outside the mainstream of public policy research. This includes tools for forecasting and exploring the future (for example, scenarios), tools for identifying and recommending policy options (for example, cost–benefit, cost-effectiveness and multi-criteria analysis) and tools for exploring different problem conceptions and frames (for example, participatory brainstorming). These tools have typically been developed to perform a different set of tasks, namely collecting, condensing and interpreting different kinds of policy relevant knowledge. Together, they are the tools of *policy formulation.*

Policy formulation is a very different stage to those that precede and/ or follow it in the well-known policy cycle. If agenda setting is essentially concerned with identifying where to go, the policy formulation stage is about determining *how* to get there. In many ways, policy formulation is the point at which some of the most critical decisions of all are made. As such, it constitutes the very essence of governing. But in comparison with the other policy stages, it is relatively difficult to observe directly and hence to study. Consequently, policy researchers have struggled to study it. But among more and more policy researchers there is a feeling that it may well constitute the final 'missing link' in policy analysis.

It should be completely natural to conceive of or study policy formulation by thinking in terms of the tools used. Yet, some time ago we were struck by the fact that the policy instruments literature remains fixated on the implementing instruments. This book represents our combined effort to remedy what we perceive to be a significant gap in our collective understanding of public policy. In it, we present the first book length account of the main policy formulation tools, coupled to an exploration of their origins, the actors involved in their development, the venues in which such tools may (or may not) be used, the capacities of actors to employ them, the uses to which they are put by different policy formulators and the effects that they eventually produce. In doing so, we seek to reveal what is gained by bringing the study of policy formulation tools back into the mainstream of public policy research. We say 'back into' because having been a central, possibly even *the* central concern of policy analysts in the 1950s and 1960s, tools in general gradually fell out of fashion. As Chapter 1 explains, although the developers of certain tools, many of them specialists in economics, computing and systems analysis, continued to push ahead in the quest for greater policy relevance, policy researchers gradually turned their attention either to the detailed design of policy implementing instruments or to understanding and explaining wider policy dynamics.

We believe that now is absolutely the right time to look afresh at policy formulation tools. Policy analysts are becoming more interested in policy formulation – one of *the* most poorly understood of all the policy process stages. Interest in policy design is also re-awakening as the number of complex problems such as climate change stack up. And having invested heavily in the tools in the past, the tool developers and practitioners are desperate to understand how – and indeed if – they perform in practice, a task which requires bridges to be built with public policy researchers.

Conscious that this still has the look and feel of a very promising subfield 'in the making', we devote considerable space in Chapter 1 to elaborating a typology and definition of the main policy formulation tools, and an analytical framework for understanding their uses and effects. Given the current state of knowledge, we believe it is especially important to engage in such foundational activities to ensure that future work develops in a cumulative fashion.

Acknowledgements

We have incurred very many debts during the writing of this book. We would like to start by thanking the European Commission for funding its production, through an EU Seventh Framework Programme Network of Excellence 'LIAISE', co-led by Sander Janssen and Klaus Jacob. We hope that the book encourages the post-LIAISE entity to more fully consider the relationship between policy tools (including but not limited to computerized models) and their uses and effects (including but not limited to impact assessment) in a more holistic, reflexive and theoretically informed fashion. LIAISE kindly funded two intensive workshops in 2012 and 2013 at which initial versions of all the chapters were presented and thoroughly discussed, and a rather innovative buy back deal which means this book is provided fully 'open access' to all in perpetuity. We would especially like to thank the authors of the chapters for believing that there is more to be gained by working together to look across the numerous and highly tool-specific literatures, and for responding so positively to our detailed editorial comments. We would also like to thank Sander and Klaus for co-managing the detailed administrative process of securing the open access agreement with the publisher. Finally, we are indebted to Alfie Kirk for administering the two workshops.

After the workshops were completed, David Benson and Tim Rayner kindly assisted us in the long process of turning the papers into a book manuscript. We are especially grateful to Tim for his 'award-winning' attention to detail and to David who turned our random scribbles into an analytical framework. We would also like to thank the four referees who provided very useful feedback on our original book proposal and to the members of the PPE reading group at UEA for their comments on Chapters 1 and 13. Responsibility for any remaining errors and omissions in these two chapters rests entirely with us, the editors and our co-authors.

Finally, we would like to thank Alex Pettifer and his team at Edward Elgar Publishing for producing and marketing this book.

Abbreviations

CBA   cost–benefit analysis
EU   European Union
GDP   gross domestic product
MCA   multi-criteria analysis
NGO   non-governmental organization
OECD Organisation for Economic Co-operation and Development

PART I

Introduction

1. The tools of policy formulation: an introduction

John R. Turnpenny, Andrew J. Jordan, David Benson and Tim Rayner

INTRODUCTION

What techniques or means do public policymakers use in their attempts to achieve policy goals? The roles of what may be termed policy instruments, tools and methods (Howlett 2011, p. 22) have attracted a great deal of attention. It is generally accepted that policy tools and instruments exist at all stages of the policy process (Howlett 2011, p. 22), ranging from policy formulation through to *ex post* evaluation (Dunn 2004). But in the public policy literature, much of the debate has focused on instruments for *implementing* agreed policy objectives, such as regulations, subsidies, taxes and voluntary agreements (Hood 1983; Hood and Margetts 2007; Salamon 2002). Recently, a second category of implementing instruments has been identified: *procedural* tools (Howlett 2000). These include education, training, provision of information and public hearings. These are procedural in the sense that they seek to affect outcomes indirectly through manipulating policy processes. The manner in which both types of instruments are selected and deployed aims to change the substance, effects and outcomes of policy, by sending signals about what is to be achieved and how government is likely to respond to target groups. Understanding these processes is critical to a better understanding of governing activities. Adopting an 'instruments perspective' on these activities has arguably contributed significantly to the study of public policy and governance in general (Lascoumes and Le Galés 2007).

There is, however, also a third category of policy tools and instruments which has largely remained outside the mainstream of policy research.[1] These tools have typically been developed by researchers and policy practitioners with the aim of performing a rather different set of tasks to the implementing instruments described above. They are variously referred to as 'analytical tools' (Radin 2013, p. viii), 'policy-analytic methods' (Dunn

2004, p. 6), decision support tools or 'analycentric' tools (Schick 1977). Radin rightly devotes a whole chapter of her book charting the development of the field of policy analysis to telling their story – on the grounds that they constitute the 'tools of the [policy analysis] trade' (Radin 2013, p. 143).

From Radin's and others' accounts it soon becomes clear that what we shall term *policy formulation tools*[2] come in many different shapes and sizes. Initially, they were designed to support a very specific task, namely the 'collection of as much information and data as were available to help decision makers address the substantive aspects of the problem at hand' (Radin 2013, p. 23). Nowadays, these tools are regarded as a means to address many other policy formulation tasks, for example understanding the nature of policy problems, estimating how they might change over time and clarifying or even eliminating some of the many possible policy response options. In fact, to understand these tools fully, we argue that policy researchers must view them in the context of the broader activities and processes of policy formulation.

Policy formulation is a very different activity to policy implementation. It is an important phase devoted to 'generating options about what to do about a public problem' (Howlett 2011, p. 29), and is inherent to most, if not all, forms of policymaking. If the agenda-setting stage in the well-known policy cycle is essentially concerned with identifying *where* to go, the policy formulation stage is all about *how* to get there (Hill 2009, p. 171). If policy formulation is 'a process of identifying and addressing possible solutions to policy problems or, to put it another way, exploring the various options or alternatives available for addressing a problem', then developing and/or using *policy formulation tools* is a vital part of that process (Howlett 2011, p. 30). We suggest that, much more than for other policy stages, it is very hard to conceive of policy formulation – let alone properly study it – without thinking in terms of tools. Based on Dunn (2004), these include tools for *forecasting* and exploring future problems through the use of scenarios, tools for identifying and *recommending* policy options (for example, cost–benefit, cost-effectiveness and multi-criteria analyses) and tools for exploring *problem structuring* or *framing* (for example, brainstorming, boundary analysis and argumentation mapping).

In recent years, the number of potentially deployable policy formulation tools has expanded massively (for an indication of what is currently in the toolbox, see Dunn (2004) and Radin (2013, p. 146)). They include types that may be considered to fall into both positivist and post-positivist categories, with the latter inspired by critiques of the role of technocratic analysis and a concern to address subtle influences that act to condition the content of policy, such as material forces, discourses and ideologies (Fischer 1995). Yet, the policy tools and instruments literature remains stubbornly fixated on implementation instruments. And while there are many individual literatures that seek to promote and/or inform the use of specific policy formulation tools, the policy analysis literature is relatively silent on how, why, when, by whom, in what settings and with what effects, the various tools are used in practice. To the extent that they devote attention to formulation as a specific stage in the policy process, most textbooks frame it around understandings of processes, interests and expertise. In many ways, the limited academic treatment that policy formulation tools have received in the period following the Second World War is symptomatic of a wider division in policy analysis between those doing policy research and those engaged in policy practice. For reasons explored more fully below, when it comes to policy formulation tools, practice has arguably run well ahead of research. In this book, we seek to bring these two wings of the policy analysis community into a closer dialogue.

More specifically, in this book we investigate – for the first time – what might be gained by bringing the study of policy formulation tools back into the mainstream of public policy research. The policy instruments literature might lead us to expect each policy formulation tool to impart a specific 'spin' (Salamon 2002) on ensuing policy dynamics. Certain other literatures, such as science and technology studies (Stirling 2008) or planning (Owens and Cowell 2002), also suggest that certain tools serve to influence policy outputs in a variety of ways. For example, use of cost–benefit analysis to develop policy has the potential to marginalize concern for equity in some sectors, in favour of outputs perceived as the most efficient use of scarce resources. But does this actually happen in practice, and if so how? At present, the various literatures are too fragmented and too detached from public policy theory to tell us. There has, of course, been a huge amount written on individual formulation tools, often by scholars who have invested a great deal in developing them and advocating their use. They are understandably eager to see them being taken up and used by policymakers. Yet we will show that many tool developers and promoters are often vexed – and sometimes deeply disappointed – by their apparent lack of use, or even outright misuse by practitioners (Shulock 1999). We feel that this is another topic which would benefit from greater interaction between those who (to employ another well-known distinction) analyse *for* policy, and those who conduct analysis *of* policy.

We believe that now is a particularly opportune moment to look afresh at policy formulation tools. Policy researchers and analysts are becoming more interested in policy formulation – arguably one of *the* most poorly understood of all the policy process stages; indeed, there is a growing belief that it may constitute the final, 'missing link' (Hargrove 1975) in policy analysis. Interest in policy design is also re-awakening, partly because of the rise to prominence of ever more complex problems such as energy insecurity and climate change that defy standard policy remedies (Howlett et al. 2014). And having invested heavily in tools in the past, tool promoters and policy practitioners are eager to understand how – and indeed if – they perform in practice.

The remainder of this chapter is divided as follows. The second section takes a step back by examining the main *actors, processes and venues* of policy formulation in a very general sense. The third section scours the various existing literatures to explore in more detail the development of the various policy formulation *tools* that could in principle be used in these venues. It also charts the subsequent turn away from these tools in mainstream public policy research, and explores some of the reasons why interest in policy formulation has recently undergone a renaissance. Section 4 explores the analytical steps that will be needed to re-assemble the various literatures into a more coherent sub-field of policy research, revolving around a series of common foci. To that end, we propose a new definition and typology of tools, and offer a means of re-assembling the field around an analytical framework focused on actors, venues, capacities and effects. We conclude by introducing the rest of the book, including our final, concluding chapter.

POLICY FORMULATION: ACTORS, PROCESSES AND VENUES

Actors: Who are the Policy Formulators?

The literature on policy formulation has expanded significantly in the last three decades (Wolman 1981; Thomas 2001; Wu et al. 2010; Howlett 2011). According to Howlett (2011, p. 29), it is the stage of the policy process 'in which options that might help resolve issues and problems recognized at the agenda-setting stage are identified, refined, appraised and formalized'. The process of identifying and comparing alternative actions is said to shape the subsequent stage – that of decision making (Linder and Peters 1990). During the formulation stage, policy analysts will typically have to confront trade-offs between legitimate public demands for action, and the political, technical and financial capabilities to address them. For many scholars, policy formulation is the very essence of public policy analysis, which Wildavsky (1987, pp. 15–16) characterized as how to understand the relationship between 'manipulable means and obtainable objectives'.

But who formulates public policies? It is generally recognized that policy formulation is a critically important but relatively inscrutable stage of the policy process (Wu et al. 2010, p.47), with many different actors interacting, often under intense and focused political pressure from special advisers, lobbyists and interest groups. There is also a widespread assumption that unlike the agenda-setting stage (in which the media, politicians and the public may be more transparently involved), policy formulation is much more of a political netherworld, dominated by those with specialist knowledge, preferred access to decision makers or a paid position in a particular government agency or department (Howlett and Geist 2012, p.19). Even though their precise role may be hard to fathom, in principle all may use or seek to use formulation tools. As we shall see, this creates a distinct set of challenges for those (like us) who want to study the use of the tools, or those who wish to design and/or promote them.

In many ways, policy formulation is the stage which the policy analysis community was originally established to understand and inform (Radin 2013, p.5). Meltsner's (1976) pioneering study of the still relatively inchoate policy analysis community distinguished between analysts with political skills and those with more technical skills. As we shall see, it was the latter that took the lead in developing and applying the first policy formulation tools. The more general literatures have focused on the role of politicians and bureaucrats (Craft and Howlett 2012, p.80). Pioneering accounts of policymaking (such as Page and Jenkins (2005) and Fleischer (2009)) have, for example, focused on the 'policy process generalists' who rarely, if ever, deal with policy tools in a substantive way and have very little training in formal policy analysis.

More specific studies of policy formulation have sought to offer a more detailed stocktake of the different policy analysts who are typically involved (Howlett 2011, p.31). Together, these actors are often said to constitute a policy advisory system, comprising: *decision makers* (chiefly politicians); *knowledge producers and/or providers*; and *knowledge brokers* (Howlett 2011, pp.31–33). Other typologies have differentiated the main participants in relation to their location (in other words, core actors – professional policy analysts, central agency officials and others); and level of influence (in other words, public sector insiders; private sector insiders; and outsiders) (Howlett 2011, p.33). Precisely who formulates policy is ultimately an empirical question. The point which we wish to make is that it is important to appreciate the variety of actors who might be involved in policy formulation activities, as they might well have rather different motives and capabilities for using particular tools – a matter to which we now turn.

Policy Formulation Processes and Tasks

One of the most common ways to comprehend the process of policy formulation is to break it down into constituent steps or tasks. For Wolman
(1981), policy formulation comprises several 'components', each impacting
heavily on overall policy performance. In his view, the 'formulating
process' starts with the 'conceptualization of the problem' by policymakers
(Wolman 1981, p. 435). Like Wolman, Thomas (2001, pp. 216–217) also
identifies an initial '[a]ppraisal phase' of data collection where 'critical
issues . . . [are] identified' by stakeholders. However, as many commentators
have observed, 'problems' themselves are not self-evident or neutral, with
Wolman (1981, p. 437) arguing that they may be contested, subjective or
socially constructed and may change through time in response to societal
values. *Problem characterization* could therefore be considered to be an
extension of the agenda-setting process. Policymakers may select certain
forms of evidence to support action on specific issues, or issues themselves
may be productive of certain types of evidence (see for example, Kingdon
2010; Baumgartner and Jones 1991).

Having established the existence of a policy problem (or problems)
through some form of data collection, the various policy-relevant dimensions of the problem are then *evaluated* to determine their causes and extent,
chiefly as a basis for identifying potential policy solutions. Inadequate
understanding at this stage creates a need for what Wolman (1981, p. 437)
terms '[t]heory evaluation and selection'. While the point is often made
that causation tends to be difficult to precisely establish, Wolman observes
that 'the better the understanding is of the causal process . . . the more
likely . . . we will be able to devise public policy to deal with it successfully' (Wolman 1981, p. 437). Understanding causation, as Wolman puts
it, is also reliant on the generation of adequate theoretical propositions in
addition to relevant data on which to support them. For Wu et al. (2010,
p. 40) '[u]nderstanding the source of the problem' is an unavoidable part of
formulation. They also make the point that rarely is there 'full agreement
over . . . underlying causes' (Wu et al. 2010, p. 40). Like initial problem
characterization, evaluation of the causes of a problem may thus involve
political conflict as different actors seek to apportion blame, reduce their
perceived complicity or shape subsequent policy responses in line with
their interests. These characteristics strongly condition the type of tools
used.

Once a broad consensus has been reached on the nature and extent
of the problem(s), policymakers turn to consider appropriate responses.
From the initial information gathering and analysis of causes, formulators engage in the '[s]pecification of objectives' (Wolman 1981, p. 438) or

'[c]larifying policy objectives' (Wu et al. 2010, p. 40) stage. Initially, this third step of *objective specification* can involve the determination of the objectives to be met and the timescales for action (Wu et al. 2010). Again, disagreements over objectives can quickly ensue but once they are established, as a fourth step, specific policy options can be *assessed* and recommendations made on policy design(s). Because any particular problem may have multiple potential solutions, each with differing costs and benefits, these options require comparative assessment to guide decision making. As Howlett (2011, p. 31) puts it, this part of the formulation process 'sees public officials weighing the evidence on various policy options and drafting some form of proposal that identifies which of these options will be advanced to the ratification stage'.

Prior to the adoption of the final policy, it undergoes a fifth step – *design*. Having determined objectives, various means are available for selection from the tool box (for example Howlett 2011; Jordan et al. 2012; Jordan et al. 2013b). Determining the preferred policy mix is central to design considerations. While typologies also abound in the instruments literature, four main categories are evident: regulations; market-based instruments; voluntary approaches; and informational measures (Jordan et al. 2013b). In addition, the instrument of public spending or budgeting may also be identified (see for example, Russel and Jordan 2014). Policymakers select from these instruments according to a range of considerations that are both internal and external to the instrument. This stage of formulation could, according to Wolman (1981, pp. 440–446), consequently involve the weighing-up of several factors: the 'causal efficacy' of the policy; 'political feasibility'; 'technical feasibility'; any 'secondary consequences' resulting from the design; instrument type (regulations or incentives); and the capacity of implementation structures.

As above, all the steps including this one may become deeply contested. After all, the final architecture of the policy could, once implemented, create winners and losers via processes of positive and negative feedback (Jordan and Matt 2014). One means of dissipating distributional conflict throughout the entire formulation process is to engage in what Thomas (2001, p. 218) terms consensus building or 'consolidation', whereby agreement is sought between the various policy formulators and their client groupings. We shall show that a number of tools have been developed specifically for this purpose. But while '[a]nticipating and addressing the . . . concerns of the various powerful social groups is essential', consultation may create associated transaction costs such as the slowing down of policy adoption (Wu et al. 2010, p. 41). A decision can be taken – the subsequent stage of the policy process – once agreement has been reached on the chosen course of action.

These five tasks constitute the standard steps or tasks of policy formulation. During the 1960s and 1970s, when the policy analysis movement was still in its infancy, policy formulation was depicted as though it were both analytically and in practice separate from agenda setting and decision making. It was the stage where policy analysts 'would explore alternative approaches to "solve" a policy problem that had gained the attention of decision makers and had reached the policy agenda' (Radin 2013, p. 23). In doing so, policy formulation could be 'politically deodorized' (Heclo 1972, p. 15) in a way that allowed policy specialists to draw on the state of the art in policy tools and planning philosophies, to ensure that policy remained on as rationally determined a track as possible (Self 1981, p. 222).

As we saw above, and shall explain more fully below, it soon became apparent that the politics could not be so easily squeezed out of policy formulation by using tools or indeed any other devices. It also became clear that some of the formulation tasks could overlap or be missed out entirely. Indeed, policy formulation may not culminate in the adoption of a discrete and hence settled 'policy': on the contrary, policies may continue to be (re) formulated throughout their implementation as tool-informed learning takes place in relation to their operational effectiveness and associated outcomes (Jordan et al. 2013a). As we shall show, many policy analysts responded to these discomforting discoveries by offering ever more strident recommendations on how policy formulation *should* be conducted (Vining and Weimer 2010; Dunn 2004); notably fewer have studied how it is *actually* practiced (Colebatch and Radin 2006; Noordegraaf 2011). In the following section we shall explore what a perspective focusing on tools and venues offers by way of greater insight into the steps and the venues of policy formulation.

The Venues of Policy Formulation

Policy formulation – like policymaking more generally – occurs in particular venues. Baumgartner and Jones (1991, p. 1045) have termed these 'venues of policy action', going on to define them as 'institutional locations where authoritative decisions are made concerning a given issue' (Baumgartner and Jones 1993, p. 32). More specifically, Timmermans and Scholten (2006, p. 1105) suggest that the venues 'are locations where policies originate, obtain support, and are adopted as binding decisions'.

To date, this notion has been explored in most depth within the 'venue shopping' literature on agenda setting; a particular sub-field of policy analysis that examines how interest groups strategically shift their demands for realizing political goals between different venues in multi-level systems of governance (Pralle 2003). Several types of venue have been detected, including, inter alia, within federal, state and local governments plus within international organizations (Pralle 2003), European Union institutions and national governments (Beyers and Kerremans 2012), and various trans-governmental co-operation mechanisms (Guiraudon 2002). Venues can include 'formal political arenas such as legislatures, executives and the judiciary, but also the media and the stock market' and so-called 'scientific venues such as research institutes, think-tanks and expert committees' (Timmermans and Scholten 2006, p. 1105). A particular role is also ascribed to the use of scientific evidence by actors to achieve agenda-setting demands in venue shopping strategies (Timmermans and Scholten 2006).

On this basis, any attempt to categorize venues for policy formulation should be cognizant of the institutional space itself and, significantly, the type of evidence used. With respect to the former, when examining formulation we can more neatly divide venues by functional power rather than institutional level or actor group. Here, in terms of relative power, it is national government executives that are still arguably dominant globally, despite increasing shifts towards multi-level governance (Jordan and Huitema 2014). To give greater analytical purchase to our conceptualizations we therefore build on Peters and Barker (1993), Baumgartner and Jones (1993) and Timmermans and Scholten (2006), and define policy formulation venues as *institutional locations, both within and outside governments, in which certain policy formulation tasks are performed, with the aim of informing the design, content and effects of policymaking activities.*

Policy formulation venues can in principle exist at different levels of governance (nation state versus supra/sub-national); and within or outside the structures of the state. There has been much work (see for example Barker 1993; Parsons 1995; Halligan 1995) on classifying policy advice systems, and two dimensions identified therein are particularly important for understanding policy formulation venues more generally. First, are the policy formulation tasks conducted externally or internally to the executive; in other words, *where* is the task undertaken? For example, internal venues may be populated wholly or mainly by serving officials or ministers and may include departmental inquiries, government committees and policy analysis units (for examples of the latter, see Page 2003). External venues may encompass legislative, governmental or public inquiries and involve non-executive actors such as elected parliamentarians, scientific advisors, think tanks, industry representatives and non-governmental organizations.

Second, are official (executive) or non-official sources of knowledge employed, that is, what knowledge *sources* do policy formulators draw upon? We distinguish between executive-sanctioned or derived knowledge,

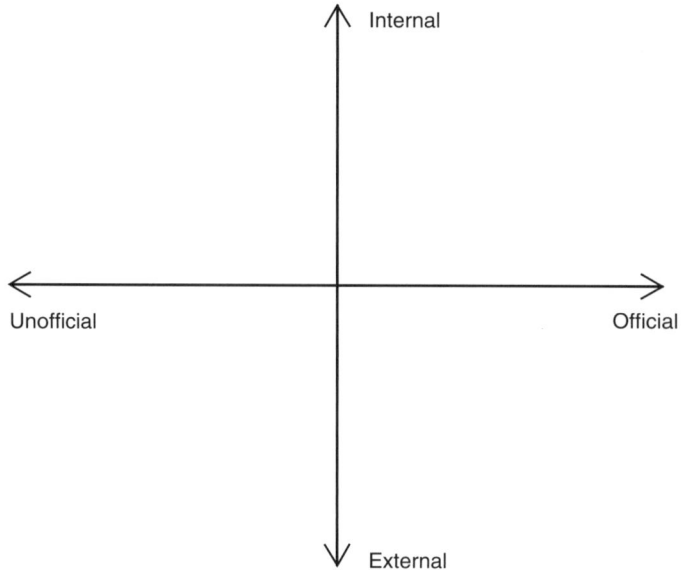

Figure 1.1　The main venues of policy formulation

and unofficial sources that may include surveys, research which appears as non-formal reports, and the outputs of research networks and public intellectuals. Rather closed processes of policy formulation can occur within internal venues using officially derived evidence, in contrast to more open external venues that draw upon non-official forms of knowledge.

Neither of these two dimensions – well known to scholars of policy advisory systems (Craft and Howlett 2012, p. 87) – are binary. For example, there are varying degrees to which the entirety of a policy formulation task is undertaken internally or externally, and varying degrees to which different types of evidence are employed at different times or for different purposes. We therefore propose to represent them by means of a 2×2 matrix (Figure 1.1).

THE TOOLS OF POLICY FORMULATION

The Analycentric Turn in Policy Analysis

As noted above, tools have always had a special place in the history of policy analysis. Modern policy analysis is often held to have developed in earnest from the 1940s onwards (DeLeon 2006). Harold Lasswell's (1971) 'policy sciences of democracy' provided a vision of analysis that drew together different academic disciplines as well as different actors in the policy formulation process – academic, bureaucrat and the person in the street – to address public problems. This was a multidisciplinary endeavour that sought to solve problems in an applied fashion (Dunn 2004, p. 41). While departments of public administration and politics were supposed to supply an understanding of how political and administrative systems operated, the assumption was that the tools of analysis would be produced by technical experts in economics, operations and systems analysis (Dunn 2004, p. 41).

The 1950s and 1960s saw the rise of the professional policy analyst, providing specialist input to policy, and institutions for formalizing such input like the Systems Analysis Unit in the US Defense Department (Radin 2013, p. 14) and, later in the UK, the Central Policy Review Staff, both staffed by experts in the latest tools and methods. The Systems Analysis Unit was charged with implementing one of the very first (and most controversial) systematic policy formulation tools, known as the Programme Planning and Budgeting System (PPBS) (Schultze 1970). The PPBS sought to integrate budgeting and policy development in the quest for greater efficiency and hence more rational decisions.

These tool-driven or 'analycentric' approaches (Schick 1977) initially developed in the fields of defence and budgeting, but from the late 1960s, as the reach of governmental action spread further into fields such as education, health and social care, the scope of analytical activities also expanded (Parsons 1995; Radin 2013, pp. 17–22; DeLeon 2006) almost as a corollary. As Schick (1977, p. 258) observed: 'whenever positive government action has been extended to a new sphere, analytic activity has been sure to follow'. Crucially, the increasingly forceful turn towards analycentric tools and methods embedded a linear-rational approach to analysis of policy problems, in which – to put it simplistically – problems were to be identified and then 'solved' using analytical tools. In his manifesto for the new policy analysis community, Dror (1971, p. 232) famously declared that the 'aim of policy analysis is to permit improvements in decision making and policymaking by allowing a fuller consideration of a broader set of alternatives, with a wider context, with the help of more systematic tools'.

Tools, in other words, were absolutely central to the rapidly emerging field of policy analysis, and were to be taken forward by a new cadre of policy analysts, who operated in small policy analysis units like the Central Policy Review Staff based at the very apex of government. A direct consequence of these developments was a major effort to integrate analytical tools into policy formulation, an activity which until then had, as noted above, been dominated by generalists and those with a legal background (Radin 2013, p. 14). These tools initially drew on techniques from operational research and economic analysis, including methods for assessing the costs and benefits of different policy alternatives, and analysis of interacting parts of complex systems. Tools such as cost–benefit analysis (CBA) and computer models were to be found in the analycentric 'backroom' (Self 1981, p. 222), where political 'irrationalities' could be tempered and policy made more 'rational'. These tools and tool-utilizing skills had originally been developed and honed during the Second World War, but as Radin (2013, p. 14) puts it rather nicely, 'the energy of Americans that had been concentrated on making war in a more rational manner now sought new directions'. The tool specialists found a willing audience amongst politicians and policymakers who were anxious to embark upon new endeavours.

The Turn Away from Policy Formulation Tools

In the Lasswellian perspective, tools were seen as having a central role in the development of an integrated approach that united policy researchers with policy practitioners. But for a number of reasons, things did not quite match up to his vision, and policy formulation tools were gradually marginalized in public policy research and some fell out of favour with policymakers.

First, when used, CBA and integrated forms of planning and budgeting such as the PPBS fell some way short of initial expectations. When the academic backlash came it pushed the study of policy formulation tools back in the direction of the 'cloistered' (Radin 2013, p. 166) backroom of policy research. Tools such as computer modelling and CBA seemed to stand for everything that was bad about positivist and 'technocratic' forms of policy analysis (Goodin et al. 2006, p. 4). Tool specialists were derided as 'econocrats' (Self 1985) and 'whizzkids' (Mintrom and Williams 2013, p. 9). Wildavsky (1987, p. xxvi), never keen on tools even when they were in vogue, viewed policy analysis more as an art and a craft than an exercise in applying 'macro-macho' policy tools such as the PPBS and CBA to solve problems. 'The technical base of policy analysis is weak', he continued. 'Its strengths lie in the ability to make a little knowledge go a long way by combining and understanding of the constraints of a situation with the ability to explore the environment constructively' (Wildavsky 1987, p. 16). Others critiqued the assumption that using tools would take the politics out of policymaking; in practice, politics all too readily intervened (DeLeon and Martell 2006, p. 33). Why, to put it bluntly, should a bureaucrat perform a sophisticated policy assessment employing state-of-the-art tools, when critical policy decisions had already effectively been made? (Shulock 1999, p. 241). Politics could also intervene more insidiously, through the values embodied and reproduced by particular, ostensibly neutral tools. CBA in particular lost legitimacy in certain policy sectors as a result (Owens et al. 2004), though hung on quite tenaciously thereafter. The very idea that policy analysis should seek to provide analytical solutions for 'elites' was challenged; rather, claims were made that analysts should concentrate on understanding the multiple actors that are involved in policy formulation (Hajer and Wagenaar 2003), and uncover the many meanings that they bring to the process and the framings they employ (Radin 2013, p. 162). So while the academic critique of tools and methods were mostly centred on the most positivist, rational variants (in other words, the PPBS and CBA) (Self 1985), its effect was eventually much more wide ranging and long lasting.

Second, policymakers also began to turn away from centralized, tool-driven forms of policy planning. The abolition of PPBS in the 1970s and of the CPRS in the early 1980s, coupled with the rise of a much more explicitly ideological approach to policymaking in the 1980s, led not to the removal of analysis altogether, but changes in the type and tools of analysis demanded. Thus, the rise of private sector management techniques in running public services (in other words, the New Public Management agenda), coupled with desire to reduce the power and scope of bureaucracy, nurtured a demand for a new set of accounting tools for contracting out public services (Mintrom and Williams 2013).

Third, the mainstream of public policy research had long before turned to other research questions. These focused more on attempts (of which Lindblom (1959) is a classic early example) to better understand the policy process itself, not as a series of stages in which rational analysis could/ should be applied, but as a much more complex, negotiated and above all deeply political process. Others built on the claim that policy formulation was actually not especially influential – that policy *implementation*, not formulation, was the missing link – and devoted their energies to post-decisional policymaking processes. Meanwhile, after Salamon's (1989) influential intervention, policy instrument scholars increasingly focused on the selection and effects of the implementing instruments.

Finally, the tool designers and developers became ever more divided into 'clusters of functional interest' (Schick 1977, p. 260). The idea of an integrated policy analysis for democracy was quietly forgotten in the rush to design ever more sophisticated tools. Indeed, some have devoted their entire careers to this task, only later to discover that relatively few policymakers routinely use the tools they had designed (Pearce 1998; Hanley et al. 1990). As Schick (1977, p. 262) had earlier predicted, they believed that the route to usefulness was via ever greater precision and rigour – but it wasn't.

The Turn Back to Policy Formulation Tools

Nowadays, interest in policy formulation tools appears to be growing strongly once again, for several reasons. First, new tasks other than knowledge creation are being found for tools such as CBA and indicators. As noted above, they are seen as a means to implement the New Public Management agenda, for example. According to Boswell et al. (Chapter 11, this volume), they seek to incentivize improvements in performance, monitor progress and ensure political accountability. In many OECD countries, tool use has been institutionalized through systems of Regulatory Impact Assessment (Turnpenny et al. 2009; Nilsson et al. 2008). In developing countries (Chapter 10, this volume), tools are being used to rationalize policymaking in situations where the public sphere is still relatively weak, *vis-à-vis* traditional forms of politics based on patronage.

Second, the emergence of ever more complex policy problems has generated a fresh wave of interest in more sophisticated policy formulation tools such as scenarios and computer-based forms of modelling. There is a growing appreciation amongst practitioners and academics that policies in these areas will not 'design themselves' (Howlett and Lejano 2013, p. 14); according to Lindquist (1992, pp. 128–129), they:

> need new analytical tools that will help them to diagnose and map the external environments of the public agencies, to recognize the inherent tensions and dynamics in these environments as they pertain to policy development and consensus building, and to develop new strategies for 'working' in these environments in the interests both of their political masters and those of the broader communities they serve.

Tools, in other words, are no longer the preserve of technocrats operating in cloistered backrooms, well away from the public gaze. Unfortunately, there remains a lack of understanding of which tools are being used and how well they are performing in relation to this considerably longer list of tasks and purposes. In the UK, the Cabinet Office was sufficiently concerned to institute a wide-ranging review, which called for 'a fundamental change in culture to place good analysis at the heart of policymaking' (Cabinet Office 2000, p. 5). It asserted that 'the use of analysis and modelling in the US is more extensive . . . and of much better overall quality' (Cabinet Office 2000, p. 99), but acknowledged that there was no systematic audit of use across jurisdictions which could be used to identify best practices. Following a major failure in the use of models in UK government, a wide-ranging review was eventually undertaken in 2013 which reported that around 500 computerized models were being used, influencing many billions of pounds of government expenditure (HM Treasury

2013, p. 33). Yet this transformation in the tools of policy formulation being used seems to have escaped the attention of most policy scholars.

Third, the growing interest in policy formulation tools could also be seen as one symptom of the gradual re-discovery of policy design as both a policy goal (in other words, through state-led policymaking) and a research topic (Howlett et al. 2014). Far from reducing the need for state involvement, the emergence of a more complex, networked society and austerity pressures, makes it more important for interventions to be carefully targeted and legitimated (Howlett and Lejano 2013, p. 12). One way the pressure upon the state to discharge these functions manifests itself is in the perceived need for tools to formulate 'better' policies. Several of the chapters in this book (for example, Chapters 3, 9 and 12) make repeated references to tools that seek to engage with complex policy problems that are uniquely interconnected and cross-jurisdictional in their scale and scope, and have a very strong public interest dimension.

Finally, the number of policy formulation tool types has grown significantly in recent years. And as they have emerged from the analycentric 'backroom' (Self 1981, p. 222), the expectation has grown that they will respond more sensitively to changing contextual conditions and public expectations, somewhat addressing Wildavsky's (1987, p. vi) call for policy to be seen as an art and a craft rather than a technocratic exercise in selecting and employing tools to 'solve' problems. In the next section we attempt to bring a greater sense of analytical order to the expanding list of tools, methods, tasks and expectations.

FORMULATION TOOLS: TOWARDS A NEW SUB-FIELD OF POLICY ANALYSIS?

The Literatures on Policy Formulation Tools: Taking Stock

In attempting to move the study of policy formulation tools back into the mainstream of public policy research, we immediately confront a problem – the relative absence of common definitions and typologies. Without these, it is difficult to believe that the literatures discussed above can be telescoped into a new sub-field. We believe that four literatures provide an especially important source of common terms and concepts, which we now briefly summarize.

The first literature describes the internal characteristics and functions of each tool, and/or offers tool kits which seek to assist policy formulators in selecting 'the right tool for the job'. On closer inspection, there are in fact many sub-literatures for all of a vast array of different tools; numerous

classic texts like Dunn (2004) and Rossi et al. (2004) introduce some of
the main ones. Generally speaking, rather fragmented into the main tool
subtypes, and rather rationalistic in its framing, this literature nonetheless remains crucial because it outlines the intrinsic features of each tool.
However (as repeatedly noted above), it does not have a great deal to say
about where, how, why and by whom (in other words, by which actors and
in which venues) they are used, and what effects they (do not) produce.

The second is dominated by typologies. Tools can be typologized in
a number of different ways, for example: by the resources or capacities
they require; by the activity they mainly support (for example, agenda
setting, options appraisal); by the task they perform; and by their spatial
resolution. Radin (2013, p. 145) opts for a more parsimonious framing,
distinguishing between two main types: the more economic tools such
as cost–benefit analysis (CBA) and what she terms the more 'systematic
approaches' such as criteria analysis and political mapping. The problem
is that dividing the field into two does not really offer much typological
variation. In an earlier analysis, we elected to subdivide the main tools into
three main types based on their level of technical complexity (Nilsson et
al. 2008):

- *Simple* tools such as checklists, questionnaires, impact tables or
  similar techniques for assisting expert judgement.
- More *formal* tools, such as scenario techniques, CBA, risk assessment and multi-criteria analysis, which entail several analytical steps
  corresponding to predefined rules, methods and procedures.
- *Advanced* tools which attempt to capture the more dynamic and
  complex aspects of societal or economic development by performing
  computer-based simulation exercises.

At the time, we noted that there was no normative ranking implied in this
typology. We also noted the basic difference between tools (such as scenarios and public participation) with more open procedures and purposes, and
those like CBA that follow a set of standard procedural steps. But we did
not relate these to the policy formulation tasks that tools could or should
perform. We return to the matter of typologies below.

The third literature adopts a more critical perspective (Wildavsky
1987; Shulock 1999; Self 1981), offering words of caution about expecting too much from tools. It appears to have left a deep impression on a
sufficient number of policy analysts, perhaps sufficient to militate against
the development of a new sub-field. However, it is clear that despite these
cautionary words, many tools have been developed and are very heavily
applied in certain venues to routinely produce effects that are not currently

understood. Hence, questions about precisely where, how, why and by whom they are used remain.

A fourth and final literature is more strongly focused on the main venues and processes of policy formulation rather than the tools. In attempting to better understand and explain how policy is made and what influences it, this literature encompasses studies of crucial factors such as the utilization of knowledge in policymaking (Radaelli 1995), and the role of power and institutions (for an excellent summary, see Sabatier 2005). The manner in which power and particular analytical practices are bound up with one another has been explored in planning/geography (see for example, Owens and Cowell 2002) and science and technology studies (Stirling 2008). Other aspects focus on the political demand for evidence-based policymaking (Sanderson 2002; Shine and Bartley 2011). Much of this literature adopts a macro- or a meso-level focus and draws on or develops theory. To the extent that it considers policy formulation tools at all, there is, however, a tendency (although by no means universal) to assume that tools are epiphenomenal and hence not warranting detailed analysis. But we shall argue that without more detailed research, these remain no more than untested assumptions.

Re-assembling the Field: A Definition and a Typology

To move forwards, we draw upon Jenkins-Smith (1990, p. 11) by defining a policy formulation tool as:

> a technique, scheme, device or operation (including – but not limited to – those developed in the fields of economics, mathematics, statistics, computing, operations research and systems dynamics), which can be used to collect, condense and make sense of different kinds of policy relevant knowledge to perform some or all of the various inter-linked tasks of policy formulation.

But what are the main tools of policy formulation and which of the interlinked formulation tasks mentioned in this definition do they seek to address? Today, the range of policy formulation tools is considerably wider and more 'eclectic' (Radin 2013, p. 159) than it was in Lasswell's time. While keenly aware that typologizing can very easily become an end in itself, developing some kind of workable taxonomy nonetheless remains a crucial next step towards enhancing a shared understanding of how policy formulation tools are used in contemporary public policymaking.

We propose that the five policy formulation tasks outlined above – problem characterization, problem evaluation, specification of objectives, policy options assessment and policy design – may be used to structure a typology of policy formulation tools, based on what might be termed the 'textbook' characteristics of what they may be capable of. We also draw on Dunn's (2004, pp. 6–7) schema of three types of tasks associated with policy formulation tools (problem structuring, forecasting and recommending), and de Ridder et al.'s (2007) typology of assessment tools (see Table 1.1). In Table 1.1, the first two tasks of 'problem characterization' and 'problem evaluation' broadly correspond to Dunn's (2004) problem *structuring* – that is, tools that produce information about what problem to solve. The remaining three tasks correspond to Dunn's *forecasting* – hence tools that produce information about the expected outcomes of policies – and also *recommending* – hence tools that produce information about preferred policies.

Following Thomas (2001, p. 218), the consensus building or 'consolidation' that can occur throughout the formulation process may draw on feedback or *consolidation* tools for communicating findings back to policy actors. These can include many of the same sorts of tools presented under 'problem characterization', such as stakeholder meetings, the elicitation of public perceptions and/or expert opinions.

An Analytical Framework

In the rest of this book, a number of experts in policy formulation tools and venues seek to shed new light on the interaction between four key aspects of these tools, which together constitute our analytical framework: *actors, capacities, venues* and *effects*.

Actors

First, we seek to elucidate those *actors* who participate in policy formulation, particularly those that develop and/or promote particular policy formulation tools. The tools literature has often lacked a sense of human agency and, as noted above, the policy formulation literature tended to ignore the tools being used. These two aspects need to be brought together. In this book we therefore seek to know who the actors are and why they develop and/or promote particular tools. Why were particular tools developed, when and by whom? And what values do the tools embody?

Venues

Second, we want to know more about by whom and in which policy formulation *venues* such tools are used, and for what purposes. What factors shape the selection and deployment of particular tools? Again the broader question of agency seems to be largely unaddressed in the four existing literatures summarized above. Tool selection is treated largely as a 'given'; indeed many studies seem to ignore entirely the reasons why policymakers

Table 1.1   A typology of policy formulation tools, linking tools to their potential use in different policy formulation tasks

Policy formulation task	Examples of the policy-relevant information tools may provide	Examples of tools
Problem Characterization	baseline information on policy problems	• environmental, social and economic indicators; • survey data; • statistical reports; • stakeholder evidence
	evidence on problem causation and scale	• geographical information systems; • maps; • expert evidence
	articulation of values through participation	• brainstorming; • boundary analysis; • argumentation mapping
Problem Evaluation	See 'Problem Characterization'	See 'Problem Characterization'
Specification of Objectives	visions on different objectives, futures and pathways	• scenario analysis
Options Assessment	comparison of potential impacts of different options	• cost–benefit and cost-effectiveness analysis; • cost–utility analysis; • multi-criteria analysis; • risk–benefit analysis; • risk assessment
	assessment of past and future trends	extrapolative or forecasting tools, including: • time-series analyses or statistical methods; • informed judgements (for example, Delphi technique); • computer simulations; • economic forecasting; • multi-agent simulation
Policy Design	evaluation of potential effectiveness of different instruments or policy mixes	See 'Options Assessment'

Source: Based on Dunn (2004); de Ridder et al. (2007).

utilize them (or do not). Finally, relatively little is known about how the various tools and venues intersect, both in theory and, as importantly, in practice.

Capacities
Third, we wish to examine the relationship between policy capacity and policy formulation tools. Policy capacity is one of a number of sub-dimensions of state capacity, which together include the ability to create and maintain social order and exercise democratic authority (Matthews 2012). Broadly, it is the ability that governments have to identify and pursue policy goals and achieve certain policy outcomes in a more or less instrumental fashion, that is, 'to marshal the necessary resources to make intelligent collective choices about and set strategic directions for the allocation of scarce resources to public ends' (Painter and Pierre 2005, p. 2). It is known to vary between policy systems and even between governance levels in the same policy system. Policy instruments and tools have long been assumed to have an important influence on policy capacity – if they did not, why use them (Howlett et al. 2014, p. 4)? The fact that they are unevenly used over time, for example, could explain why the policy capacity to get things done also varies across space and time (Bähr 2010; Wurzel et al. 2013).

The chapters of this book seek to examine the relationship between policy capacity and tools in three main ways. First, they conceive of the policy formulation or policy analytic capacities that inhere within each tool (in other words, Table 1.1). For example, scenarios and foresight exercises provide policymakers with the capacity to address the problem characterization and problem evaluation tasks, particularly in situations of high scientific uncertainty. By contrast, tools such as CBA and multi-criteria analysis (MCA) provide a means to complete the policy assessment of option and policy design stages of the policy formulation process.

Second, the chapters also tackle the question of what policy capacities are in turn required by policymakers to employ – and perhaps even more fundamentally to *select* – certain policy formulation tools. For example, relatively heavily procedural tools such as MCA and CBA arguably require specialist staff and specific oversight systems. When these are weak or absent, the use made of tools may tend towards the symbolic. Thus, several questions may be posed. What *capacities* do actors have – or need – to employ specific policy formulation tools? And what factors enable and/ or constrain these capacities?

Finally, the chapters open up the potentially very broad – but equally important – question of what factors might conceivably enable or constrain the availability of these capacities. The fact that critical supporting capacities may not be available in every policy system is something which is raised in several of the chapters.

Effects
Finally, what *effects*, both intended and actual, do the various tools generate when they are employed? As we explained above, our original expectation was that the tools would produce some quite specific epistemic and political effects. But while some evidence is available on their wider effects, much more is required. The policy instruments literature has been struggling to address this question, at least for implementation tools, ever since Salamon (2002, p. 2) speculated that each tool imparts its own distinctive spin or twist on policy dynamics. *Substantive* effects include learning in relation to new means to achieve given policy goals (a feature which is predominant amongst the more structured procedural tools such as CBA, but also computer modelling tools) through to the heuristic-conceptual effects on problem understandings (see for example Chapters 2 and 3, this volume). The *procedural* effects could be similarly wide ranging including (re-)channelling political attention, opening up new opportunities for outsiders to exert influence and uncovering political power relationships. The chapters examine whether or not these and other effects occurred, and whether they were, or were not, originally intended.

Plan of this Book

The chapters are grouped into two main parts. Those in Part II provide – in some cases, for the very first time – a systematic review of the literature on particular tools. They are written by tool experts according to a common template and draw upon examples from across the globe. Given space constraints, we elected to focus on six of the most widely known and commonly advocated tools, which broadly reflect the range of tool types and policy formulation tasks summarized in Table 1.1. Thus, Matthijs Hisschemöller and Eefje Cuppen begin by examining *participatory tools* (Chapter 2), Marta Pérez-Soba and Rob Maas cover *scenarios* (Chapter 3) and Markku Lehtonen reviews *indicators* (Chapter 4). Then, Martin van Ittersum and Barbara Sterk summarize what is currently known about *computerized models* (Chapter 5), Catherine Gamper and Catrinel Turcanu explore forms of *multi-criteria analysis* (Chapter 6) and Giles Atkinson concludes by reviewing the literature on *cost–benefit analysis* (Chapter 7).

The chapters in Part II explore the relationship between actors, venues, capacities and effects from the perspective of each tool. By contrast, the authors in Part III cut across and re-assemble these four categories by looking at tool–venue relationships in Europe, North America and

Asia. Some (for example, Chapters 8 and 9) turn the analytical telescope right around and examine the use made of multiple tools in one venue. Each chapter employs different theories to interpret freshly collected empirical information to test explanations and identify pertinent new research questions. In broad terms, the first two chapters in Part III examine the use of multiple tools in one or more venues, whereas those that follow focus on the application of specific tools in one or more venues. Thus in their chapter, Michael Howlett and colleagues explore the distribution of all tools across many venues in Canada (Chapter 8), whereas John Turnpenny and colleagues explore the use of all the tools in the single venue of policy-level appraisal within Europe (Chapter 9). Sachin Warghade examines the use of two tools in a number of different venues in India (Chapter 10), and Christina Boswell et al. investigate the use of indicators in the UK (Chapter 11). Finally, Paul Upham and colleagues explore the application of a particular type of computerized model in a range of different policy formulation venues in the UK (Chapter 12). In the final Chapter (13), we draw together the main findings of the book and identify pertinent new policy and analytical research challenges. Conscious that this still has the look and feel of a sub-field of policy analysis 'in the making' we attempt to draw on these findings to critically reflect back on our typology, our definition of formulation tools and our analytical framework.

More generally, in Chapter 13 we seek to explore what a renewed focus on policy formulation tools adds to our understanding of three important matters. First, what stands to be gained in respect of our collective understanding of the tools themselves, which as we have repeatedly noted have often been studied in a rather isolated, static and descriptive manner? Second, what does it reveal in relation to policy formulation and policy-making more generally? Policy formulation is arguably the most difficult policy 'stage' of all to study since it is often 'out of the public eye . . . [and] in the realm of the experts' (Sidney 2007, p. 79). Howlett has argued that it is a 'highly diffuse and often disjointed process whose workings and results are often very difficult to discern and whose nuances in particular instances can be fully understood only through careful empirical case study' (Howlett 2011, p. 32). Aware of the challenges, in this book we seek to investigate what a renewed focus on tools is able to add to the current stock of knowledge. In doing so, we seek to directly challenge the conventional wisdom about tools as epiphenomenal, that is, wholly secondary to ideas, interests, power and knowledge. Finally, what does it add to our collective understanding of the politics of policymaking? This is an extremely pertinent question because many of the tools were originally conceived as a means to take the political heat *out* of policymaking.

Rationalism no longer holds the same grip on policy analysis as it once did, but the perceived need to 'design' policy interventions as effectively and as legitimately as possible remains as strong as ever. Therefore, whether or not the tools succeed in these tasks is something we believe will interest mainstream political scientists, as much as policy analysts and experts in the tools.

NOTES

1. Hood and Margetts' (2007) concept of 'detector' tools for harvesting policy relevant information corresponds only to one of a number of different policy formulation tasks.
2. Although we regard the terms tool and instrument as being broadly synonymous, henceforth we use the term 'tools' mainly to differentiate policy formulation tools from policy implementation instruments.

REFERENCES

Bähr, H. (2010), *The Politics of Means and Ends*, Farnham: Ashgate.

Barker, A. (1993), 'Patterns of decision advice processes: a review of types and a commentary on some recent British practices', in B.G. Peters and A. Barker (eds), *Advising West European Governments: Inquiries, Expertise and Public Policy*, Edinburgh: Edinburgh University Press, pp. 20–36.

Baumgartner, F.R. and B.D. Jones (1991), 'Agenda dynamics and policy subsystems', *The Journal of Politics*, **53**, 1044–1074.

Baumgartner, F.R. and B.D. Jones (1993), *Agendas and Instability in American Politics*, Chicago, London: The University of Chicago Press.

Beyers, J. and B. Kerremans (2012), 'Domestic embeddedness and the dynamics of multilevel venue shopping in four EU Member States', *Governance*, **25**, 263–290.

Cabinet Office (2000), *Adding It Up*, London: Cabinet Office.

Colebatch, H.K. and B.A. Radin (2006), 'Mapping the work of policy', in H.K. Colebatch (ed.), *The Work of Policy*, New York: Rowman and Littlefield, pp. 217–226.

Craft, J. and M. Howlett (2012), 'Policy formulation, governance shifts and policy influence', *Journal of Public Policy*, **32** (2), 79–98.

DeLeon, P. (2006), 'The historical roots of the field', in M. Moran, M. Rein and R. Goodin (eds), *The Oxford Handbook of Public Policy*, Oxford: Oxford University Press, pp. 39–57.

DeLeon, P. and C. Martell (2006), 'The policy sciences: past, present and future', in B.G. Peters and J. Pierre (eds), *Handbook of Public Policy*, London: Sage, pp. 31–48.

de Ridder, W., J. Turnpenny, M. Nilsson and A. von Raggamby (2007), 'A framework for tool selection and use in integrated assessment for sustainable development', *Journal of Environmental Assessment Policy and Management*, **9**, 423–441.

Dror, Y. (1971), *Ventures in Policy Sciences*, New York: Elsevier.

Dunn, W. (2004), *Public Policy Analysis: An Introduction*, Upper Saddle River, New Jersey: Pearson/Prentice Hall.

Fischer, F. (1995), *Evaluating Public Policy*, Chicago: Nelson Hall.

Fleischer, J. (2009), 'Power resources of parliamentary executives: policy advice in the UK and Germany', *West European Politics*, **32** (1), 196–214.

Goodin, R., M. Moran and M. Rein (2006), 'The public and its policies', in M. Moran, M. Rein and R. Goodin (eds), *The Oxford Handbook of Public Policy*, Oxford: Oxford University Press, pp. 3–35.

Guiraudon, V. (2002), 'European integration and migration policy: vertical policy-making as venue shopping', *Journal of Common Market Studies*, **38** (2), 251–271.

Hajer, M. and H. Wagenaar (2003), *Deliberative Policy Analysis*, Cambridge: Cambridge University Press.

Halligan, J. (1995), 'Policy advice and the public service', in B. Guy Peters and D.T. Savoie (eds), *Governance in a Changing Environment*, Montreal: McGill-Queen's University Press, pp. 138–172.

Hanley, N., S. Hallett and I. Moffatt (1990), 'Research policy and review 33: why is more notice not taken of economists' prescriptions for the control of pollution', *Environment and Planning A*, **22**, 1421–1439.

Hargrove, E.C. (1975), *The Missing Link: The Study of the Implementation of Social Policy*, Washington: Urban Institute.

Heclo, H. (1972), 'Modes and moods of policy analysis', *British Journal of Political Science*, **2** (1), 131.

Hill, M. (2009), *The Public Policy Process*, 5th edition, Abingdon: Routledge.

HM Treasury (2013), *Review of Quality Assurance of Government Analytic Models*, London: HM Treasury.

Hood, C. (1983), *The Tools of Government*, London: Macmillan.

Hood, C. and H. Margetts (2007), *The Tools of Government in the Digital Age*, Basingstoke: Palgrave.

Howlett, M. (2000), 'Managing the hollow state. Procedural policy instruments and modern governance', *Canadian Public Administration*, **43** (4), 412–431.

Howlett, M. (2011), *Designing Public Policies: Principles and Instruments*, Abingdon: Routledge.

Howlett, M. and S. Geist (2012), 'The policy making process', in E. Araral, S. Fritzen, M. Howlett, M. Ramesh, and X. Wu (eds), *Routledge Handbook of Public Policy*, London: Routledge, pp. 17–28.

Howlett, M. and R. Lejano (2013), 'Tales from the crypt: the rise and fall (and rebirth?) of policy design', *Administration and Society*, **45** (3), 357–381.

Howlett, M., J.J. Woo and I. Mukherjee (2014), 'From tools to toolkits in policy design studies: the new design orientation towards policy formulation research', *Policy and Politics*, **42**, http://dx.doi.org/10.1332/147084414X13992869118596.

Jenkins-Smith, H. (1990), *Democratic Politics and Policy Analysis*, Pacific Grove, CA: Brooks/Cole.

Jordan, A.J. and D. Huitema (2014), 'Innovations in climate policy: the politics of invention, diffusion and evaluation', *Environmental Politics*, **23** (5), 715–734.

Jordan, A. and E. Matt (2014), 'Designing policies that intentionally stick: policy feedback in a changing climate', *Policy Sciences*, **47** (3), 227–247.

Jordan, A.J., M. Bauer and C. Green-Pedersen (2013a), 'Policy dismantling', *Journal of European Public Policy*, **20** (5), 795–805.

Jordan, A., R. Wurzel and A. Zito (2013b), 'Still the century of "new" environmental policy instruments?', *Environmental Politics*, **22** (1), 155–173.

Jordan, A.J., D. Benson, R. Wurzel and A.R. Zito (2012), 'Environmental policy: governing by multiple policy instruments?', in J.J. Richardson (ed.), *Constructing a Policy Making State?*, Oxford: Oxford University Press, pp. 104–124.

Kingdon, J.W. (2010), *Agendas, Alternatives and Public Policies*, Harmondsworth: Longman.

Lascoumes, P. and P. Le Galés (2007), 'Introduction: understanding public policy through its instruments', *Governance*, **20** (1), 1–22.

Lasswell, H. (1971), *A Pre-view of Policy Sciences*, New York: Elsevier.

Lindblom, C.E. (1959), 'The science of "muddling through"', *Public Administration Review*, **19** (2), 79–88.

Linder, S.H. and B.G. Peters (1990), 'Policy formulation and the challenge of conscious design', *Evaluation and Program Planning*, **13**, 303–311.

Lindquist, E. (1992), 'Public managers and policy communities', *Canadian Public Administration*, **35**, 127–159.

Matthews, F. (2012), 'Governance and state capacity', in D. Levi-Faur (ed.), *The Oxford Handbook of Governance*, Oxford: Oxford University Press, pp. 281–293.

Meltsner, A.J. (1976), *Policy Analysts in the Bureaucracy*, Berkeley: University of California Press.

Mintrom, M. and C. Williams (2013), 'Public policy debate and the rise of policy analysis', in E. Araral, S. Fritzen, M. Howlett, M. Ramesh and X. Wu (eds), *Routledge Handbook of Public Policy*, London: Routledge, pp. 3–16.

Nilsson, M., A. Jordan, J. Turnpenny, J. Hertin, B. Nykvist and D. Russel (2008), 'The use and non-use of policy appraisal tools in public policy making', *Policy Sciences*, **41** (4), 335–355.

Noordegraaf, M. (2011), 'Academic accounts of policy experience', in H. Colebatch, R. Hoppe and M. Noordegraaf (eds), *Working for Policy*, Amsterdam: University of Amsterdam Press, pp. 45–67.

Owens, S. and R. Cowell (2002), *Land and Limits: Interpreting Sustainability in the Planning Process*, London and New York: Routledge.

Owens, S., T. Rayner and O. Bina (2004), 'New agendas for appraisal: reflections on theory, practice and research', *Environment and Planning A*, **36**, 1943–1959.

Page, E.C. (2003), 'The civil servant as legislator: law making in British administration', *Public Administration*, **81** (4), 651–679.

Page, E.C. and B. Jenkins (2005), *Policy Bureaucracy: Governing with a Cast of Thousands*, Oxford: Oxford University Press.

Painter, M. and J. Pierre (2005), 'Unpacking policy capacity: issues and themes', in M. Painter and J. Pierre (eds), *Challenges to State Policy Capacity*, Basingstoke: Palgrave, pp. 1–18.

Parsons, W. (1995), *Public Policy*, Aldershot, UK and Brookfield, VT, USA: Edward Elgar Publishing.

Pearce, D.W. (1998), 'Cost–benefit analysis and policy', *Oxford Review of Economic Policy*, **14** (4), 84–100.

Peters, B.G. and A. Barker (1993), 'Introduction: governments, information, advice and policy-making', in B.G. Peters and A. Barker (eds), *Advising West European Governments: Inquiries, Expertise and Public Policy*, Edinburgh: Edinburgh University Press, pp. 1–19.

Pralle, S.B. (2003), 'Venue shopping, political strategy, and policy change: the internationalization of Canadian forest advocacy', *Journal of Public Policy*, **23**, 233–260.

Radaelli, C. (1995), 'The role of knowledge in the policy process', *Journal of European Public Policy*, **2** (2), 159–183.

Radin, B. (2013), *Beyond Machiavelli*, Washington, DC: Georgetown University Press.

Rossi, P.H., M.W. Lipsey and H. Freeman (2004), *Evaluation*, London: Sage.

Russel, D. and A. Jordan (2014), 'Embedding the concept of ecosystem services? The utilisation of ecological knowledge in different policy venues', *Environment and Planning* C, **32** (2), 192–207.

Sabatier, P. (2005), *Theories of the Policy Process*, 2nd edition, Boulder: Westview Press.

Salamon, L. (1989), *Beyond Privatisation*, Washington: Urban Institute Press.

Salamon, L. (2002), 'The new governance and the tools of public action: an introduction', in L. Salamon (ed.), *Tools of Government*, Oxford: Oxford University Press, pp. 1–47.

Sanderson, I. (2002), 'Evaluation, policy learning and evidence-based policy making', *Public Administration*, **80** (1), 1–22.

Schick, A. (1977), 'Beyond analysis', *Public Administration Review*, **37** (3), 258–263.

Schultze, C. (1970), *The Politics and Economics of Public Spending*, Washington: Brookings Institution.

Self, P. (1981), 'Planning: rational or political?', in P. Baehr and B. Wittrock (eds), *Policy Analysis and Policy Innovation*, London: Sage, pp. 219–236.

Self, P. (1985), *Econocrats and the Policy Process*, Basingstoke: Macmillan.

Shine, K.T. and B. Bartley (2011), 'Whose evidence base? The dynamic effects of ownership, receptivity and values on collaborative evidence-informed policy making', *Evidence and Policy*, **7** (4), 511–530.

Shulock, N. (1999), 'The paradox of policy analysis: if it is not used, why do we produce so much of it?', *Journal of Policy Analysis and Management*, **18** (2), 226–244.

Sidney, M.S. (2007), 'Policy formulation: design and tools', in F. Fischer, G.J. Miller and M.S. Sidney (eds), *Handbook of Public Policy Analysis: Theory, Politics and Methods*, New Brunswick, NJ: CRC Taylor & Francis, pp. 79–87.

Stirling, A. (2008), '"Opening up" and "closing down": power, participation, and pluralism in the social appraisal of technology', *Science, Technology, and Human Values*, **33** (2), 262–294.

Thomas, H.G. (2001), 'Towards a new higher education law in Lithuania: reflections on the process of policy formulation', *Higher Education Policy*, **14** (3), 213–223.

Timmermans, A. and P. Scholten (2006), 'The political flow of wisdom: science institutions as policy venues in the Netherlands', *Journal of European Public Policy*, **13** (7), 1104–1118.

Turnpenny, J., C.M. Radaelli, A. Jordan and K. Jacob (2009), 'The policy and politics of policy appraisal: emerging trends and new directions', *Journal of European Public Policy*, **16** (4), 640–653.

Vining, A.R. and D.L. Weimer (2010), 'Foundations of public administration: policy analysis', *Public Administration Review, Foundations of Public Administration Series*, retrieved from http://www.aspanet.org/public/ASPADocs/PAR/FPA/FPA-Policy-Article.pdf (accessed 20 January 2014).

Wildavsky, A. (1987), *Speaking Truth to Power: The Art and Craft of Policy Analysis*, New Brunswick: Transaction Books.

Wolman, H. (1981), 'The determinants of program success and failure', *Journal of Public Policy*, **1** (4), 433–464.

Wu, X., M. Ramesh, M. Howlett and S.A. Fritzen (2010), *The Public Policy Primer: Managing the Policy Process*, London: Routledge.

Wurzel, R.K.W., A.R. Zito and A.J. Jordan (2013), *Environmental Governance in Europe: A Comparative Analysis of New Environmental Policy Instruments*, Cheltenham, UK and Northampton, MA, USA: Edward Elgar Publishing.

PART II

Tools of policy formulation

2. Participatory assessment: tools for empowering, learning and legitimating?

Matthijs Hisschemöller and Eefje Cuppen

INTRODUCTION

Since the 1960s, a large number of participatory assessment tools and methods have been developed for use in a wide variety of policy venues and fields. There are many opinions on what participatory tools are about. As will be explained, these relate in large part to ongoing debates about the goals of participation. Hence, there is no shared authoritative definition of participatory tools and this chapter has no intention of developing one. Rather pragmatically, it distinguishes between participatory *methods*, which refer to procedures, and participatory *tools*, which relate to steps in a procedure. Just as an authoritative definition of participatory assessment tools and methods is lacking, so too is consensus over the outcome they aim at. What they have in common and what makes them distinct from other (social) science methods and tools is that they assist in bringing people together at a specific location (which could include the Internet) and facilitate some sort of joint assessment (Hisschemöller 2005). Hence, the distinctive features of participatory methods and tools are that they facilitate *dialogue* as a way to come to grips with complex (unstructured) decision problems that cannot be addressed by scientific expertise alone. Given this definition, participatory tools overlap with some of the other policy formulation tools that also employ stakeholder involvement (for example, participatory modelling or participatory multi-criteria analysis (MCA)).

Participatory assessment needs to be distinguished from legal procedures for political participation that are mandatory in many countries and sometimes also prescribed by international law. Its use is broadly recommended and facilitated by international organizations, for example the World Bank (1996), UNHCR (2006) and the World Food Programme (2001).

Participatory assessment tools and methods are used to assist mandatory fact-finding procedures, such as social or environmental impact assessment, which inform decision makers and the public at large as to the consequences of policy choices. Much EU legislation, including for example the Water Framework Directive, assigns a key role to European citizens in the preparation of policy plans. However, participatory tools themselves are normally (see section 3) not prescribed by law.

This chapter cannot provide a complete overview of all participatory assessment tools and methods. It focuses on tools designed for facilitation of actual dialogue in a face-to-face setting. This means that the huge range of computer tools currently available for stakeholder participation is beyond its scope (but on this, see Chapter 5, this volume). This chapter is also unable to cover all venues where participatory tools are applied. Examples reflect the authors' expertise in environmental studies, but our discussion of participatory tools does have relevance well beyond this field.

Section 2 traces the various origins of participatory assessment tools and methods and discusses the basic rationales for participation. Section 3 presents a four-stage model of policy formulation and shows where participatory tools fit in. Section 4 then goes into more detail on methods and tools that are relevant for the four stages of the policy formulation process. Section 5 addresses the practice of participatory assessment. Section 6 then wraps up and concludes.

ORIGINS AND RATIONALES OF PARTICIPATORY ASSESSMENT TOOLS

The emergence and popularity of participatory assessment tools and methods can be related to the rise of social movements since the 1960s, which aimed at democratizing decision making at all levels of society. Participation has been intrinsically linked to the idea of empowering groups who are less able to make themselves heard, enabling them to effectively defend their interests against the powerful. Criticizing mainstream political theories that legitimized distance between the governors and the governed, social scientists increasingly abandoned Schumpeter's (1942, 1976) radical notion that citizens are incapable of rational involvement in the political process. Focusing instead on structural disempowerment of the poor, non-white and women, critics took exception to the normativity of the 'pluralist' conception of the policy arena as a market place that, as Berelson et al. put it, 'makes for enough consensus to hold the system together and enough cleavage to make it move' (Berelson et al. 1954, p. 318). Political science witnessed a revival of 'classical' political ideas, of which

Carole Pateman's (1979) discussion of Rousseau's social contract remains an eloquent example to this day.

The classical democratic ideal, expressed by the likes of Rousseau and J.S. Mill, sketches a polity where people open-mindedly engage in an enriching process of *learning* (see Held 1987). Learning is central to Habermas' (1984) famous notion of the ideal speech situation, where persons with different views interact without obstruction by differences in power and influence. Policy scientists inspired by Habermas criticized mainstream 'technocratic' practices in policymaking and policy analysis (see for example, Fischer 1990). What counts in the end for these policy scientists, or at least what *should* prevail in the context of good governance, is the quality of policy argument (Dunn 1982; Fischer and Forester 1993).

The participatory wave provided fertile ground not only to analyse and theorise, but also to develop and apply tools to facilitate participation. The notion of participation as empowerment, as put forward by Freire (2004), inspired scholars in the field of development studies to create tools known as *Participatory Action Research* (Fals Borda and Rahman 1991; Hall 2005) and *Participatory Rural Appraisal* (Chambers 2008; for an overview see Tufte and Mefalopulos 2009). Urban planning experimented with deliberative tools such as, in Germany, *Planungszelle* and *Citizens' Fora* (Renn 2004). The 1980s witnessed harsh controversies related to environmental and technological risk, such as the worldwide concerns over nuclear power, hazardous waste and (transboundary) water pollution. The rise of tools such as citizens' and science courts (Kantrowitz 1967; Seley 1983), citizens' juries (Huitema et al. 2007), scientific mediation (Abrams and Primack 1980) and consensus conferences (see for example, Einsiedel et al. 2001) corresponded with this period. The invention and application of participatory tools to help policy officials in 'dealing with an angry public' (Susskind and Field 1996) was also witnessed. Apart from new tools, existing tools were reinvented and/or adjusted, such as focus groups (Merton and Kendall 1946) and brainstorming (Osborn 1963).

Although the conceptual link between participation and learning is echoed among a wide group of policy scientists, it would be incorrect to trace the origins of participatory assessment tools and methods to the participatory ideology exclusively. Before the Cold War, the US Defense establishment recognized the critical importance of avoiding tunnel vision and 'group-think' among decision makers in situations characterized by stress and uncertainty. Tools for *simulation* and *gaming* (see Chapter 3, this volume), originally developed in the military and international relations studies, have found wide use in participatory settings (Mayer 1997). Critical notions developed in decision science found their way through many science disciplines, especially that of the 'wicked problem' (Rittel and Webber 1973) and related notions such as 'type 3 error' – solving the 'wrong problem' (Raiffa 1968) – and bounded rationality (Simon 1973). A *wicked, ill-structured* or *unstructured* problem is defined in terms of uncertainty or conflict with respect to the (relevance of) knowledge and values at stake (Hisschemöller and Hoppe 2001). Interestingly, for Rittel and his followers the participatory wave was not the starting point but the necessary consequence of so-called second generation design. The appearance of so many 'wicked' problems he considered a good reason to transfer the ways in which the large-scale NASA and military-type technological problems had been approached into civilian or other design areas (Bayazit 2004). Management science also delivered its own contribution to participatory tool development, inspired by notions from decision science and philosophers like Ackoff (1978), Churchman (1967) and Dewey (1932).

At this point we may understand why assessing the specific qualities of participatory tools for policy formulation is far from easy. This is because there is persistent ambiguity in political thought with respect to the moral and practical benefits of participation. Participation, as scholars tend to agree, can serve three purposes: empowerment, learning and legitimization or, in the terminology introduced by Fiorino (1990), normative, substantive and instrumental. The normative view relates to the very concept of democracy, which means rule by the people (the *demos*) and the idea that every citizen has the right to speak and be heard. Learning relates to the substantive rationale for participation. In this view, participation is a method for knowledge production. The connection between the normative and the substantive has become reflected in statements that 'lay people are experts with respect to their own problems' (Mitroff et al. 1983) or that 'citizens are the best judges of their own interests' (Fiorino 1990, p. 228). For participatory assessment tools and methods this implies that they must be able to incorporate a maximum of diversity (Stirling 2008). Diversity enhances learning, because it helps articulate marginal viewpoints that have more probative value than mainstream thinking (Dunn 1997). Participation as knowledge production is the focus of transdisciplinary research (Funtowicz and Ravetz 1993; Gibbons et al. 1994). Third, legitimization relates to implementation, which in Fiorino's terminology is the instrumental rationale for participation. A decision is likely to be accepted if the process is considered fair, even by those who have lost the struggle over the outcome.

Notwithstanding an inclination among advocates of participation to tie these three features neatly together, they are not by definition compatible. The notion of diversity appears especially problematic. From the instrumental perspective, too much diversity endangers effective and legitimate decisions. Yet, from the perspective of empowerment, (too much) diversity would undermine the unity needed to effectively oppose the powers-that-be. A closer look into the history of political thought reveals that diversity has not consistently or exclusively been an ingredient of democratic theories. Instead, the necessity of (managing a certain amount of) diversity can (also) be traced to political thought of Machiavelli (1970), who is not usually considered a democrat at all. Machiavelli argues that diversity and social conflict are conditions allowing states to adapt to changing realities, safeguarding their people from war and disaster. In a mild way, this argument has been adopted by pluralist theorists as manifest in the 'intelligence of democracy' (Lindblom 1965).

PARTICIPATORY ASSESSMENT AND THE POLICY FORMULATION PROCESS

In typologies of participatory tools (for example, van Asselt and Rijkens-Klomp 2002; Rowe and Frewer 2005), one theme has returned over time, which can probably be best labelled as 'opening-up' versus 'closing down' (Stirling 2008). This theme relates to the critical features of political rationality: *differentiation* and *unification* (Diesing 1962). Differentiation relates to *problem structuring*, that is, collecting as much (contradictory) information as possible on the issue at stake, and therefore requires a maximum degree of participation. Unification relates to choosing an intervention perspective based on at least part of the information available. Policy formulation heuristics normally echo this distinction in that they identify distinct stages. The first stages, namely agenda setting and problem conceptualization, normally show a degree of differentiation, whereas later in the process of policy formulation unification becomes prominent, especially through the ranking of policy alternatives and the final decision. However, neither in reality nor for Diesing (1962) is policy formulation a linear process, because differentiation and unification are in constant tension. Table 2.1 presents a simple four-stage model of policy formulation leading to decision making in the left-hand column and in the right-hand column a four-step model of participatory methodology. We pragmatically assume that both models are compatible, and that each step of the participatory methodology precedes, or provides input to, the related stage of the policy formulation process.

The decision heuristic works toward a final decision, narrowing down step-by-step the scope and focus of the issue under consideration (moving from differentiation to unification). As Table 2.1 also shows, each step in policy formulation allows for differentiation but is simultaneously aimed at reaching some form of unification. Stage 1 concludes with a

Table 2.1   *A comparison of the different stages in the policy formulation process and the main steps in participatory methodology*

Policy formulation process leading to a decision		Participatory assessment methodology (Cuppen 2010)	
Stage 1	Agenda setting, (initial) problem conceptualization	*Step 1*	Stakeholder identification and selection, identification of divergent viewpoints
Goal/ deliverable	Decision on problem boundaries	*Goal/deliverable*	Probing of problem boundaries (diversity)
Stage 2	Specification of policy objectives	*Step 2*	Articulation of perspectives
Goal/ deliverable	Decision on policy objectives	*Goal/deliverable*	Sharing/exploring ideas and approaches
Stage 3	Identification and appraisal of potential policy options	*Step 3*	Confrontation of perspectives
Goal/ deliverable	Ranking of preferences, assessing intervention perspectives	*Goal/deliverable*	Appraisal of alternative policy options: arguments for/against policy alternatives; understanding differences and similarities across perspectives; sometimes ranking
Stage 4	Decision making	*Step 4*	Synthesis, policy advice
Goal/ deliverable	Decision, policy paper, and so on	*Goal/deliverable*	Dialogue outcomes reported (often agreement to disagree)

conceptualization of the problem, stage 2 with a choice of policy objectives and stage 3 with a ranking of alternatives. Hence, Table 2.1 emphasizes the persistent tension between the two basic features of political rationality. The same is true for the steps in participatory assessment. In the course of the policy process, participatory assessment tools and methods are capable of opening-up to the extent allowed for by the constraints set in previous stages. The range of alternatives to be explored in stage 3 is highly dependent on the range of policy objectives specified in stage 2. And the range of policy objectives considered is constrained by the problem conceptualization in stage 1. The problem conceptualization, in turn, is largely dependent on the variety of stakeholders and perspectives identified.

The extent to which each step is covered by participatory methods and tools varies. A wide range of methods and tools is available that supports the articulation of perspectives (step 2) and the appraisal of alternative policy options (step 3). Notably few tools, however, focus on synthesis and follow-up, which suggests that participatory tools and methods are used mainly to open up policy appraisal (Stirling 2008) or, in the words of Diesing (1962), aim at differentiation rather than unification.

PARTICIPATORY METHODS AND TOOLS

This section discusses participatory assessment tools and methods with specific relevance for different stages in the policy formulation process.

Stage 1: Agenda Setting and Problem Conceptualization

Ultimately, it is the identification of stakeholders and the range of divergent views they represent which, apart from the organization of the dialogue itself, shapes the contents of the participatory assessment. Remarkably, participatory assessments often identify stakeholders in a rather intuitive way, according to their (assumed) position with respect to a certain issue (Hisschemöller 2005). They may use techniques such as random, stratified or snowball sampling. While these techniques may be helpful to assure representative, large sample sizes in quantitative research, their use for participatory assessment is disputable (Cuppen 2010; 2012a). From a learning perspective, representation implies the balanced inclusion of the variety of perspectives. Such 'discursive representation' (Dryzek and Niemeyer 2008, p. 281) asks for tools that enable a selection based on measured rather than assumed stakeholder perspectives. Examples of such tools are Q Methodology (for example, Cuppen et al. 2010) and the Repertory Grid Technique (van de Kerkhof et al. 2009), which allow for both qualitative and quantitative analysis. As for Q Methodology, a limited sample of respondents sort a set of subjective statements on a policy issue, according to a bell-shaped distribution that represents salience to the individual ('most agree' versus 'most disagree'). A subsequent quantitative analysis results in a number of (usually two to six) factors which can be interpreted as perspectives. The quantitative analysis enables the identification of respondents who can 'represent' each of the perspectives in a dialogue (Cuppen et al. 2010). The combined use of qualitative and quantitative research techniques via Q Methodology or Repertory Grid Technique reveals that perspectives cannot simply be 'read off' from stakeholders' affiliations with business, environmental NGOs or other stakeholders. Actor types have been found to be heterogeneous with regard to perspectives (Cuppen et al. 2010; Vasileiadou et al. 2014).

Stage 2: Specification of Policy Objectives

In this stage, participatory assessment tools and methods must be geared towards the articulation of diverse stakeholder perspectives in order to share and explore these. A wide range of tools exists for this step, some of which were already addressed for step 1 (for example, Repertory Grid Technique, Q Methodology). Others are dealt with under stage 3.

A widely applied tool that deserves mentioning is Focus Group methodology. Originally developed for marketing, this tool has been adjusted to the context of environmental policy formulation (Greenbaum 1998; Wilkinson 2004; Gerger Swartling 2006). Its basic idea is to arrange for a conversation in a (small) group on a topic presented in a more or less detailed way in order to find out about peoples' impressions and opinions. Focus Group methodology in fact covers a diversity of approaches, ranging from more to less structured, low to high diversity in the group or from little to much information presented. Climate change modelling has used focus groups for receiving feed-back on scientific models and scenarios (see also Chapter 5, this volume).

Stage 3: Identification and Appraisal of Potential Policy Options

Much experience has been gained with tools to support participatory technology assessments on controversial issues such as genetic modification. Examples include Consensus Conferences, Planning Cells and Citizens' Juries. These tools aim at facilitating a dialogue between experts and laypersons in homogeneous (either experts or laypersons) and heterogeneous (experts and laypersons together) groups. As a common feature, these tools often a priori allocate 'knowledge' to the expert domain and 'values' to the domain of laypeople. Separating 'facts' and 'values' in such a way is at odds, however, with the findings of studies into risk perception indicating that both are intertwined (Cuppen et al. 2009). These tools and methods tend to be based on the assumption that differences in judgement mainly exist between experts and laypersons. However, there may be as many differences *within* layperson and expert groups as there are *between* them.

Another 'family' of participatory assessment tools and methods originating from management science aims at improving the quality of (business) plans by assessing conflicting stakeholder assumptions. Well-known examples are Devil's Advocate (Schwenk and Cosier 1980; Schweiger et al. 1986), Policy Delphi (Turoff 1975) and Dialectical Methodology (Mason and Mitroff 1981). The underlying idea of these tools and methods is that the appraisal of competing alternatives benefits from the articulation of stakeholders' contradictory (but hidden) assumptions rather than from invoking 'objectified' expert judgement. These participatory assessment tools and methods differ from Consensus Conferences, for example, in that they recognize different realms of stakeholder expertise, including practical knowledge, alongside scientific (academic) expertise, and treat them as equally valuable. Thus they do not separate stakeholders into an expert and lay group. However, they also make assumptions that have an impact on the structuring of the dialogue process. One assumption is that stakeholder debate can be negatively influenced by differences in power and authority of those involved. Therefore, participatory assessment tools and methods may structure stakeholder interaction in such a way that participants do not know each others' identity (for example, in classical delphi), a practice in line with Habermas' notion of the ideal speech situation. Sometimes, the Devil's Advocate technique is organized as a game: the advocate pretends to be against the proposed plan but actually plays a role. Evaluation research suggests that such role playing (artificial conflict) contributes little to learning, while so-called authentic conflict contributes more (for example, Nemeth et al. 2004).

Yet another approach for appraisal of policy options is backcasting, developed as an alternative to forecasting (see Chapter 3, this volume). Participatory Backcasting first identifies a particular (desirable) future end-point and then works backward from it to the present, as if it were already realized. Backcasting can be a powerful tool to assess the feasibility of a (desired) future state and the interventions needed to reach that point (Robinson 2003). It is able to avoid the conservatism inherent in forecasting, as it encourages reflection on the breaking of dominant trends through 'out-of-the-box' thinking (Dreborg 1996).

Stage 4: Decision Making

Some participatory assessment tools and methods are specifically aimed at reaching a decision, such as joint fact finding (McCreary et al. 2001) and the decision seminar (Lasswell 1960). A well-known example of such methodology is Consensus Building, which aims to 'forge agreements that satisfy everyone's primary interests and concerns' (Susskind et al. 1999, p. xvii). Grounded in the theory and practice of interest-based negotiation and mediation (Innes 2004), this problem-solving approach is essentially different from those participatory assessment tools and methods that focus on problem structuring. The notion of consensus is critical in many participatory assessment tools. In essence, consensus tends to be regarded as preferable to dissent, if only because disagreement might cause troublesome personal relationships, which people working in a (small) group would like to avoid. In case of irreconcilable values, consensus may be artificial or symbolic (Kupper 2006). Such consensus obstructs learning and may lead to the adoption of invalid assumptions or inferior choices (Janis 1972; Gregory et al. 2001; Stasser and Titus 1985; Coglianese 1999). It should be noted that artificial or symbolic consensus is not necessarily negative, as it keeps the process moving and enables parties to develop trust (Hisschemöller and Hoppe 2001).

Despite many criticisms, consensus building is, to our knowledge, the only participatory assessment tool and method with an institutionalized sibling. The US Negotiated Rulemaking Act prescribes the negotiation of the terms of a particular proposed rule, hence the name.

PARTICIPATORY ASSESSMENT IN PRACTICE

Unfortunately there is a lack of systematic evaluation of the policy impact and effectiveness of participatory assessment tools and methods or participatory assessment in general. One of the main reasons for this probably relates to the conflicting (and hidden) aims of participation noted above. There is often a discrepancy between how particular tools and methods are applied in practice and how they are prescribed by theory. While this chapter focuses on participatory assessment tools and methods for policy formulation, in practice they are often used to legitimize already decided policy. This has repercussions, for example when different expectations exist with regard to the role and intended impact of a participatory assessment. The policy evaluation literature shows numerous examples of disappointments among participants who have invested energy in participatory assessments only to find out in the end that policymakers did not use – or

BOX 2.1   PARTICIPATORY ASSESSMENT TOOLS AND METHODS: VENUES AND IMPACTS

Example 1: Consensus Conference (CC)

Consensus Conferences (CCs) have been documented for Denmark (below), New Zealand (Goven 2003), the UK (Joss 2005; Irwin et al. 2012), Norway (Oughton and Strand 2004), Belgium (Vandenabeele and Goorden 2004), Canada and Australia (Einsiedel et al. 2001), and the Netherlands (Jelsma 2001). Most CCs have been commissioned by government and organized by an external institute, either affiliated to parliament (e.g. the Danish Board of Technology, an NGO since late 2011) or independent. Evaluations of specific CCs show that practice may deviate from theory due to particular contextual and venue-specific factors. For example, limited interaction between citizens and experts was reported for a Belgian and Austrian CC (Vandenabeele and Goorden 2004, Joss and Bellucci 2002). Too little time for public debate, lack of transparency and overall mistrust were reported for CCs in the UK and the Netherlands (Joss 2005, Jelsma 2001). In Denmark, where parliament has recognized CC as an important policymaking tool, CCs have provided a base for policy directions (Grundahl 1995), but have not had an immediate policy impact (Einsiedel et al. 2001; Vandenabeele and Goorden 2004; Joss and Bellucci 2002). At best, evaluations report learning among the participating citizens and experts.

Example 2: Participatory Backcasting (PB)

Participatory Backcasting (PB) has been widely applied in cases ranging from: the future of natural areas in Canada (Tansey et al. 2002; VanWynsberghe et al. 2003); energy futures for the Netherlands (Hisschemöller and Bode 2011; Breukers et al. 2013), for the UK (combined with multi-criteria appraisal; Eames and McDowall 2010) and for Belgium (Keune and Goorden 2002); sustainable households in five countries (Green and Vergragt 2002); and long-term changes of Swedish city life (Carlsson-Kanyama et al. 2003). Participants are usually stake-holders, representing different sectors and groups. There is no evidence for imme-diate policy impact of PB. Yet, as Quist (2007) shows, it may encourage higher order learning among participants as well as follow-up programmes. Venue-specific factors shape how PB works out in practice. An example is provided by the Dutch Hydrogen Dialogue (2004–2008), funded by the Dutch Organization for Scientific Research. This addressed the question of how hydrogen can contribute to a future sustainable energy system (Hisschemöller and Bode 2011).

About 60 stakeholders (from the Netherlands and abroad) participated, includ-ing energy companies, small innovative firms, knowledge institutes, vehicle lease and transport companies, NGOs and one association of home owners considering the establishment of a hydrogen-based energy system in their neighbourhood. Since participants valued the utilization of policy-relevant results highly, the project team committed three former Dutch MPs as independent chairs of three dialogue groups. Participants were invited based on the outcome of a Repertory Grid exer-cise (van de Kerkhof et al. 2009), which unfolded three perspectives on a 'hydrogen economy'. PB was then used for developing (competing) hydrogen pathways.

At a 'Confrontation Workshop', the pathways were reviewed by international keynote speakers, a national Advisory Board including experts and policymakers, and the participants themselves. In this application of PB, creative conflict was a central design issue, intended to stimulate learning through interaction between stakeholders from different (inter)national networks. However, the anticipated learning effect was hampered because the conflict on substance turned into a conflict of interests. Eventually, the participants from the national Energy Research Institute distanced themselves from the entire dialogue report, because in their view the dialogue facilitators did not sufficiently distinguish energy experts' views from non-expert opinions.

The dialogue did not have an immediate impact on policy. However, a few years later the Dutch National company, Gasunie, started implementing the option most controversial throughout the dialogue, adding large quantities of H_2 into a local gas infrastructure. The actors taking most advantage of the dialogue were small innovative entrepreneurs, seeking like-minded stakeholders to start up transition experiments.

even abused – their contribution. Processes considered unfair, biased or as pseudo-participation generally do not contribute to public acceptance. A related explanation for the lack of systematic evaluation may be that (hidden) conflicts between instrumental, substantive and normative aims of participation also undermine the evaluation itself, especially as the (main) goal, of gaining acceptance, remains implicit or is covered under the veil of substantive or normative aims.

Some authors observe resistance among policymakers and their techno-scientific advisers to participatory exercises (for example, Irwin et al. 2012). Participatory assessments and public participation in general increase uncertainty among policymakers with respect to the timing and actual outcome of a policy formulation process (Hisschemöller and Hoppe 2001). Whereas policymakers may like the idea that participatory assessments contribute to the public acceptance of policies, they dislike the idea that successful participatory processes may diminish their control. Hence, they may not have an interest to know about the impact of participatory assessment tools and methods.

Another explanation for the lack of systematic evaluation relates to difficulties in measuring the impact of such tools and methods. First of all, policy learning is a slow process, as is generally the case with the utilization of research. Evaluating effectiveness is difficult, as policy change is a complex process that takes place over periods of at least a decade (Sabatier 1999). Participatory assessments may therefore have an impact only in the longer term, which may be difficult to measure. Difficulties in measuring the impact of participatory assessments also relate to the fact that the impact may not be restricted to changes in governmental policy, but may affect other domains and actors as well. There is evidence that stake-holders learned, especially about the different perspectives on the topic (Cuppen 2012b). Academics, companies, innovative entrepreneurs, NGOs and (local) government officials then initiate follow-up activities beyond the level of (national) government (Quist 2007). Surprisingly, the authors' own participatory assessments on climate and energy have led to techno-logical inventions and initiatives for collaboration among stakeholders. This may also confirm that the impacts of participatory assessments may be especially significant in the longer term.

Interestingly, this suggests that participatory assessment tools and methods are not primarily used in the venues where they were initiated. It suggests that participatory assessments, like participatory processes in general, can themselves *create* venues as well. Participatory assessment tools and methods are a vehicle for bringing together different actors, exchanging ideas and viewpoints and mobilizing resources. In other words, they create new networks, most of these starting as informal and at some distance from state policy venues. However, over time these venues may expand into new institutions for deliberating on policy objectives, options and strategies, as for example, Sabatier (1999) shows.

A last point to be mentioned here is that there are many participatory assessments of varying quality, which makes it hard to systematically evaluate their impacts. For some examples, it is even questionable whether they may legitimately be described as 'participatory'. In an evaluation of the Austrian trans-disciplinary programme, Felt et al. (2012) find that the researchers on the one hand strongly convey the participatory discourse, but simultaneously tend to protect the privileged position of the researcher *vis-à-vis* societal stakeholders.

In conclusion, there is still much work to do in evaluating the real impact and quality of participatory assessment tools and methods, starting with developing methodologies for categorizing and measuring these impacts. This may support quality and usefulness of future tools and methods.

CONCLUSIONS

This chapter has highlighted the great variety of participatory assessment tools and methods applied in many policy sectors and venues across the world. These tools and methods have in common that they facilitate some sort of dialogue between people with different views on a specific topic: participatory methods arrange for a procedure along the various stages of the policy formulation process, whereas tools can be applied in only one or few stages. Participatory assessment tools and methods can easily be integrated into other policy formulation tools that require feedback from stakeholders, such as environmental modelling (see Chapter 5, this volume) or multi-criteria appraisal (see Chapter 6, this volume).

We find that only a few participatory assessment tools and methods seriously address the issue of stakeholder identification and selection, despite the fact that this first step determines the process and outcome to a high degree. Most participatory assessment tools and methods can be used for identifying objectives or for exploring alternative courses of action.

In assessing the potential of participatory assessment tools and methods, two issues are of critical importance. First, we find that different (sometimes irreconcilable) views on participation have immediate consequences for their design and application. Some focus on reaching consensus, in order to facilitate decisions on controversial issues, while others focus on articulating conflicting perspectives to enhance learning with respect to developing new policy approaches and options. Second, the practice of applying participatory assessment tools and methods often suffers from contradictory objectives among participants and disappointments that policymakers are more interested in legitimizing already decided measures than in gaining new ideas for addressing intractable issues. These two observations may also explain the observed lack of systematic evaluation of participatory assessment tools and methods in practice.

The critical evaluation this chapter offers is meant to present a state of the art with a fair assessment of the challenges in the field. We do not intend it to discourage readers from studying and employing participatory approaches. After all, despite much scepticism and resistance in policy venues, openness to new insights is and must remain a major feature of good policy formulation and governance.

REFERENCES

Abrams, N.E. and J.R. Primack (1980), 'Helping the public decide, the case of radioactive waste management', *Environment*, **22** (3), 14–40.

Ackoff, R.L. (1978), *The Art of Problem Solving*, New York: John Wiley & Sons.

Bayazit, N. (2004), 'Investigating design: a review of forty years of design research', *Design Issues*, **20** (1), 16–29.

Berelson, B.R., P.F. Lazarsfeld and W.N. McPhee (1954), *Voting*, Chicago: University of Chicago Press.

Breukers, S., M. Hisschemöller, E. Cuppen and R.A.A. Suurs (2013), 'Analysing the past and exploring the future of sustainable biomass: participatory stakeholder dialogue and technological innovation systems research', *Technological Forecasting and Social Change*, **81**, 227–235.

Carlsson-Kanyama, A., K.H. Dreborg, R. Engstrom and G. Henriksson (2003), *Possibilities for Long-term Changes of City Life: Experiences of Backcasting with*

Stakeholders, Fms-report 178, Stockholm: Environmental Strategies Research Group.

Chambers, R. (2008), 'PRA, PLA and pluralism: practice and theory', in P. Reason and H. Bradbury (eds), *The Sage Handbook of Action Research: Participative Inquiry and Practice*, London: Sage, pp. 297–318.

Churchman, C.W. (1967), 'Wicked problems' (guest editorial), *Management Science*, **14** (4), B-141, B-142.

Coglianese, C. (1999), 'The limits of consensus', *Environment*, **41**, 1–6.

Cuppen, E. (2010), 'Putting perspectives into participation', PhD dissertation, Amsterdam: VU University of Amsterdam.

Cuppen, E. (2012a), 'Diversity and constructive conflict in stakeholder dialogue: considerations for design and methods', *Policy Sciences*, **45** (1), 23–46.

Cuppen, E. (2012b), 'A quasi-experimental evaluation of learning in stakeholder dialogue on bio-energy', *Research Policy*, **41**, 624–637.

Cuppen, E., M. Hisschemöller and C.J.H. Midden (2009), 'Bias in the exchange of arguments: the case of scientists' evaluation of lay viewpoints on GM food', *Public Understanding of Science*, **18**, 591–607.

Cuppen, E., S. Breukers, M. Hisschemöller and E. Bergsma (2010), 'Q methodology to select participants for a stakeholder dialogue on energy options from biomass in the Netherlands', *Ecological Economics*, **69**, 579–591.

Dewey, J. (1932), *Ethics*, New York: Holt and Company.

Diesing, P. (1962), *Reason in Society: Five Types of Decisions and their Social Conditions*, 2nd edition, Westport, Connecticut: Greenwood Press.

Dreborg, K.H. (1996), 'Essence of backcasting', *Futures*, **28**, 813–828.

Dryzek, J.S. and S. Niemeyer (2008), 'Discursive representation', *American Political Science Review*, **102**, 481–492.

Dunn, W.N. (1982), 'Reforms as arguments', *Knowledge: Creation, Diffusion, Utilization*, **3**, 293–326.

Dunn, W.N. (1997), 'Probing the boundaries of ignorance in policy analysis', *American Behavioral Scientist*, **40**, 277–298.

Eames, M. and W. McDowall (2010), 'Sustainability, foresight and contested futures: exploring visions and pathways in the transition to a hydrogen economy', *Technology Analysis & Strategic Management*, **22** (6), 671–692.

Einsiedel, E.F., E. Jelsoe and T. Breck (2001), 'Publics at the technology table: the consensus conference in Denmark, Canada, and Australia', *Public Understanding of Science*, **10**, 83–98.

Fals Borda, O. and M.A. Rahman (1991), *Action and Knowledge*, Lanham, Maryland: Rowman and Littlefield.

Felt, U., J. Igelsböck, A. Schikowitz and T. Völker (2012), 'Challenging participation in sustainability research', *International Journal of Deliberative Mechanisms in Science*, **1** (1), 4–34.

Fiorino, D.J. (1990), 'Citizen participation and environmental risk: a survey of institutional mechanisms', *Science Technology & Human Values*, **15**, 226–243.

Fischer, F. (1990), *Technocracy and the Politics of Expertise*, Newbury Park, CA: Sage.

Fischer, F. and J. Forester (eds) (1993), *The Argumentative Turn in Policy Analysis and Planning*, Durham: Duke University Press.

Freire, P. (2004), *Pedagogy of Hope. Reliving Pedagogy of the Oppressed*, New York: Continuum.

Funtowicz, S.O. and J.R. Ravetz (1993), 'Science for the post-normal age', *Futures*, **25**, 739–755.
Gerger Swartling, A. (2006), *Focus Groups*. Sustainablity A-TEST, 15-4-0013, retrieved from http://www.ivm.vu.nl/en/Images/PT6_tcm53-161511.pdf (accessed 5 January 2014).
Gibbons, M., C. Limoges, H. Nowotny, S. Schwartzman, P. Scott and M. Trow (1994), *The New Production of Knowledge*, London: Sage.
Goven, J. (2003), 'Deploying the consensus conference in New Zealand: democracy and de-problematization', *Public Understanding of Science*, **12**, 423–440.
Green, K. and P. Vergragt (2002), 'Towards sustainable households: a methodology for developing sustainable technological and social innovations', *Futures*, **34**, 381–400.
Greenbaum, T.L. (1998), *The Handbook for Focus Group Research*, 2nd edition, Thousand Oaks, CA: Sage.
Gregory, R., T.L. MacDaniels and D. Fields (2001), 'Decision aiding, not dispute resolution: creating insights through structured environmental decisions', *Journal of Policy Analysis and Management*, **20**, 415–432.
Grundahl, J. (1995), 'The Danish consensus conference model', in S. Joss and J. Durant (eds), *Public Participation in Science: The Role of Consensus Conferences in Europe*, London: Science Museum, pp. 31–40.
Habermas, J. (1984), *The Theory of Communicative Action. Reason and the Rationalization of Society*, vol. 1, Boston, MA: Beacon Press.
Hall, B.L. (2005), 'In from the cold: reflections on participatory action research from 1970–2005', *Convergence*, **38** (1), 5–24.
Held, D. (1987), *Models of Democracy*, Cambridge: Polity Press.
Hisschemöller, M. (2005), 'Participation as knowledge production and the limits of democracy', in S. Maasen and P. Weingart (eds), *Democratization of Expertise? Exploring Novel Forms of Scientific Advice in Political Decision-Making – Yearbook Sociology of the Sciences*, **24**, Dordrecht: Kluwer, pp. 189–208.
Hisschemöller, M. and R. Bode (2011), 'Institutionalized knowledge conflict in assessing the possible contributions of H_2 to a sustainable energy system for the Netherlands', *International Journal of Hydrogen Energy*, **36** (1), 14–24.
Hisschemöller, M. and R. Hoppe (2001), 'Coping with intractable controversies: the case for problem structuring in policy design and analysis', in M. Hisschemöller, R. Hoppe, W.N. Dunn and J. Ravetz (eds), *Knowledge, Power and Participation in Environmental Policy Analysis. Policy Studies Review Annual*, **12**, 47–72.
Huitema, D., M. van de Kerkhof and U. Pesch (2007), 'The nature of the beast: are citizens' juries deliberative or pluralist?', *Policy Sciences*, **40**, 287–311.
Innes, J. (2004), 'Consensus building: clarification for the critics', *Planning Theory*, **3**, 5–20.
Irwin, A., T.E. Jensen and K.E. Jones (2012), 'The good, the bad and the perfect: criticizing engagement practice', *Social Studies of Science*, **43**, 118–135.
Janis, I.L. (1972), *Victims of Groupthink: Psychological Studies of Foreign Policy Decisions and Fiascoes*, Boston: Houghton-Mifflin.
Jelsma, J. (2001), 'Frame reflective policy-analysis in practice: co-evolution of a policy regime and an intractable controversy in biotechnology', in M. Hisschemöller, R. Hoppe, W.N. Dunn and J. Ravetz (eds), *Knowledge, Power and Participation in Environmental Policy Analysis. Policy Studies Review Annual*, **12**, 201–229.

Joss, S. (2005), 'Between policy and politics', in S. Maasen and P. Weingart (eds), *Democratization of Expertise? Exploring Novel Forms of Scientific Advice in Political Decision-making – Yearbook Sociology of the Sciences*, **24**, Dordrecht: Kluwer.

Joss, S. and S. Bellucci (2002), *Participatory Technology Assessment – European Perspectives*, London: Centre for the Study of Democracy (CSD), University of Westminster.

Kantrowitz, E. (1967), 'Proposal for an institution for scientific judgement', *Science*, **12**, 763–764.

Keune, H. and L. Goorden (2002), *Interactieve Backcasting: Een Duurzame Energietoekomst voor Belgie*, Universiteit Antwerpen, Vakgroep Milieu, Technologie en Technologiemanagement STEM.

Kupper, F. (2006), *Democratizing Animal Biotechnology. Inquiry and Deliberation in Ethics and Governance*, PhD Dissertation, Amsterdam, VU.

Lasswell, H.D. (1960), 'Technique of decision seminars', *Midwest Journal of Political Science*, **4**, 213–236.

Lindblom, C.E. (1965), *The Intelligence of Democracy*, New York: Free Press.

Machiavelli, N. (1970), *The Discourses*, edited by Bernard Crick, Harmondsworth: Pelican Classics.

Mason, R.O. and I.I. Mitroff (1981), *Challenging Strategic Planning Assumptions: Theory, Cases and Techniques*, New York: Wiley.

Mayer, I. (1997), *Debating Technologies. A Methodological Contribution to the Design and Evaluation of Participatory Policy Analysis*, Tilburg: Tilburg University Press.

McCreary, S., J. Gamman and B. Brooks (2001), 'Refining and testing Joint Fact-Finding for environmental dispute resolution: ten years of success', *Mediation Quarterly*, **18**, 329–348.

Merton, R.K. and P.L. Kendall (1946), 'The focused interview', *American Journal of Sociology*, **51**, 541–557.

Mitroff, I.I., R.O. Mason and V.P. Barabba (1983), *The 1980 Census: Policymaking amid Turbulence*, Lexington: Lexington Books.

Nemeth, C., B. Personnaz, M. Personnaz and J.A. Goncalo (2004), 'The liberating role of conflict in group creativity: a study in two countries', *European Journal of Social Psychology*, **34**, 365–374.

Osborn, A.F. (1963), *Applied Imagination. Principles and Procedures of Creative Problem-solving*, New York: Charles Scribner's Sons.

Oughton, D.H. and P. Strand (2004), 'The Oslo consensus conference on protection of the environment', *Journal of Environmental Radioactivity*, **74**, 7–17.

Pateman, C. (1979), *The Problem of Political Obligation. A Critical Analysis of Liberal Theory*, Chichester: John Wiley.

Quist, J. (2007), *Backcasting for a Sustainable Future: The Impact after 10 years*, Delft: Eburon Academic Publishers.

Raiffa, H. (1968), *Decision Analysis. Introductory Lectures on Choices Under Uncertainty*, Reading, MA: Addision-Wesley.

Renn, O. (2004), 'The challenge of integrating deliberation and expertise: participation and discourse in risk management', in T. McDaniels and M. Small (eds), *Risk Analysis and Society*, New York: Cambridge University Press, pp. 289–366.

Rittel, H.W.J. and M.M. Webber (1973), 'Dilemmas in a general theory of planning', *Policy Sciences*, **4**, 155–169.

Robinson, J. (2003), 'Future subjunctive: backcasting as social learning', *Futures*, **35**, 839–856.

Rowe, G. and L.J. Frewer (2005), 'A typology of public engagement mechanisms', *Science Technology & Human Values*, **30**, 251–290.

Sabatier, P. (ed.) (1999), *An Advocacy Coalition Lens on Environmental Policy*, Cambridge: The MIT Press.

Schumpeter, J.A. (1942, 1976), *Capitalism, Socialism and Democracy*, New York: Harper & Row.

Schweiger, D.M., W.R. Sandberg and J.W. Ragan (1986), 'Group approaches for improving strategic decision making: a comparative analysis of dialectical inquiry, devil's advocacy and consensus', *The Academy of Management Journal*, **29**, 51–71.

Schwenk, C.R. and R.A. Cosier (1980), 'Effects of the expert, devil's advocate, and dialectical inquiry methods on predicting performance', *Organization Behavior and Human Performance*, **26**, 409–424.

Seley, J.F. (1983), *The Politics of Public Facility Planning*, Lexington: Lexington Books.

Simon, H.A. (1973), 'The structure of ill-structured problems', *Artificial Intelligence*, **4**, 181–201.

Stasser, G. and W. Titus (1985), 'Pooling of unshared information in group decision making: biased information sampling during discussion', *Journal of Personality and Social Psychology*, **48**, 1467–1478.

Stirling, A. (2008), '"Opening up" and "closing down": power, participation, and pluralism in the social appraisal of technology', *Science Technology & Human Values*, **33**, 262–294.

Susskind, L. and P. Field (1996), *Dealing with an Angry Public: The Mutual Gains Approach to Resolving Disputes*, New York: Free Press.

Susskind, L., S. McKearnan and J. Thomas-Larmer (1999), *The Consensus Building Handbook*, Thousand Oaks, CA: Sage Publications.

Tansey, J., J. Carmichael, R. VanWynsberghe and J. Robinson (2002), 'The future is not what it used to be', *Global Environmental Change*, **12** (2), 97–104.

Tufte, T. and P. Mefalopulos (2009), *Participatory Communication: A Practical Guide*, Paper 170, Washington, DC: The World Bank.

Turoff, M. (1975), 'The policy delphi', in M. Turoff and H.A. Linstone (eds), *The Delphi Method. Techniques and Applications*, Boston: Addison-Wesley, pp. 84–101.

UNHCR (2006), *UNHCR Tool for Participatory Assessment in Operations*, retrieved from http://www.unhcr.org/450e963f2.html (accessed 28 May 2014).

van Asselt, M. and N. Rijkens-Klomp (2002), 'A look in the mirror: reflection on participation in integrated assessment from a methodological perspective', *Global Environmental Change*, **12**, 167–184.

van de Kerkhof, M., E. Cuppen and M. Hisschemöller (2009), 'The repertory grid to unfold conflicting positions: the case of a stakeholder dialogue on prospects for hydrogen', *Technological Forecasting and Social Change*, **76**, 422–432.

Vandenabeele, J. and L. Goorden (2004), 'Consensus conference on genetic testing: citizenship and technology', *Journal of Community and Applied Social Psychology*, **14**, 207–213.

VanWynsberghe, R., J. Moore, J. Tansey, J. Carmichael (2003), 'Towards community engagement: six steps to expert learning for future scenario development', *Futures*, **35**, 203–219.

Vasileiadou, E., M. Hisschemöller, A.C. Petersen et al. (2014), 'Adaptation to extreme weather: identifying different societal perspectives in the Netherlands', *Regional Environmental Change*, **14**, 91–101.

Wilkinson, S. (2004), 'Focus group research', in D. Silverman (ed.), *Qualitative Research: Theory, Method and Practice*, London: Sage, pp. 177–199.

World Bank (1996), *The World Bank Participation Sourcebook*, Washington DC: World Bank.

World Food Programme (2001), *Participatory Techniques and Tools – A WFP Guide*, Rome: World Food Programme, retrieved from http://toolkit.ineesite. org/toolkit/INEEcms/uploads/1033/Participatory_Techniques_EN.pdf (accessed 28 May 2014).

3. Scenarios: tools for coping with complexity and future uncertainty?

Marta Pérez-Soba and Rob Maas

INTRODUCTION

We cannot predict the future with certainty, but we know that it is influenced by our current actions, and that these in turn are influenced by our expectations. This is why future scenarios have existed from the dawn of civilization and have been used for developing military, political and economic strategies. Does the existence of scenarios help to accomplish the desired outcomes? It is fair to say that in most cases the answer to this question is no, simply because history is normally an open, undetermined process, where sudden and unexpected events can play a decisive, disruptive role. Could the French Revolution have been prevented if Louis XVI's counsellors had had the imagination to develop a shock-scenario, foreseeing the impact of the volcanic eruptions in Iceland and Japan, and the consequent crop failures in 1784 and 1785 and food scarcity in France – often cited as a proximate cause of the French Revolution in 1789? This is debatable to say the least.

However, scenarios have become a key tool in the policy formulation process because they help with identifying possible solutions to policy problems or exploring the various options available (Howlett 2011). As former EU Environment Commissioner Janez Potočnik has put it:

> We tend not to plan well for the future and lags prevent us from reaching our goals unless we act early. We have path-dependency. For future success in almost any area, we have to incorporate future effects into our current policy-making. (EC 2010)

Regarding definitions, words such as 'futures', 'foresight', 'scenarios' and 'forecasts' are often used interchangeably in policy documents. In this chapter we use 'futures studies' as a broad term that includes different approaches for dealing with complexity and future uncertainty, that is, an interdisciplinary collection of methods, theories and findings described as narratives, images, statistical trends, models and recommendations. 'Foresight' describes the process of envisioning, inventing and constructing scenarios. 'Scenarios' are one such method of exploring the future. They are internally consistent and coherent descriptions of hypothetical futures, often with a time horizon of more than 20 years, and are usually used in futures studies. The futures analysed can be probable, imaginable, surprising, desirable or frightening, but the likelihood of realization remains unknown. In the remainder of this chapter we also use the word 'scenario' to describe a surprise-free forecast or future projection. 'Forecasts' are more focused on an accurate quantitative prediction. They could include a sensitivity analysis to include uncertainty margins. Theoretically, forecasts are more 'certain' than scenarios. However in practice both approaches overlap and, as discussed more fully below, are often used in combination.

What is it that makes scenarios such an important tool in policy formulation? Four reasons can be identified:

1. They seek to *avoid risks*, preparing decision makers for what might be coming and enabling thinking about possible actions to avoid risks, for example, increasing cereal production when weather forecasts predict poor harvests in other parts of the world;

2. They have potential to *enhance policy performance*: to know whether the benefits of measures are robust; in other words, whether policy targets can still be met if circumstances change. For example, will an investment in a new airport runway still pay off if economic growth is lower than expected? Will Member States still be able to fulfil EU environmental obligations with higher than expected economic growth?

3. They attempt to *expand creativity*: they offer a catchy, 'outside the box' image that unites different stakeholders and sets a time path for social and technological innovations. President Kennedy's 'man-on-the-moon' vision provides one example. Imagining possible futures could lead to new breakthroughs that at the time were considered unlikely;

4. They seek to *stimulate open discussion and the reaching of consensus* via processes of deliberation, thereby allowing participants to compare different perspectives on the future to see whether consensus on certain no-regret actions is possible. For example, what are sensible next steps given the different views on the causes of climate change and the different beliefs in market mechanisms or intergovernmental coordination to bring a solution?

Scenarios seek to support different activities in the policy formulation process. It is particularly in problem definition where they can help answer the question of whether current trends and policies are robust. In addition, they can help to identify policy alternatives that can be an input into the functioning of other tools such as cost–benefit analysis and multi-criteria analysis.

In this chapter we discuss the role of scenarios as tools to deal with complexity and future uncertainty in the policy formulation process. The first part focuses on scenario use in theory, and the second on their use in 'real world' venues of policy action. The first part sets the scene by discussing the specific functions of scenarios when dealing with complexity and uncertainty in the policy formulation process, links this with scenario selection and design considering the standard stages and tasks of policy formulation, and reflects on issues of credibility, legitimacy and salience. It also describes potential links and overlaps with other policy formulation tools. It ends by briefly reviewing the historical development of scenarios. Part two summarizes a selection of cases where scenarios played a decisive role. It identifies the factors that enhanced their use in particular policy venues. It investigates why a foresight process was undertaken and in which context. It explores what knowledge sources underpinned the scenarios and how they were deployed in policy formulation activities. This chapter concludes with a reflection on the importance of acknowledging the particular needs of policymakers in policy formulation processes when dealing with complexity and uncertainty.

SCENARIO USE IN THEORY

Uncertainty and Complexity: The Raison d'Être of Scenarios as Policy Formulation Tools

Policymakers are faced with the complexity and uncertainty of possible future circumstances inherent in a highly dynamic, globalizing world. According to de Jouvenel (2004), policymakers often justify their decisions by claiming they had no other choice, but in truth they no longer had a choice because of a lack of foresight. In addition, politicians themselves are an important source of uncertainty by making changes in the structure of government throughout their term in office (Kelly et al. 2010). Scenarios are commonly prescribed as a tool to avoid constantly being forced to react to emergencies. They help to deal with uncertainty and complexity, and therefore enhance decision performance by supporting the definition of solutions for potential challenges.

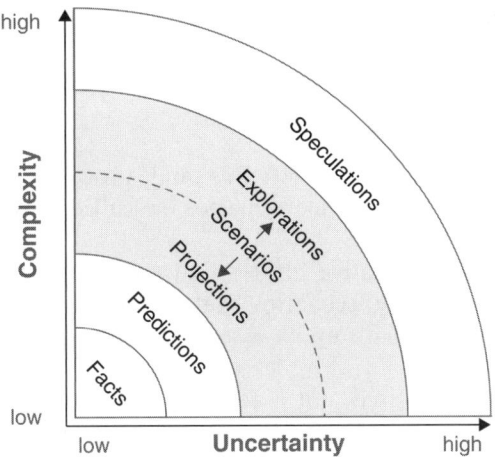

Complexity

low

low   **Uncertainty**   high

Speculations

Explorations

Scenarios

Projections

Predictions

Facts

Source: Zurek and Henrichs (2007).

Figure 3.1   Ways to explore the future depending on its uncertainty and complexity

Zurek and Henrichs (2007) use uncertainty and complexity as the main axes to define ways of exploring the future, specifically: (1) how uncertain we are about future developments of key drivers; and (2) how well we understand the complexity of the system and its causalities (see Figure 3.1).

Figure 3.1 helps to identify the type of futures study needed in policy formulation, depending on the degree of uncertainty and complexity of the policy question. Forecasting methods include trend extrapolations or model calculations and might be used to assess the consequences of assumed changes in policy measures, such as a rise in taxes or reduction in the number of immigrants. Speculations are often the best that can be achieved when levels of uncertainty and complexity are both relatively high. Scenarios, on the other hand, lie somewhere in between forecasts and speculations, that is, when the degree of uncertainty and complexity is of an intermediate level. The definition of scenarios used in the Millennium Ecosystem Assessment (MEA 2005) reflects this understanding of a scenario, describing them as plausible and often simplified descriptions of how the future may develop, based on a coherent and internally consistent set of assumptions about key driving forces and relationships. Scenarios therefore have an exploratory character. They could assume changes in external drivers that cannot be directly influenced by policy measures (for example, higher frequency of natural hazards, higher energy prices, and so on), as well as in internal drivers, such as certain policy changes.

We can distinguish three types of scenarios based on their degree of uncertainty and complexity:

1. Those extrapolating current trends and processes, for example, business-as-usual or reference scenarios (so-called *prospective* or *predictive* scenarios);
2. Those exploring alternative futures that are plausible, surprising or shocking, for example, scenarios that assume technological break-throughs or events that impose a security risk (so-called *explorative* scenarios);
3. Those describing desired, not necessarily expected futures (so-called *descriptive* or *normative* scenarios). Visions are an example of norma-tive scenarios.

It is interesting to note that in practice, tensions can occur between forecasters (for example, modellers, economists) and visionary, creative scenario developers who focus on discontinuities and desirable futures, as described by van 't Klooster (2007) during the development of spatial planning scenarios.

The Selection and Design of Scenarios as a Policy Formulation Tool

The Dutch Scientific Council for Policy (WRR) argues that since the future is fundamentally unpredictable and not every imaginable future is possible, policies should not be based on a single, surprise-free futures study (WRR 2010). Every futures study should really start with two critical questions (see Figure 3.2). Answering these two questions leads to different types of futures studies:

1. Is it wise to assume stability and continuity of the system? If not, uncertainty should be central in the study and one surprise-free fore-cast will be insufficient;
2. Is it sensible to assume normative consensus about what future is desirable? If the answer is yes, different scenarios should grasp the uncertainty range. If the answer is no, divergent normative perspec-tives on the future are needed.

According to the WRR, there is often a blind spot for developing diver-gent normative perspectives, which present a range of policy choices with explicit indications for whom these choices are desirable.

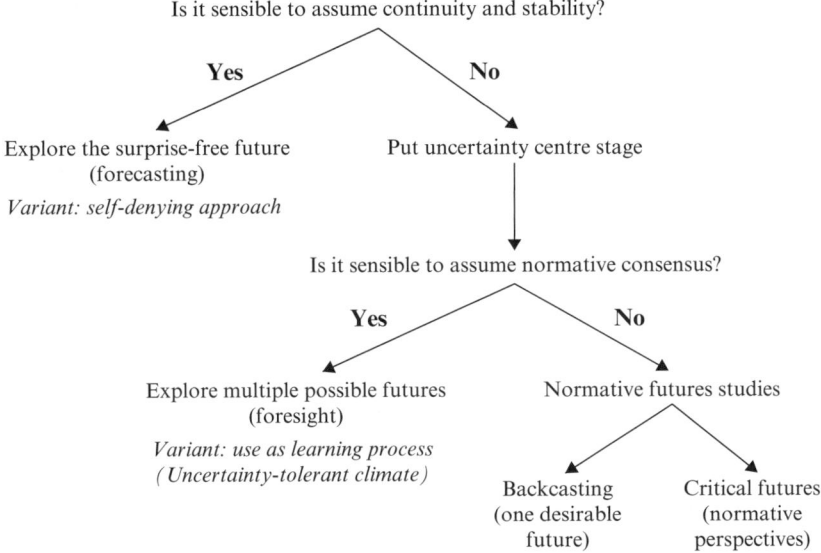

Critical questions

Is it sensible to assume continuity and stability?

Yes   **No**

Explore the surprise-free future
(forecasting)
Variant: self-denying approach

Put uncertainty centre stage

Is it sensible to assume normative consensus?

Yes   **No**

Explore multiple possible futures
(foresight)
*Variant: use as learning process
(Uncertainty-tolerant climate)*

Normative futures studies

Backcasting
(one desirable
future)

Critical futures
(normative
perspectives)

Source: WRR (2010).

Figure 3.2   *A decision tree that considers the degree of future uncertainty and normative consensus*

In developing scenarios, we can distinguish different phases in any policy formulation process (Schwartz and Ogilvy 1998; de Jouvenel 2004; Metzger et al. 2010):

1. *Problem characterization*
   A specific scenario exercise will have to start with the definition of the policy issue at stake, for example, energy security, climate change, and so on, and, related to that, the system boundaries, that is, what is the spatial scale of the subject and the relevant time horizon? For example, when developing scenarios for city planning, global scenarios for the next 100 years will not be necessary, although they can give input to the process in defining relevant exogenous factors.

2. *Problem conceptualization*
   This phase identifies the drivers that impact the system under analysis. The drivers can be exogenous/external (for example, technological

developments or oil prices), exogenous/internal (for example, policy choices) or endogenous factors (drivers that are dependent on other drivers, for example, energy demand as the result of traffic development or energy saving). Literature surveys, analyses of statistical trends, surveys with Delphi methods, and stakeholder workshops can all produce inputs for a scenario development. A morphological analysis of relevant factors and relationships, a scheme with causes and effects, such as the Drivers–Pressures–State–Impacts–Responses (DPSIR) scheme (EEA 1999) is one means to frame the problem. Workshops and (qualitative) modelling or systems analysis techniques can help to create a common understanding or find out where views on how the world works differ. The result of this phase is the identification of key drivers that affect the subject directly or indirectly.

3. *Scenario framing*

In this phase, the logic of the scenarios is defined. The certainty of future development of the key drivers is identified. Can continuity be assumed and trends extrapolated (for example, on energy use)? Alternatively, for which exogenous drivers are contrasting scenarios needed because the uncertainty range is large or discontinuities cannot be excluded (for example, the oil-price development, or new European regulation on electric vehicles)? If so, what are the main drivers and do these need contrasting scenarios? If there are many uncertain drivers, the number of possible scenarios can become quite large and this would lead to a set of scenarios that becomes incomprehensible to users. In such cases, a *tree structure* can be used to create some order. For example, a high versus low economic growth scenario can be assumed, each split into a fossil fuel and renewable energy scenario. All four scenarios can be further split into a high or low oil price variant, and so on.

In order to limit the total number of scenarios to a manageable number, the main drivers have to be selected, or assumptions made about different drivers with a high mutual dependency can be merged into a set of contrasting coherent scenarios (for example, combining high oil prices with fast technological developments). The latter approach requires the development of a credible storyline or narrative.

Triangles, scenario-axes or pentagons can be used to explain the contrasts in such coherent scenarios. *Triangles* and *pentagons* can be used to illustrate that scenarios have been designed from a certain perspective (economy, society or environment; or from a citizen, public or private company perspective). This can assist in identifying trade-offs and looking for compromises. *Axes* can be used when two dominant drivers (or groups of drivers) have been identified that are independent of each other. Use of the deregulation–regulation axis versus the globalization–regionalization axis is quite common. In this phase, it is also good to consider the inertia in the system and to check if the chosen time horizon is still valid.

4. *Scenario description*

Here, each scenario comes to life, that is, it is described in a credible and salient way, for example, using figures, images, narratives and metaphors. According to van der Heijden (2005), a scenario that will actually be used in policy formulation is internally consistent, links historic events with hypothetical ones in the future, carries storylines that can be expressed in simple diagrams, is as plausible as other scenarios, reflects elements that are already determined, and identifies indicators or 'signposts' that show that the scenario is already occurring. The narrative should not only be written in scientific or economic terms; it should also be based on different 'ways of knowing' (Lejano et al. 2013) and include memorable metaphors (Wack 1985). Participatory approaches can help to enrich the plausibility of the scenarios, and increase the acceptance for use in the policy process.

5. *Scenario assessments*

In this final phase, potential policy options are identified and assessed. Many questions typically emerge in this phase. What, for example, is the impact of policy options in each scenario? What trade-offs do policymakers have to face? Can no-regrets options (in other words, measures that are right in all scenarios) be defined? How can the cost-effectiveness of policies be optimized? Numerical models can be an important tool to use, but in the last few years (serious) gaming has often been used as an option to better understand the attitudes of key players in a scenario and to define robust policy recommendations.

Surprising Futures

The crucial question in each scenario exercise is whether all uncertainties have been taken into account, or whether something vital has been overlooked. What would cause surprises or abrupt changes? And do we need (additional) 'what-if' scenarios to address such surprises?

There are many examples in futures analysis where factors have interacted in complex ways, due to non-linear feedback loops, and produced sometimes surprising futures. The combination of systems analysis and qualitative storylines enables the inclusion of factors that are difficult to formalize – such as technological breakthroughs or shifts in values – and demonstrates their impacts.

Brooks (1986) identifies methods to spot surprises that might subsequently be explored via systems analysis:

- assume non-linearities;
- amplify responses to small random changes/events;
- change the (perceived) scarcity or thresholds;
- assume delayed effects;
- assume human ingenuity and transitions towards another carrier for economic development.

Saritas and Nugroho (2012) distinguish discontinuities, but also wild cards and weak signals as sources for surprise, which can be identified (and prioritized) in surveys. Wild cards are trend-breaking assumptions, fault lines or external shocks, for example on social or political stability. Weak signals are less prominent trends that might eventually become important game changers, for example the sudden availability and exploitation of 'big data', the sudden uptake and use of a new technology such as electric bicycles, or an increased focus on new behaviours such as consuming healthy food.

What Policy Formulation Tasks do Scenarios Aim to Perform?

Scenarios may, in principle, perform several tasks at the same time in the policy formulation process, as defined in the first chapter of this book:

1. Characterization of the current situation: this is a usual starting phase in foresight analysis, as a reference to the current state is needed to measure the impact of the policy option and assess its policy relevance;
2. Problem conceptualization: this is the core business of any foresight exercise. There are two contrasting conceptual approaches in scenario development: the 'exploratory' (how the future *could* be) and the 'normative' (how the future *should* be). As part of the exploratory scenarios, frightening scenarios may enable precautionary policy, security policy and improved crisis management (preparedness). Pessimistic assumptions about the environment (for example, scarcity, natural disasters, major accidents), economic system (economic cycles, growing inequality, financial bubbles) or the behaviour of actors (crime, lack of enforcement of laws, conflicts) may make it possible to assess worst-case developments;

3. The identification of policy options: scenario techniques include the identification of options or alternatives for the future: 'exploratory' methods begin from the present, and see where events and trends might take us; 'normative' methods begin from the future, asking what trends and events would take us there (EC et al. 2005). Scenarios can focus on the short term (close to the 4–8 years regional and national policy cycle) or on the longer term (usually more than 20 years, used in global policy formulation processes);

4. The assessment of potential policy options: this is the last phase in scenario development (see previous section).

In addition, the scenario building process offers opportunities to open up debate and involve government policymakers and stakeholders outside the official state machinery, seek consensus on a policy strategy and increase the legitimacy of policy measures.

What Expertise/Knowledge is Needed in Scenario Development?

A broad awareness of what is happening in the world is a basic requirement for any scenario developer. Useful information can come from the existing literature, statistics, news programmes, experience or conversations with experts and non-professionals. Scenario developers are often interdisciplinary generalists, interested in history, as well as economic, physical and social processes. They should be able to work directly with real world decision takers or with scenario consultants/trainers, and translate scenario findings into practical and robust policy recommendations. In addition, awareness is needed about the way in which individuals select and discard information without being aware of doing so. As far as possible, scenario developers should be aware of their own biases and be as reflexive and open-minded as possible. Scenario developers are trained in finding key trends and imagining attitudes of key players. They analyse flows and what factors may disrupt them. Where knowledge is lacking or inconclusive, value-laden opinions become an inevitable part of a scenario exercise. Ideological questions regularly arise in scenario-based policy formulation processes. For example, is market liberalization or more government regulation the best way forward?

Surveys, workshops and Delphi methods are techniques that can help generate future expectations shared by a larger group. According to Swart et al. (2004), a successful scenario study requires a sufficiently large group of participants and adequate time for problem definition, knowledge-based development, iterative scenario analysis, and for review and outreach. The development of coherent, engaging stories about the future, including potential surprise events or seeds of change, has to place the focal problem in a broader context. Last but not least, it is vital to be clear for whom scenarios are made and for which purpose. Normative judgements and political worldviews have to be made explicit in scenario development (Metzger et al. 2010).

Successful scenario development meets three fundamental characteristics (Alcamo and Henrichs 2008). *Credibility* refers to the scientific rigour and internal coherence of the scenario. *Legitimacy* is linked to the scenario development process. Finally, *saliency* refers to the appropriateness of scenarios in responding to information needs. These criteria can be further specified as follows (Rounsevell and Henrichs 2008):

Credibility:

- addressing the subjectivity of scenario developers and stakeholders involved (biases, prejudices, expectations, ideology);
- quantifying uncertainty in scenario assumptions (differences in drivers' uncertainty or in interpretation of stakeholders' inputs);
- quantifying uncertainty within models (data, calibration).

Legitimacy:

- including stakeholder participatory approaches can help to facilitate societal acceptance;
- ensuring transparency and traceability of the scenario development process and its political context (aim, who built it/funded it).

Saliency:

- designing scenario processes that ensure relevance to the policy question and stakeholder perspectives (for example, stakeholder participation, focal questions, and so on);
- stimulating and capturing creativity, by allowing the exploration of 'surprises';
- presenting and communicating scenarios in an accessible manner.

These criteria are not, however, necessarily followed in practice (see below) (Rounsevell and Henrichs 2008).

Links with Other Policy Formulation Tools

In principle, scenarios have close links with other policy formulation tools, especially those to assess potential impacts of policy options, like modelling, cost–benefit analysis (CBA) (see Chapter 7, this volume), cost-effectiveness analysis (CEA) and trade-off analysis. In fact, these tools arguably become more policy relevant when based on futures studies, as their outcomes greatly depend on underlying assumptions about present and future circumstances.

Exploratory scenarios are largely based on multivariate systems analysis and cause–effect models. Normative forecasting relies more on Bayesian statistics, linear and dynamic programming. For both exploratory and normative approaches, dynamic modelling is very relevant to identify the feedback mechanisms. Modelling (see Chapter 5, this volume) is intrinsically linked to the use of scenarios because models provide artificial experiments to explore system behaviour in the future where facts are not freely available (Matthews et al. 2007). Models help assess the complex interactions between system components and therefore support the development of quantitative pathways. This is the reason why model-based scenarios are often prescribed in *ex ante* assessments of policies (see Chapter 5, this volume; Bennett et al. 2003; Rounsevell et al. 2006; Helming and Pérez-Soba 2011). 'Story-And-Simulation' is the state-of-the-art of linking scenario narratives and models, thus enabling interaction between scientists and a range of other stakeholders (see Chapter 2, this volume). The framework is on the one hand flexible enough to use in conjunction with additional tools, and on the other sufficiently strict to separate clearly the roles of stakeholders and scientists and allow for co-production of knowledge (Kok et al. 2011). Most studies use a traditional 'Story-And-Simulation' approach coupling qualitative stories with (spatially explicit) mathematical models. More recently, the addition of other tools such as conceptual models and Fuzzy-Sets has shown their potential in facilitating the quantification of stakeholder input, for example directly obtaining estimates for model parameters. The potential for using these (and other related tools) has barely been touched upon in the literature.

Uncertainty management is another tool that is intrinsically linked to the credibility of scenarios. If continuity in trends can be assumed, uncertainties for investment decisions can be assessed in a quantitative way by attaching probabilities to different quantitative forecasts in order to calculate pay-off periods under different assumptions. Decisions can be optimized and project risks can be included in the required discount rate for an investment. For government policy, robustness can be increased by assessing whether a measure is still effective in meeting a policy target when scenario assumptions are changed. Policymakers could choose to limit the policy to no-regret measures (saving money and accepting the risks of non-compliance with the policy targets) or extend the policy strategy with additional measures to ensure that targets will be met under different scenario assumptions (the precautionary approach).

SCENARIOS: THEIR USE IN PRACTICE

The Historical Evolution of Scenarios as a Policy Influencing Tool

In this overview we briefly describe the evolution of scenarios in decision making, highlighting the particular role they played in certain policy
formulation venues. *Utopia* by Thomas More (1516) offers a very early
example of a visionary scenario, aimed at stimulating social change in
Renaissance society (More 2012). By contrast, Malthus' *Essay on the
Principle of Population* (1798) was based on a statistical analysis of trends
and warned that limitations in agricultural productivity would halt population growth. Other types of 'frightening' scenarios have been published in
more recent decades (for example, on climate change or resource scarcity),
and were intended to provoke action to address risks.

Are futures studies, we might ask, science, fiction, or science-fiction?
The future cannot be tested empirically because there are no data. In his
article *The Discovery of the Future*, H.G. Wells was the first to discuss the
possibilities of exploring the future as a scientific activity (Wells 1913).
Later on, techniques and methods were developed that systematically
included the future in policy strategies and planning. Although science-
fiction literature, futuristic 'megatrends' or mystical prophecies can be a
source of inspiration for policymakers, in this chapter we have focused on
scenarios developed by scientists.

Futures studies nowadays closely relate to 'strategic planning', which
aims at meeting a certain goal and choosing the required means, depending on the (possible) circumstances and reactions from other parties.
Originally, strategic planning had a military meaning, inspired by 2400-
year old lessons on the 'art-of-war' (Sun Tzu 400BC), but later on was
also used by private companies. In the private sector, Royal Dutch Shell
first developed scenarios in the 1970s to prepare for the impact of sudden
changes in oil prices. Pierre Wack acknowledged that uncertainties and
potential discontinuities made traditional surprise-free forecasts less useful
and introduced the development of alternative scenarios (Wack 1985).

The US military think tank RAND first used scenarios in the 1940s
for strategic planning. After the Second World War, the RAND corporation became a leading institute for technologically oriented futures
studies. RAND's Herman Kahn was one of the lead authors of *The
Year 2000* (Haydon 1967), an optimistic study about the possibility of
political control and technological and societal progress. In sharp contrast, the *Limits to Growth* report to the Club of Rome, produced by the
System Dynamics Group of the Massachusetts Institute of Technology
(MIT) (Meadows et al. 1972), presented (in Malthusian style) political

challenges including resource scarcity and pollution of the atmosphere that remain important. Several countries started to develop economic forecasts after the Second World War to optimize economic policies and to assess the need for infrastructural investments. Some, including the Netherlands and Belgium, institutionalized this activity in Central Planning Bureaus.

In the more recent past, the range of topics covered by futures studies has widened, from national security and technology development, to social and environmental policies. In some European countries, futures studies are common practice in government institutes, with the UK's Foresight Horizon Scanning Centre (and formerly the Central Policy Review Staff), and the Netherlands' economic, social and environmental planning offices providing prominent examples. In international policy venues, futures studies have become especially indispensable. The celebrated Brundtland report, for example, set out an influential vision in *Our Common Future* (WCED 1987). Since the 1980s, the Convention on Long-Range Transboundary Air Pollution has used cost-minimized policy scenarios as a starting point for policy negotiations, and the UN Framework Convention on Climate Change derived political greenhouse gas reduction targets from the scenarios of the Intergovernmental Panel on Climate Change (Swart et al. 2004; Robinson et al. 1996). The OECD has been involved in futures studies since the 1970s. In 1979 it published the 'Interfutures' report *Facing the Future: Mastering the Probable and Managing the Unpredictable*. More recently, the OECD (2013) started a web-based knowledge bank for futures studies.

The relevance of future studies for European policy formulation is shown by the institutionalization of foresight activities. For example, in 1989 European Commission president Jacques Delors established a Forward Studies Unit as a think tank to evaluate European integration on the basis of long-term prospects and structural tendencies. This interdisciplinary unit is now known as the Bureau of European Policy Advisers (BEPA). A Forward-Looking Information and Scenarios (FLIS) working group was created in 2010 by the European Environment Agency Strategic Futures group as part of EIONET (European Environment Information and Observation Network) to share the latest developments between their members (for example, tools for visions building, environmental goal setting).

The next section explores issues of use by investigating a selection of environmental, economic and spatial planning scenarios that were used by policy formulators. We describe why particular scenarios were developed, how they were applied in combination with other policy formulation tools, and what the impact was on policy decisions. We focus on one international experience (the abatement of air pollution), and a national one in the Netherlands. The chosen cases offer examples of policy formulation venues where 'official' (government sanctioned) scenarios were developed 'externally' by experts (and not 'internally' by policymakers). We conclude with lessons learned and recommendations for forthcoming scenario development as a policy formulation tool.

The Use of Scenarios in International Policy Venues

Scenarios are used across various policy venues. In general, quantitative scenarios are widely adopted in economic policymaking, for example the European Commission and the International Monetary Fund apply model based scenarios for tracking expected budget deficits. They are also commonly used for several aspects of physical planning, for example demographic trends, traffic projections, expected sea level rise, or the land use requirements for biofuels. In environmental policy planning, scenarios for national emissions of greenhouse gasses and air pollutants must be reported to the United Nations periodically. All the above-mentioned scenarios are typically developed by (external) experts, where needed with some input from policymakers (for example, on envisaged policy measures), and are relatively undisputed. The time horizon and the indicators used are generally well defined.

Scenarios are also indispensable for the impact assessment of (large) investment projects. At least a reference scenario (in other words, future without the project) and a scenario including the project are needed. The time horizon and the set of relevant indicators are less well defined, may vary from project to project, and are often subject to public debate (for example, for a shale gas project, an extension of an airport, or a plan to prevent flooding). Meaningful scenarios and indicators are often co-produced by experts and stakeholders.

International Environmental Negotiations: Transboundary Air Pollution

Since 1979, international negotiations to reduce air pollution have resulted in agreements (protocols) with emission reduction obligations for European countries. The scientific community has played a key role in providing measurements, modelling and information on air pollution impacts and the cost-effectiveness of available abatement measures. From the beginning of the 1990s, flat rate reduction targets were replaced by protocols aiming at a cost-effective, effect-oriented approach, meaning that measures should be taken that offer the best protection for health and ecosystems at the lowest costs. This approach causes emission reduction obligation percentages to vary widely among countries. For example, in a less densely populated area, in principle, fewer measures are needed.

Scenario calculations by the International Institute for Applied Systems Analysis (IIASA) using the GAINS model are the basis for political negotiations. GAINS delivers optimization results: given (politically chosen) ambition levels to protect health and ecosystems, the model gives the minimum cost solution for a target year (with a 10–20 year time horizon). Scenario results give insights to policymakers (in other words, negotiators) on the relationship between environmental protection ambitions and the costs for their country. This is effectively a backcasting scenario and addresses the following question: 'what do we need to do today to reach that desired level of protection?'

The scenarios describe the most likely future of emissions and their impacts, and are based on model extrapolations of drivers (for example, population, GDP, energy use, transport, agriculture), emission factors (influenced by abatement measures), dispersion models, dose–response relationships for health and ecosystems, and costs of (additional) abatement measures. Scenario selections are made by the policymakers, namely the leaders of the various national delegations. Differences between scenarios are the result of differences in policy measures (policy variants). In order to increase trust in the GAINS model, much effort has been spent on the review of the quality of all the input data. Country experts check and improve data on emissions, base-year activity and existing policies, the assumptions made for the development of drivers and ecosystem data. Countries are stimulated to deliver their own national projection. The GAINS team at IIASA checks the consistency of the data officially delivered by the countries. Conflicts can be managed by a Task Force on Integrated Assessment Modelling, which oversees the process (Reis et al. 2012).

The use of scenario-derived knowledge in the last thirty years has been highly significant. However, uncertainty management is likely to become steadily more important in the future, as most of the low-cost measures have already been taken and the complexity increases as air pollution and climate change interactions become more important. Uncertainty analysis will also be needed to deal with systematic biases in the scenario approach: potentially optimistic assumptions about the (full) implementation of additional policies, and pessimistic assumptions about (the absence of) emerging new technologies and behavioural change.

The Use of Scenarios in National Policy Venues

Scenario planning in the Netherlands has a long history. After the Second World War, Nobel Prize Winner Jan Tinbergen became the first director of the Central Planning Bureau (CPB) which was legally mandated to provide economic forecasts for *economic policy*. The need to optimize public investments in rebuilding the post-war economy and a strong belief in the possibility of influencing economic development were the main drivers behind this mandate. In addition, trade unions and employers agreed to use the CPB forecasts as the basis for wage agreements. Forecasts have used econometric models based on the latest macroeconomic knowledge and historical data, and assumptions on external factors (such as the development of world trade, oil prices and the population projection) and on existing or new policy measures (taxes, expenditures, social security, and so on). The CPB has the legal mandate to define the baseline scenario that includes existing policy measures. In an iterative process involving the Ministry of Finance, additional policy measures have been formulated that would be needed to meet policy targets, for example on employment, income distribution or government debt. Ultimately the cabinet of ministers have decided on policy changes. The organization's role in policy formulation grew in the 1980s, due to an agreement by political parties to subject their election manifestos to assessment by the CPB.

Due to the Netherlands' high population density, *spatial planning* is important to make the most efficient use of available land. It became the mandate of the Spatial Planning Bureau (currently entitled the Netherlands Environmental Assessment Agency) to define the scenarios that are to be used as the basis for the political spatial planning process. Long-term economic forecasts of the CPB form a quantitative input for scenario development on land use, transport, energy and environment. However, contrasting normative scenarios have proved to be more important in stimulating public debate.

Spatial plans are formulated at different government levels, where the national plan describes the long-term vision (the desirable future, but consistent with CPB forecasts) in the form of a land-use map for the Netherlands 25 years ahead, and a list of government investment projects. The national plan contains political choices, for example on suburbanization or concentration of housing, on the protection of valuable nature areas and landscapes, or on the direction of investments (to harbours and airports or to the development of rural areas). Provinces have the task of translating the national plan into regional plans, which in turn are the basis for detailed land designation maps by the local governments. The latter are decisive for acquiring a building permit. At each government level a participatory approach in the development of spatial plans has been successfully applied. Participatory spatial planning has proved to be a good vehicle to discuss desirable developments in neighbourhoods, regions or the country as a whole.

Development of environmental forecasts for the coming 25 years started in the Netherlands in the 1980s. The first *environmental scenarios* were developed to support the national energy debate: should the country use coal, gas or nuclear energy for power production or should it focus more on energy saving and renewables? While the public debate focused on the safety risks of nuclear energy and the health and ecosystem risks of coal, the long-term environmental scenarios (based on the economic forecasts of the CPB) were important to assess the costs and impacts of different options.

In the study by RIVM (National Institute for Public Health and Environment) *Concern for Tomorrow* (RIVM 1988), the focus of the scenarios was broadened to other issues, such as pollution of air and water, toxic chemicals, manure, waste treatment and climate change. The scenario method was rather simple: extrapolations based on trends in population growth, activity levels and available technologies. However, the comprehensive approach gave new insights into the urgency and common drivers of environmental problems, the limitations of end-of-pipe technologies and the need for structural changes, for example in waste treatment, energy, transport and agriculture. After *Concern for Tomorrow*, RIVM was given a legal mandate to develop environmental forecasts on a regular basis and to make *ex ante* environmental impact assessments of policy proposals. RIVM (now renamed the Netherlands Environmental Assessment Agency) received a legal mandate to develop both a baseline scenario and a maximum feasible scenario that includes technical and non-technical measures (and their additional costs). This frames the policy formulation envelope. It remains the responsibility of policymakers to decide on the measures that will be included in the National Environmental Policy Plan.

In order to maintain credibility, broad consensus among experts on data, methods and results proved to be important. Therefore, RIVM organized close cooperation with expert institutes in the field of agriculture, transport, energy and nature conservation. Participatory methods with representatives from government, industry and NGOs were limited to the definition of ambition levels for environmental protection and the identification of new measures. Although uncertainties in economic developments were grasped using high, medium and low economic growth forecasts produced by the CPB, in practice policymakers were often unable to use the uncertainty ranges and simply adopted the medium projection as the basis for policymaking.

The 'surprise-free' approach was quite effective as long as the need for environmental protection was relatively undisputed and the authority of experts was accepted. This changed in the beginning of the twenty-first century when scepticism about environmental problems grew and the

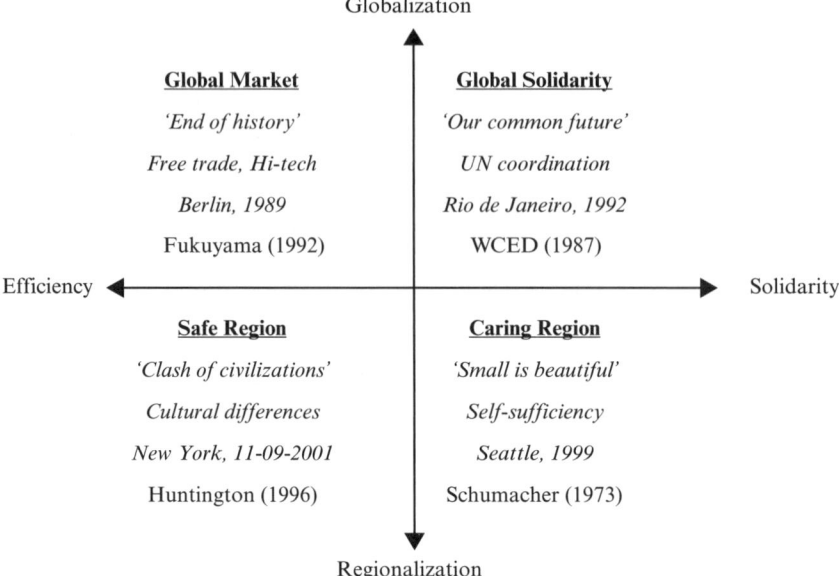

*Figure 3.3   Four normative futures developed in the RIVM Sustainability
                Outlook, symbolized by four emblematic books*

monopoly enjoyed by experts over knowledge declined, due in part to the
expansion of the Internet. Many environmental issues (not only climate
change, but also air pollution, nitrate in groundwater, electromagnetic
fields or pesticides) were perceived as 'wicked' problems, with a high
degree of scientific controversy and of conflicting interests or values.

'Sustainable development' is perhaps the most 'wicked problem' of
all, with many different opinions on what it means and what should be
done. In order to facilitate the development of a sustainable development
strategy, in 2004 RIVM was asked by the Dutch Cabinet to develop a
Sustainability Outlook with four normative futures (see Figure 3.3; RIVM
2004). From a survey among 40,000 people, four major worldviews were
selected. For each of these, the main trends, worries and desired policy
measures were identified via additional surveys among 2500 people. In
four focus groups of about 20 selected people each (representatives of a
certain worldview), narratives, cause–effect diagrams and images for the
scenarios were developed. The scenarios were thus the result of a broad
participatory approach. Quantitative figures were not crucial, but only
used for illustration (and derived from CPB forecasts). Each normative

scenario contained a consistent storyline: trends, external developments and chosen policy strategies would lead to the desired future (a so-called 'utopia').

What each group thought of the scenarios developed by the others was also analysed. It soon became clear what the main weaknesses were in each of the four scenarios, for example risk of excessive bureaucracy, overly optimistic assumptions about the ability of markets to produce timely technological solutions, too much emphasis on voluntary contributions without a solution for free-rider problems. The analysis of weaknesses made it possible for policymakers to make their policy strategy more robust. Moreover, it was possible to identify which policy measures would be no-regret in all scenarios (for example, efficiency improvements) and which measures would face strong opposition (for example, stricter regulation). During simulated negotiation sessions with experts and policymakers, possibilities for consensus were identified. For example, emissions trading was identified as a compromise between the taxation and regulation of CO_2.

CONCLUSIONS

In theory, scenarios are tools that aim to deal with the increasing complexity and future uncertainty of modern life. The real world examples presented in this chapter indicate that they have become indispensable tools in policy formulation processes and are used in very different policy venues. Scenarios are fundamentally linked to the initial, problem conceptualization stage of the policy formulation process. However, a full foresight process is closely interwoven with the other phases and important tasks. Scenarios can, for example, be used to acquire and consolidate ideas on the long-term effects of possible policy decisions, and can facilitate evaluation of the trade-offs that would result from adopting different policy options.

The two examples described above highlight the three 'golden rules' that make futures studies more successful in informing the policy formulation process: credibility, legitimacy and saliency. Credibility is perhaps the critical factor: trust in the sources (in other words, who gave information, the data quality), in the foresight process (addressing the developers' and stakeholders' subjectivities), in the models used (data, calibration), the framing (narrative, metaphor) as well as the dissemination of the results (who communicates and in what context) (Selin 2006). Explorative scenarios *seem* to be more credible in the eyes of policymakers because they are based on the knowledge of experts in the fields at stake that understand the current state and possible future trends. Normative scenarios tend to have lower credibility because their development relies upon 'crystal-ball gazing' and leaping inferentially to what will occur in a (usually probabilistic) future. However, little objective evidence exists to defend these assertions. The inputs to explorative scenarios could be biased as well, consciously or unconsciously, and not in a systematic manner.

As regards saliency, scenario processes that ensure relevance to the policy context combine different scenario development methods (mainly explorative and normative) to expand the range of possible alternative futures. In this way, they increase the number of possible pathways to the future and enhance flexibility in the policy formulation process. The lack of diversity in scenario types is often the main limitation in scenario-based policy formulation activities. Focusing on one 'most probable' or 'most wishful' scenario makes policy formulation easier, but may constrain innovation, limit strategic thinking, and distract policymakers from the more creative solutions that are widely perceived to be needed in the environmental sector. Rosy futures with optimistic assumptions about policy effectiveness increase the risk of problem mis-diagnosis and eventually policy failure (Neugarten 2006). In addition, the integration of normative and explorative methods will enhance legitimacy (as different methods allow a broader participation of society in the development of narratives). However this has proved to be challenging because it requires dynamic system modelling techniques including feedback relationships that are not yet fully developed.

As nobody has a monopoly on knowledge of the future, broad participation and communication with relevant stakeholders is a critical factor to ensure greater legitimacy. However, involving more stakeholders often leads in practice to new problems (Tonn 2003): a high turnover among process participants and a lack of credibility because some participants miss expert authority. If some are unwilling to reveal their values and stakes, tensions between participants (for example, from different departments and government levels) could prevent creative thinking.

In practice, the belief in a scenario is limited to the people involved in their construction (Schoonenboom 2003). The theoretical solution would be to involve 'internal' policymakers in the scenario development process. However, involvement of policymakers could block the development of alternative futures, as many policymakers are not willing to have the existing policy criticized. In practice, many policymakers have difficulties in dealing with uncertain futures (especially when scenarios are also value-laden). They may expect experts to deliver certainty, as shown by the examples in this chapter which were developed by experts 'external' to the government.

Theoretically, scenarios need to be credible, legitimate and salient to be successfully used in policy formulation. Understanding the characteristics of the relevant policy venue at the start of scenario development activities, considering who will use the scenarios, for what purpose and in what political context (in other words, the values and stakes of those involved), is more likely to make the scenario a more successful tool in informing policy formulation. For example, in relation to really complex issues such as the 'sustainable development' of a country or the development of a 'smart city', legitimacy and credibility are crucial and therefore participatory approaches are a 'must' for successful scenarios.

Finally, as an additional way to reduce uncertainty and understand complexity, policymakers are starting to request periodic *ex post* evaluations of the actual realization of scenarios and policy plans (for example, mid-term assessment of Europe 2020, mid-term review of EU Common Agricultural Policy) in order to draw lessons for future forecasts and plans. Optimism on the actual implementation of envisaged policy measures (for example, on energy saving or clean vehicles) often causes a structural bias in scenarios (Maas 2000). The challenge is to either accept the risks of non-compliance with the policy targets, or to develop robust scenarios that include reserve measures in the policy package that can substitute for those that do not survive the implementation phase.

REFERENCES

Alcamo, J. and T. Henrichs (2008), 'Towards guidelines for environmental scenario analysis', in J. Alcamo (ed.), *Environmental Futures: The Practice of Environmental Scenario Analysis*, vol. 2, London: Elsevier, pp. 13–35.

Bennett, E.M., S.R. Carpenter, G.D. Peterson, G.S. Cumming, M. Zurek and P. Pingali (2003), 'Why global scenarios need ecology', *Frontiers in Ecology and the Environment*, **1**, 322–329.

Brooks, H. (1986), 'The typology of surprises in technology, institutions, and development', in W.C. Clark and R.E. Munn (eds), *Sustainable Development of the Biosphere*, Cambridge: Cambridge University Press, UK, pp. 325–350.

de Jouvenel, H. (2004), *Invitation à la Prospective*, Paris: Edition Futuribles.

EC (2010), 'Looking ahead on climate change', speech by Commissioner Potočnik, Green Alliance Conference, London, 15 September 2010, retrieved from http://europa.eu/rapid/press-release_SPEECH-10-450_en.htm?locale5en (accessed 30 December 2013).

EC, JRC and IPTS (2005), 'Exploratory versus normative methods', retrieved from http://forlearn.jrc.ec.europa.eu/guide/4_methodology/meth_explo-norma.htm http://forlearn.jrc.ec.europa.eu/guide/4_methodology/meth_explo-norma.htm (accessed 30 December 2013).

EEA (1999), *Environmental Indicators: Typology and Overview*, Technical Report No. 25, Copenhagen: European Environment Agency.

Fukuyama, F. (1992), *The End of History and the Last Man*, New York: Free Press.

Haydon, B.W. (1967), *The Year 2000*, Santa Monica, California: RAND Corporation, retrieved from http://www.rand.org/pubs/papers/P3571 (accessed 30 December 2013).

Helming, K. and M. Pérez-Soba (2011), 'Landscape scenarios and multifunctionality: making land use impact assessment operational', *Ecology and Society*, **16** (1), 50 [online], retrieved from http://www.ecologyandsociety.org/vol16/iss1/art50/.

Howlett, M. (2011), *Designing Public Policies: Principles and Instruments*, New York: Routledge.

Huntington, S. (1996), *The Clash of Civilizations and the Remaking of World Order*, New York: Touchstone.

Kelly, A., J. Lumbreras, R. Maas, T. Pignatelli, F. Ferreira and A. Engleryd (2010), 'Setting national emission ceilings for air pollutants: policy lessons from an ex-post evaluation of the Gothenburg Protocol', *Environmental Science & Policy*, **13**, 28–41.

Kok, K., M. Gramberger, K-H. Simon, J. Jäger and I. Omann (2011), 'Report on the new methodology for scenario analysis, including guidelines for its implementation, and based on an analysis of past scenario exercises', Deliverable 3.1 CLIMSAVE project, retrieved from www.climsave.eu/climsave/outputs.html (accessed 30 December 2013).

Lejano, R.P., J. Tavares-Reager and F. Berkes (2013), 'Climate and narrative', *Environmental Science and Policy*, **31**, 61–70.

Maas, R.J.M. (2000), 'De toekomst van Gisteren, de emissieplafonds in het Bestrijdingsplan Verzuring en de veranderde inzichten in de afgelopen tien jaar', *Tijdschrift Lucht*, **17** (1), 6–8.

Malthus, T. (1798), *Essay on the Principle of Population*, London: J. Johnson.

Matthews, R., N. Gilbert, A. Roach, J. Polhill and N. Gotts (2007), 'Agent-based land-use models: a review of applications', *Landscape Ecology*, **22**, 1447–1459.

MEA (Millennium Ecosystem Assessment) (2005), *Ecosystems and Human Wellbeing: Our Human Planet*, Washington: Island Press.

Meadows, D.H., D.L. Meadows, J. Randers and W. Behrens III (1972), *The Limits to Growth*, New York: Universe Books.

Metzger, M.J., M.D.A. Rounsevell, H. van den Heiligenberg, M. Pérez-Soba and P. Soto Hardiman (2010), 'How personal judgment influences scenario development: an example for future rural development in Europe', *Ecology and Society*, **15** (2), 5 [online], retrieved from http://www.ecologyandsociety.org/vol15/iss2/art5/ (accessed 30 December 2013).

More, T. (2012), *Utopia*, London: Penguin Classics.

Neugarten, M.L. (2006), 'Foresight – are we looking in the right direction?', *Futures*, **38**, 894–907.

OECD (2013), 'Futures Thinking – overview of methodologies', retrieved from www.oecd.org/site/schoolingfortomorrowknowledgebase/futuresthinking/scenarios/ (accessed 30 December 2013).

Reis, S., P. Grennfelt, Z. Klimont et al. (2012), 'From acid rain to climate change', *Science*, **338**, 1153–1154.

RIVM (1988), *Concern for Tomorrow, a National Environmental Survey 1985–2010*, Bilthoven: RIVM.

RIVM (2004), *Quality and the Future, Sustainability Outlook*, Bilthoven: RIVM.

Robinson, J., C. van Bers and D. McLeod (1996), 'Life in 2030: the sustainable society project', in A. Dale and J. Robinson (eds), *Achieving Sustainable Development*, Vancouver: UBC Press, pp. 3–23.

Rounsevell, M. and T. Henrichs (2008), 'Scenario development for impact assessment and land use change', Seminar presentation at International Conference on Impact Assessment of Land Use Changes, Humboldt University, Berlin.

Rounsevell, M.D.A., I. Reginster, M.B. Araújo et al. (2006), 'A coherent set of future land use change scenarios for Europe', *Agriculture, Ecosystems and Environment*, **114**, 57–68.

Saritas, O. and Y. Nugroho (2012), 'Mapping issues and envisaging futures: an evolutionary approach', *Technological Forecasting & Social Change*, **79**, 509–529.

Schoonenboom, J. (2003), 'Toekomstscenarios en beleid', *Tijdschrift voor Beleid, Politiek en Maatschappij*, **30**, 212–217.

Schumacher, F. (1973), *Small is Beautiful*, London: Blond and Briggs.

Schwartz, P. and J.A. Ogilvy (1998), 'Plotting your scenarios', in L. Fahey and R. Randall (eds), *Learning from the Future*, New York: John Wiley & Sons, pp. 57–80.

Selin, C. (2006), 'Trust and the illusive force of scenarios', *Futures*, **38**, 1–14.

Sun Tzu (400BC), *The Art of War*, http://classics.mit.edu/Tzu/artwar.html.

Swart, R.J., P. Raskin and J. Robinson (2004), 'The problem of the future: sustainability science and scenario analysis', *Global Environmental Change*, **14**, 137–146.

Tonn, B.E. (2003), 'The future of futures decision making', *Futures*, **35**, 673–688.

van der Heijden, K. (2005), *Scenarios: The Art of Strategic Conversation*, 2nd edition, Chichester, UK: Wiley.

van 't Klooster, S.A. (2007), *Toekomstverkenning: Ambities en de Praktijk*, PhD dissertation, University of Maastricht, Delft: Eburon.

Wack, P. (1985), 'Scenarios – shooting the rapids', *Harvard Business Review*, **85**, 73–89.

WCED (World Commission on Environment and Development) (1987), *Our Common Future*, Oxford: Oxford University Press.

Wells, H.G. (1913), *The Discovery of the Future*, New York: B.W. Huebsch.

WRR (Scientific Council for Government Policy) (2010), *Exploring Futures for Policymaking*, in M. van Asselt, N. Faas, F. van der Molen and S. Veenman (eds), *Uit zicht ('Out of Sight'): over toekomstverkennen met beleid*, summary in English of report WRR-Verkenningen 24 (ISBN 978 90 8964 263 9), Amsterdam: Amsterdam University Press.

Zurek, M.B. and T. Henrichs (2007), 'Linking scenarios across scales in international environmental scenarios', *Technological Forecasting and Social Change*, **74**, 1282–1295.

4. Indicators: tools for informing, monitoring or controlling?

Markku Lehtonen

INTRODUCTION: INDICATORS AS GOVERNANCE TOOLS

Today, indicators are produced and used worldwide; across all levels and sectors of society; by public, private and civil society actors; for a variety of purposes, ranging from knowledge-provision to administrative control. While the use of quantitative data as policy support, including policy formulation, has a long history, recent decades have seen the rise of what some have called an 'indicator industry' (for example, Hezri and Hasan 2004), focused especially on the production of environmental and sustainability indicators, within a framework variously called 'governance by numbers' (Miller 2001; Lascoumes and Le Galès 2005; Jackson 2011), 'management by numbers' in public service (for example, Hood 2007) or 'numbers discourse' (Jackson 2011, p. 23). Indicators are generally expected to enhance the rationality of policymaking and public debate by providing a supposedly more objective, robust, and reliable information base. Indicators can operate as 'boundary objects' (for example, Turnhout 2009; Star 2010), catering to both technocratic and deliberative ideals, by combining 'hard facts' and modelling with collective reasoning and 'speculation'. Hence, indicators draw much of their power from being perceived as exact, scientific and objective information on the one hand and a policy-relevant, tailor-made and hence partly subjective type of evidence on the other.

The antecedents of the ongoing proliferation of indicators can be traced to the development of economic indicators, most notably that of GDP, in the aftermath of the Great Depression, and their worldwide adoption following the Second World War (Godin 2003, p. 680; Cobb and Rixford 1998, p. 7; Morse and Bell 2011). In a broader sense, the origins of indicators can be traced as far back as the work of the 'social reformers' in Belgium, France, England and the US in the 1830s (Cobb and Rixford 1998, p. 6). Subsequent waves included the 'social indicator movement' in the 1960s and 1970s (Hezri 2006; Cobb and Rixford 1998,

p. 8), science, technology and innovation (STI) indicators in the 1950s (Godin 2003), and since the 1980s, performance management indicators – as an essential element of New Public Management and evidence-based policy – today most widely applied in the UK through sectoral perform-ance indicator systems, league tables and rankings at various governance levels (Hood 2007, p. 100; Le Galès 2011; Jackson 2011, p. 17). Since the 1970s, national statistics offices and international organizations (espe-cially the OECD) have pioneered the development of environmental and natural resource indicators, intended to support 'state of the environment' reporting, various types of assessment, multilateral environmental agree-ments (MEAs) and the development of environmental policy instruments (OECD 1991; Pintér et al. 2005, p. 2; Hezri 2006, p. 161). Most recent developments include the evolution of environmental indictors towards interdisciplinary and cross-sectoral approaches (Hezri 2006, p. 162), the introduction of sustainable development indicators at various levels of governance, and the proliferation of various composite indicators of sustainability, societal progress and wellbeing (for example, Stiglitz et al. 2010; Sébastien and Bauler 2013; Seaford 2013).

Research and development work in the area has hitherto overwhelm-ingly concentrated on improving the technical quality of indicators, while the fate of indicators in policymaking and the associated sociopoliti-cal aspects have attracted little attention. This chapter focuses on this neglected area of indicator research, by providing an overview of the multiple types of existing indicators, as well as their use and influence in various venues of policymaking. Empirical examples are drawn mainly from the fields of environmental and sustainability indicators.

The remainder of this chapter is structured as follows. Section 2 out-lines the different types of indicators and their intended functions, with particular emphasis on their role in policy formulation, and distinguishing between the concepts of use and influence. Section 3 looks at the actual practice, that is, the empirical evidence concerning the roles that indica-tors actually play in various policy venues. The section first examines the extent to which indicators fulfil their intended functions, and then turns to the broader, unintended consequences that indicator work has in society. Section 4 concludes.

TYPES AND PURPOSES OF INDICATORS

Indicators constitute a heterogeneous policy tool, with a range of purposes, functions, disciplinary backgrounds, application areas and levels, and theo-retical and normative underpinnings. An often-cited definition perceives indicators as 'variables that summarize or otherwise simplify relevant information, make visible or perceptible phenomena of interest, and quantify, measure, and communicate relevant information' (Gallopin 1996, p. 108). Jackson (2011, p. 15), in defining a performance indicator as an 'unbiased estimate of true performance which cannot be measured directly', captures two essential features of indicators, namely that of 'indication', entailing the idea that an entity that is not directly measurable can nevertheless be 'assessed using a limited set of measurable parameters' (Turnhout 2009, p. 403), and that of 'signalling' – an indicator needs to be interpreted and given meaning (Jackson 2011, p. 15). According to Gudmundsson (2003, p. 4), the existence of an underlying conceptual framework distinguishes indicators from data or statistics. Such a framework determines the criteria and logic for the choice of specific indicators, anchors indicator systems in theory and ensures comparability and communicability (Gudmundsson 2003, p. 4; Pintér et al. 2005, p. 16). Godin (2003, p. 681) highlights the early warning trend-observation functions, while Jackson (2011, p. 24) underlines the imprecision inherent in indicators. Views diverge on whether indicators should necessarily be underpinned by a causal model (Godin 2003, p. 681; Cobb and Rixford 1998), or whether indeed indicators differ from evaluations in that only the latter necessarily seek to establish cause–effect relationships (Gudmundsson 2003, p. 2). Finally, Gudmundsson (2003, p. 4) evokes the objective of utilization as a defining characteristic of indicators, and distinguishes three alternative *'utilization frameworks'*, which classify indicators according to their function as providing information, monitoring or control. *Information frameworks* entail descriptive indicators, *monitoring frameworks* are designed to provide regular feedback through a combination of descriptive and performance indicators (for example, OECD Environmental Performance Indicators and the EU Lisbon Process competitiveness indicators), while *control frameworks* entail a stronger link to action through, for example, resource allocation and the associated sanctions. The question of indicator functions will be addressed in more detail later in this chapter. The next section will suggest a typology of different indicators.

Types of Indicators: Descriptive, Performance and Composites

A distinction can be made between descriptive, performance and composite indicators. *Descriptive indicators* 'can be dichotomous, number, grade, time series, or ratios or other derived functions', and indicate the state of a system (for example, the environment), while leaving specific policy interpretations aside (Gudmundsson 2003, p. 3). The absence of explicit interpretations obviously does not imply neutrality or objectivity. *Performance indicators* compare indicator values against a standard, target value or benchmark, measuring how well 'someone' is performing, thereby implying that this 'someone' has agency, that is, capacity to influence the course of events. Performance indicators can concern policy inputs, processes, outputs, outcomes, effectiveness or efficiency (Carter et al. 1993). By their very nature, performance indicators therefore already entail a specific type of intended use. Hood (2007, pp. 100–101) further distinguishes *target systems*, designed to measure performance against an aspirational standard and to help raise levels of performance; *ranking systems* that compare performance of a given unit with that of another, similar unit; and *intelligence systems* that do not rank or compare to a standard, but aim merely to build a knowledge base.

Finally, the production of *composite indicators*[1] that aggregate a series of individual indicators into one or a few numbers, on the basis of an underlying model of the multidimensional concept that is being measured (for example, Grupp and Schubert 2010), especially when single indicators cannot capture the richness of a multidimensional concept, has greatly expanded in the past years. While GDP remains the hegemonic composite indicator, recent efforts have concentrated on developing alternative indicators of sustainability, progress and wellbeing as well as an increasing variety of league tables and rankings of countries, public services, and so on (for example, Pintér et al. 2005). The constitution of composite indicators presents methodological challenges relating to choice, weighting and aggregation. A 'milder' variant of composite indicators are 'headline indicators' – a selection of key indicators in a given policy domain, designed to communicate in a concise manner to high-level policymakers and the general public the essence of progress towards main policy objectives.

Intended Functions of Indicators

As a specific means of operationalizing the concept of evidence-based policy, indicators can serve multiple functions, in particular those of communication and awareness raising (Rosenström and Lyytimäki 2006, p. 33), monitoring and evaluation of performance, supporting policy evaluation, early warning, political advocacy, control and accountability, transparency, and improving the quality of decisions. Further functions attributed to indicators include guidance to policy analysis and formation, improvement of government effectiveness (Moldan and Billharz 1997), setting targets and establishment of standards, promotion of the idea of integrated action, and focusing of policy discussion (Briguglio 2003). Indicators can serve as 'signals' that enable or prescribe an action or management function, and condense information in situations characterized by complexity (Gudmundsson 2003). Seen from such an instrumental

Table 4.1   Performance indicator functions: different types

Purpose	Question the performance indicator can help to answer
Evaluate	How well the organization is performing
Control	Whether the employees are doing 'the right thing'
Budget	Which programmes, people, or projects will be allocated funding?
Motivate	How to inspire staff, mangers, citizens, and so on, in order to improve performance?
Promote	How to convince external stakeholders that the organization is performing well?
Celebrate	Cause for celebration of success
Learn	Which measures and activities are successful/unsuccessful?
Improve	What measures can improve performance?

Source: From Behn (2003).

perspective, indicators help policymakers to decide whether or not to act (Gudmundsson 2003, p. 2). Whichever the primary objective, indicators are expected to simplify and facilitate communication by reducing ambiguity.

Descriptive indicators are closest to 'pure' data or statistics in that they do not presuppose a specific type of use, and the ways in which they enter into policymaking are largely unpredictable. Descriptive indicators often constitute the essential building blocks of performance and composite indicators.

The generic function of *performance indicators* is to strengthen accountability, in particular by helping to ensure an efficient and appropriate use of public money in the pursuit of commonly agreed societal goals. In practice, performance indicators are also expected to serve functions typically attributed to policy evaluation, such as learning, improvement, and 'symbolic' functions (Table 4.1).

Composite indicators are expected to focus attention on important policy issues, offer more rounded assessments of performance, and present the 'big picture' in a manner accessible to a range of audiences – in contrast with the potentially contradictory information provided by indicator sets that examine a phenomenon from multiple perspectives. Rankings and league tables can be used to signal quality of service and inform choice; for performance benchmarking, accountability and resource allocation; or the attribution of rewards (Jackson 2011, p. 20). Precisely because of the simplification inherent in their construction, composites cannot identify causal relationships and alone provide a sufficient knowledge basis for specific policy decisions (for example, Grupp and Schubert 2010, p. 77). The composites therefore can influence policy indirectly, by informing the

Table 4.2   Indicators: main types and functions

	Indicators	
Planning stage	Type	Function
Diagnosis	Descriptive	Monitoring and description of the initial situation
	Analytical	Analysis of the initial situation
Programming, realization	Prognostic	Characterization of expected or potential development
	Programming	Reflection on overall goals
	Planning	Reflection on medium- and long-term goals
	Social normatives	Quantification of goals and means
Evaluation	Control	Description of the final situation
	Impact indicators	Reflection on outcomes
	Effectiveness indicators	Reflection on effectiveness

Source: From Illner (1984).

public and the political debate about specific social objectives and policy trade-offs, making explicit the underlying assumptions, challenging the dominant models of measurement, helping the public to hold politicians to account, and so on (Seaford 2013).

Illner's (1984) typology of indicator types and functions at different stages of a policy cycle is one among the many attempts to determine the expected and potential roles of indicators in policymaking (Table 4.2).

Seaford (2013) has identified the potential roles that composite indicators of subjective wellbeing could play at different phases of a policy cycle (Figure 4.1).

Seaford emphasizes the largely indirect political and conceptual functions such as public accountability, agenda-setting and assessment of policy objectives, while Illner's account stresses more the direct and instrumental functions of indicators.

The *level of governance* (a key aspect of policy venue – see Chapter 1, this volume) decisively shapes the appropriate underlying framework, type (descriptive, performance, composite), and expected functions of the indicators in question. For instance, the various national-level composite indicators of sustainable development, environment and wellbeing have their counterparts at the sub-national and community levels, yet the functions of these indicators differ. While both seek to raise awareness, the community-level indicators aim at empowering communities and citizens. Performance measurement indicators, in turn, are typically designed to

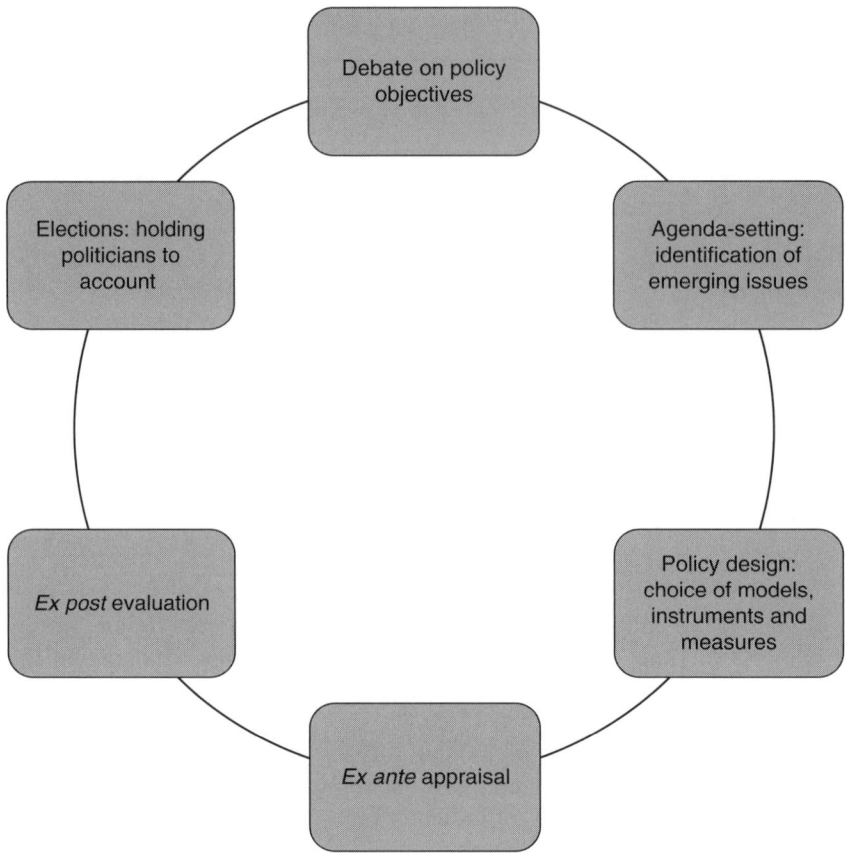

Source: Adapted from Seaford (2013).

*Figure 4.1   The potential roles of subjective wellbeing indicators at
            different stages of the policy cycle*

facilitate control of the civil service by decision makers at the relevant
governance level – and to enable the civil service to improve its day-to-day
performance.

Indicators and Policy Formulation

Many of the expected functions of indicators fall outside of the scope
of policy formulation as defined in Chapter 1: in particular composite
and headline indicators are designed to influence phases preceding policy
formulation, notably agenda-setting and problem identification. In policy

formulation, indicators can be crucial in *characterizing the current situation*; already the choice of the indicators for describing the current policy situation both reflects and shapes perceptions of which elements in decision making situations are deemed important. By virtue of their perceived rigour and accuracy, indicators can assist *problem conceptualization* – for instance by informing the development of formal or informal models (Seaford 2013), and construction of scenarios. More generally, by quantifying and simplifying, indicators render problems more manageable. Indicators also help to shape perceptions of which policies are deemed viable and relevant, that is, the *identification of policy options*. For instance, the choice of the parameters to constitute an air pollution index, or the choices of the appropriate biodiversity or climate change indicators shape the range and viability of alternative policy responses. Indicators are frequently used in *assessing and comparing potential policy options*. Finally, while indicators are not designed to *recommend and/or propose a specific policy design*, in reality they are frequently used to justify a given (often a pre-existing) policy design.

Instrumental, Conceptual and Political Functions of Indicators

The types of intended use of indicators often tend to focus on what the knowledge-utilization literature terms *instrumental* use (for example, Weiss 1999), entailing in our case the use of indicators as direct input to specific decisions, in line with the linear rational-positivist model of policymaking, typically involving 'single-loop' learning concerning the consequences of specific actions or policy options (Argyris and Schön 1978). Expectations concerning performance management indicators typically fall within this category. Yet many of the intended functions mentioned above can be considered as *conceptual*, as indicators are expected to constitute a part of a broad information base for decisions, shape conceptual frameworks and mental models of actors, and ultimately generate 'enlightenment' (Weiss 1999). Hence, indicators should foster especially the more complex types of social learning in the spirit of Habermasian 'communicative rationality'. Finally, some of the expected functions are *political*, especially when indicators are expected to influence agenda-setting and problem definition, highlight neglected issues, or (de)stabilize and (de)legitimize prevailing frameworks of thought.

Often the political use of indicators is overlooked and portrayed in a negative light, as misuse, abuse, attempts to conceal, cheat, delay and manipulate (for example, Hezri 2006). Alternatively, the absence of proof that indicators have influenced policy is often taken as a proof of failure. 'Indicator advocates' hence often regret the fact that indicators are either ignored or used selectively, or 'misused' for strategic (in other words, illegitimate) purposes, without due regard for their inherent technical limitations. Numerous measures are then often suggested to minimize 'misuse', such as informing and educating the users or the introduction of 'statistical health warnings' (for example, Jackson 2011, p. 20; Pintér et al. 2005, p. 7; Hood 2007, p. 100; Grupp and Schubert 2010, p. 76). But the 'political' use of indicators can involve more than outright legitimization of decisions already made and 'symbolic' use. It can also entail necessary efforts to strengthen the legitimacy of democratic decision making, or advocacy for socially progressive objectives (Parris and Kates 2003). Regarding the former, Stirling (2006) qualifies this potentially constructive type of legitimization as 'weak' justification, targeted at legitimizing processes and/or institutions, whereas 'strong' justification would focus on justifying substantive policy outcomes (in other words, *ex post* legitimization of decisions that have been made on other grounds than those explicitly mentioned). Political use and functions of indicators can involve double- or triple-loop learning, including 'political learning', which concerns the 'political feasibility of a given idea or prospects for advancing a given problem through manoeuvring within and manipulation of policy processes' (Hezri 2006, p. 101).

As Table 4.1 (Behn 2003) suggests, the roles of indicators extend well beyond the direct policy formulation tasks, covering in particular crucial feedback functions of evaluation, control, learning, motivation and even various 'symbolic' functions. Such functions are, however, de facto rather than intended consequences of indicators. The following sections will review the empirical experience concerning the actually observed and potential unintended consequences of indicators.

INDICATORS 'IN PRACTICE': ARE THEY USED AND DOES 'USE' IMPLY INFLUENCE?

The discussion above focused merely on the intended, desired objectives of indicators – their 'legitimate' functions. However, the actual use, influence and broader consequences of indicators in practice often prove to be quite different from those foreseen by their designers and advocates. These well-intentioned and as such necessary recommendations reflect a limited perception of the political role of indicators, and hence often turn out ineffective. This section will set aside the issue of the 'correct' use of indicators, and adopt a less normative perspective, by examining the various ways in which indicator work in reality influences policy formulation.

Indicator Use and Indicator Influence

The discussion above focused on the use and intended functions of indicators, yet a first step towards analysing the broader roles of indicators in policymaking is to distinguish between (1) the use of indicators, that is, their handling (for example, receiving, processing, communicating and reporting) in a variety of policy venues, and (2) the influence on policy formulation processes stemming from the indicators or indicator sets, or from the processes through which indicators are developed or applied. Indicator influence can concern the targeted policy or broader processes in society, such as administrative structures or the operation of democratic institutions. It can entail new or reconfirmed decisions and actions, shared understandings, and networking among, or changes in, the legitimacy of policy or policy actors (Valovirta 2002; Hezri and Dovers 2006; Pollitt 2006; Zittoun 2006; Lehtonen 2013). Indicators are not always used as intended, and the resulting influence may conflict with the objectives sought, or produce negative unintended effects (for example, Perrin 1998; 2002; Jackson 2011). Use is therefore not always a 'good thing', nor is the learning entailed in indicator work automatically desirable or undesirable per se.

The (Lack of) Intended Use of Indicators – and Ways of Enhancing Use

The degree to which indicators are used for their intended purposes varies greatly across indicator types and policy areas. In particular, there seems to be a rather strong dichotomy between the wide use of established economic (for example, GDP, unemployment rate, levels of government debt and budget deficits) and performance management indicators on one hand, and the far more infrequent use of the various sectoral, cross-sectoral and sustainability indicators on the other. Government performance measures are certainly used for their intended control purposes. This can take place in internal venues, and draw on official sources of knowledge, when central government departments and agencies use performance indicators to allocate resources, or public service managers to motivate employees to improve performance; to trigger corrective action; to compare, identify and encourage 'best practice'; to plan and budget. The use of indicators by auditors and regulators to evaluate the provision of value for money by public sector organizations can, in turn, be defined as use in external venues, drawing on a variety of official and unofficial knowledge sources. The degree to which the various sectoral indicators (including for example, indicators for monitoring national sustainable development strategies) are used varies widely. Perhaps most frequent is the use of these indicators in mandatory reporting exercises by government departments, which may take place in either internal (for example, annual sectoral reporting, or public sector performance measurement) or external venues (for example, obligatory EU policy assessments, OECD country reviews). These exercises draw mainly on official sources of knowledge, including those produced by international organizations.

The 'alternative' composite indicators of progress, wellbeing and sustainable development, in turn, are actively used in particular by their producers and policy advocates in order to promote their preferred worldviews, in other words, in venues external to the government, drawing on unofficial data sources. The uptake of such indicators by national and EU-level administrations in their daily work and decision making is far less widespread, probably largely due to the 'unofficial' status of the data underpinning the indicators. Some composite environmental and sustainability indicators, in particular the ecological footprint, have found a certain echo in the media and to a limited extent in public debate (for example, Morse 2011). The recent and ongoing effort by various governments – including collaboration with national statistics offices – to develop 'official' alternative indicators of progress and wellbeing (for example, Seaford 2013; Sébastien et al. 2014) marks a shift in this indicator work towards the internal-official quadrant of the scheme in Chapter 1. However, the main expectation is that these indicators operate in the external venues, through public debate, and subsequent uptake by policymakers (for example, Seaford 2013). The extent of actual use and influence of these indicators still remains uncertain, not least because of the frequent doubts about their scientific credibility and technical robustness (Sébastien et al. 2014). Finally, in many cases indicators are not used, simply because the potential users are not even aware of their existence – a phenomenon that also obtains for indicators within the internal-official quadrant (for example, Lehtonen 2013).

The hope that users would consider for instance sustainability or environmental indicator sets in their totality, reflecting upon the trade-offs between the various indicators, has proven largely illusory. Especially in external venues, indicators are used selectively, interpreted out of their context, used as political ammunition rather than as a rational input to policy, or simply ignored. This is often a combined result of attributes relating to the indicators themselves, the actor 'repertoires' – 'stabilized ways of thinking and acting (on the individual level) or stabilized codes, operations and technology (on other levels)' (van der Meer 1999, p. 390) – and the broader policy context. Relevant factors may include excessively loose linking between reporting schemes and policymaking; lack of trust of potential users in the indicators (government actors may be institutionally prevented from using 'unofficial' data sources, while external actors may mistrust government data); lack of resources within the administration; or neglect of user concerns in the design of indicator systems. Several preconditions have hence been identified for instrumental use of indicators: relevance for the intended user (representative, simple and easy to interpret, reflecting ongoing changes in society, ability to clearly communicate success or failure), scientific and technical quality (ideally based on international standards and norms, and on a clear conceptual framework), measurability, context-specificity and adaptability, linking with regular monitoring and evaluation exercises, and clear identification of target groups and expected indicator functions (Pintér et al. 2005, p. 16; Hezri 2006, p. 172; Bell et al. 2011, p. 5; Seaford 2013). There should be an adequate but imperfect match between the 'repertoires' of the indicator users and the conceptual framework conveyed by the indicator, in other words, indicators should be salient, credible and legitimate to their expected users (see Chapter 3, this volume; Cash et al. 2002). The relationships and determinants of salience, credibility and legitimacy are complex, and there are obvious trade-offs between the three criteria. For example, the frequent debates and disputes concerning the validity of rankings conducted by international organizations illustrate the vagueness and fluidity of the distinction between 'official' and 'unofficial' sources of knowledge.

The temporal aspects are also vital in determining indicator use. Frequent complaints by potential users include the lack of timely, up-to-date indicator information (for example, Rosenström and Lyytimäki 2006) and the claim that backward-looking indicators are not useful in policy formulation – hence the greater appeal of forward-looking policy formulation tools such as cost–benefit analyses (see Chapter 7, this volume) and scenarios (see Chapter 3, this volume; Lehtonen 2013).

These perceived indicator qualities, in turn, are strongly shaped by the process of indicator production – the extent to which the actors participating in indicator processes are seen as legitimate and credible. Collaborative processes of indicator development may foster agreement on problem definitions, policy objectives and policy measures (Bell et al. 2011). In line with findings from evaluation research, the process of indicator production – through social learning, networking, problem framing, focus and motivation – is often equally or even more influential than the 'use' of the final, published indicator (for example, Mickwitz and Melanen 2009; Lehtonen 2013; see also Chapter 2, this volume).

Among the factors relating to the policy setting, those that shape indicator use include the existence (or absence) of an 'indicator culture', the weight of the policy area in question among policy priorities (for example, Sébastien et al. 2014), and the degree of agreement among key actors on

Table 4.3   Examples of indicators and their use in different policy venues

	Unofficial	Official
Internal		• Government performance indicators • Mandatory (annual) reporting • Sustainable development (SD) indicators • State of the environment indicators • GDP; economic indicators • Resource allocation, control, identification and encouragement to adopt 'best practice'
External	• Composites: Ecological footprint, Genuine Progress Indicator, Transparency indicators • Community SD indicator sets • Advocacy for specific worldviews; community empowerment and capacity building; monitoring of progress by non-governmental actors	• GDP; government economic and social indicators; science and technology indicators; sectoral performance indicators; government initiatives for new indicators of progress and wellbeing; state of the environment indicators • Auditing and evaluation by external agencies, intl. organizations (auditing offices, rating agencies, OECD, EU. . .) • Debate in the media, parliaments, drawing on the indicator reports and data; 'ammunition' in political debates

problem definitions, policy objectives and policy measures (for example, Turnhout et al. 2007; Bell et al. 2011, p. 108). Use tends to be enhanced when the policy agenda in question has remained stable over time (Bell et al. 2011, p. 10), yet situations of crisis can open 'windows of opportunity' for enhanced indicator use, as the prevailing institutions and frameworks of thought are called into question (Hezri 2006, p. 172).

Table 4.3 presents a number of selected examples of indicators and their intended and actual use, classified according to the distinctions between internal and external venues, and between official and unofficial sources of knowledge.

Institutionalization, Codification and Mandatory Use

Institutionalization through the integration of new indicators into mainstream policy mechanisms and existing statistical, measurement and reporting systems is frequently seen as a key objective and success criterion and as a means of enhancing indicator influence (for example, Pintér et al. 2005, p. 3). Typically, institutionalization involves processes whereby the credibility of hitherto unofficial indicator information is strengthened by giving it an official 'seal' of credibility. Mandatory application of indicators can foster such institutionalization. Mandatory use in internal venues may also trigger use in external venues, through public debate generated for example as a result of the publication of government reviews. In practice, such spillover effects have been rare. Indicator production and use have been institutionalized through the establishment of guidelines, mandates and designated venues for their production and use, with international organizations (for example, the OECD, Eurostat and the various UN organs) and processes (for example, Local Agenda 21), and national statistics offices in leading roles (Srebotnjak 2007; Stiglitz et al. 2010). Forms of institutionalization have ranged from the establishment of academic journals (for example, Social Indicators Research, Ecological Indicators), and regular international expert collaboration (Hezri 2006, p. 158), codification – and hence 'officialization' – of indicators through frameworks such as the System of National Accounts (SNA) and the System of Integrated Environmental and Economic Accounts (SEEA) (for example, Pintér et al. 2005, pp. 22–23), and manuals for indicator production (Godin 2003, p. 687).

Indicator Constituencies?

The creation of an 'indicator industry', and the associated codification and institutionalization of indicators, has been decisively fostered by groups advocating the use of their favourite indicators. These groups can alternatively be perceived as 'instrument constituencies' (Voß and Simons 2014), epistemic communities (Haas 1992) or advocacy coalitions (Sabatier 1988). Statisticians, especially at national statistics offices and international organizations, still play a central role in such groups, yet the more recent processes such as the development of community-level and composite sustainability indicators and alternative indicators of progress have seen an increasing involvement of actors outside the government, for example think tanks, NGOs and grassroots community groups (for example, Sébastien and Bauler 2013; Sébastien et al. 2014). Indicator development processes tend to be highly sector-specific, variously led either by users or producers, and often highly international in nature. Depending on their status in policymaking hierarchies, such constituencies of like-minded experts and policy actors not only foster institutionalization of the indicator systems, but also shape the extent to which a sector or an organization develops an 'indicator culture'. Furthermore, the use of especially sustainable development indicators is often confined to an 'inner circle' of indicator producers and the obligated users of the indicators (Rinne et al. 2013), hence breaking the clear-cut distinction between the 'users' and 'producers' of indicators introduced above (for example, Bell et al. 2011; cf. Pintér et al. 2005, p. 18).

Beyond Intended Use: Unanticipated Consequences of Indicators

A central lesson from research on the role of indicators in policymaking is that their policy influence mostly stems not from direct use in policymaking to guide decisions, but instead from the multiple forms of indirect and largely unintended and uncontrollable pathways, best categorized as 'conceptual' and 'political' influence. The following brief survey will focus on three themes that have emerged as central in research concerning the influence of indicators: the theoretical approaches applied for examining influence, the debate on the broader societal impacts of performance indicators, and the 'paradoxes' concerning the use and influence of indicators.

Theoretical Approaches

A number of theoretical approaches have been suggested for the analysis of the broader, indirect roles of indicators. These include scholarship on governmentality (for example, Rydin 2007), 'government/management by numbers' (Lascoumes and Le Galès 2005; Hood 2007), and indicators as boundary objects capable of connecting science, policy and society (Turnhout et al. 2007; Star 2010; Sébastien et al. 2014). A primary criticism brought forward by these strands of literature is the tendency of indicators to 'depoliticize', that is, to reduce value conflicts and normative debates to supposedly neutral and commonly agreed numbers perceived as incontestable facts (Jany-Catrice 2010, p. 95). Urban studies (sociology, geography and urban planning) have called into question the presumed ability of indicators to foster socially desirable objectives, and highlighted the inseparability of indicator systems from the broader dynamics and trends in policymaking (for example, Hezri 2006, pp. 159–160; Rydin et al. 2003; also Rydin 2007).

Le Galès (2011) highlights the 'revolutionary' consequences from indicator systems, which engender behaviours that conform to the demands of market society. Zittoun (2006) hence refers to the processes of 'instrumentation', whereby indicators embody power, by virtue of their participation in the processes of problem formulation and the design of problem solutions (see also Lascoumes and Le Galès (2005, p. 12), who describe instrumentation of public policy as the whole of the problems generated by and involved in the choice and use of instruments – techniques, operational modes, policy instruments – that make it possible to materialize and operationalize government action). Through simplification, indicators make problems accessible to non-experts, while at the same time legitimizing the power of experts as the only ones capable of truly 'mastering the numbers'.

The distinction between rationalist–technocratic and constructivist–interpretive models of policymaking is arguably even more pronounced in the case of indicators than in, for instance, evaluation and assessment practice. This is due to the quantitative and presumably accurate nature of indicators on one hand, and their ambition towards policy relevance on the other (for example, Rametsteiner et al. 2011). Hence, indicators are expected to 'close down', enabling better management and control by providing robust, accurate, quantitative and unambiguous information for the purposes of political advocacy and day-to-day policymaking, but they are increasingly also seen as a means of 'opening up' via the highlighting of uncertainties, trade-offs and neglected issues in policymaking (for example, Stirling 2008; Rafols et al. 2012; see also Chapter 2, this volume). Such a 'challenge function' is inherent in alternative indicators of progress, for example. The 'science-driven' statisticians who often drive indicator development are typically reluctant to abandon what they consider a 'non-political', objective and science-based position (for example, Srebotnjak 2007), while the indicator users call for policy-relevant, rough-and-tumble indicators. At least implicitly, policy formulators often tend to adhere to a 'science-driven' and 'apolitical' perception of indicators (Rametsteiner et al. 2011), seeing the involvement of politics in indicator work as undesirable (for example, Lehtonen 2013), while the central role of statisticians in indicator development further accentuates the dominance of the rationalist – technocratic perspective.

THE INFLUENCE OF PERFORMANCE MEASUREMENT: PARADOXES AND DILEMMAS

The evaluation literature has provided plenty of useful lessons concerning the broader impacts of performance measurement – of which indicators constitute an essential element. For example, lessons from the literature concerning the impact of public sector performance measurement on decision making are far from conclusive (Hezri 2006, pp. 156–157). Norman (2002) characterizes the debate as a battle between three groups: the 'true believers' who highlight benefits such as new investment in data capture, harmonization of measurement methods across institutions, and behavioural changes; the 'critics and doubters' who stress problems in the use, interpretation and societal relevance, lack of political will, bureaucratic inertia, and use of indicators for propaganda purposes; and the 'pragmatic sceptics' (for example, van der Knaap 2006) who see active contestation as a sign of an evolution towards better theory and practice. As a counterpoint to the promise that indicators would provide greater accountability, efficiency and citizen control over policymakers, there is a considerable body of literature highlighting numerous negative features of performance measurement. These can be summarized as follows (for example, Perrin 1998; 2002; Blalock 1999; Davies 1999; van der Knaap 2006; Hood 2007; Jackson 2011; Le Galès 2011):

- complexity and opacity, which reduce potential for dialogue and deliberation;
- disincentives to responsibility, innovation, creativity and achievement;
- goal-shifting and 'gaming';
- dissimulation and distortion of data or even lying and cheating;
- reductionism and the suppression of the plurality of values and points of view;
- a management rhetoric inappropriate in sectors with a 'non-managerial' tradition;
- legitimization and reinforcement of prevailing power structures;
- 'misuse' and misunderstanding resulting from ignorance of the sources, definitions and methods underlying the indicators;
- potential systemic effects: loss of public trust, risk of a system collapse (Hood 2007, p. 102).

The problems of performance measurement can be seen as a subset of the more generic paradoxes and dilemmas involved in indicator work. Hence, it is precisely the widespread use and institutionalization of performance indicators – policy 'success' – that accentuates their risks and downsides.

The absence of a linear connection between use and influence represents an example of the many paradoxes, dilemmas and trade-offs involved in indicator work. These include tensions between:

- deductive and inductive approaches (whether indicators should serve to test theory and hypotheses, or whether the inquiry should progress from data gathering towards theory-building);
- use of indicators as inputs for the design and implementation of public policies versus as tools for monitoring and evaluation;

- international comparability and national/regional/local relevance;
- description and prescription;
- objectivity and normativity; and
- academic and practitioner emphasis, in other words, whether the quality of an indicator should be defined by the scientific quality or practical usefulness of the indicator (Cobb and Rixford 1998, pp. 3–4; Rosenström and Lyytimäki 2006).

Four further tensions merit particular attention:

- *The 'paradox of conservatism'.*[2] The factors enhancing instrumental use – institutionalization, consensus on data, policy and conceptual frameworks – are often in conflict with the challenge function of indicators, in other words, their capacity to destabilize prevailing practices, frameworks of thought, and 'hegemonic discourses' (Driscoll Derickson 2009, p. 904). For instance, the paradigmatic consensus underpinning the GDP as a proxy measure for wellbeing has guaranteed its resistance against pervasive criticism (Morse and Bell 2011).
- *Matching supply with demand.* The objective of better matching supply with demand emphasizes the instrumental role of indicators and single-loop learning, while the more complex types of learning entail shaping demand rather than merely responding to the existing demand.
- *Process versus product.* Indicator research and practice tends to overwhelmingly concentrate on the quality of the indicator as the 'final product', despite the growing evidence of the importance of indicator production processes as a crucial source of especially conceptual influence (for example, Mickwitz and Melanen 2009; Bell et al. 2011; Lehtonen 2013).
- *Aggregation, quantification, scientific rigour and policy relevance.* Aggregate and composite indicators can be powerful tools for communication, comparison and peer pressure (for example, Pagani 2003), yet aggregation can feed reductionism, over-simplification and disregard for contextual differences. For instance, in the area of Social Impact Assessment, strong disagreements prevail between the defenders (for example, European Commission 2009) and critics (for example, Esteves et al. 2012, p. 40) of quantitative indicators.

CONCLUSIONS

The partly overlapping waves of indicator development have closely followed the political and societal agendas of their time. The Great Depression and the needs to manage the war economy stimulated the development of national economic accounting systems, the 'civilization critique' of the 1960s gave rise to the 'social indicators movement', environmental indicators developed together with environmental concern in the 1970s, while neo-liberalism brought along the performance management movement in the 1980s. The sustainable development indicator work in the wake of the Rio Conference in 1992 has been followed by a new kind of growth criticism, in the form of alternative indicators of progress and wellbeing. While the different indicators vary both in their form (descriptive, performance or composite) and specific purpose (monitoring, control, awareness-raising, advocacy, knowledge-production), they share the objective of providing a better, simpler and less ambiguous yet scientifically robust knowledge base for decision making. Largely due to its double ambition of policy relevance and scientific robustness, indicator work is typically characterized by a range of tensions and ambiguities, notably between the attempt to 'close down' by reducing ambiguity, and 'open up' via highlighting uncertainties, and challenging of established frameworks of thought and power structures.

The intended functions of indicators cover most of the policy formulation tasks identified in Chapter 1, but extend beyond policy formulation in the strict sense, from agenda-setting and problem formulation in the 'upstream' stages to *ex post* evaluation and monitoring in the 'downstream'. Indicators constitute an 'auxiliary' policy formulation tool typically applied in conjunction with other tools: both *ex ante* assessment and *ex post* policy evaluation make wide use of indicators; scenario-building draws increasingly upon 'forward-looking' indicators to characterize and assess the impacts of alternative scenarios (see Chapter 3); and participation of the relevant stakeholders (see Chapter 2) in indicator development has been repeatedly pinpointed as crucial if indicators are to be relevant for their intended users.

In practice, the high hopes concerning the ability of indicators to rationalize policymaking and change policy have often remained unfulfilled. Two contrasting experiences can be identified: the performance management indicators have clearly been directly used for control and management, often as part of mandatory monitoring, reporting, assessment, evaluation and performance measurement frameworks, many of which are internal to the government (or intergovernmental processes) and draw upon 'government-certified' information sources. By contrast, the voluntary use and media uptake of various sectoral and 'alternative' indicators of progress (sustainability, wellbeing, and so on), in venues outside of the government, have been far more rare and unpredictable. The lack of adoption and use cannot be attributed solely to the lack of credibility of 'unofficial' indicators and data sources, because the sectoral indicators typically carry a government 'label' of authority. Furthermore, indicator use often remains within a small circle of 'insiders' and specialists, in venues outside or at the margin of policy formulation in the strict sense. With the exception of performance management frameworks, indicators seldom directly influence policy. By contrast, the true power of indicators as policy formulation tools lies in their indirect, unintended, and partly intractable long-term impacts through learning, political advocacy and systemic effects. Indeed, at times, the greater the use of indicators, especially in the policy venues internal to the government, the weaker the potential of the indicators to challenge the prevailing frameworks of thought and institutional structures. The effects from the use of indicators in such situations are by no means negligible, even though the desirability of impacts such as routinization, conservatism and entrenchment of power structures embodied in the indicator systems may be called into question.

Policymakers and potential indicator users frequently criticize the poor policy relevance of indicators, yet the bulk of the attention in indicator research and development (and especially within the government) focuses on ensuring their scientific credibility. The production of 'alternative' indicators is certainly more driven by concerns for their political usability and relevance, but the debate around these – and the criticism against them – mostly addresses questions of technical quality. What is often at stake in controversies concerning 'governance by numbers' are the trust, credibility and reputation of the different organizations producing indicators – ultimately the public trust in science and 'official' expertise. The processes of indicator production usually receive little attention beyond the call for broad participation of stakeholders, as do the potential systemic effects from the application of indicator schemes. While key questions for indicator work concern the most appropriate theoretical frameworks for examining the broader unintended and systemic impacts of indicators, the future of indicators in policy formulation practices remains as uncertain as ever. Indicators will certainly survive as a major type of policy formulation tool, yet uncertainty prevails particularly over the shape and even the survival of performance management frameworks and the increasingly numerous composite indicators, as well as over the persistence of the arguably 'revolutionary' impacts that especially the former have on public policy and organizational culture. Some commentators indeed predict a rather radical transformation of performance management frameworks, arguing that 'techniques such as league tables will probably be abandoned and consigned to the history of policy failures' (Jackson 2011, p. 24).[3]

NOTES

1. See also the OECD glossary of statistical terms: http://stats.oecd.org/glossary/detail. asp?ID56278.
2. I am grateful to Henrik Gudmundsson for having coined this term.
3. The abandonment by the UK's new coalition government in summer 2010 of the highly elaborate government performance management framework developed over the past three decades may represent a test case for the strength of institutionalization and the resilience of the 'indicator culture' created in UK public sector management.

REFERENCES

Argyris, C. and D. Schön (1978), *Organisational Learning: A Theory of Action Perspective*, Reading, MA: Addison Wesley.
Behn, R.D. (2003), 'Why measure performance? Different purposes require different measures', *Public Administration Review*, **63**, 586–606.
Bell, S., K. Eason and P. Frederiksen (eds) (2011), *A Synthesis of the Findings of the POINT Project. POINT – Policy Use and Influence of Indicators, Deliverable 15*, with contributions from Z. Baránková, T. Bauler, L. Cassar, E. Conrad, H. Gudmundsson, Z. Izakovièová, P. Kautto, M. Lehtonen, J. Lyytimäki, S. Morse, L.K. Petersen, J. Rinne, L. Sébastien and K. Hedegaard Sørensen, http://www.pointeufp7.info/storage/POINT_synthesis_deliverable%2015.pdf.
Blalock, A.B. (1999), 'Evaluation research and the performance management movement: from estrangement to useful integration?', *Evaluation*, **5**, 117–149.
Briguglio, L. (2003), The usefulness of sustainability indicators. Paper prepared for the Symposium Sustainability Indicators for Malta, in SI-MO MALTA, Foundation for International Studies (ed.), *Symposium Sustainability Indicators for Malta*, Valletta, Malta, 19 February 2003.
Carter, N., R. Klein and P. Day (1993), *How Organizations Measure Success. The Use of Performance Indicators in Government*, London: Routledge.
Cash, D., W. Clark, F. Alcock, N. Dickson, N. Eckley and J. Jäger (2002), *Salience, Credibility, Legitimacy and Boundaries: Linking Research, Assessment and Decision Making*. Faculty Research Working Papers Series RWP02-046, Harvard: John F. Kennedy School of Government.
Cobb, C.W. and C. Rixford (1998), *Lessons Learned from the History of Social Indicators*, San Francisco: Redefining Progress.
Davies, I.C. (1999), 'Evaluation and performance management in government', *Evaluation*, **5**, 150–159.
Driscoll Derickson, K. (2009), 'Gendered, material, and partial knowledges: a feminist critique of neighborhood-level indicator systems', *Environment and Planning A*, **41**, 896–910.
Esteves, A.M., D. Franks and F. Vanclay (2012), 'Social impact assessment: the state of the art', *Impact Assessment and Project Appraisal*, **30**, 35–44.

European Commission (2009), *European Commission Impact Assessment Guidelines*, Brussels: European Commission.

Gallopin, G.C. (1996), 'Environmental and sustainability indicators and the concept of situational indicators. A systems approach', *Environmental Modelling and Assessment*, **1**, 101–117.

Godin, B. (2003), 'The emergence of S&T indicators: why did governments supplement statistics with indicators?', *Research Policy*, **32**, 679–691.

Grupp, H. and T. Schubert (2010), 'Review and new evidence on composite innovation indicators for evaluating national performance', *Research Policy*, **39**, 67–78.

Gudmundsson, H. (2003), 'The policy use of environmental indicators – learning from evaluation research', *The Journal of Transdisciplinary Environmental Studies*, **2**, 1–12.

Haas, P.M. (1992), 'Epistemic communities and international policy coordination: introduction', *International Organization*, **46**, 1–35.

Hezri, A.A. (2006), *Connecting Sustainability Indicators to Policy Systems*, unpublished PhD thesis, the Australian National University.

Hezri, A.A. and S.R. Dovers (2006), 'Sustainability indicators, policy and governance: issues for ecological economics', *Ecological Economics*, **60**, 86–99.

Hezri, A.A. and M.N. Hasan (2004), 'Management framework for sustainable development indicators in the State of Selangor, Malaysia', *Ecological Indicators*, **4**, 287–304.

Hood, C. (2007), 'Public service management by numbers: Why does it vary? Where has it come from? What are the gaps and the puzzles?', *Public Money & Management*, **27**, 95–102.

Illner, M. (1984), 'On functional types of indicators in social planning', *Social Indicators Research*, **14**, 275–285.

Jackson, P.M. (2011), 'Governance by numbers: what have we learned over the past 30 years?', *Public Money & Management*, **31**, 13–26.

Jany-Catrice, F. (2010), 'La longue marche vers de nouveaux indicateurs sur les territoires', *Revue Savoir/Agir*, 93–101.

Lascoumes, P. and P. Le Galès (eds) (2005), *Gouverner par les instruments*, Paris: Les Presses de Science Po.

Le Galès, P. (2011), 'Rencontre avec Patrick Le Galès: Management public, le laboratoire Britannique', *Sciences Humaines*, 7, No. 228.

Lehtonen, M. (2013), 'The non-use and influence of UK energy sector indicators', *Ecological Indicators*, **35**, 24–34.

Mickwitz, P. and M. Melanen (2009), 'The role of co-operation between academia and policymakers for the development and use of sustainability indicators – a case from the Finnish Kymenlaakso Region', *Journal of Cleaner Production*, **17**, 1086–1100.

Miller, P. (2001), 'Governing by numbers: why calculative practices matter', *Social Research*, **68**, 379–396.

Moldan, B. and S. Billharz (eds) (1997), *Sustainability Indicators: Report on the Project on Indicators of Sustainable Development, SCOPE 58*, Chichester: Wiley.

Morse, S. (2011), 'Attracting attention for the cause. The reporting of three indices in the UK national press', *Social Indicator Research*, **101**, 17–35.

Morse, S. and S. Bell (2011), 'Sustainable development indicators: the tyranny of methodology revisited', *Consilience: The Journal of Sustainable Development*, **6**, 222–239.

Norman, R. (2002), 'Managing through measurement or meaning? Lessons from experience with New Zealand's public sector performance management systems', *International Review of Administrative Sciences*, **68**, 619–628.

OECD (1991), *Environmental Indicators: A Preliminary Set*, Paris: OECD.

Pagani, F. (2003), *Peer Review: An OECD Tool for Co-operation and Change*, Paris: OECD.

Parris, T.M. and R.W. Kates (2003), 'Characterizing and measuring sustainable development', *Annual Review of Environmental Resources*, **28**, 1–28.

Perrin, B. (1998), 'Effective use and misuse of performance measurement', *American Journal of Evaluation*, **19**, 367–379.

Perrin, B. (2002), 'How to – and how not to – evaluate innovation', *Evaluation*, **8**, 13–28.

Pintér, L., P. Hardi and P. Bartelmus (2005), *Indicators of Sustainable Development: Proposals for a Way Forward. Discussion Paper Prepared under a Consulting Agreement on behalf of the UN Division for Sustainable Development, UNDSD/ EGM/ISD/2005/CRP.2*, PLACE: IISD – International Institute for Sustainable Development.

Pollitt, C. (2006), 'Performance information for democracy: the missing link?', *Evaluation*, **12**, 38–55.

Rafols, I., T. Ciarli, P. van Zwanenberg and A. Stirling (2012), 'Towards indicators for "opening up" science and technology policy'. Presentation at the conference, *Internet, Politics, Policy 2012: Big Data, Big Challenges?* Oxford Internet Institute, University of Oxford, 20–21 September 2012.

Rametsteiner, E., H. Pülzl, J. Alkan-Olsson and P. Frederiksen (2011), 'Sustainability indicator development – science or political negotiation?', *Ecological Economics*, **11**, 61–70.

Rinne, J., J. Lyytimäki and P. Kautto (2013), 'From sustainability to well-being: lessons learned from the use of sustainable development indicators at national and EU level', *Ecological Indicators*, **35**, 35–42.

Rosenström, U. and J. Lyytimäki (2006), 'The role of indicators in improving timeliness of international environmental reports', *European Environment*, **16**, 32–44.

Rydin, Y. (2007), 'Indicators as a governmental technology? The lessons of community-based sustainability indicator projects', *Environment and Planning D: Society and Space*, **25**, 610–624.

Rydin, Y., N. Holman and E. Wolff (2003), 'Local sustainability indicators', *Local Environment*, **8**, 581–589.

Sabatier, P.A. (1988), 'An advocacy coalition framework of policy change and the role of policy-oriented learning therein', *Policy Sciences*, **21**, 129–168.

Seaford, C. (2013), 'The multiple uses of subjective well-being indicators', *Social Indicator Research*, **114**, 29–43.

Sébastien, L. and T. Bauler (2013), 'Use and influence of composite indicators for sustainable development at the EU-level', *Ecological Indicators*, **35**, 3–12.

Sébastien, L., M. Lehtonen and T. Bauler (2014), 'Can indicators fill the gap between science and policy? An exploration of the (non) use and (non) influence of indicators in EU and UK policymaking', *Nature & Culture*, **9** (3), 316–343.

Srebotnjak, T. (2007), 'The role of environmental statisticians in environmental policy: the case of performance measurement', *Environmental Science and Policy*, **10**, 405–418.

Star, S.L. (2010), 'This is not a boundary object: reflections on the origin of a concept', *Science, Technology & Human Values*, **35**, 601–617.

Stiglitz, J.E., A. Sen and J-P. Fitoussi (2010), *Mismeasuring our Lives. Why GDP Doesn't Add Up. The Report by the Commission on the Measurement of Economic Performance and Social Progress*, New York and London: New Press.

Stirling, A. (2006), 'Analysis, participation and power: justification and closure in participatory multi-criteria analysis', *Land Use Policy*, **23**, 95–107.

Stirling, A. (2008), '"Opening up" and "closing down": power, participation, and pluralism in the social appraisal of technology', *Science, Technology & Human Values*, **33**, 262–294.

Turnhout, E.M. (2009), 'The effectiveness of boundary objects: the case of ecological indicators', *Science and Public Policy*, **36**, 403–412.

Turnhout, E.M., M. Hisschemöller and H. Eijsackers (2007), 'Ecological indicators: between the two fires of science and policy', *Ecological Indicators*, **7**, 215–228.

Valovirta, V. (2002), 'Evaluation utilization as argumentation', *Evaluation*, **8**, 60–80.

van der Knaap, P. (2006), 'Responsive evaluation and performance management: overcoming the downsides of policy objectives and performance indicators', *Evaluation*, **12**, 278–293.

van der Meer, F-B. (1999), 'Evaluation and the social construction of impacts', *Evaluation*, **5**, 387–406.

Voß, J.-P. and A. Simons (2014), 'Instrument constituencies and the supply-side of policy innovation', *Environmental Politics*, **3** (5), 735–754.

Weiss, C.H. (1999), 'The interface between evaluation and public policy', *Evaluation*, **5** (4), 468–486.

Zittoun, P. (2006), Indicateurs et cartographie dynamique du bruit, un instrument de reconfiguration des politiques publiques? *Développement durable et territoires, Dossier 8: Méthodologies et pratiques territoriales de l'évaluation en matière de développement durable*, online since 13 December 2006 (accessed 4 February 2014) http://developpementdurable.revues.org/index3261.html.

5. Computerized models: tools for assessing the future of complex systems?

Martin K. van Ittersum and Barbara Sterk

INTRODUCTION

Models are commonly used to make decisions. At some point all of us will have employed a mental model, that is, a simplification of reality, in an everyday situation. For instance, when we want to make the best decision for the environment and consider whether to buy our vegetables in a large supermarket or a local farm shop, we will use our own mental model of what is good, and less good, for the environment. But it was the advent of computers that gave a boost in particular to quantitative models. They have been on the scene roughly since the Second World War. Since the 1950s, engineers have studied complex dynamic systems using computer models, inspiring biologists to apply similar techniques in their disciplines. Such models assist in understanding the behaviour of a system, that is, a limited part of reality that contains interrelated elements. This understanding generally refers to how the different elements (components) of a system interact and determine the state of the system at a certain moment, as well as how it may change over time. Once this understanding of historical and present behaviour has been achieved, models are used to forecast future states of the system.

In reality, different computer models serve different policy formulation purposes. As the literature uses a variety of often inconsistent terms to categorize computer models, in this chapter we first try to shed some light on terminology, and more importantly on different classes of computerized models and their purposes in forecasting future states of systems (Section 2). We then introduce the various ways in which computer models can be used in a policy formulation process and how this relates to other tools as described in this book (Section 3). To properly understand the role of computer models in policy formulation processes we need to have a closer look at what evidence and knowledge they deliver to such processes, which is the subject of Section 4.

After these introductory sections we are ready to have a somewhat more detailed look at practical cases in which computer models played a role in policy formulation processes to derive insights from hindsight. Modesty is justified when it comes to the use of models in such processes: while almost every scientific paper presenting a model or application in a case study claims (potential) usefulness for decision and policymaking processes, few have documented real-life applications with a demonstrated analysis of policy impact. This is not to say that models are rarely used in societal processes, but rather that analysis and documentation of the (non-)use in the literature is scarce. In Section 5 we therefore present lessons learned from a number of case studies in which models did play an important role and from this we try to achieve a deeper understanding of the utility of computer models in policy formulation, their users, and when and how models are employed in practice. Although we focus on cases where models have been used, the reasons why in many other cases they have not been used logically follow from the analysis, because one or several of the conditions for use have not been met. In Section 6 we conclude with a discussion of key factors that are important in the effective use of computerized models in policy formulation processes, and highlight possible new research on this important, policy-relevant topic.

COMPUTER MODELS AND THEIR PURPOSES

There are many types of quantitative systems models and hence many classifications of them. Here we present a few common terms and classifications that are used in the literature to label the type of methods that we will focus on in this chapter. We concentrate on computer models that aim to provide new insights into future states of fairly complex systems. Examples will be drawn from models that represent complex natural resource management (NRM) systems, where the authors have particular experience.

For studies analysing future states of systems, three rather different terms can be used (van Asselt et al. 2010): forecasting (analysing the likely 'surprise-free' futures, that is futures that are plausible and that logically follow from past and present trends); foresight (analysing different 'possible' futures); and normative future explorations (exploring different 'desired' futures). Forecasting and foresight studies (see Chapter 3, this volume) can also be labelled as, respectively, 'projective' and 'predictive studies'; that is, they try to model the actual, likely or probable evolution of systems, taking the objectives of actors as being more or less implicit. Normative approaches, on the other hand, try to find ('explore') the optimal, desired or alternative solutions to a given problem by keeping the objectives explicit. Predictive (in economic literature also often called positive) studies are generally more policy-oriented: they take system properties, including the human behaviour component, as a given and try to 'predict' the future state(s) of the system in response to alternative policies. Often, explorative or normative future studies are more resource-oriented: they analyse possible futures based on availability and limitations of (natural) resources, while assuming certain objectives of agents and optimum behaviour to realize such objectives.

Today, many models are used for the purpose of so-called integrated assessment and/or in the context of the impact assessment of policies (see Chapter 9, this volume). Here, we refer to integrated assessment as a research process, while we use impact assessment to refer to the political process of assessing the expected impact of new policies or technologies (Adelle et al. 2012). Integrated assessment has been defined as 'an interdisciplinary and participatory research process combining, interpreting and communicating knowledge from diverse scientific disciplines to allow a better understanding of complex phenomena' (Rotmans and van Asselt 1996, p. 327). Integrated assessment and modelling (IAM) has been proposed as a means of enhancing the management of complex systems and to improve integrated assessment (Parson 1995; Harris 2002; Parker et al. 2002). It is based on systems analysis as a way to consider, in a more holistic fashion, the biophysical, economic, social and institutional aspects of a system under study. The term is used for models that consider biophysical and socio-economic aspects and have multi-level capabilities, for instance analysis at regional, farm and field level. The assumption underlying IAM is that computerized tools contribute to better informed *ex ante* impact assessments of new policies and technologies, as for instance employed by the European Commission since 2003 in the EU's policy formulation process (EC 2005).

Models that aim to contribute to the impact assessment of policies need to have some predictive capacity, that is, they must be able to predict likely systems changes as a result of policy changes, and must therefore allow modelling of the responses of actors. So actor behaviour must somehow be captured in the models. In contrast, more explorative and normative models address system responses or optimum configurations with more 'what-if' type questions and scenarios coming to the fore. For example, how would the system change or what would be an optimum system configuration assuming a certain objective (or prioritization of objectives) of actors? The quality of these studies is not measured in terms of the likelihood that the outcomes of the models will actually happen, but rather in showing the ultimate consequences of different priorities or choices. Crucially, they can help to reveal trade-offs between conflicting objectives. The terms predictive and explorative can be further explained and defined

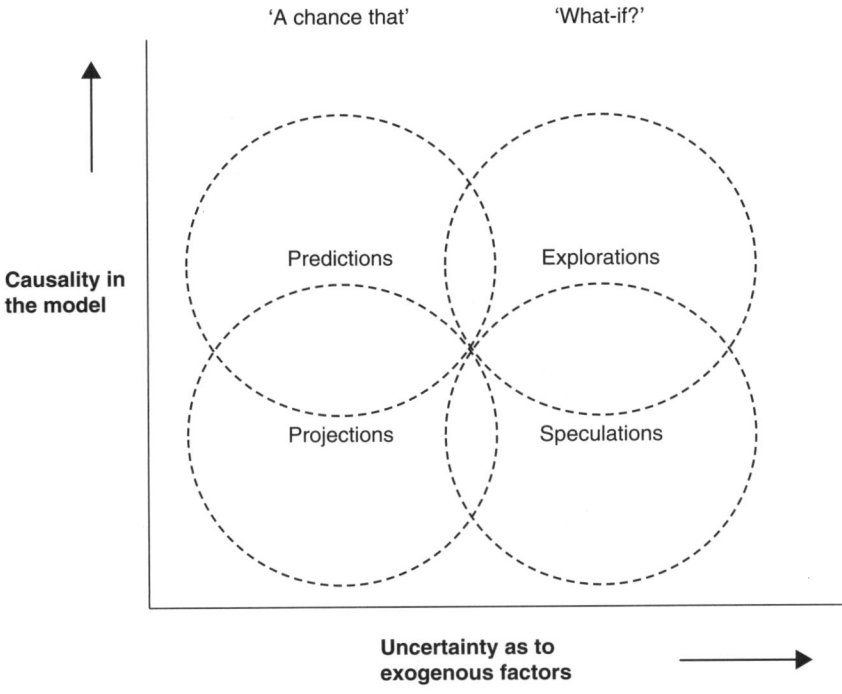

Source: van Ittersum et al. (1998) and Becker and Dewulf (1989).

Figure 5.1 Typical model-based future studies as classified by the degree of future uncertainty and the causality in the model

in a classification that relates future studies to systems models. It employs four classes based on two criteria (Figure 5.1). The first criterion is the level of uncertainty, with respect to assessing future values of system parameters and exogenous factors, for example in relation to land use, population growth, trade and market developments. Usually, the longer the time horizon of a study, the higher the level of uncertainty in these factors. It is here that a scenario approach (see Chapter 3, this volume) might be useful. The effects of making specific estimates for exogenous variables (for example, population growth) may be revealed in scenarios. The whole set of scenarios should represent the extremes of possible values for the uncertain parameters. The second criterion is the level of causality in the model of a given system, used to forecast possible future states. The level of causality is reflected in the type of model that is used for the study. Models may have a strong statistical/descriptive basis or a more mechanistic/explanatory basis with information on causes of certain developments. In more mechanistic models, behaviour or possible behaviour of a system at a higher level is explained completely by characteristics of components at lower hierarchical levels. Regional and farming systems are often too complex to model mechanistically. However, it may well be possible to model certain aspects of the systems, for example the biophysical aspects, and make explicit assumptions about others, for example the socio-economic aspects, in a scenario analysis.

These two criteria classify model-based future studies into four categories (Figure 5.1). *Projections* are based on a low level of causality in the model employed and in fact are only useful under low levels of uncertainty. If more information on causality and relations behind a projection is available, projections may gradually evolve into *predictions*. The distinction between projections and predictions is a matter of judgement, but a prediction claims a certain degree of predictability of the described developments, whereas a projection merely transplants current knowledge and information into the future (van Latesteijn 1995). In both, extrapolations of past and current trends are used and system performance is used as an input. Use is often made of actual and historical data of an empirical and statistical nature. Predictive and projective studies are generally done for the short term (less than 10 years). If the level of uncertainty increases, a projection might evolve into a *speculation* and, if more information is available on how different processes and developments are related, a speculation changes into an *exploration* of the future (see also Chapter 3, Figure 3.1, this volume). Explorations show options for future developments given explicit assumptions about uncertain developments. They usually concern strategic (occurring over >10 years) issues.

In the terminology used by van Asselt et al. (2010), that is, forecasting, foresight and normative future studies, forecasting comes close to projections, foresights are close to predictions and normative future studies generally belong to the class of explorations. However, van Asselt et al. also use the word 'explore' to describe forecasting and foresight, illustrating the ambiguity evident in both the literature and daily practice when it comes to classifying and describing future studies using computer models.

MODELS AND POLICY FORMULATION

What Policy Formulation Tasks do Models Seek to Perform?

Computer models frequently aim to provide information that informs various steps in the policy cycle. A cycle in which policies are formulated

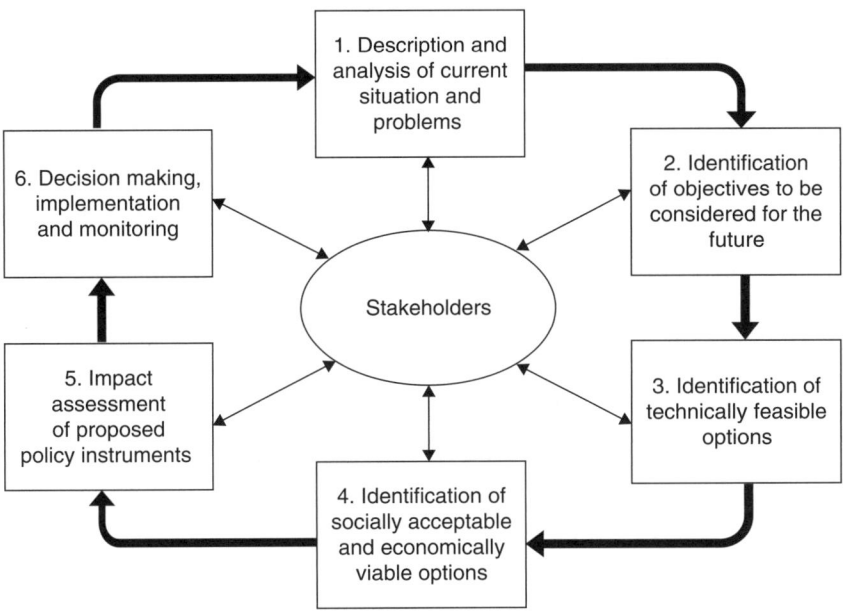

Note: Steps 1–5 are part of policy formulation.

Figure 5.2 *The development cycle for natural resource management policies*

is a highly complex, non-linear and iterative process. Howlett (2011) sub-divides it in terms of agenda setting, policy formulation, decision making, implementation and evaluation. Computer models as discussed in this chapter are aimed primarily at supporting the stage in which options that might help resolve issues and problems recognized at the agenda-setting stage are identified, refined, appraised and formalized (Howlett 2011, p. 29). Applied to land use and natural resource management problems, the policy formulation step can be structured as in Figure 5.2 (van Ittersum et al. 2004; Dent and Ridgway 1986). Again, this is highly stylized and hypothetical compared with the reality. In the first step, the current situation and the resource base are described and analysed to make an inventory of problems (in other words, problem definition and diagnosis); creation of awareness is very important in this phase. In the second step, objectives are identified that steer policy formulation. Stakeholders should agree about a set of objectives and the way they are quantified. In the third and fourth steps, natural resource-use options are explored; especially the degree to which they satisfy a range of objectives. In the third step, the emphasis is on biophysically feasible options, meaning that system designs are explored which are possible from a biophysical and technical point of view, while little is said about how feasible or desirable they are from a socio-economic point of view. In the fourth step, socially acceptable and economically viable options are identified. In the fifth step, policy measures are assessed in an analytical and participatory process.

It is important to mention that the term 'policies' as used here includes specific projects and programmes, that is, we are not only talking about, for example, a price or input subsidy policy, but also about projects to construct, for example, an irrigation scheme or a road, or an extension programme. In the sixth step, the selected options are implemented and their impact is monitored and evaluated. This can then lead to a new policy cycle and the (re-)formulation of existing policies. The cycle is centred on the stakeholders, including the different actors affected by the policies. This facilitates the endorsement of both the *process* of policy formulation and its eventual *outcomes*, and prevents the procedure becoming too top-down (Dent et al. 1994; Fresco 1994).

Explorative studies are thought to be useful in steps 3 and 4 of Figure 5.2, that is, to identify ways to realize objectives and ultimate consequences of particular objectives. In Stirling's (2008) terms, these studies aim to 'open up' (as opposed to 'close down') the future; they must not take for granted past and present states and evolutions of the system, but indicate which (strategic) options for change exist. The required longer time horizon of such models implies greater uncertainty (see Figure 5.1). In step 3, the emphasis is on exploration of biophysically and technically feasible options, under different societal priorities; hence the studies have a relatively strong biophysical orientation. Predictive studies (Figure 5.1) can play a role particularly in steps 4 and 5. In step 4 economically viable and socially acceptable options must be identified, with the studies requiring a relatively strong socio-economic orientation. In the phase of identification of policy measures (step 5), predictive studies are introduced, particularly to estimate which policy instruments lead to the desired outcome in terms of defined indicators. This is a core activity in impact assessment procedures, as for instance employed in the European Commission.

How do Computerized Models Link to Other Policy Formulation Tools?

Computer models are normally combined with other policy formulation tools to make them (more) effective in decision making processes (cf. Ewert et al. 2009). For example, scientists use participatory methods (see Chapter 2, this volume) to translate policy problems and views into researchable questions, scenarios and indicators. This is crucial for engagement and contextualization of the modelling work and something that has been ignored too often in past modelling studies. Scenarios are employed to benchmark a policy change against a baseline situation in which policies do not change, or to explore explicit assumptions on drivers of change that are not part of the model (exogenous as opposed to endogenous variables which are part of the model) (see Chapter 3, this volume; Thérond et al. 2009). Scientists also use indicators (see Chapter 4, this volume) to characterize different dimensions, aspects and criteria of sustainability; computer models allow for their quantitative assessment (Alkan Olsson et al. 2009). Aggregated or summary indicators can also be used to aggregate and present complex outcomes of computer models. For that purpose various kinds of visualization tools can also be employed, ranging from GIS, spider webs and various kinds of diagrams.

Cost–benefit analysis (see Chapter 7, this volume) can also be part of computer models (Janssen and van Ittersum 2007; Britz et al. 2012), though an important distinction is that the models as covered in this chapter try to present objectives and indicators in their own physical units rather than expressing everything in monetary terms. To weigh different criteria or objectives, for instance economic versus environmental, multi-criteria assessment methods (see Chapter 6, this volume) may be used *ex post* (Paracchini et al. 2011), after the model has been used; the objectives or indicators quantified by the model can be weighed using MCA techniques to reveal trade-offs between objectives and to identify optimal compromises. Although this step may be appealing for stakeholders or decision makers to arrive at 'single best options or solutions', the danger of weighing is that differences in opinion and relevance are rendered implicit. In the end, this may hinder transparent discussions and decisions.

WHAT KINDS OF KNOWLEDGE DO COMPUTER MODELS SEEK TO FEED INTO POLICY FORMULATION?

Scientists have choices in how they relate to decision makers. These choices have important effects on decisions or other outcomes arising from the science–policy interface. In his book *The Honest Broker*, Roger Pielke (2007) describes four roles a scientist can take in this respect: Pure Scientist, Science Arbiter, Issue Advocate and Honest Broker. A Pure Scientist is not involved in policy – (s)he publishes or presents his or her scientific work, without engaging with policymakers. A Science Arbiter responds to questions without expressing an opinion on related policy choices, in contrast to an Issue Advocate who takes a clear position and argues for specific policy action, using scientific knowledge. Finally, the Honest Broker engages in the policy process to use scientific information to expand or clarify the scope of choice available to the decision maker. In this role, the scientist reveals the different options and their possible consequences, without taking a stance.

Following Pielke, we work from the premise that the prime and preferred role of the scientist is that of an Honest Broker. However, it is virtually impossible for a scientist to take a value-free stance in societal and political issues. Scientists often have to make choices on what to include or exclude in their analysis for reasons of data availability, importance and resource (including time) availability; such choices are often affected by normative and personal factors. Yet, a key stated aim of a great deal of science is to better inform policymaking processes – through assessing proposed options in all relevant dimensions of sustainable development, and through revealing alternative options and their consequences – while not advocating particular solutions. This requires transparency about all kinds of choices made in the research process. It also requires a degree of engagement with the decision maker to make sure all relevant alternatives are investigated, and that the scientific analysis is indeed useful and understandable.

Quantitative systems models constitute an important means of learning, in the context of professional practice connected to human values (Leeuwis 2004). Learning through experience could be labelled experiential learning (Kolb 1984) through a continuous interaction and iteration between thinking and action. Models often seek to enhance such learning and thus seek to play a heuristic role. By their very nature, computer models are strong in handling all kinds of interactions between sub-components of the system and between different processes that determine its state. This may assist in providing insight into important processes and drivers of systems behaviour, thus contributing to meaning and knowledge. Scientific and policy-oriented research relies on this use of system models for all sorts of levels, ranging from the level of the gene (as in the case of Genetically Modified Organisms) to planetary systems (as in the case of the Intergovernmental Panel on Climate Change). Models may also be used to structure thinking about implications of systems configurations that do not yet exist, thus supporting *ex ante* or *ex post* assessment and evaluation of policies. Finally, if transparent, models may enhance learning by diversifying the solution space, revealing trade-offs and synergy among objectives, and supporting the selection of 'suitable' alternatives. Other proposed roles of models are relational (mediation of conflicts between stakeholders or actors and contributions to community-building) and symbolic (raising awareness and putting issues on the agenda). The extent to which these high aspirations are actually delivered is discussed in the next section.

BY WHOM, WHEN AND HOW ARE COMPUTER MODELS USED IN PRACTICE?

The aim of the remainder of this chapter is to present insight from hindsight (lessons learned) in terms of factors determining the use and usefulness of computer models in everyday policymaking. Specific references are made to experiences from land use and natural resource management (NRM) models. The work draws heavily on Sterk (2007), who investigated the use (in societal problem solving) of a number of whole farm models and a range of land use and NRM models. A synthesis paper based on her work (Sterk et al. 2011) concluded that a number of conditions need to be met before a model can be used successfully, for instance to create awareness of a problem (phase 1 in Figure 5.2), define policy objectives (phase 2) or assess proposed policies (phase 5). These factors are necessary conditions, but do not automatically lead to successful application. However, by focusing on these conditions, application of a model is not merely a matter of luck but becomes something that can be managed to some degree. The section also brings in reflections on, and lessons learned from, a major European project to develop research models for *ex ante* impact assessment (van Ittersum et al. 2008).

Model Impact and Utility in 'Real World' Policy Formulation Activities?

Sterk (2007) demonstrated how land use models may contribute to societal problem solving and concludes that the uses are rather diverse, including heuristic, symbolic and relational. Cases where a land use model had an impact combined a heuristic role with at least one other, for example a relational or symbolic role (Shackley 1997; Sterk et al. 2009a; 2011). Also, the models fed into different policy formulation venues, ranging from high-level negotiations with directors of ministries, to far more technical policy analysis and support units of ministries or directorates (see below).

A heuristic role refers to learning about land use and NRM systems, but also to learning about the views, norms and values of other actors. Land use models are especially appreciated for their study of interactions between the components of systems; they allow integration and synthesis of fragmented knowledge on processes and components of the system to arrive at a more holistic view. All successful introductions of land use models described by Sterk et al. (2009a) fulfilled such a heuristic role. Another demonstrated role of land use and NRM models is relational, referring to the enhancement of mediation of conflicts between stakeholders or actors and contributions to community-building (facilitating the definition of common ground and purpose). EURURALIS (Westhoek et al. 2006; Verburg et al. 2006) is an example of a model which had this quality. It assessed the effects on landscape of plausible changes at the European level in different political and socio-economic conditions. To this end, EURURALIS assessed scenarios of plausible changes as defined by drivers of globalization and the control of governments over societal developments. In terms of our classification (Section 2), the model had predictive qualities. In 2002, Wageningen University and Research Centre and the Netherlands Environmental Agency were asked by the Dutch Ministry of Agriculture, Nature and Food Quality to develop a partly quantitative decision support tool. Parallel to the development of EURURALIS, the Dutch Ministry of Agriculture initiated a European network of national policymakers to address the future of rural areas and to develop an EU rural policy agenda. It was similar to existing networks on water and nature conservation. Reflecting upon the role of the model in the process, an informant in the Ministry claimed the new network would cease to exist if the EURURALIS modelling work were no longer part of the network (Sterk et al. 2009a). According to the scientists and employee of the Ministry involved, the rural area directors especially appreciated the possibility of employing the EURURALIS tool as a card index and the visualization of output in land use maps because these features helped the users to get an overview of the diversity in developments and interdependencies in the rural area at both national and European levels. Respondents explicitly referred to its community-creating role, that is, the model facilitated the definition of common ground and purpose. Furthermore, its heuristic role was acknowledged, that is, EURURALIS helped the users to develop an idea of relevant aspects and interdependencies at both national and European levels.

The third demonstrated role of land use models is symbolic, that is, they may help put issues on the agenda. The *Ground for Choices* study (Rabbinge and van Latesteijn 1992) carried out by the Netherlands Scientific Council for Government Policy (WRR), is a paradigm case of a land use study of explorative nature that fulfilled a symbolic role as well as a heuristic one. It was highly successful in putting the need for further reforms to the EU's Common Agricultural Policy (CAP) onto the agenda in the early 1990s, just after the so-called MacSharry reforms initiated a process of price liberalization with direct income support measures substituting price support. The study revealed the extreme consequences of prioritizing market liberalization, rural development, environmental or nature conservation objectives in a set of agricultural land use scenarios. It showed the enormous potential of increasing agricultural production and resource use efficiency in the EU (at that time comprising only 12 Member States) when exploiting technical potentials and concentrating agriculture on the land with best climate and soils. The study also made clear that policy objectives matter: consequences in terms of optimum land use are very different depending on what objective, for example market liberalization or rural development (still an important aim of the CAP), is prioritized. Though the study did not directly assess policies nor lead to immediate policy changes, the WRR itself and its collaborators in the study claimed that the Dutch government and agricultural and nature conservation organizations became convinced of the need for further consideration of the options to integrate environmental, nature and forest objectives with agricultural objectives in response to *Ground for Choices*. In the years after publication of the study, the focus shifted from 'agricultural' to developing 'rural' policy. This change of mindset is a typical quality of explorative studies; one which is especially important in the early stages of policy formulation.

When and How are Computer Models Used in Practice?

We argue that computer models and knowledge emerging from them *may*, but not necessarily *will*, be used, if a number of circumstances converge. More precisely, the specific phase of the problem solving or policy formulation cycle, the role of model, type of model and the so-called boundary arrangement between science and policy need to match (Figure 5.3). The chances that the computer models (or the knowledge emerging from them) actually *will* be used increase if this matching occurs in a process of contextualization and networking.

Problem solving dynamics and the main phases of policy formulation (Section 3), different roles of models (Section 4) and different types of models (Section 2) have been introduced earlier in the chapter. Boundary arrangements describe how actors conceive of the division of labour between science and policy. They characterize the institutional science–policy space and help to explain experiences of interactions between science and policy. Building on the work of Hoppe (2005), Sterk et al. (2009b) define four boundary arrangements based on two criteria: (1) who is perceived to initiate the research, that is, 'science' or 'policy', and (2) how logical and appropriate it is to integrate scientific knowledge and policy. Acknowledging the different existing boundary arrangements makes explicit the institutional space in which modellers function and the arrangements or facilitators that may assist in model introduction.

The actual matching of the four factors and the chances for model use are supported by 'contextualization' and 'network building'. Contextualization is the process that encompasses the explication of underlying values and aspirations of the modeller, fitting the model to a

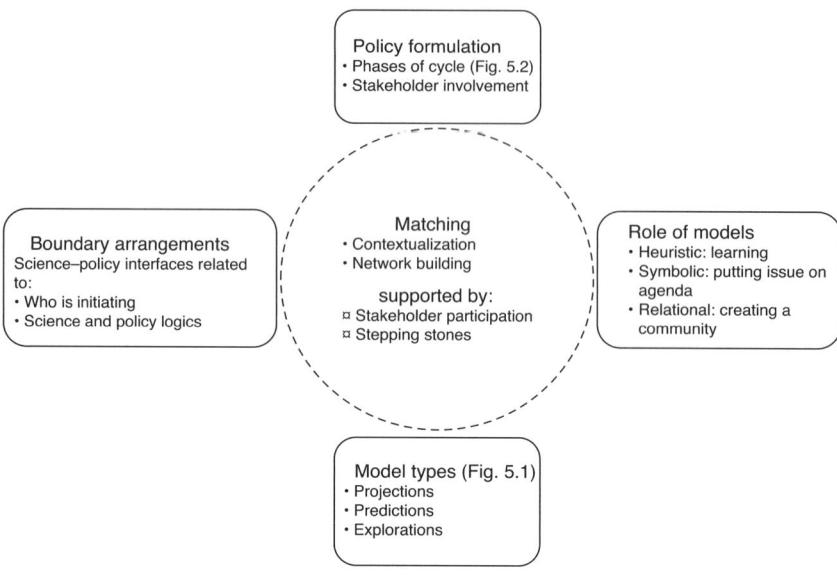

Source: Sterk et al. (2011).

Figure 5.3   *Conditions that favour model application in policy*
                formulation: matching of four factors through a process of
                model contextualization and network building

social and biophysical context and interpretation of the model (and its
results) in relation to other knowledge sources such as expertise and the
experiences of other involved actors. Network building, mostly led by
the scientists, is about becoming linked to other societal stakeholders and
fostering feelings of interdependency. In building a network, modellers,
potential users, other stakeholders as well as the land use model itself
take on roles. In the cases where land use models contributed to problem
solving, substantial investments have always been made in network building and contextualization. It was not one specific actor (group) that made
these investments; we came across examples where both modellers and
future users took the initiative.

   In the analysis of contextualization and network building processes, two
'critical leverage points' were identified (Sterk et al. 2011): first, participation of stakeholders and/or envisaged users in model development, and
second, availability of 'stepping stones', the latter referring to the closer
involvement of researchers or professionals other than the modeller within
the policy sphere. A stepping stone is a person (or small group of people)

that functions as a guide when a modeller starts to work in an unknown problem setting or moves into a different boundary arrangement.

Participation of stakeholders in model development has been a frequently debated aspect of modelling research (for example, Parker et al. 2002; Walker 2002; Jakeman et al. 2006). The argument holds that more participation increases the relevance and commitment of the involved stakeholders and consequently leads to greater impact of modelling outside science. Crucially, the cases where a land use model contributed to problem solving exhibited some degree of participation in model development, ranging from a few meetings to discuss the problem definition and research questions, informing the envisaged users about progress and fine-tuning the research further, to collaborative data collection of modellers and stakeholders. The observed consistent employment of participatory modelling suggests that it is a viable approach, although the implementation varied.

Practical Lessons Learned in the Matching Process of a Large Computer Modelling Framework

The integrated project SEAMLESS, funded by the European Commission, aimed at developing an integrated framework of models that can be employed to better inform *ex ante* impact assessments of EU agricultural and environmental policies (van Ittersum et al. 2008). It was funded by DG Research (the European Commission's Directorate-General responsible for funding and implementing European research programmes) as one of a series of integrated projects aimed at developing research tools to underpin *ex ante* impact assessment. In the case of SEAMLESS, DG Research perceived that the European Commission's Directorate-General (DG) for Agriculture (and perhaps other DGs) would have need for this type of model-based framework, to be used by or to provide information to the policy analysts and policy support units in the DGs. In the course of the SEAMLESS project, around 20 meetings took place in Brussels with DG Research and/or DG Agriculture and representatives of various other DGs to define the potential role of the project. DG Research and the research consortium defined the role as being essentially heuristic; symbolic and relational roles were never demanded nor discussed. Concrete topics on model development and contextualization – which were discussed in the course of the many interactions in Brussels – as well as the responses of the project's modellers, are summarized in Table 5.1.

Next to the 'extrinsic' factors (for example, making a policy impact) that will be further discussed below, there are of course '*intrinsic*' methodological and technical requirements of models that must be satisfied. Peer review and publication of all model components – and their integration – in international journals are a necessity to build credibility. Model

Table 5.1   The Integrated Framework: a comparison of potential user requirements* and the responses from the SEAMLESS project

Requirement of (foreseen) users	Response of research project	References
Flexible and open framework	Component-based structure	van Ittersum et al. (2008); Ewert et al. (2009)
Link with the EC's Impact Assessment procedure	The framework and user interface was structured in pre-modelling, modelling, post-modelling phases	Ewert et al. (2009); Bäcklund et al. (2010)
Relevance for users with different focus and expertise (different 'policy formulation venues')	Graphical User Interface for Integrative Modeller and Policy Expert	van Ittersum et al. (2008); Ewert et al. (2009)
Transparency and consistency of the framework	Extensive documentation and adoption of ontologies	www.seamlessassociation.org; Janssen et al. (2009)
Adopt and relate to existing indicators	Indicator library and indicator framework	Alkan Olsson et al. (2009)
Information on uncertainty	User-oriented uncertainty analysis approach	Gabbert et al. (2010)
Maintenance and future of the framework and components	Establishment of a post-project SEAMLESS Association	www.seamlessassociaton.org

Note: *As defined and discussed in a series of workshops in Brussels.

documentation is a second obvious requirement, but is far from trivial in practice. Third, the models should preferably be freely available, that is, open source, such that those interested in the model and its code can, in principle, themselves evaluate or use the model. In a recent overview article, Britz et al. (2012) present a number of other intrinsic qualities of integrated assessment models in agriculture. These include consistent linkages between different organization levels, often the micro and macro level (in other words, farm to regional or market level), model calibration and validation and uncertainty analysis. The model description and documentation must explicate underlying assumptions. In an uncertainty analysis, consequences of model assumptions and all sorts of uncertainties as to processes and data can be investigated by the modellers. The challenges of doing this in a scientifically sound yet meaningful manner for users are far from trivial. Gabbert et al. (2010) explored a user-oriented approach, but uncertainty analysis is clearly an intrinsic model quality that requires more attention to avoid 'black box' syndromes of research models and their application. This is a quality contributing to a successful contextualization of computer models for policy assessment.

As to the *extrinsic* factors, a number of lessons learned became apparent to the project coordinator (the lead author of this chapter) while reflecting on the process of science–policy interaction. First, research project formulation and execution require careful attention to *expectation management*. Project proposals (for Framework Programmes of the EU and other funding agencies alike) must be ambitious and promise well-defined outputs to win funding. In the case of SEAMLESS it was not possible – it was strongly discouraged by DG Research – to interact with potential users during the definition of the project. Yet the proposal had to be precise in its deliverables, and the complexity of the consortium of 30 research institutions (with over 150 scientists) required a precise work allocation and plan of work. Once the project had been approved and started, interactions with foreseen users were initiated and both the funder (DG Research) and foreseen users (mainly from DG Agriculture) strongly encouraged the project to raise its ambitions (Table 5.1) and sometimes to deviate from the original project proposal. The latter requires a level of flexibility which is sometimes difficult to attain in a research consortium in which the partners and individual scientists have their own specific roles. Also, although the project was funded primarily to achieve methodological advances, there was a continuous push to analyse 'hot' political topics. The project had to manage expectations in terms of what could be delivered in that respect, that is, a tension exists between *methodology development* and *application*. The methodology-application tension is a particular issue when the work is carried out by universities and institutes primarily motivated by research rather than commercial/policy applications.

Already at an early stage in the policy formulation interactions in Brussels, the issue of *maintenance and continuity* of the research tools was brought up by the foreseen users. While originally DG Research had suggested that it would take responsibility for continuity in the event of a successful project, it subsequently became clear that continuity was to be first and foremost a responsibility of the research consortium, despite various intermediate project reviews being very positive. As no single consortium member (university or institute) was able to maintain and apply all the computer models of the framework, it was essential to identify the key partners needed to maintain, further develop and apply the core components of the framework. Just before completion of the project, the SEAMLESS Association was established with around 10 core members from the consortium. The budget of the Association was modest and composed of membership fees from each partner. Though DG Research favoured the establishment of an association, neither it nor DG Agriculture felt responsible for providing financial support. The establishment of the Association is precisely the type of institutional mechanism that the knowledge utilization literature (Nutley et al. 2007) argues is required to institutionalize knowledge use over the longer term.

Finally, two important overarching lessons were learned from the science–policy interface during the SEAMLESS project. First, a *stepping stone* must be created in Brussels to network and contextualize the models and their representation of systems. It seems indispensable to post an intermediate person (cf. knowledge broker – Ward et al. 2009) in Brussels, to work on the science–policy interface on a daily basis. Working on this issue remotely, in the case of the SEAMLESS project from Lund and Wageningen, is not sufficient, whatever the level of personal commitment. A second lesson learned is the crucial *role of the funder*, as well as the agency responsible for drafting the research call, in this case DG Research. Much can and should be expected from efforts of the research consortium to contextualize the research models and to ensure a proper matching of methodologies to the politically relevant questions and processes. However, the donor(s) can play the crucial role of stepping stone in a networking process which potentially greatly facilitates the contextualization and uptake of the developed models.

CONCLUSIONS

Many computer models are being developed in research, with many either claiming political relevance or being financed precisely with that objective in mind. The challenges surrounding actual use of computer models in policy formulation are far from trivial, but are rarely investigated and documented in detail. Here, we would like to plead for more studies documenting both model use and non-use. Analysis of cases of non- or very partial use may be at least as enlightening as 'successful' cases, although modellers may find the results uncomfortable reading. In this chapter we have tried to conceptualize and summarize lessons learned, identifying by whom, when and how computer models are used in policy formulation, based on a number of demonstrated cases of land use and NRM where models *did* make a difference in policy formulation. We believe that some of the insights from hindsight may be generally applicable to other types of models and policy domains, but some may not be. Nevertheless, valuable general lessons can be learned.

The factors 'problem solving dynamics', 'boundary arrangements', 'model types', 'roles of models' and the 'matching' process allow insight regarding the who, when and how questions as to land use and NRM modelling. Based on this analysis and the further experience obtained in the example presented in Section 5, we conclude that in designing a modelling strategy with a promising opportunity for model use, equal attention must be paid to the technical requirements for model development and to the embedding of the work in a given or intended societal context. Contextualization and network building are essential to embed a model in the societal context, and to avoid modelling becoming too much of a scientific or technocratic purpose in itself.

A number of activities are particularly relevant for the matching process in various stages of the actual model development work. During the preparation, the scientists can clearly influence the proper choice of model type depending on the problem formulation dynamics and the required role of the model. Models are generally appreciated for their capability to address interactions between components of systems and between different environmental, economic and social aspects, including analysis of trade-offs. Policy questions that are likely to benefit from an integrative systems approach will allow better chances for model introduction. Studying the boundary arrangement will greatly facilitate the identification of a proper pathway for model introduction. Finally, stepping stones may be helpful when working in new or difficult boundary arrangements.

During the actual model development process, continuous attention is needed to match the possible and desired roles of the model in the specific phase(s) of policy formulation. Second, model contextualization requires attention, which implies that the underlying values and aspirations of the modellers are made explicit continuously and that these fit the social and biophysical context of the system and its stakeholders. Stepping stones in the science–policy interaction may continue to be highly instrumental in realizing this matching and contextualization.

A distinct quality of computer models is their heuristic role, that is, their potential contribution to learning, especially social learning (Muro and Jeffrey 2008; Reed et al. 2010), which can be defined as the convergence of stakeholder perspectives on the problem and possible solutions (De Kraker et al. 2011). Social learning can form the basis for integrated solutions that require collective support and/or concerted action of various stakeholders. In recent research, attempts have been made to measure social learning, with an emphasis on the role of computer models (van der Wal et al., 2014). It is our hypothesis that a more precise understanding of whether and how social learning is facilitated by models may strengthen the understanding of how they must be developed, both technically and socially. This, together with enhanced insight into the factors determining the introduction of a model, seem crucial steps towards a better understanding and use of computer models in policy formulation processes.

ACKNOWLEDGEMENTS

The authors would like to thank Andy Jordan, John Turnpenny and Tim Rayner for their valuable advice and assistance in the finalizing of this chapter.

REFERENCES

Adelle, C., A. Jordan and J. Turnpenny (2012), 'Proceeding in parallel or drifting apart? A systematic review of policy appraisal research and practices', *Environment and Planning C: Government and Policy*, **30** (3), 401–415.

Alkan Olsson, J., C. Bockstaller, L. Stapleton et al. (2009), 'A goal oriented indicator framework to support impact assessment of new policies for agri-environmental systems', *Environmental Science and Policy*, **12**, 562–572.

Bäcklund, A.K., J.P. Bousset, S. Brogaard, S. Macombe, M. Taverne and M.K. van Ittersum (2010), 'Science – policy interfaces in impact assessment procedures', in F. Brouwer and M.K. van Ittersum (eds), *Environmental and Agricultural Modelling: Integrated Approaches for Policy Impact Assessment*, Dordrecht: Springer, pp. 275–294.

Becker, H.A. and G. Dewulf (eds) (1989), *Terugkijken op Toekomstonderzoek*, ISOR, Utrecht: University of Utrecht.

Britz, W., M.K. van Ittersum, A. Oude Lansink and T. Heckelei (2012), 'Tools for integrated assessment in agriculture. State of the art and challenges', *Bio-based and Applied Economics*, **1**, 125–150.

De Kraker, J., C. Kroeze and P. Kirschner (2011), 'Computer models as social learning tools in participatory integrated assessment', *International Journal of Agricultural Sustainability*, **9**, 297–309.

Dent, D.L. and R.B. Ridgway (1986), *Land Use Planning Handbook for Sri Lanka*, Colombo: Ministry of Lands and Land Development.

Dent, D.L., D.B. Dalal Clayton and R.B. Ridgway (1994), 'The future of the land lies in the capability of its people and their institutions', in L.O. Fresco, L. Stroosnijder, J. Bouma and H. van Keulen (eds), *The Future of the Land: Mobilising and Integrating Knowledge for Land Use Options*, Chichester, UK: Wiley, pp. 81–86.

EC (2005), *Impact Assessment Guidelines*, SEC(2005) 791, Brussels: European Commission.

Ewert, F., M.K. van Ittersum, I. Bezlepkina, et al. (2009), 'A methodology for enhanced flexibility of integrated assessment in agriculture', *Environmental Science & Policy*, **12**, 546–561.

Fresco, L.O. (1994), 'Planning for the people and the land of the future', in L.O. Fresco, L. Stroosnijder, J. Bouma and H. van Keulen (eds), *The Future of the Land: Mobilising and Integrating Knowledge for Land Use Options*, Chichester, UK: Wiley, pp. 395–398.

Gabbert, S., M.K. van Ittersum, C. Kroeze, S. Stalpers, F. Ewert and J. Alkan Olsson (2010), 'Uncertainty analysis in integrated assessment: the users' perspective', *Regional Environmental Change*, **10**, 131–143.

Harris, G. (2002), 'Integrated assessment and modeling – science for sustainability', in R. Costanza and S.E. Joergensen (eds), *Understanding and Solving Environmental Problems in the 21st Century*, London: Elsevier, pp. 5–17.

Hoppe, R. (2005), 'Rethinking the science–policy nexus: from knowledge utilization and science technology studies to types of boundary arrangements', *Poiesis and Praxis*, **3**, 199–215.

Howlett, M. (2011), *Designing Public Policies*, Abingdon: Routledge.

Jakeman, A.J., R.A. Letcher and J.P. Norton (2006), 'Ten iterative steps in development and evaluation of environmental models', *Environmental Modelling & Software*, **21**, 602–614.

Janssen, S. and M.K. van Ittersum (2007), 'Assessing farm innovations and responses to policies: a review of bio-economic farm models', *Agricultural Systems*, **94**, 622–636.

Janssen, S., F. Ewert, H. Li et al. (2009), 'Defining assessment projects and scenarios for policy support: use of ontology in integrated assessment and modelling', *Environmental Modelling & Software*, **24**, 1491–1500.

Kolb, D.A. (1984), *Experiential Learning: Experience as the Source of Learning and Development*, Case Western Reserve University, Englewood Cliffs, NJ: Prentice Hall Inc.

Leeuwis, C. (2004), *Communication for Rural Innovation: Rethinking Agricultural Extension*, Oxford, UK: Blackwell Science.

Muro, M. and P. Jeffrey (2008), 'A critical review of the theory and application of social learning in participatory natural resource management processes', *Journal of Environmental Planning and Management*, **51**, 325–344.

Nutley, S.M., I. Walter and H.T.O. Davis (2007), *Using Evidence: How Research can Inform Public Service*, Bristol: The Policy Press.

Paracchini, M.L., C. Pacini, M.L.M. Jones and M. Pérez-Soba (2011), 'An aggregation framework to link indicators associated with multifunctional land use to the stakeholder evaluation of policy options', *Ecological Indicators*, **11**, 71–80.

Parker, P., R. Letcher, A. Jakeman et al. (2002), 'Progress in integrated assessment and modelling', *Environmental Modelling & Software*, **17**, 209–217.

Parson, E.A. (1995), 'Integrated assessment and environmental policy making', *Energy Policy*, **23**, 463–475.

Pielke, R.A. (2007), *The Honest Broker: Making Sense of Science in Policy and Politics*, Cambridge: Cambridge University Press.

Rabbinge, R. and H.C. van Latesteijn (1992), 'Long-term options for land use in the European community', *Agricultural Systems*, **40**, 195–210.

Reed, M.S., A.C. Evely, G. Cundill et al. (2010), 'What is social learning?', *Ecology and Society*, **15** (4), retrieved from http://www.ecologyandsociety.org/vol15/iss4/resp1/ (accessed 28 May 2014).

Rotmans, J. and M.B.A. van Asselt (1996), 'Integrated assessment: growing child on its way to maturity. An editorial essay', *Climatic Change*, **34**, 327–336.

Shackley, S. (1997), 'Trust in models? The mediating and transformative role of computer models in environmental discourse', in M. Redclift and G. Woodgate (eds), *International Handbook of Environmental Sociology*, Cheltenham, UK and Lyme, NH, USA: Edward Elgar Publishing, pp. 237–260.

Sterk, B. (2007), *A Window of Opportunities*, unpublished PhD thesis, University of Wageningen.

Sterk, B., C. Leeuwis and M.K. van Ittersum (2009a), 'Land use models in complex societal problem solving: plug and play or networking?', *Environmental Modelling & Software*, **24**, 165–172.

Sterk, B., P. Carberry, C. Leeuwis et al. (2009b), 'The interface between land use systems research and policy: multiple arrangements and leverages', *Land Use Policy*, **26**, 434–442.

Sterk, B., M.K. van Ittersum and C. Leeuwis (2011), 'How, when, and for what reasons does land use modelling contribute to societal problem solving?', *Environmental Modelling & Software*, **26**, 310–316.

Stirling, A. (2008), '"Opening up" and "closing down": power, participation, and pluralism in the social appraisal of technology', *Science, Technology and Human Values*, **33** (2), 262–294.

Thérond, O., H. Belhouchette, S. Janssen et al. (2009), 'Methodology to translate policy assessment problems into scenarios: the example of the SEAMLESS Integrated Framework', *Environmental Science and Policy*, **12**, 619–630.

van Asselt, M.B.A., A. Faas, F. van der Molen and S.A. Veenman (eds) (2010), *Uit zicht: toekomstverkennen met beleid*, Wetenschappelijke raad voor het regeringsbeleid, Den Haag, Amsterdam: Amsterdam University Press.

van der Wal, M., J. De Kraker, A. Offermans, C. Kroeze, P.A. Kirschner and M.K. van Ittersum (2014), 'Measuring social learning in participatory approaches to natural resource management', *Environmental Policy and Governance*, **24** (1), 1–15.

van Ittersum, M.K., R. Rabbinge and H.C. van Latesteijn (1998), 'Exploratory land use studies and their role in strategic policy making', *Agricultural Systems*, **58**, 309–330.

van Ittersum, M.K., F. Ewert, T. Heckelei et al. (2008), 'Integrated assessment of agricultural systems – a component-based framework for the European Union (SEAMLESS)', *Agricultural Systems*, **96**, 150–165.

van Ittersum, M.K., R.P. Roetter, H. van Keulen et al. (2004), 'A systems network (SysNet) approach for interactively evaluating strategic land use options at sub-national scale in South and South-east Asia', *Land Use Policy*, **21**, 101–113.

van Latesteijn, H.C. (1995), 'Scenarios for land use in Europe: agro-ecological options within socio-economic boundaries', in J. Bouma, A. Kuyvenhoven, B.A.M. Bouman, J.C. Luyten and H.G. Zandstra (eds), *Eco-regional Approaches for Sustainable Land use and Food Production*, Dordrecht: Kluwer Academic Publishers, pp. 43–63.

Verburg, P.H., M.D.A. Rounsevell and A. Veldkamp (2006), 'Scenario-based studies of future land use in Europe', *Agriculture, Ecosystems & Environment*, **114**, 1–6.

Walker, D.H. (2002), 'Decision support, learning and rural resource management', *Agricultural Systems*, **73**, 113–127.

Ward, V., A. House and S. Hamer (2009), 'Knowledge brokering: the missing link in the evidence to action chain?', *Evidence and Policy*, **5**, 267–279.

Westhoek, H.J., M. van den Berg and J.A. Bakkes (2006), 'Scenario development to explore the future of Europe's rural areas', *Agriculture, Ecosystems & Environment*, **114**, 7–20.

6. Multi-criteria analysis: a tool for going beyond monetization?

Catherine D. Gamper and Catrinel Turcanu

INTRODUCTION

Multi-criteria analysis (MCA) has emerged from the field of operational research and management science as an appraisal tool able to handle complex multi-factorial decision problems that affect several stakeholders and where an equitable, inclusive and transparent decision process is sought. According to the International Multi-Criteria Decision Society (IMCDM 2013), multi-criteria analysis dates back to the 1950s when analysts started to consider multiple objectives for optimality conditions in non-linear programming – so-called 'Goal Programming'. Since then, a multitude of MCA methods have been developed (some of which will be discussed below) and their use has gone far beyond the realm of operational and business research, as we will demonstrate later in the chapter. To assess the worth of different policy options, MCA aggregates the results on *multiple* evaluation *criteria* into indicators of the overall performance of options without enforcing the transformation of criteria and their results to a common – what is in many other tools a monetary – scale. In its role as a decision *aiding*, rather than a decision *making* tool, MCA seeks to render the evaluation of policy options transparent to the decision maker and other stakeholders, instead of 'replacing the decision maker with a mathematical model' (Roy and Vincke 1981, p. 208). MCA thereby seeks to promote 'good decision making' (Keeney and Raiffa 1972, p. 65) by offering a clearer illustration of the different inputs that typically go into a policy formulation process, and by dealing in a structured way with multiple, conflicting objectives and value systems. In particular, the problem-structuring phase of the policy formulation process – during which the goals of policy, the options to be evaluated and the criteria according to which this is to be done are defined – is recognized as a useful learning opportunity to which MCA can contribute (Marttunen and Hämäläinen 1995). In this phase, MCA stimulates discussion between the various stakeholders (French et al. 1993) and helps decision makers to better comprehend the decision problem, as well as the values and priorities involved (Belton and Stewart 2002).

Numerous case studies in the literature suggest that MCA has seen widespread application across different policy venues, spanning many policy areas concerning the environment, public transport and health, analysis of vulnerability to natural and man-made hazards, and many others. Indeed, MCA has been recognized by a number of governments, NGOs and international organizations as the preferred way to analyze complex decisions. It has even been legally prescribed in some cases. The tool's ability to open up to different value systems by directly representing stakeholders' preferences (through participation in the evaluation process) has particularly appealed to critics of other evaluation tools that can integrate preferences only in indirect ways, such as through monetary evaluation in CBA (see Chapter 7, this volume).

To evaluate the tool's merits, we will first take a close look at the main methodological aspects of MCA, before analyzing its application across different policy venues. This will lead us to an evaluation of the tool's added value and caveats which policymakers and analysts have to bear in mind when applying MCA in policy formulation processes. We will also provide insight into the venues that are most favourable to its application. This should hopefully inform the future application and development of MCA across different policy venues and sectors.

MAIN METHODOLOGICAL ASPECTS OF MULTI-CRITERIA ANALYSIS

In common with some other policy formulation tools, for instance CBA (cost–benefit analysis) or CEA (cost-effectiveness analysis) – covered in Chapter 7 – MCA provides an integrative decision making methodology, from problem and objectives definition, through evaluation of policy options, to ranking/comparing options. The underlying methodology, however, is different.

Multi-criteria analysis may be structured in several steps (see for example, Keeney 1992; Roy 1996; Dodgson et al. 2000; Munda 2004): characterization of the decision context (for example, individual or group decision making, need for participation, and so on) and the type of recommendation needed (for example, ranking, choice of best option, and so on); definition of options; elaboration of evaluation criteria; assessment of options' impact with respect to these criteria; preference modelling and aggregation of preferences; sensitivity and/or robustness analysis.

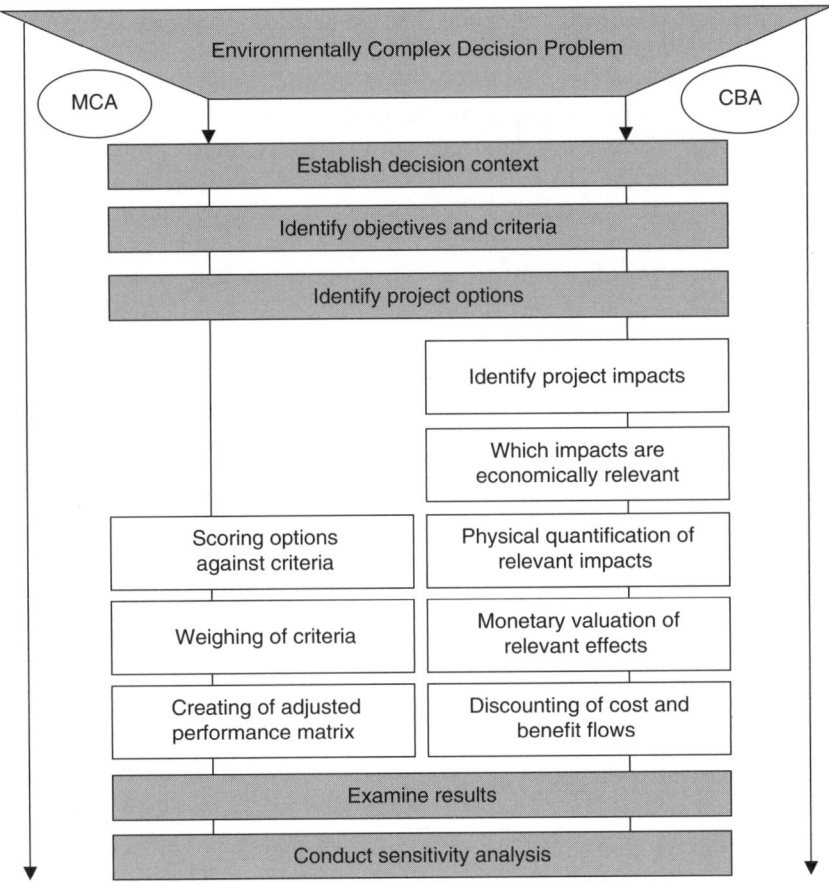

Source: Gamper et al. (2006, p. 294).

Figure 6.1 Multi-criteria analysis and cost–benefit analysis: a comparison of the different steps in the process

Figure 6.1 shows the similarities and differences between MCA and CBA, which is also frequently applied to inform policy formulation processes.

CBA, though following similar steps in the policy formulation process, identifies positive and negative impacts of policy options quite differently, as it uses a single evaluation criterion and requires the valuation of all impacts in monetary terms. Such a simplified logic makes input elements very straightforward to compare and has therefore attracted widespread application across diverse policy venues and sectors, from public health and transport to the environment. The monetization process demands a high degree of methodological rigour to avoid biases and maintain internal validity. This has raised issues in the practical application of this approach. For instance, putting a price tag on the marginal costs of a loss of biodiversity is not only technically elaborate, but may prove unacceptable to those who believe that the intrinsic existence value of nature is unmeasurable in money terms. In practice, when rigorous monetary evaluation proves too time- and resource-intensive, CBA often leaves some values out of the equation altogether, rendering its results technically invalid (see for example Joubert et al. 1997; Brouwer and van Ek 2004). MCA offers scope for resolving some of these issues by accepting the multiplicity of impact dimensions and hence evaluation criteria for complex policy issues, such as the environment or health. This proves especially useful in the case of 'soft' or intangible factors, such as ethical, social, cultural or ecological ones, for which monetization of impacts may be exceedingly difficult and/or contentious (Gamper and Turcanu 2007).

MCA allows for consideration of several value systems and for participation to take into account the preferences of different stakeholders. Gamper et al. (2006) and Lebret et al. (2005) argue that MCA should be the preferred method if consensual solutions to resolve conflicts need to be found. For a detailed discussion of the methodological differences see Tietenberg (2001), Edwards-Jones et al. (2000), Munda et al. (2004), Gamper et al. (2006).

Identifying Objectives and Criteria

Decision makers' and stakeholders' values or preferences may be explicitly included in a MCA model through a set of criteria against which the impact of the potential policy options is evaluated. This may include environmental criteria, such as the protection of natural habitats for certain species, or economic criteria, such as the job and economic development opportunities or costs arising from an infrastructure development policy. Evaluation criteria can be built in two ways. The top-down approach starts from a main objective and builds a hierarchical tree structure of fundamental objectives (Keeney 1992) or key concerns (Bana e Costa and Beinat 2005). The bottom-up approach starts from the impacts of policy options and builds a consistent family of evaluation criteria (Roy 1996) by partial synthesis of related and non-conflicting items. In practice, a combination of the two approaches may prove the most efficient (Bana e Costa and Beinat 2005).

Numerous studies in the MCA literature have addressed the desirable properties of a good set of criteria: the most important include (1) *exhaustiveness* (the criteria selected characterize completely the evaluation of any policy option); (2) *cohesiveness* (partial preferences with respect to each individual criterion have to be consistent with the global preference); and (3) *non-redundancy* (elimination of any criterion from the chosen set of criteria leads to violation of at least one of the previous properties) (Roy 1996). The second in this list means for instance that an improvement of an option with respect to some criteria should not lead to a worse 'global' evaluation. Roy and Bouyssou (1993) give an example involving a 'reliability' criterion, proving that in some cases this property might not be valid: two cost values might be indifferent if they both have a low reliability, but the lower cost could be strictly preferred if the higher cost is obtained with a higher reliability. Keeney (1992) argues that the evaluation criteria should also be *operational*, that is, allowing impact assessment for the available policy options within reason given available time and resources. Related to the latter, one should note that in the presence of uncertainty, the evaluation of an option with respect to a criterion might not be a unique element, but rather an interval, a distribution or a fuzzy set.

Identifying Policy Options to Achieve the Set of Objectives

The set of possible policy options taken into consideration in the policy appraisal process should include those considered realistic by at least one of the actors, or assumed as such by the analyst (Roy and Bouyssou 1993), and that contribute to the achievement of objectives. The definition of policy options depends both on the problem itself and the actors involved, and strongly influences the subsequent methodological steps. The set of options can be *comprehensive*, if every option is exclusive of any other, or *fragmented*, if certain combinations of individual options have to be considered.

Since MCA can and should ideally be based on an iterative process, the initial set of options might be modified during the policy formulation process, but should always include a comparison with the option of remaining with the status quo.

Evaluating Policy Options

In the MCA literature (Vincke 1992; Roy 1996; Belton and Stewart 2002), three main categories of approach are highlighted. However, it is recognized that these categories do not have sharp boundaries and that combinations of two such approaches can be envisaged (Roy 1996). The categories are: (1) *multi-attribute utility (MAUT) methods*, seeking to aggregate all points of view into a unique function which is to be optimized; (2) *outranking methods*, which construct and exploit a synthesizing relation based on the decision maker's preferences; and (3) *interactive/trial-error methods*, which explore the space of feasible options through a dialogue with the decision maker(s). Some guidelines exist on choosing a specific MCA approach (for example, Guitouni and Martel 1998), as well as recommendations on the desired properties it should have (for example, Munda 2004). In the following, the main MCA methods are summarized. For more details on the underlying assumptions and the related theoretical aspects, the interested reader may consult the references provided in the text.

Multi-attribute Utility/Value Methods

Multi-attribute utility methods (MAUT) (Keeney and Raiffa 1976) are based on the assumption that the decision maker's preferences are coherent with some increasing real function U called utility, which (s)he attempts to maximize. In other words, an option a is preferred over another option b, if and only if $U(a) > U(b)$.

In the additive model, which is most commonly used, the utility of an option a is expressed as a sum of the partial utilities:

$$U(a) = \sum_{i=1}^{n} U_i(g_i(a)),$$

where U_i are single-attribute utility functions corresponding to the evaluation criteria g_i and n is the number of criteria. An extensive literature has been dedicated to building the additive model, for example Fishburn (1967) and Jacquet-Lagrèze and Siskos (1982). Fishburn (1967) has formulated sufficient and necessary conditions for the existence of an additive utility function. A necessary condition for the validity of the additive model is, for instance, that any subset of criteria is preferentially independent of the remaining criteria.[1] Keeney (1992) provides other examples of relatively simple (for example, multi-linear) utility functions and the conditions for the validity of the corresponding models.

When uncertainties are not taken into account, the model becomes a multi-attribute *value* model. The additive value model can be formulated as the maximization of a value function V given by:

$$V(a) = \sum_{i=1}^{n} w_i \cdot V_i(g_i(a)),$$

where the weights w_i are scaling constants that indicate value trade-offs between criteria. These weights can be determined by various techniques, as illustrated for example in Hämäläinen (2002).

The uncertainty and imprecision in MAUT models can be modelled by means of probability theory. It is interesting to note that the shape of the utility function has a direct relation with the attitude to risk of the decision makers. A concave utility function corresponds to *risk aversion*, a linear function to *risk neutrality* and a convex function to *risk proneness* (Keeney 1992).

Outranking Methods

Outranking methods (Roy 1985) were developed to address some difficulties experienced with the MAUT approach in dealing with practical problems. Bouyssou (2001) notes that outranking methods do not require establishing trade-offs between criteria in order to derive overall preferences and that they are mostly non-compensatory. This implies for instance that a very weak performance on an important criterion (say, health effects) cannot be compensated by better performances on a number of less important criteria, as it could be in the case for MAUT methods.

Outranking methods may involve the use of a more general criterion model, called pseudo-criterion, which is characterized by two thresholds describing the concepts of *indifference* and *strong preference*. These thresholds are related in some cases to the uncertainty inherent in the evaluation of certain criteria. The analysis of options in outranking methods entails pairwise comparison of options on each criterion, and subsequently building an overall preference relation (also called outranking relation) aggregating these partial preferences. The underlying principle is 'democratic majority, without strong minority'. Accordingly, an option *a* outranks option *b*, or in other words *a* is at least as good as *b*, if a majority (or more important set) of criteria supports this assertion and if the opposition of the other criteria (their number or their importance) is 'not too strong' (Bouyssou 2001, pp. 249–250). The outranking relation can be further exploited to derive the best option(s) and issue a recommendation.

Some of the outranking methods, such as ELECTRE I-III (Roy and Bouyssou 1993) and PROMETHEE (Brans et al. 1984), also require assigning weights to criteria. However, for such methods weights represent the intrinsic importance of the evaluation criteria, instead of value trade-offs, as in the case of MAUT. Some outranking methods such as MELCHIOR (Leclercq 1984) or ELECTRE IV (Roy 1996) can also cope with situations when criteria weights cannot be assessed.

Interactive Methods

Interactive methods (Steuer 1986; Vanderpooten and Vincke 1989; Vincke 1992; Lee and Olson 1999) alternate the computation steps with interaction steps in which the analyst gradually specifies or revises preference information, in accordance to the decision maker's or other stakeholders' requests.

In the early stages of investigation, the set of decision options may be itself an outcome of this interaction.

The underlying principle of this MCA approach is inspired by Simon's theory of satisficing (Simon 1976), the goal being to find a satisfactory compromise solution. This is especially appropriate (Belton and Stewart 2002) for the case when the participants in the decision process have some good a priori ideas about the realistically achievable levels for the evaluation criteria.

Interactive methods can be seen to function in a search-oriented or learning-oriented framework. In the latter setting, the set of non-dominated solutions is freely explored, the current solution found being compared with the most preferred up to that stage. Therefore, a solution discarded at some step might be reconsidered at a later stage.

Sensitivity and Robustness Analysis

Data uncertainty and imprecision are inherent characteristics of real-life applications and equally affect MCA models. A classical way to deal with this is to undertake sensitivity analysis. This seeks to determine the parameters which contribute most to the variance in the MCA results or how much the model parameters (for example, criteria weights) may vary such that the conclusion of interest (for example, that a policy option achieves the best rank) still holds.

An alternative way to address uncertainty and imprecision in MCA is robustness analysis. The notion of robustness may have different interpretations (Dias 2006). Roy and Bouyssou (1993, p. 315) use the term '*robust*' for a result or conclusion that is not 'clearly invalidated' for any possible instance of the decision model parameters (for example, weights or thresholds). Connected to that, the *robustness analysis* is the process of elaborating recommendations founded on robust conclusions. Dias and Clímaco (1999) identify two types:

- *Absolute robust* conclusion, in other words, a statement referring to one option only, which is valid for all admissible instances of the MCA model parameters, for example, 'option *a* has the utility $U(a) > 0.5$';
- *Relative robust* conclusion, in other words, a statement referring to one option in relation to others, and which is valid for all admissible instances of the MCA parameters, for example, 'option *a* has a better rank than option *b*' or 'option *a* has the best rank'.

For instance, if the range of a criterion's weight is estimated as [0.3, 0.5], sensitivity analysis may point out for example that the ranking of the different policy options changes if this weight becomes larger than 0.4. Robustness analysis can indicate instead that a given option will always outperform another, no matter what the particular value of the weight in the given interval.

MULTI-CRITERIA ANALYSIS IN POLICY PRACTICE

In the following we will look at aspects of usage, the policy venues where it occurs, the quality of implementation, and the legitimacy and policy relevance of MCA. We first ask why and under what circumstances the application of MCA was initiated and by whom it is used, whether its application has been driven by decision analysts or whether it has been more formally adopted in legal frameworks prescribing it as a tool to evaluate policy options. We then assess the quality of policy formulating processes with MCA based on: (1) their transparency and legitimacy (for example, integration of stakeholders in the process) and (2) the degree to which the results of the policy formulating process through MCA were relevant for actual policymaking.

Multi-criteria Analysis: Its Venues

In this section we discuss venues favourable to the application of MCA. As will be seen, MCA is applied at different levels of governance, with different triggering factors. To get a better insight into the real potential and use of MCA, we go beyond the definition of venues as introduced in Chapter 1. Accordingly, we look not only at the institutional environments where MCA has been applied, but also the processes by which it became relevant to policy appraisal (for example, formal requirement versus experts' decision), the predominant application fields and the policy context.

The users
MCA has been used by various actors to inform policy formulation processes. While the use of the tool is often initiated by analysts as support for local, regional or even national policy formulation processes (for example, Bana e Costa and Oliveira 2002; Petras 1997), governments themselves have also used and recommended its application (Del Rio Vilas et al. 2013; Munda 2004; van Gennip et al. 1997). International organizations have also applied MCA, as shown for example in the UN Environment Programme's use of the method for the evaluation of emissions abatement options (Borges and Villavicencio 2004). In still further cases, a MCA-based research study initiated by analysts without governmental involvement or

participation later informed a policymaking process, as was the case in a French study where MCA results became part of the government's strategic programme for flood prevention (Azibi and Vanderpooten 2003).

The main policy areas
MCA studies have been applied as policy formulation tools across a number of policy areas (see examples in Table 6.1), most notably environment,

Table 6.1   Examples of MCA: methods used, degree of stakeholder involvement and decision level

Application field	MCA method	Actors involved	Outcome and decision level	Country
Water uses conflict	PROMETHEE	Wide involvement (multiple stakeholders, experts, public)	Outcome not reported in follow-up academic publications	Germany
Water uses conflict	Additive value function		Methodological investigation to support acceptance of the tool	South Africa
Greenhouse gas emissions reductions	PROMETHEE, AHP		Results presented to government	Peru
Forest management conflicts	MAUT		Shared strategy evolved	Australia
Agro-resources conflicts	ELECTRE TRI	Experts and government authorities	Results used for consultation with farmers	France
Wind energy scenarios	NAIADE	Analysts only	No information provided	Italy
Transport	MACBETH	Stakeholders as 'actors'	Basis for policy proposal	Portugal
Public health	Additive value function	Ministerial delegates	Direct influence on health policy	Netherlands
Management of municipal housing stock	MACBETH	Experts and municipal authorities	Informally used for decisions	Portugal
Radioactive waste disposal	PROMETHEE	Experts	Direct influence on state policy	Croatia

Source: Adapted from: Gamper and Turcanu (2007).

public transport, health, and natural and man-made hazards. Probably the widest application of MCA for public policy can be found in environmental decision making. It has been applied to water and forest use and resources issues in Germany, South Africa and China (Messner et al. 2006; Joubert et al. 1997; Ananda and Hearth 2005; Arondel and Girardin 2000; Wu et al. 2012), fishery governance in Australia (Dichmont et al. 2013), protection against natural hazards in Bangladesh (Haque et al. 2012), management of urban wastewater in Australia (Tjandraatmadja et al. 2013), evaluation of policy options for greenhouse gas emissions reduction in Peru (Borges and Villavicencio 2004) and energy policies in Italy and the USA (Cavallaro and Ciraolo 2005; Hobbs and Horn 1997).

Other public policy areas where MCA has been quite frequently applied are public health and infrastructure. For example, Bana e Costa et al. (2001) have analyzed the case of a Portuguese railway line, van Gennip et al. (1997) used MCA to rank the most common diseases in the Netherlands in order to come up with a prioritization strategy for the government's financing of public health, while Del Rio Vilas et al. (2013) applied MCA as a decision-support tool for the Veterinary Risk Group in the UK.

Formal Requirements Prescribing MCA

In contrast to other tools (such as CBA) which are frequently legally pre-scribed (for example in large infrastructure projects in the Netherlands or the United Kingdom especially) and for natural hazard management (for example, in Austria, Switzerland), MCA has not received such widespread legal backing. Gamper and Turcanu (2007) identify some of the difficul-ties linked to the application of MCA at governmental level, including the variety of MCA tools which makes standardization problematic; the difficult inter-comparison of case studies (different methods may yield dif-ferent results) and the technical complexity of MCA modelling. A recent survey by Adelle et al. (2011) among 124 specialists in charge of Impact Assessment showed that only 6 per cent thought that the use of MCA is encouraged in their country, while this rose to 27 per cent for monetary evaluation tools such as CBA and CEA (see also Chapter 9, this volume).

Nevertheless, some notable examples of legal requirement for MCA do exist. For example, the Italian law for public works (ANAC 2011) stipu-lates that project selection should be done using a multi-attribute value method, ELECTRE, or any other MCA method recognized in the scien-tific literature (AHP, TOPSIS, and so on). Another example can be found in Spain where the acquisition of data-processing equipment by the central public administration offices has to be conducted based on MCA (Barba-Romero 2001). According to Joubert et al. (1997), MCA is also implicitly required by law in the USA for water resource planning. The increased focus on MCA is currently reflected by the inclusion of the tool in policy guidance documents elaborated at governmental level (Dodgson et al. 2000; Brooks et al. 2009). For instance, Brooks et al. (2009, p. 46) recommend MCA as 'particularly suitable for participatory decision making'.

A number of European Union and United Nations documents currently recommend the use of MCA. The UN Framework Convention on Climate Change (UNFCCC), for example, recommends MCA if evaluation criteria cannot (easily) be accommodated in monetary evaluation (UNFCCC 2002) and FAO (the UN's Food and Agriculture Organization) proposes cost–utility analysis based on an additive utility model for the evaluation of food quality systems as an alternative to other tools such as CBA (Krieger et al. 2007).

The Reasons for Choosing MCA

The results reported in the literature show that a general motivation for choosing MCA over other tools is to gain a better insight into the complexity of decisions on public policies and their consequences when these are felt not only on one, but on multiple dimensions, including economic, social, environmental or institutional. The tool is applied for systematic comparison and ranking of policy options, sometimes in combination with other tools such as CEA (Wu et al. 2012) or Life Cycle Analysis (Tjandraatmadja et al. 2013). MCA is also applied to lay out the basis for future policies, for instance by evaluating and prioritizing emerging threats and vulnerabilities (Del Rio Vilas et al. 2013).

MCA is chosen when trading between different objectives (for example, sustainability objectives and economic objectives) is difficult (Dichmont et al. 2013, p. 130), where its appeal comes from its 'attention on impacts related to specific objectives, thus reducing potential bias'. Similarly, for Hobbs and Horn (1997, p. 357), MCA was chosen in an energy planning application because it makes 'choices more explicit, rational and efficient', which is accomplished, among other ways, by displaying trade-offs among criteria so that 'planners, regulators and the public can understand the advantages and disadvantages of alternatives'.

However, the potential of MCA is most evident in situations involving a complex policy context, with multiple, potentially competing objectives and value systems, which cannot be easily quantified (for example, environmental issues) let alone translated into monetary terms, due to their intangible nature (for example, social, cultural or psychological issues). This applies particularly to resolving conflicts around public policy decisions that spread over jurisdictional borders, where no established decision making procedures are in place, and conflict potential may arise, as demonstrated for example by the case of managing water users' interests on the river Spree in Germany (Messner et al. 2006).

But MCA's capabilities go further than that: it can structure and facilitate stakeholders' involvement in decision processes. This is a key aspect, since through participation it contributes to the democratization of the policy formulation process and to its enhanced fairness and overall efficiency (Stirling 2008), potentially increasing the quality of decisions (Beierle 2002) and resulting in more widely accepted policy options (for an example see Linkov et al. 2006). The European Commission's *Evaluation of Socio-Economic Development* Guide (EC 2013, p. 135) suggests that MCA provides a framework facilitating the participation of all actors in decision making and in problem solving, which may help in 'reaching a compromise or defining a coalition of views, without dictating the individual or collective judgement of the partners'. Some case studies in the literature mention the participatory framework provided by MCA as among the main reason for choosing the tool. For instance, Haque et al. (2012) have used MCA following the recommendations of the UNFCCC (2002), to develop a 'participatory integrated assessment' of adaptation options for flood protection in Bangladesh.

The Quality and Legitimacy of Multi-criteria Analysis in Practice

Opening up the policy formulation process can increase or undermine the legitimacy of a MCA study
Among the advantages of policy formulation with MCA is its opening to different value systems, as mentioned above, which is particularly fostered by a transparent and inclusive participatory process (see Chapter 2, this volume). Although a generic MCA cannot be considered as a participatory tool in itself, stakeholders can participate in some or all stages of the policy formulation process when MCA is used. Some MCA tools specifically designed for opening up the decision making process to participation, such as multi-criteria mapping (Stirling and Mayer 2001), are listed among the current tools for participatory policy assessment (see Chapter 2).

In practice, the extent to which stakeholder inclusion in MCA takes place largely depends on the people steering the process and brings with it challenges inherent to any participatory assessment exercise. In reported case studies (see Table 6.1) its inclusion has sometimes involved fairly narrow approaches, such as when only experts and/or authorities are included (Bana e Costa and Oliveira 2002; van Gennip et al. 1997; Petras 1997; Brouwer and van Ek 2004). Broader participation entails sharing the involvement and responsibilities in the policy formulation process more widely, as shown by Borges and Villavicencio (2004) or Marttunen and Hämäläinen (1995). In these cases, experts built the scenarios, as well as the criteria, while the evaluation and the weighting process were performed by wider stakeholder groups. Or, as in the case described by Bombaerts et al. (2007), the options can be identified in a participatory manner, such as was done for low-level radioactive waste disposal options elaborated in a dialogue between a radioactive waste agency, local communities and local individuals. Examples where stakeholders participated in all phases of the policy formulation analysis, including the definition of alternatives and criteria, are provided for example by Joubert et al. (1997) and Messner et al. (2006).

Opening up the appraisal processes to a wider stakeholder group has other clear benefits, not only in making the outcome of a policy formulation process with MCA more legitimate, but also in terms of clarifying the problem, both between the public and experts, as well as between experts of different fields (Kontić et al. 2006). In a larger participative context, including the general public, Renn et al. (1993) propose a three step procedure relying on MCA, but making a division of decision making tasks between three levels of society: evaluation criteria are to be constructed by involvement of all relevant stakeholders; identification and impact assessment for the decision options are mainly carried out by experts; and weighting should be done by citizens' panels.

Early involvement of stakeholders (Banville et al. 1998) can give a more pragmatic dimension to MCA and contribute to an increased acceptance of the final result. Stakeholder processes are, however, costly and time consuming and, in terms of legitimacy, may on some occasions not contribute in the manner suggested by advocates (see Chapter 2, this volume). In some cases they may even lead to a stalling of the decision process. Therefore, difficult questions remain over which stakeholders should get involved, at what time and through which processes.

In addition, politics may sometimes constrain wide stakeholder involvement. Political actors may not wish to openly express their priorities, or may have their own hidden agendas. Bana e Costa et al. (2001) describe a case where direct participation was replaced – at the request of one of the actors – by an analyst simulating the viewpoints of all relevant stakeholders. Similarly, Brouwer and van Ek (2004) report on a stakeholder analysis, where experts judged the effect different strategies might have on the elicited stakeholder groups, but the MCA was then performed without them.

Another challenge relates to knowledge and information sharing, which means on the one hand making technical information understandable to all stakeholders, and on the other making technical specialists aware of the social and political dimensions of the problem they face (Bardos et al. 2002, p. 19). This brings with it a necessary reduction of complexity, but carries the risk that participants consider that the evaluation criteria employed in the final analysis oversimplify the underlying problem (Marttunen and Hämäläinen 1995).

MCA is sometimes regarded as challenging the expert's prerogatives since it may be interpreted as making specialist knowledge subject to non-expert evaluation. In a study on the use of decision aid tools including MCA in environmental management, Joliveau et al. (2000) show that experts may oppose such tools due to several factors, including inter alia hesitation in changing the usual procedures, fear that the model will collide with their recommendations or reluctance to share their power of decision. By contrast, Belton and Stewart (2002, p. 160) emphasize that an important role of MCA is to provide a 'sounding board' against which experts and decision makers can test their intuitions. They illustrate a good number of MCAs for which analysis and intuition were 'successfully reconciled' (Belton and Stewart 2002, p. 288), for example due to creation of new decision alternatives, or to the reconsideration of preferences.

MCA results can be directly and indirectly policy-relevant
Even though the essential contribution of MCA in a policy formulation process lies in decision *aiding*, rather than *making*, it is still relevant to understand whether it actually informs policymaking or is employed instead as a symbolic planning tool. The latter can render participatory processes ineffective, once participants sense that the decision has already been taken regardless of their inclusion. In practice, the final decision may or may not comply with the recommendations derived from the MCA. However, the analysis itself, the questions raised and the type of reasoning promoted (Bouyssou et al. 2000) can have a positive impact on the decision process, in that preferences are revealed and can thus be considered by the final decision maker (thereby avoiding the interests of some being favoured automatically over those of other affected stakeholders).

The usefulness and integration of the MCA outcomes in policy formulation are not easily observed through a desk review. This information is rarely tangible and seldom reported in the case study results, partly because it may take time after the process until the actual decision by policymakers is taken. A more in-depth understanding would require research among analysts, stakeholders and policymakers to understand the actual translation of outcomes in the policymaking process. Some indicative information can nevertheless be found. For example, in the Dutch case reported by van Gennip et al. (1997), the results of the MCA were directly discussed in the Dutch parliament to formulate health policy options. Also in the study of Bana e Costa and Oliveira (2002, p. 390) the results are 'informally used for deciding which requests for building works should be given priority in each year'. The case reported by Borges and Villavicencio (2004) presents another example of a MCA study the outcome of which subsequently formed the basis for the policy options presented by the Peruvian government in its National Communication to the UN Framework on Climate Change (Borges and Villavicencio 2004). Finally, Fletcher et al. (2010) present a case where the priorities derived by the application of MCA for the evaluation of ecological assets in the West Coast Bioregion of Australia by the Department of Fisheries process form now the basis for the Department's budget planning process.

CONCLUSION

This chapter has shown that MCA's policy relevance is observed beyond its legal prescription in national laws or directives, being frequently encountered – in one approach or another – in situations requiring a transparent, well-structured and inclusive policy formulation process. As we have shown, one has to look deeper into the structure, initiation and the participating partners to assess its potential and impact on policy appraisal decisions. The actual relevance of MCA as a policy formulation tool is twofold. First, a number of successful applications in various policy domains show that MCA can cope with multi-factor, multi-stakeholder decision problems, its outcome being supported by stakeholders and decision makers in a good number of cases. Second, the mutual learning among experts and stakeholders promoted by MCA means that the findings or difficulties encountered can be used for improving the policy formulation process in various ways. This may involve developing new policy options (for example, Bana e Costa et al. 2001), broadening the group of stakeholders participating in the policy formulation process or incorporating the results of the procedure in new regulations (for example, van Gennip et al. 1997). Therefore MCA could be of use not only when embedded as a means of appraisal in new regulations, but also indirectly, in order to support the evaluation of current policies, while orientating future ones (Stirling and Mayer 2001).

However, MCA results can be seen as highly subjective, due to the emphasis on 'the judgement of the decision making team, in establishing objectives and criteria, estimating relative importance weights and, to some extent, in judging the contribution of each option to each performance criterion' (Dodgson et al. 2000, p. 20). For this reason, some authors (for example, Bardos et al. 2002; Lebret et al. 2005) advocate a need for international standardization and harmonization in the use of tools like

MCA in order to increase their applicability. While weighting the different criteria is certainly dependent on the societal context, technical (legal) guidelines could be drafted for specific application domains, in terms of criteria and indicators to be considered, MCA methods to be used or stakeholder processes to be developed. This would facilitate the application of MCA by providing a generic comprehensive framework based on which policymakers and analysts could customize the method to their particular appraisal needs.

NOTE

1. A subset of criteria S is called preferentially independent, if the preference between options differing only on criteria from S does not depend on their evaluation on the remaining criteria. For instance, comfort and fuel consumption might not be preferentially independent from price because the importance of comfort may increase with price (Marichal and Roubens 2000).

REFERENCES

Adelle, C., A. Jordan, J. Turnpenny et al. (2011), *A Summary of User Needs and Expectations with Regards to Impact Assessment.* Deliverable D1.3 of EC FP7 LIAISE project (Linking Impact Assessment Instruments to Sustainability Expertise). Project no. 243826. Network of Excellence FP7 Environment (including Climate Change).

ANAC (2011), Determinazione n. 7 del 24 novembre 2011, Gazzetta Ufficiale n. 291 del 15–12–2011. Retrieved from http://www.avcp.it/portal/public/classic/AttivitaAutorita/AttiDellAutorita/_Atto?ca54846 (accessed 15 July 2014).

Ananda, J. and G. Hearth (2005), 'Evaluating public risk preferences in forest land-use choices using multi-attribute utility theory', *Ecological Economics*, **48**, 408–419.

Arondel, C. and P. Girardin (2000), 'Sorting cropping systems on the basis of their impact on groundwater quality', *European Journal of Operational Research*, **127**, 467–482.

Azibi, R. and D. Vanderpooten (2003), 'Aggregation of dispersed consequences for constructing criteria: the evaluation of flood risk reduction strategies', *European Journal of Operational Research*, **144**, 397–411.

Bana e Costa, C. and E. Beinat (2005), *Model Structuring in Public Decision Aiding.* Working paper LSEOR 05.79, London: London School of Economics and Political Science.

Bana e Costa, C. and R.C. Oliveira (2002), 'Assigning priorities for maintenance, repair and refurbishment in managing a municipal housing stock', *European Journal of Operational Research*, **138**, 380–391.

Bana e Costa, C., F. Nunes da Silva and J.C. Vansnick (2001), 'Conflict dissolution in the public sector: a case-study', *European Journal of Operational Research*, **130**, 388–401.

Banville, C., M. Landry, J-M. Martel and C. Boulaire (1998), 'A stakeholder approach to MCDA', *Systems Research*, **15**, 15–32.

Barba-Romero, S. (2001), 'The Spanish government uses a discrete multicriteria DSS to determine data-processing acquisitions', *Interfaces*, **31**, 123–131.

Bardos, P., A. Lewis, S. Nortcliff, C. Matiotti, F. Marot and T. Sullivan (2002), *CLARINET Report: Review of Decision Support Tools for Contaminated Land Management and their use in Europe*. Vienna: Austrian Federal Environment Agency. Retrieved from http://www.umweltbundesamt.at/fileadmin/site/umweltthemen/altlasten/clarinet/final_report_1102.pdf (accessed 2 January 2014).

Beierle, T.C. (2002), 'The quality of stakeholder-based decisions', *Risk Analysis*, **22**(4), 739–751.

Belton, V. and T.J. Stewart (2002), *Multiple Criteria Decision Analysis: An integrated approach*, Dordrecht: Kluwer.

Bombaerts, G., C. Carlé and F. Hardeman (2007), 'A multi-criteria analysis was carried out to help choose between a surface and a deep repository for low-level radioactive waste', *Nuclear Engineering International*, **52** (631), 14–18.

Borges, P.C. and A. Villavicencio (2004), 'Avoiding academic and decorative planning in GHG emissions abatement studies with MCDA: the Peruvian case', *European Journal of Operational Research*, **152**, 641–654.

Bouyssou, D. (2001), 'Outranking methods', in C.A. Floudas and P.M. Pardalos (eds), *Encyclopedia of Optimization*, vol. 4, Dordrecht: Kluwer, pp. 249–255.

Bouyssou, D., T. Marchant, M. Pirlot, P. Perny, A. Tsoukias and P. Vincke (2000), 'Evaluation and decision models: a critical perspective', *International Series in Operations Research & Management Science*, vol. 32, Dordrecht: Kluwer Academic Publishers.

Brans, J.P., B. Mareschal and P. Vincke (1984), 'PROMETHEE: a new family of outranking methods in multicriteria analysis', in J.P. Brans (ed.), *Operational Research*, IFORS '84, North Holland, Amsterdam, pp. 477–490.

Brooks, M., F. Gagnon-Lebrun, H. Harvey and C. Sauve (2009), *Prioritizing Climate Change Risks and Actions on Adaptation: A Review of Selected Institutions, Tools and Approaches*, Ottawa: Government of Canada.

Brouwer, R. and R. van Ek (2004), 'Integrated ecological, economic, and social impact assessment of alternative flood control policies in the Netherlands', *Ecological Economics*, **50**, 1–21.

Cavallaro, F. and L. Ciraolo (2005), 'A multicriteria approach to evaluate wind energy plants on an Italian island', *Energy Policy*, **33**, 235–244.

Del Rio Vilas, V.J., F. Voller, G. Montibeller et al. (2013), 'An integrated process and management tools for ranking multiple emerging threats to animal health', *Preventive Veterinary Medicine*, **108** (2–3), 94–102.

Dias, L.C. (2006), *A Note on the Role of Robustness Analysis in Decision Aiding Processes*. Working paper, INESC-Coimbra: Institute of Systems Engineering and Computers.

Dias, L.C. and J.N. Clímaco (1999), 'On computing ELECTRE's credibility indices under partial information', *Journal of Multi-Criteria Decision Analysis*, **8**, 74–92.

Dichmont, C.M., S. Pascoe, E. Jebreen, R. Pears, K. Brooks and P. Perez (2013), 'Choosing a fishery's governance structure using data poor methods', *Marine Policy*, **37**, 123–131.

Dodgson, J., M. Spackman, A. Pearman and L. Phillips (2000), *Multi-Criteria Analysis: A Manual*, London: Department of the Environment, Transport and the Regions.

EC (2013), *EVALSED Sourcebook – Methods and Techniques*, European Commission Guidance Documents on Evaluating Socio-Economic Development, DG Regional Policy, Brussels: European Commission.

Edwards-Jones, G., B. Davies and S. Hussain (2000), *Ecological Economics. An Introduction*, London: Blackwell Science.

Fishburn, P.C. (1967), 'Methods for estimating additive utilities', *Management Science*, **14**, 335–378.

Fletcher, W.J., J. Shaw, S.J. Metcalf and D.J. Gaughan (2010), 'An ecosystem based fisheries management framework: the efficient, regional-level planning tool for management agencies', *Marine Policy*, **34**, 1226–1238.

French, S., O. Walmod-Larsen and K. Sinkko (1993), *Decision Conferencing on Countermeasures after a Large Nuclear Accident*, Risoe-R-676(EN) Report, Roskilde: Risoe National Laboratories.

Gamper, C.D. and C. Turcanu (2007), 'On the governmental use of multi-criteria analysis', *Ecological Economics*, **62** (2), 298–307.

Gamper, C.D., M. Thöni and H. Weck-Hannemann (2006), 'A conceptual approach to the use of cost–benefit and multi criteria analysis in natural hazard management', *Natural Hazards and Earth System Sciences*, **6**, 293–302.

Guitouni, A. and J-M. Martel (1998), 'Tentative guidelines to help choosing an appropriate MCDA method', *European Journal of Operational Research*, **109**, 501–521.

Hämäläinen, R.P. (2002), 'Value Tree Analysis. Multiple Criteria Decision Analysis e-Learning Site', retrieved from http://mcda.aalto.fi/ (accessed 2 January 2014).

Haque, A.N., S. Grafokos and M. Huijsman (2012), 'Participatory integrated assessment of flood protection measures for climate adaptation in Dhaka', *Environment and Urbanization*, **24**, 197–213.

Hobbs, B.J. and G.T.F. Horn (1997), 'Building public confidence in energy planning: a multi-method MCDM approach to demand-side planning at BC gas', *Energy Policy*, **25** (3), 357–375.

IMCDM (2013), 'International Society for Multi-Criteria Decision Making'. http://www.mcdmsociety.org/facts.html.

Jacquet-Lagreze, E. and J. Siskos (1982), 'Assessing a set of additive utility functions for multicriteria decision making, the UTA method', *European Journal of Operational Research*, **10** (2), 151–164.

Joliveau, T., N. Molines and S. Caquard (2000), *Méthodes et outils de gestion de l'information pour les démarches territoriales participatives*, Centre de Recherches sur l'Environnement et l'Aménagement CNRS – UMR 5600, Université Jean Monnet – Saint Etienne.

Joubert, A.R., A. Leiman, H.M. de Klerk, S. Katua and J. Coenrad Aggenbach (1997), 'Fynbos (fine bush) vegetation and the supply of water: a comparison of multi-criteria decision analysis and cost–benefit analysis', *Ecological Economics*, **22**, 123–140.

Keeney, R.L. (1992), *Value-Focused Thinking: A Path to Creative Decision-Making*, Cambridge, MA: Harvard University Press.

Keeney, R.L. and H. Raiffa (1972), 'A critique of formal analysis in public sector decision making', in A.W. Drake, R.L. Keeney and P.M. Morse (eds), *Analysis of Public Systems*, Cambridge, MA: The MIT Press, pp. 64–75.

Keeney, R.L. and H. Raiffa (1976), *Decisions with Multiple Objectives: Preferences and Value Tradeoffs*, New York: John Wiley & Sons.

Kontić B., M. Bohanec and T. Urbančič (2006), 'An experiment in participative environmental decision making', *The Environmentalist*, **26**, 5–15.

Krieger, S., G. Schiefer and C.A. da Silva (2007), *Costs and Benefits in Food Quality Systems: Concepts and a Multi-Criteria Evaluation Approach*. Working paper. Agricultural Management, Marketing and Finance Service (AGSF). Rome: Food and Agriculture Organization of the United Nations, retrieved from http://www.fao.org/docrep/016/ap298e/ap298e.pdf (accessed 2 January 2014).

Lebret, E., K. Leidelmeijer and H.F.P.M. van Poll (2005), *MCA en MKBA: Structureren of Sturen?*. Report 630500001/2005, RIVM Rijksinstituut voor Volksgezondheid en Millieu, retrieved from www.rivm.nl/bibliotheek/rapporten/630500001.html (accessed 2 January 2013).

Leclercq, J.P. (1984), 'Propositions d'extension de la notion de dominance en présence de relations d'ordre sur les pseudo-critères: MELCHIOR', *Revue Belge de Recherche Opérationnelle, de Statistique et d'Informatique*, **24** (1), 32–46.

Lee, S.M. and D.L. Olson (1999), 'Goal programming', in T. Gal, T.J. Stewart and T. Hanne (eds), *Multicriteria Decision Making: Advances in MCDM Models, Algorithms, Theory and Applications*, Boston: Kluwer Academic Publishers, pp. 203–235.

Linkov, I., F.K. Satterstrom, G. Kiker et al. (2006), 'Multicriteria decision analysis: a comprehensive decision approach for management of contaminated sediments', *Risk Analysis*, **26**, 61–78.

Marichal, J.L. and M. Roubens (2000), 'Determination of weights of interacting criteria from a reference set', *European Journal of Operational Research*, **124** (3), 641–650.

Marttunen, M. and R.P. Hämäläinen (1995), 'Decision analysis interviews in environmental impact assessment', *European Journal of Operational Research*, **87**, 551–563.

Messner, F., O. Zwirner and M. Karkuschke (2006), 'Participation in multicriteria decision support for the resolution of a water allocation problem in the Spree River basin', *Land Use Policy*, **23**, 63–75.

Munda, G. (2004), 'Social multicriteria-evaluation: Methodological foundations and operational consequences', *European Journal of Operational Research*, **158**, 662–677.

Munda, G., P. Nijkamp and P. Rietveld (2004), 'Environmental decision making: a comparison between cost–benefit analysis and multicriteria decision aid', in P. Nijkamp (ed.), *Environmental Economics and Evaluation, Selected Essays of Peter Nijkamp*, Volume 4, Cheltenham, UK and Northampton, MA, USA: Edward Elgar Publishing, pp. 165–176.

Petras, J.C.E. (1997), 'Ranking the sites for low- and intermediate-level radioactive waste disposal facilities in Croatia', *International Transactions in Operational Research*, **4** (4), 237–249.

Renn, O., T. Webler, H. Rakel, P. Dienel and B. Johnson (1993), 'Public participation in decision making: a three step procedure', *Policy Sciences*, **26**, 189–214.

Roy, B. (1985), *Méthodologie Multicritère d' Aide à la Décision*, Paris: Economica.

Roy, B. (1996), *Multicriteria Methodology for Decision Aiding*, Dordrecht: Kluwer.

Roy, B. and D. Bouyssou (1993), *Aide Multicritère à la Décision: Méthodes et Cas*, Paris: Economica.

Roy, B. and P. Vincke (1981), 'Multicriteria analysis: survey and new directions', *European Journal of Operational Research*, **8** (3), 207–218.

Simon, H.A. (1976), *Administrative Behaviour*, New York: The Free Press.

Steuer, R. (1986), *Multiple Criteria Optimization: Theory, Computation and Application*, New York: Wiley.

Stirling, A. (2008), '"Opening up" and "closing down": power, participation, and pluralism in the social appraisal of technology', *Science, Technology and Human Values*, **33** (2), 262–294.

Stirling, A. and S. Mayer (2001), 'A novel approach to the appraisal of technological risk: a multicriteria mapping study of a genetically modified crop', *Environment and Planning C*, **19**, 529–555.

Tietenberg, T. (2001), *Environmental Economics & Policy*, New York: Addison Wesley Longman.

Tjandraatmadja, G., A.K. Sharma, T. Grant and F. Pamminger (2013), 'A decision support methodology for integrated urban water management in remote settlements', *Water Resource Management*, **27**, 433–449.

UNFCCC (United Nations Framework Convention on Climate Change) (2002), *Input of the Least Developed Countries Expert Group on the Improvement of the Guidelines for the Preparation of National Adaptation Programmes of Action*. FCCC/SBI/2002/INF.14, United Nations Office Geneva, Switzerland, retrieved from www.unfccc.int/resource/docs/2002/sbi/inf14.pdf (accessed 2 January 2014).

van Gennip, C.E.G., J.A.M. Hulshof and F.A. Lootsma (1997), 'A multi-criteria evaluation of diseases in a study for public-health planning', *European Journal of Operational Research*, **99**, 236–240.

Vanderpooten, D. and P. Vincke (1989), 'Description and analysis of some representative interactive multicriteria procedures', *Mathematical and Computer Modelling*, **12** (10), 1221–1238.

Vincke, P. (1992), *Multicriteria Decision-Aid*, Chichester: John Wiley & Sons.

Wu J., J. Wu, X. Wang and M. Zhong (2012), 'Securing water for wetland conservation: a comparative analysis of policy options to protect a national nature reserve in China', *Journal of Environmental Management*, **94**, 102–111.

7. Cost–benefit analysis: a tool that is both useful and influential?

Giles Atkinson[1]

INTRODUCTION

The recommendation that policymakers should go ahead with public policies and projects *only if* the benefits of these proposals outweigh the costs has a common-sensical appeal. Articulating this intuition more rigorously in policy formulation is the domain of cost–benefit analysis (CBA), or variants which draw on the same conceptual framework. There is an extensive academic literature on CBA, some of which may not use the term 'cost–benefit analysis' but instead refers to 'benefit–cost analysis', 'policy evaluation' or 'project appraisal'. Numerous texts and manuals have appeared covering CBA generally (for example, Boardman et al. 2011), in developing countries (for example, Londero 2003) and applications such as environment (Hanley and Barbier 2009; Pearce et al. 2006). A number of characteristics make CBA distinctive as a policy formulation tool. Perhaps most notably, it is an attempt to quantify costs and benefits in monetary terms. This, in turn, relies on an assessment of how people whose wellbeing is affected by policy actions value those losses and gains.

But while economic texts give every impression that CBA has all the answers, in practice there is some recognition that CBA is only one input to policy formulation decisions. The very act of carrying out a CBA presupposes, for example, that physical impacts have been understood sufficiently to bring them into the ambit of an economic appraisal. In addition, CBA sits side-by-side with a number of assessment tools and metrics all purporting, in different ways, to indicate the worth of a policy action. Moreover, none of these mechanical tools (including CBA) is a substitute for human judgement. The decision process here might be conceived of as policymakers having all this multidimensional information at their disposal and using it to inform a rational (or at least a sensible) choice that represents an overall improvement for society.

That, at least, might be the notion in principle. So while this chapter begins by setting out what makes CBA distinctive and how it is intended to be used, in what follows, the main purpose is to consider how CBA operates in the 'real world': the actual world of policy formulation beyond the textbook. This discussion reviews evidence regarding two related but distinct concerns: whether CBA is actually *used* in policy formulation and whether it is *influential* in this process (perhaps in the sense of what policy outputs and outcomes are actually adopted). Published evidence is somewhat sparse, especially in the latter dimension. However, what seems clear is that policymakers cannot simply be assumed always to be choosing actions so as to achieve societal improvements as CBA practitioners might like to assume. In these respects, CBA might be downgraded or given less prominence than other (non-CBA) evidence used in informing decisions. Understanding what these decision makers actually do is critical too from the perspective of making sense both of how the policy formulation process actually works and how guidance, which might enhance this process, can be more influential in future.

WHAT IS COST–BENEFIT ANALYSIS?

The conceptual case for thinking about costs and benefits in formulating policy is typically cast in the relatively narrow terms of welfare economics. In practical terms, this places an emphasis on the efficiency with which, for example, public funds are spent. This conceptual foundation offers considerable strength, built as it is on an intellectual tradition which dates back many decades (see, for the history of CBA, Pearce 1998 and Persky 2001). It confers a weakness too: well-known problems identified, in theory, with these welfare economic foundations also become a problem for the practical application of CBA (see Gowdy (2004) as an exemplary critique in this vein).

A broader rationale for CBA, however, is put forward by Randall (2002). There are many reasons, he argues, why a policy action can be viewed as a good thing (or otherwise). But broadly speaking, two such reasons relate to the 'rightness' of the action and its consequences. In this respect, CBA 'exists' to say something more tangible about the former. That is, the likely benefits and costs of actions can be viewed as one important input needed to make sensible decisions about whether policy proposals are good or otherwise. Put this way, CBA is not just the transfer of cold market logic to all policy venues, which can then simply be rejected if one chooses to reject the underlying premise for this transfer. Instead, costs and benefits are something that 'benign and conscientious' policymakers *should* be interested in more generally if they are concerned with creating good consequences as a result of their decisions (Randall 2007, p. 92).

From this starting point, CBA can be interpreted as constructing an elaborate policy formulation tool that enables the quantification of these costs and benefits to the fullest extent possible. Stokey and Zeckhauser (1978, p. 134) define it as:

> the principal analytical framework used to evaluate public expenditure decisions. The approach requires systematic counting of all costs and benefits, tangible and intangible, whether readily quantifiable or difficult to measure, that will accrue to all members of society if a particular project is adopted.

According to this quotation, the scope of CBA is truly vast, the ambition level is high and the ensuing economic evaluation apparently trumps all else in informing any decision. For example, it is not circumscribed by looking at the worth of an action from the standpoint of any particular stakeholder or interest group. Instead CBA works on the basis that any gain or loss to anyone who has standing (in other words, who counts) must be included. Nor is the approach, in principle, restricted to any particular policy venue. We discuss what this might mean in practice in the section below.

What is Distinctive about Cost–Benefit Analysis as a Policy Formulation Tool?

While the practical details can vary, the basic structure of any cost–benefit analysis takes the same form the world over. It involves summing the monetary value of net benefits (benefits minus costs) over the lifetime of a project or a policy. For a typical intervention, there will be costs now in return for benefits later. This leads to a crucial point: this stream of net benefits is *discounted*. What this means is that the value of net benefits in each period are not just added together but are treated differently depending on when they occur in time. Specifically, less and less weight is given to costs or benefits the further these impacts are in the future. These discounted net benefits are summed to estimate the net present value (NPV) of the project or policy. The decision rule in CBA is to recommend that the action goes ahead if the sum of (discounted) net benefits is greater than zero: that is, NPV>0. If we are choosing between mutually exclusive projects, then a CBA would recommend the project with the greatest net benefits.

The emphasis of conventional CBA is on *securing overall net gains* rather than their *distribution*. Placing this spotlight on total costs and total benefits does not necessarily reflect a judgement that distributional concerns 'do not matter'. Rather it assumes that the issue of who gains and who loses can be dealt with separately to the issue of making decisions, so as to generate as much overall 'goodness' of action as possible.[2]

Nevertheless, there are well-known procedures in CBA to deal with the benefits received and costs incurred by different societal groups. Indeed, in the UK, official guidance on CBA clearly states that:

> Any distributional effects identified should be explicitly stated and quantified as far as possible. At a minimum, this requires appraisers to identify how the costs and benefits accrue to different groups in society . . .. Where it is considered necessary and practical, this might involve explicitly recognising distributional effects within a project's NPV. (HM Treasury 2003, p. 91)

Yet it is rare for such advice to be followed to the letter. Some deviation is understandable. What distributional weights should be applied is a matter of significant debate and uncertainty. Cost–benefit analysts can be forgiven perhaps for steering clear of these deep waters. However, it is harder to justify why relatively simple steps – such as identifying and cataloguing how costs and benefits are distributed – are seldom seen.

Another distributional dilemma surrounds discounting which, on the face of it, appears inconsistent with the spirit of 'intergenerational equity'. The reason is that the higher the discount rate used the more likely it is that (other things being equal) decisions are shifted towards actions which bring more immediate net benefits. Moreover, impacts occurring relatively far into the future receive almost no weight for any positive discount rate. Not surprisingly then, the choice of discount rate for policies with long-term consequences is especially controversial. For example, in the case of assessing the economic burden of climate change, this debate has highlighted fundamental differences between those economists who see a role for the practitioner to make, or reflect, explicit moral judgements about intergenerational equity and those who argue for a more objective approach based on information revealed in actual economic decisions about how much people care about the future (IPCC 1996; Stern 2007; Weitzman 2007). Resolving such debates is far from straightforward and faces profound questions on which, to quote Beckerman and Hepburn (2007, p. 198), 'reasonable minds may differ'. While it is important, therefore, that cost–benefit appraisal codifies and accommodates these differences, this may incur a penalty in the sense of less decisive recommendations.

Current interest in CBA stems from a variety of motivations. In part, however, the growing ability of practitioners to place robust money values on intangible impacts has surely played a crucial role. In environmental applications of CBA, for example, the estimation of these non-market values has given rise to a proliferation of methods.[3] Some involve estimating original values by looking at *actual* behaviour. An example here would be the costs that visitors incur (in terms of out-of-pocket expenses and time costs of visits) to participate in nature-based recreation. Other methods elicit values by looking at *intended* behaviour. These stated preference methods involve people being asked more directly about the value they place on a policy change (see, for example, Alberini and Kahn 2006). Critical scrutiny of such techniques has also been prominent however. Grounds for criticism vary. For some, all non-market valuation appears to be controversial. Others make a distinction between certain classes of (non-market) goods which morally should be beyond valuation (for example, Kelman 2005), or technically defy robust valuation given the state-of-the-art in valuation practice (for example, Bateman et al. 2008; 2010). None of this criticism is necessarily a bad thing. A healthy dose of scepticism is important in the application, use and interpretation of any empirical methodology and non-market valuation is no exception.

Policy Venues and Cost–Benefit Analysis

The policy venues in which CBA might be used and, in turn, influence policy formulation can be viewed from a number of perspectives. First, there is use according to (the scale of a) particular intervention. While such interventions are typically conceived as discrete projects, these can be relatively large or relatively small. Quite often there is a cost threshold above which the need for a CBA is triggered (see, for example, European Commission, (2008), in the context of the EU). Indeed, some of these projects might have economic and social consequences across a significant geographical area and population (for example, in the UK, the proposals for a high-speed rail network). In many instances, the 'project' might be better construed as a (change in) policy (for example, the introduction of the London Congestion Charge) or even an entire strategy (which may itself imply that a range of policies are initiated or reformed). The use of CBA in the UK's air quality management strategy would be one example of the latter (see Defra 2007). It is also worth noting that CBA has been used for an agenda-setting role too. In the UK, the Stern Review on the Economics of Climate Change (Stern 2007) and the National Ecosystems Assessment (NEA 2011) are prominent examples of this.

Second, there is use as classified by tier of government or institution. In the UK, national government (or those performing appraisals on its behalf) is arguably the principal user of CBA. There is less (if any) evidence of use amongst local government authorities. However, in the environmental sector, a range of public bodies also employ this approach, including the Environment Agency as well as other regulatory agencies such as OfGEM (the Office of Gas and Electricity Markets) for the electricity sector, and OfWAT (the Water Services Regulation Authority) for the water sector.

Moreover, social CBA is also used in the private sector. Companies in the water industry in England and Wales, for example, must use social CBA as one element of the investment case that they put forward to OfWAT under the periodic pricing reviews that the sector is subject to.

Third, there is use of CBA by characteristic of the policy sector, be this transport, environment or criminal justice for example. In the UK, impact assessment obligations provide the institutional impetus behind CBA (see Chapter 9, this volume), a feature shared by many countries. Perhaps unsurprisingly it is the policy department in the UK that is most associated with economic policy – HM Treasury – that is both custodian of how CBA is done and responsible for extending its use across government. Focal to this is the detailed guidance on how to value costs and benefits in monetary terms in what is popularly known as the *Greenbook* (HM Treasury 2003). In effect, such guidelines are the bridge between the CBA textbook world and the real world of practical implementation. Some organizations develop this guidance further. The Department for Transport's WebTAG (its online Transport Appraisal Guidelines: www.dft.gov.uk/webtag/) is the UK exemplar here. Dunn (2012) provides detailed guidance on non-market valuation of environmental impacts which has the status of supplementary *Greenbook* guidance. What this more specific guidance reflects is not only the increasing use of CBA in environmental policy but also the growing need for 'non-environment' ministries nevertheless to appraise the environmental impacts of their own proposals. For some policy departments, the application of CBA is less firmly established. Criminal justice and policing is one broad example here. However, this does not mean that economic approaches are absent altogether from policy thinking, as illustrated by the publication of figures estimating the UK costs of crime (Dubourg and Hamed 2005).

Other countries also have their own specific CBA guidance (see Chapter 9, this volume) although general principles will be broadly similar. For example, in the environmental policy context in the USA, CBA is widely used and the Environmental Protection Agency (EPA) has its own extensive guidelines (US EPA 2000) for preparing economic analyses of regulations. In many of these cases, the driving force for the use of CBA still comes from central government. Important centres of guidance have come from other institutions too. The European Commission is committed to applying some form of cost–benefit test to its directives. CBA has been used in guiding decisions about disbursing the EU's Structural and Cohesion Funds which, over the period 2007–2013, amounted to more than €300 billion. How best to spend this money is thus a very real challenge although the high-level objectives are plain enough: the assistance of socially and economically disadvantaged areas of the EU through the financing of projects which are net beneficial on the basis of a cost–benefit assessment. How parties applying to the EU's Structural and Cohesion Funds (SCF) should carry out this CBA is illustrated in a guidance document (European Commission 2008). The World Bank also has its own formal (practice) guidelines entitled *Operational Policy on the Economic Evaluation of Investment Operations* (Belli et al. 1998).

Cost–Benefit Analysis and Other Decision Making Procedures

CBA examines the social justification for a policy proposal. It is thus distinct from a financial assessment which looks only at the bottom-line for the implementing agency. In many instances, however, economic appraisal will consist of both social CBA and the financial case. For example, when a regional authority applies for financial support – under the SCF – to invest in its conventional rail network or a water treatment plant, it will do so first by demonstrating that the relevant project has a social NPV that is positive. However, the EU is also concerned about evidence regarding the financial case for the project. If the financial net benefits are greater than zero then the project will not be financed by the EU. Put another way, this project pays its own way and is judged not to need external financing under the SCF. Put another way, funding is only approved if the project has a social CBA justification but is not financially viable for the authority making the application.

In some circumstances, the monetary value of impacts might be highly uncertain or defy sensible calculation altogether. In such cases, cost effectiveness analysis (CEA) could be used to ascertain the cost at which a proposal is able to secure a unit of some specified benefit. In its simplest form, there is a single indicator of effectiveness, E, which is compared with a cost of C. The usual procedure is to produce a cost-effectiveness ratio (CER): $CER = E/C$. For example, this ratio might be read as £ per life saved. From this perspective, multi-criteria analysis (MCA), discussed in Chapter 6, is similar to CEA but involves multiple indicators of effectiveness.

A key distinction between CBA and both CEA and MCA is that while all offer guidance on which of several alternative policies (or projects) to select, the latter two approaches are silent on whether or not it is worth adopting any policy action at all. The notion of 'worth doing' only has meaning if costs and benefits can be compared in a manner that enables a judgement to be made about whether costs are greater (or smaller) than benefits. And this, in turn, requires that costs and benefits have a common *numeraire* which in CBA is money. Nor is it clear how MCA deals with issues of time. How time is treated in CBA is sometimes controversial. But it is at least explicit, whereas in MCA it is implicit. More positively, distributional implications are usually chosen as one of the objectives in an MCA and hence equity concerns can be clearly accommodated. All of this adds to the impression that MCA and CBA are complements rather than substitutes.

Even where costs and benefits can be valued,[4] these impacts may have complex pathways. Tracing and quantifying such impacts over the economic life of the project or policy is the necessary precursor to valuing them. Environmental applications of CBA provide perhaps the best illustration here. Measuring physical impacts needs to be based on a sound body of natural science. For example, in the case of evaluating air quality management proposals, this requires an understanding of how air pollutants (reduced from some emission source) otherwise would have been dispersed. This is important because the chief benefit of these proposals is likely to be improved health enjoyed by people currently exposed to reduced pollution. Assessment of these changes in health states (reduced mortality or reduced morbidity) requires an understanding of the epidemiology of exposure and health impact. Only after all this is estimated can the resulting impacts be valued in money terms.

This creates an obvious linkage of CBA to those assessment techniques which seek to quantify physical impacts of policy actions. Environmental Impact Assessment (EIA) is one example. EIA can be thought of as a procedural venue that hosts a number of different appraisal tools. However, it is also the point at which basic information about the physical consequences for the environment of a proposal are measured and collected. In this way, EIA is also an essential input to CBA. CBA covers the other impacts of projects and policies, and goes one stage further than EIA by attempting to put money values on the environmental impacts. Unlike CBA, EIA has no formal decision rule attached to it: for example that benefits must exceed costs. However, analysts would typically argue that its purpose is to look at alternative means of minimizing the environmental impacts without altering the benefits of the project or policy. Whatever the case, EIA and CBA are not substitutes for one another.

Strategic environmental assessment (SEA) provides a further possibly complementary role. Instead of single projects or policies, SEA considers broader programmes of investments or policies. The goal is to look for the synergies between individual policies and projects and to evaluate alternatives in a more comprehensive manner. The emphasis on *strategic* is important. A weakness of the cost–benefit approach is that, in practice, it does tend to deal with decisions incrementally and in isolation.

An example is the evaluation of impacts on the natural environment that a transport infrastructure project might have. It is important to see the changes in landscape and ecology that might occur here not just in terms of the specific location affected by this specific project but also in terms of the cumulative effect of past decisions (as well as potential future decisions). This strategic view is highly useful if the policy concern is that (some aspect of) the natural environment is maintained overall. What this does is make a principle of 'ecological sustainability' applicable to the portfolio of policy actions. A strategic view, in this respect, would be essential for assessing whether this constraint is being observed.

HOW AND WHERE DOES CBA WORK IN THE REAL WORLD?

The existence of official procedures for undertaking CBA for policy formulation, discussed above, provides a prominent and focal indicator of potential use of economic appraisal. However, the existence of such procedures cannot be taken as an indication that CBA is actually used or that it is influential. To make such claims, further evidence about actual practice must be sought (Hahn and Dudley 2007; Hahn and Tetlock 2008). 'Use', for example, might be equated to actual uptake – that is, its presence in an impact assessment – although this should also involve asking questions about how comprehensive these uses were as well as their quality. Assessing 'influence' on policy outputs and ultimately outcomes is arguably more difficult still, requiring further quantitative and qualitative investigation. In what follows, we comment on a selection of the evidence that appears to throw light on some of these issues.

The Use and Quality of CBA

One sobering reflection on the use of CBA in the World Bank was revealed in a recent assessment by the Independent Evaluation Group (IEG 2011). The most striking headline was that the requirement for CBA formally codified in the Bank's operational procedures (OP10.04) was followed far less in practice (see also Little and Mirrlees 1994). The proportion of World Bank projects using CBA dropped significantly from 1970 to 2000. According to the Independent Evaluation Group (IEG 2011), one (proximate) explanation for this trend was a shift in investment portfolio from policy sectors with a tradition of using CBA (for example, energy, transport and urban development) to those which do not (for example, education, environment and health). Nonetheless, the group's report still found a significant reduction in the use of CBA in traditional sectors in which the World Bank remains heavily committed in terms of its investments (for example, physical infrastructure). Moreover, given the strides made in extending CBA thinking and practice to novel project venues, a question inevitably arises as to why this progress has not been translated into actual appraisal in these new sectors.

How generalizable are such findings? While not straightforward to judge systematically, an earlier report by OECD (2004) states that despite the desirability of CBA, it is not used in many of its member countries because of the difficulties of placing money values on a comprehensive range of costs and benefits. In the US, a review of 74 impact assessments issued by the US EPA from 1982 to 1999 found that while all of the policy actions contained in these assessments monetized at least some costs, only about half monetized some benefits (Hahn and Dudley 2007). Fewer still (about a quarter on average), provided a full monetized range of estimates of benefits, although the number doing so increased notably over the sample period. This raises important points. Clearly, there is more to do to increase the use of CBA, not least to bring actual practice in line with official guidelines. However, it is not the case that use of economic appraisal is entirely lacking; it is usually present but often partial.

A logical further question is whether, when applied, CBA applications were any good in the sense of conforming to good practice, following official guidance that an institution itself has adopted or being judged as good quality according to some recognized criteria. Some of the indicators assembled by Hahn and Dudley (2007) for the US identify a number of relevant issues. For example, even for those (US EPA) applications which estimated costs and/or benefits, it was relatively uncommon for these estimates to be complete (rather than monetizing a small subset of impacts) and for point estimates to be accompanied by a range (that is, low and high estimates of the value of a given impact). Moreover, the consideration of different options or alternatives, in cost–benefit terms, was also infrequent. More commonly, practice involved simply comparing some (presumably) favoured single option for a policy change with the status quo. A similar finding emerged from another recent study of EU studies of environmental projects for which financing was requested under regional assistance schemes (COWI 2011).

Another way in which quality might be assessed is by asking how accurate CBA is in what it attempts to measure. Testing this might involve a mechanical exercise to compare the results of *ex ante* and *ex post* CBA studies of the same intervention. An *ex ante* CBA is essentially a forecast of the future: estimating likely net benefits in order to inform a decision to be made. *Ex post* CBA – that is, conducting further analysis of costs and benefits of an intervention at a later stage – can be viewed therefore as a 'test' of that forecast. In other words, what can we learn – for example, for future, similar applications or regarding the accuracy with which CBA is undertaken generally – with the benefit of this hindsight?

Flyvbjerg et al. (2003) provide a meta-study of the *ex ante* and *ex post* costs of transport infrastructure investment in Europe, USA and other countries (from the 1920s to the 1990s). The results are revealing: *ex post* cost escalation affected 90 per cent of the projects they examined. Nor are cost escalations a thing of the past according to these data. This illustrates one aspect of a broader problem afflicting real world CBA of 'appraisal optimism': offering *ex ante* estimates of costs that are lower than they turn out to be in reality. In reaction to this, HM Treasury (2003) states that capital costs estimates for UK public appraisal of physical infrastructure investments should be increased in any CBA by about two-thirds. This direction of bias is evident for projects which involve large investment in physical infrastructure. The opposite can be found in the case of policy regulations. For example, MacLeod et al. (2009) find evidence across the EU for lower regulatory costs *ex post* than predicted *ex ante*, a finding they attribute to firms affected by these burdens finding more cost-effective ways of complying with policy. For the US, however, Hahn and Tetlock (2008) find no systematic evidence of such bias.

The Influence of CBA

The fact that the quality of many CBA applications falls short – and possibly far short – of what is specified in textbooks and official guidelines might lead to scepticism about whether politicians are seriously committed to using economic appraisal to guide policy formulation. It may even be the case that CBA is seen simply as a box to tick, perhaps because it is an obligation (COWI 2011). While it would be a mistake to claim that CBA has no influence at all, it would be equally erroneous to claim it is nearly always influential.

Yet, determining the extent of influence is far from straightforward. For example, IEG (2011) find *relatively* higher returns for World Bank projects for which *ex ante* CBA had been undertaken. Yet, disentangling the influence of appraisal from other confounding factors is a challenge. Hahn and Tetlock (2008) review evidence of influence of economic appraisal on a number of health and safety regulations in the US. This appears to indicate little effect in weeding out regulations which protect life and limb at inexplicably high cost. Moreover, where influence can be identified it tends to be on formulating the details of a specific proposal rather than using this same economic thinking to inform more broadly what the options are.

The fact that decisions are often inconsistent with, or downplay, CBA can be squared with the reality that, in practice, CBA is only one input to the decision and, in some circumstances, other considerations trump economic thinking (see Chapter 9, this volume). The experience of the London Congestion Charge illustrates how economic considerations are balanced in this way. The scheme requires that those motorists entering the congestion charge zone around central London during designated hours must pay a charge. The cost–benefit case for a charge in London was arguably long-standing (Newbery 2006). However, the (initial) £5 daily charge appears to have been largely politically determined. That is, it was not an amount which would provide Londoners with the maximum net benefits (Santos and Fraser 2006). Even so, the official CBA which accompanied the proposal for the congestion charge showed that it would create benefits in excess of costs. In addition, distributional concerns shaped the formulation of the charge: certain groups are exempted or face a lower charge. Such provisions plausibly entail some sacrifice in the cost–benefit gain. Presumably decision makers surmised that this sacrifice was justified if it helped allay public perceptions about the acceptability of the charge.

In other cases, it may be that decision makers have taken an extreme stance on some of the criticisms of CBA: whether it is sufficiently deliberative in the sense of ensuring groups have some sway over decision making (in addition to having their costs and benefits counted in a CBA) (Turner 2007) or whether estimates of costs and benefits are sufficiently robust to base serious decisions on. The evaluation of London's 'Supersewer' perhaps provides an example of this. This project is a major physical investment in London's sewage system proposed by Thames Water plc, which would be financed by higher water charges for customers. The benefits of this are largely intangible, stemming from a substantial decrease in the wastewater discharges into the River Thames that occur currently. The assessment of this proposal involved two cost–benefit studies. The first found a case on economic grounds by looking only at the costs and benefits to households in the Thames Water region (for example, see Mourato et al. 2005). Even so, the project was rejected by the water sector regulator apparently because of a mix of concerns about the reliability of benefit estimates, the way in which higher water bills might impact on poorer households as well as whether different investment options had been adequately considered.

A second CBA study (of the same project) was undertaken a few years later. Notably, this re-valued the intangible benefits on the basis of new ecological data as well as looking at benefits to people beyond the Thames region (given the cultural significance of the River Thames). While this second study found the cost–benefit case lacking if only Thames Water customers were considered, if benefits to people living beyond that area were included, the project was justified. This time around the project gained the necessary political support and was approved. What circumstances changed between these two studies is a matter of speculation. However, it would be difficult to sustain the argument that the primary reason was that the second CBA was simply better and more credible (although, to confound matters, it possibly was). More generally, while there is genuine complexity in undertaking a full CBA, it is probably more likely that such concerns often provide a flag of convenience behind which other (more political) motives might hide.

In the case of London's bid to host the 2012 Summer Olympic Games, the decision to bid was essentially political (although presumably sporting criteria also played some part) and economic analysis largely an afterthought. Yet, the cost of London 2012 was comparable with many large infrastructure investments (and indeed was probably more than twice the likely cost of the London Supersewer project). Indeed, the evident costs of London 2012 did necessitate some search for evidence; but with the political onus to prove that the Games must surely be value for money. Interestingly, nowhere in this defence was there any consideration of the economic assessment of benefits that had been undertaken by the organizations responsible for the bid (see Atkinson et al. 2008 and Blake 2005). There was also an equally pressing wish to show that the benefits would be evenly distributed across the UK. This was important because the costs of paying for the Games are likely to be evenly spread across UK taxpayers.

The case of London 2012 is somewhat exceptional as a policy venue. Yet the way in which economic assessment has (and has not) influenced policy formulation in a venue with a more deep-rooted tradition of using CBA is just as interesting. The HS2 project is a proposed transport investment linking London with the Midlands and North of England by high speed rail. CBA formed part of the official case for the government's financial support for this wholly new rail infrastructure and purchase of required new rolling stock. This economic case, it appears, is fairly marginal: a finding to put in the context of the general *ex post* experience elsewhere of lower benefits and/or higher costs than anticipated *ex ante* (de Rus and Nash 2007). There has been significant scrutiny of the official CBA of HS2, not just restricted to the likely rising financial cost of the project. Discussion has also focused on costs which were left out; particularly the landscape changes and biodiversity losses that the new infrastructure may cause. Debate has also surrounded the estimation of time savings for business travellers that a faster train service provides. What is interesting here is the way in which cost–benefit arguments have contributed to shaping this debate and that, moreover, the economic content of this debate has not been the sole preserve of technical experts. Whether this is genuine influence or whether – given CBA's prominence in the venue of transport policy – this is the way that arguments 'must' be couched to be heard is another matter.

As Hahn and Tetlock (2008) note, policy decisions are by their very nature political. It is probably also the case that this is more overt in some policy venues than others. Discussions about the influence of CBA clearly need to consider its 'political economy' (see Chapter 9, this volume). That is, rather than merely choosing what is best for social wellbeing as assumed in CBA textbooks, governments and their constituent decision makers are faced with political realities that necessitate the reconciliation of conflicting, or satisfying of particular, interests. Favouring CBA might not be the best way of serving those ends (Pearce et al. 2006). In this sense, decisions which have already been made – and the need to justify those decisions – end up constraining the analysis and the evidence (IEG 2011). Undertaking a thorough CBA from the outset of the policy formulation process might strike decision makers as politically risky. Put another way, CBA might provide a different answer to the one that a policymaker wants; something that David Pearce (1998) refers to as CBA removing flexibility in politics.

Another way in which these political economy considerations might be important is in explaining, in part, apparently technical phenomena such as appraisal optimism. This has been explored by Florio and Sartori (2010) in the context of the EU appraisal of the Structural and Cohesion Funds discussed earlier. The problem here arises because in making its decision to approve financing for projects, the EU is reliant on the information (about costs and benefits) that it receives from those in eligible regions proposing the action. This might be a regional or national authority which in turn could be using information provided by private agents (for example, a contractor of some description). COWI (2011, p. 13) illustrates the incentive problem starkly here in the following quotation from a Member State representation, suggesting that appraisal is: 'a matter of making the financial analysis look as bad as possible in order to increase the funding need, and to make the economic analysis to look as positive as possible in order to justify the public funding'. There is an increasing suspicion that such incentives could explain a lot of what were previously thought to be simply technical-analytical shortcomings. De Rus (2011) is particularly concerned about rail projects: demand forecasts always seem too high and cost forecasts always seem to be too low, viewed from an *ex post* perspective. Forecasting is undoubtedly challenging and so may result in technical errors being made. However, strategy possibly plays its part as well.

DISCUSSION AND CONCLUSIONS

Cost–benefit analysis has been developed over a long period of time and most of its advocates would argue that even if policies are not solely formulated on the basis of CBA, decisions at least should be informed by it. Thus, CBA is a normative policy formulation tool for making recommendations to policymakers about what they should do. However, there is a greater role than currently obtains for positive analysis of when and why CBA is relied upon to formulate some actual policy decisions but not others, as well as understanding at what stage in the policy process this assessment actually takes place.

Some of the evidence to date should provide pause for those who believe that CBA is always used, is always done well and is always influential in policy formulation. Yet the finding that 'real world' decisions routinely downplay CBA also needs to be interpreted with care and could well be a matter of degree across different policy venues. For example, CBA is only one input to the decision in many (or most) cases. There are other complementary decision making procedures, as we have discussed, which vie for consideration and will help shape policy outputs and outcomes.

Nevertheless, there is growing recognition of the political motives that could explain both the use and influence (or otherwise) of CBA on policy decisions (Hahn and Tetlock 2008). Some of these considerations are factors which might have a bearing on how *any* form of evidence informs decisions: for example using formal evidence simply to justify decisions which, for all intents and purposes, already have been made. Yet, it could be that CBA is relatively more prone to these political machinations. All of this is clearly important to placing policy appraisal, including CBA, within a realistic understanding of how the policy formulation process *actually* works. Critically, however, it does not change the fundamental role of CBA. This remains the crucial task of explaining how a policy should look if an economic approach is considered to be consequential to that judgement. Indeed, if decision makers are genuinely interested in this policy formulation tool then what is known about actual use and influence of CBA should also be translated into practical implications for enhancing its role.

For example, while official CBA guidelines are no guarantee of actual use, these remain focal publications, setting the bar for how appraisal should be done. It is important that these guidelines reflect, in a practical way, the frontier of knowledge. Translating them into action, however, requires an additional range of considerations. Some of this may involve increasing the economic literacy needed to undertake good quality appraisals (Pearce et al. 2006), particularly in those policy venues with relatively little experience in this respect.

Political considerations may also raise the risk of biased appraisals and put a premium on understanding better the institutional process for undertaking CBA. This involves asking questions not only about how CBA is undertaken but also by whom, how and in what policy venue it is organized (Florio and Sartori 2010; IEG 2011). The starting point for this might be the insight that responsibility for conducting CBA should not be assigned solely to those with a critical stake in a project's implementation (IEG 2011). In the case of EU Regional Policy, this has involved expanding the role for *ex post* cost–benefit assessment as a way of creating incentives for good studies to be done *ex ante* by member states applying for regional funds. Other proposals involve a separation of responsibilities for conducting *ex ante* studies in terms of 'who' is doing the analysis. In this way, those appraising a proposal are placed at arm's length from the project or policy (perhaps based in a central agency) rather than the analysis being done by beneficiaries of the proposed action.

Of course, no policy system is likely to be perfect in all these respects and each will be associated too with different political considerations. For example, there may be little appetite amongst politicians for adding costly *ex post* studies to look at decisions which are literally history and a potential source of political embarrassment (Hahn and Tetlock 2008; see also Chapter 8, this volume). A central agency for conducting *ex ante* assessment may need to rely on information from parties that the separation was designed to keep at greater distance from the analysis. Nonetheless, consideration of these and other policy capacity-related challenges (see Chapters 8 and 9, this volume) is crucial if policy formulators are serious about addressing the gap between the imagined and actual use and influence of CBA in the 'real world'.

NOTES

1. This chapter draws on and updates Pearce et al. (2006) and Atkinson and Mourato (2008).
2. The Kaldor–Hicks 'compensation principle' establishes this more formally, through the idea of hypothetical compensation as a rule for deciding on policies and projects in real-life contexts (Hicks 1939; 1943; Kaldor 1939). What this amounts to is the recognition that projects and policies entail (almost inevitably) losses to some groups and individuals as well as gains to others. This alone is not a reason, according to this tradition, to reject proposed actions. So long as actions create gains which are greater than the losses, there is scope for gainers *potentially* to compensate losers (and still be better off).
3. There are many comprehensive reviews of economic valuation methods more generally (for example, Bateman et al. 2002; Champ et al. 2003; Freeman 2003; Pearce et al. 2006; Hanley and Barbier 2009).
4. The CBA approach to decision making is based on 'individual values' in the sense of adding up how individuals value a proposed policy change. For some this is in conflict

with notions of 'shared values' (see, for example, Fish et al. 2011). This has roots in earlier discussions about how people value changes, in the context of environmental policy, as consumers or citizens (Sagoff 1988). The current emphasis on shared values considers the way in which the environment has collective meaning and significance for communities of people and how the appraisal process might ignore this insight. How these shared values might be more formally incorporated in policy appraisal remains work-in-progress.

REFERENCES

Alberini, A. and J. Kahn (eds) (2006), *Handbook on Contingent Valuation*, Cheltenham, UK and Northampton, MA, USA: Edward Elgar Publishing.

Atkinson, G. and S. Mourato (2008), 'Environmental cost–benefit analysis', *Annual Review of Environment and Resources*, **33**, 317–343.

Atkinson, G., S. Mourato, S. Szymanski and E. Ozdemiroglu (2008), 'Are we willing to pay enough to "back the bid"? Valuing the intangible impacts of hosting the Summer Olympic Games', *Urban Studies*, **45** (2), 419–444.

Bateman, I.J., D. Burgess, W.G. Hutchinson and D.I. Matthews (2008), 'Contrasting NOAA Guidelines with learning design contingent valuation (LDCV): preference learning versus coherent arbitrariness', *Journal of Environmental Economics and Management*, **55**, 127–141.

Bateman, I.J., B. Fisher, E. Fitzherbert, D. Glew and R. Naidoo (2010), 'Tigers, markets and palm oil, market potential for conservation', *Oryx*, **44** (2), 230–234.

Bateman, I.J., R.T. Carson, B. Day et al. (2002), *Economic Valuation with Stated Preference Techniques*, Cheltenham, UK and Northampton, MA, USA: Edward Elgar Publishing.

Beckerman, W. and C. Hepburn (2007), 'Ethics of the discount rate in the Stern Review on the economics of climate change', *World Economics*, **8**, 187–210.

Belli, P., J. Anderson, H. Barnum, J. Dixon and J-P. Tan (1998), *Handbook on Economic Analysis of Investment Operations*, Washington, DC: The World Bank.

Blake, A. (2005), *The Economic Impact of the London 2012 Olympics*, Christel De Haan Tourism and Travel Research Institute, Nottingham University Business School.

Boardman, A.E., D.H. Greenberg, A.R. Vining and D.L. Weimer (2011), *Cost–Benefit Analysis, Concepts and Practice*, 4th edition, New Jersey: Prentice-Hall.

Champ, P.A., K.J. Boyle and T.C. Brown (eds) (2003), *A Primer on Nonmarket Valuation*, Dordrecht: Kluwer Academic Publishers.

COWI (2011), *Ex post Evaluation of Cohesion Policy Interventions 2000–2006 Financed by the Cohesion Fund (including former ISPA) Work Package C – Cost Benefit Analysis of Environment Projects. Final report*, Brussels: European Commission Directorate-General Regional Policy.

de Rus, G. (2011), *Introduction to Cost–Benefit Analysis: Looking for Reasonable Shortcuts*, Cheltenham, UK and Northampton, MA, USA: Edward Elgar Publishing.

de Rus, G. and C.A. Nash (2007), *In what Circumstances is Investment in HSR Worthwhile?*, Institute for Transport Studies, University of Leeds.

Defra (Department for Environment, Food and Rural Affairs) (2007), *The Air*

Quality Strategy for England, Scotland, Wales and Northern Ireland, Volume 2, London: Defra.

Dubourg, W.R. and J. Hamed (2005), *The Economic and Social Costs of Crime Against Individuals and Households 2003/04*, London: Home Office.

Dunn, H. (2012), *Accounting for Environmental Impacts, Supplementary Green Book Guidance*, London: HM Treasury/Defra.

European Commission (2008), *Guide to Cost–Benefit Analysis of Investment Projects*, Brussels: European Commission Directorate General Regional Policy.

Fish, R., J. Burgess, A. Church and K. Turner (2011), 'Shared values for the contributions ecosystem services make to human well-being', in NEA (National Ecosystem Assessment), *The UK National Ecosystem Assessment Technical Report*, Cambridge: UNEP-WCMC, pp. 1183–1193.

Florio, M. and D. Sartori (2010), *Getting Incentives Right: Do We Need Ex Post CBA?*, Milan: Working Paper No. 01/2010, Centre for Industrial Studies.

Flyvbjerg, B., M.K. Skamris Holm and S.L. Buhl (2003), 'How common and how large are cost overruns in transport infrastructure projects?', *Transport Reviews*, **23** (1), 71–88.

Freeman, A.M. III (2003), *The Measurement of Environmental and Resource Values*, Washington, DC: Resources for the Future.

Gowdy, J. (2004), 'The revolution in welfare economics and its implications for environmental valuation and policy', *Land Economics*, **80**, 239–257.

Hahn, R.W. and P.M. Dudley (2007), 'How well does the US Government do benefit–cost analysis?', *Review of Environmental Economics and Policy*, **1**(2), 192–211.

Hahn, R.W. and R.C. Tetlock (2008), 'Has economic analysis improved regulatory decisions?', *Journal of Economic Perspectives*, **22** (1), 67–84.

Hanley, N. and E.B. Barbier (2009), *Pricing Nature, Cost–Benefit Analysis and Environmental Policy*, Cheltenham, UK and Northampton, MA, USA: Edward Elgar Publishing.

Hicks, J.R. (1939), 'Foundations of welfare economics', *Economic Journal*, **49**, 696–712.

Hicks, J.R. (1943), 'The four consumer's surpluses', *Review of Economic Studies*, **11**, 31–41.

HM Treasury (2003), *The Green Book, Appraisal and Evaluation in Central Government*, London: HM Treasury.

IEG (Independent Evaluation Group) (2011), *Cost–Benefit Analysis in World Bank Projects*, Washington, DC: World Bank.

IPCC (Intergovernmental Panel on Climate Change) (1996), *Climate Change 1995, Economic and Social Dimensions of Climate Change*, Cambridge: Cambridge University Press.

Kaldor, N. (1939), 'Welfare propositions of economics and interpersonal comparisons of utility', *Economic Journal*, **49**, 549–552.

Kelman, S. (2005), 'Cost–benefit analysis: an ethical critique (with replies)', in R.N. Stavins (ed.), *Economics of the Environment: Selected Readings*, 5th edition, New York: W.W. Norton & Company, pp. 260–275.

Little, I. and J. Mirrlees (1994), 'The costs and benefits of analysis, project appraisal and planning twenty years on', in R. Layard and S. Glaister (eds), *Cost–Benefit Analysis*, 2nd edition, Cambridge: Cambridge University Press, pp. 199–234.

Londero, E.H. (2003), *Shadow Prices for Project Appraisal, Theory and Practice*, Cheltenham, UK and Northampton, MA, USA: Edward Elgar Publishing.

MacLeod, M., P. Ekins, R. Vanner and D. Moran (2009), *Understanding the Costs of Environmental Regulation in Europe*, Cheltenham, UK and Northampton, MA, USA: Edward Elgar Publishing.

Mourato, S., G. Atkinson, J. Newcombe and E. Ozdemiroglu (2005), 'Cost–benefit test or statutory duty? The case of options to clean-up the River Thames', *Water International*, **30** (2), 174–183.

NEA (National Ecosystem Assessment) (2011), *National Ecosystem Assessment Technical Report*, UK National Ecosystem Assessment, UNEP-WCMC, Cambridge.

Newbery, D. (2006), 'Discussion', *Economic Policy*, April, 305–307.

OECD (2004), *Regulatory Impact Analysis (RIA), Inventory*, Paris: Organisation for Economic Co-operation and Development (OECD).

Pearce, D.W. (1998), 'Cost–benefit analysis and environmental policy', *Oxford Review of Economic Policy*, **14** (4), 84–100.

Pearce, D.W., G. Atkinson and S. Mourato (2006), *Cost–Benefit Analysis and the Environment, Recent Developments*, Paris: Organisation for Economic Co-operation and Development (OECD).

Persky, J. (2001), 'Cost–benefit analysis and the classical creed', *Journal of Economic Perspectives*, **15** (4), 199–210.

Randall, A. (2002), 'Taking benefits and costs seriously', in H. Folme and T. Tietenberg (eds), *The International Yearbook of Environmental and Resource Economics*, Cheltenham, UK and Northampton, MA, USA: Edward Elgar Publishing, pp. 250–272.

Randall, A. (2007), 'Benefit Cost Analysis and a Safe Minimum Standard', in G. Atkinson, S. Dietz and E. Neumayer (eds), *Handbook of Sustainable Development*, Cheltenham, UK and Northampton, MA, USA: Edward Elgar Publishing, pp. 91–105.

Sagoff, M. (1988), *The Economy of the Earth*, Cambridge: Cambridge University Press.

Santos, G. and G. Fraser (2006), 'Road pricing, lessons from London', *Economic Policy*, April, 263–310.

Stern, N. (2007), *The Economics of Climate Change – The Stern Review*, Cambridge: Cambridge University Press.

Stokey, E. and R. Zeckhauser (1978), *A Primer for Policy Analysis*, New York: W.W. Norton & Company.

Turner, R.K. (2007), 'Limits to CBA in UK and European environmental policy: retrospects and future prospects', *Environmental and Resource Economics*, **37** (1), 253–269.

US EPA/US Environmental Protection Agency (2000), *Guidelines for Preparing Economic Analyses*, Washington, DC: US EPA.

Weitzman, M. (2007), 'A review of the Stern Review on the Economics of Climate Change', *Journal of Economic Literature*, **45**, 703–724.

PART III

Actors, capacities, venues and effects

8. Policy formulation, policy advice and policy appraisal: the distribution of analytical tools

Michael Howlett, Seck L. Tan, Andrea Migone, Adam Wellstead and Bryan Evans

INTRODUCTION: ANALYTICAL TOOLS AND POLICY ANALYSIS

At its heart, policy analysis is what Gill and Saunders (1992, pp. 6–7) have characterized as 'a method for structuring information and providing opportunities for the development of alternative choices for the policy-maker'. An important part of the process of policy formulation, policy analysis involves policy appraisal: providing information or advice to policymakers concerning the relative advantages and disadvantages of alternative policy choices (Mushkin 1977; Wildavsky 1979; Sidney 2007; Howlett et al. 2009).

Such advice comes from a variety of different actors operating in a wide range of venues both internal and external to government. And policy workers operating in these venues employ many different types of analytical techniques or 'policy formulation tools' in this effort (Mayer et al. 2004; Colebatch et al. 2011). These tools generally are designed to help evaluate current or past practices and aid decision making by clarifying or eliminating some of the many possible alternative courses of action mooted in the course of policy formulation. They play a significant role in structuring policy-making activity and in determining the content of policy outputs and thus policy outcomes (Sidney 2007) and are a worthy subject of investigation in their own right.

Unfortunately, although many works have made recommendations and suggestions for how formulation *should* be conducted (Vining and Weimer 2010; Dunn 2004), very few works have studied how it is *actually* practiced, on the ground (Colebatch 2005 and 2006; Colebatch and Radin 2006; Noordegraaf 2011). This lack of knowledge is generally true of many of the tasks and activities involved in policy formulation (DeLeon 1992;

Linder and Peters 1990), and data is limited on virtually every aspect of the policy appraisal activities in which governments engage and on the nature of the advice they receive in so doing (Page 2010; Page and Jenkins 2005).

Fortunately, however, some progress has been made on this front in recent years as evidence has begun slowly to be gathered on the nature of policy work and the different types of analytical tools practiced in different venues by different actors (Mayer et al. 2004; Boston et al. 1996; Tiernan 2011; Sullivan 2011). Several analysts, for example, have made considerable progress in mapping many of the activities involved in both *ex post* and *ex ante* policy evaluation (Nilsson et al. 2008; Hertin et al. 2009; Turnpenny et al. 2008 and 2009). And these efforts have been joined by other work done in Australia and elsewhere on regulatory impact assessments and the use of other similar tools and techniques in formulation activities (Carroll and Kellow 2011; Rissi and Sager 2013).

More recently the authors and their colleagues published a series of studies examining the activities of governmental and non-governmental policy actors in Canada which has helped push the frontiers of knowledge on these subjects forward. These studies have joined others in probing the backgrounds and activities of professional policy analysts in government (Bernier and Howlett 2011; Howlett and Newman 2010; Howlett and Wellstead 2011; Howlett and Joshi-Koop 2011); those working for NGOs (Evans and Wellstead 2013); ministerial staffers (Eichbaum and Shaw 2007; 2011; Shaw and Eichbaum 2012; Connaughton 2010; Fleischer 2009); policy consultants (Saint-Martin 1998a; 1998b; 2005; Speers 2007; Perl and White 2002) and many other prominent members of national and sub-national policy advisory systems (Dobuzinskis et al. 2007; Halligan 1995; Craft and Howlett 2012a).

Consistent with the pattern found in the UK by Page and Jenkins (2005), Australia (Tiernan 2011), New Zealand (Eichbaum and Shaw 2011), and Ireland (Connaughton 2010), these studies have found most policy workers in Canadian government to be engaged primarily in *process-related* tasks and activities. However, the work published to date has several limitations. First, although it has distinguished between regional and central level activities (Wellstead et al. 2009; Wellstead and Stedman 2010) and has found some significant variations in analytical tools practiced at these levels, it has generally not distinguished very carefully between different organizations and functions of government within departments and units (for an exception to this rule see Howlett and Joshi-Koop 2011).

Second, it has generally explored differences between government-based and non-governmental analysts and analysis, without taking into account the activities of the 'third set' of so-called 'invisible' analysts (Speers 2007);

that is, the ever-growing legion of consultants who work for governments on policy matters, in some cases supplanting or replacing internal analysis and analysts (Howlett and Migone 2013; Momani 2013; Lindquist and Desveaux 2007). A more complete picture of policy formulation tools and the roles played by policy analysts in these venues is needed if the nature of contemporary policy work, analytical techniques and formulation activities is to be better understood.

This chapter addresses both these concerns. First, it briefly summarizes the results of published national and sub-national surveys conducted in 2006–2009 of internal Canadian policy analysts and sets out what is known about their formulation and appraisal activities, focusing on the techniques they employ in their work. Second, it re-examines the original datasets used in these studies to tease out their findings with respect to differences in the use of analytical tools across departments and functional units of government. Third, it draws on two new surveys of policy consultants and those who manage them completed in December 2012, and two surveys of NGO analysts conducted in 2010–2011, in order to compare and assess what kinds of tools are practiced by the private sector and non-governmental counterparts of professional policy analysts in government.

Since the questionnaires used in the studies are almost identical, this data provides useful material that can start to fill out a comprehensive picture of similarities and differences across different venues for policy work. Combined, the data from these three studies provides more precise description of the frequency of use of specific kinds of policy formulation tools used in government and in other policy formulation venues outside government. As the chapter shows, the frequency of use of major types of analytical tool in policy formulation is not the same between the different sets of actors and also varies within venues of government by department and agency type. Nevertheless some general patterns in the use of policy appraisal tools in government can still be discerned, with all groups employing process-related tools more frequently than 'substantive' content-related technical ones, reinforcing the procedural orientation in policy work identified in earlier studies.

THE 'LUMPY' HYPOTHESIS: THE (UNEVEN) DISTRIBUTION OF POLICY ANALYSIS ACROSS GOVERNMENT

In his contribution to a 2007 book on the state of the art of policy analysis in Canada, the former head of the federal government Policy Research Initiative (Voyer 2007) suggested that the distribution of analytical capacities among government agencies was by nature 'lumpy' or uneven. That is, different units do not just have different supplies of analytical services – the usual subject of academic analyses – but also different *demands*. Therefore, in practice, not all units require the same capacity or capabilities in terms of policy analysis and aggregate measures of overall government capacity require nuanced application with respect to determining the needs and gaps encountered by specific agencies and activities.

It is also the case that the venues of policy research extend beyond the governmental confines which Voyer (2007) discussed. That is, policy analysis and advice is not the exclusive purview of professional analysts in government agencies but extends beyond them to the non-governmental sector in the form of analysis conducted by consultants and by a range of NGOs, including think tanks and research councils among others (Craft and Howlett 2012a). The distribution of capacities among non-governmental policy workers is even less well understood than within governments – until very recently virtually the exclusive focus of research into policy work – and the relationships existing between the governmental and non-governmental components of policy advisory systems are also almost completely unknown.

A plausible hypothesis, however, is to suggest that Voyer's 'lumpiness thesis' within government can be extended to the external components of overall policy advisory systems. That is, given supply and demand conditions overall and within each organization, not only should the distribution of policy formulation tools, tasks and capacities be expected to vary across governments, but also across non-governmental analysts, and between governmental and non-governmental actors, as well.[1]

In what follows empirical evidence from the above-mentioned three sets of surveys into the activities of professional analysts in government, policy consultants, and analysts working for NGOs in Canada undertaken by the authors over the period 2006–2013 is presented, along with data examining the distribution of capacities within government. This data allows us to examine for the first time the distribution of techniques across governmental and non-governmental venues in some detail.

DATA AND METHODS

The first set of surveys mentioned above focused on the activities of professional policy analysts employed by federal and provincial governments in 2006–2009. This set of 15 studies examined the behaviour and attitudes of core civil service policy actors in all senior Canadian 'policy bureaucracies' (Page and Jenkins 2005); that is, a 'typically' structured, Weberian,

Table 8.1   Sample responses

	Sample frame	Sample	Respondents (n)	Response rate (%)
Federal	Census members of Regional Federal Council	1,937	1,125	56.8
Federal	Random sample of National Capital Region-based policy employees	725	395	56.4
Provincial	Census of publicly listed provincial and territorial policy employees	3,856	1,357	35.2
Total		6,518	2,877	44.1
Usable responses			2,730	41.9

multi-level (federal) system of professional policy advice (Halligan 1995; Waller 1992).[2]

Data on the federal government came from two surveys conducted in 2006–2007. The first was a census of 1937 people identified by members of the Regional Federal Council (an organization of senior federal civil servants located outside Ottawa) from all provinces and territories that undertook policy-related work. The second was a random sample of 725 National Capital Region-based (Ottawa-Hull) policy employees identified from the Government Electronic Directory of Services (GEDS) (Wellstead and Stedman 2010; Wellstead et al. 2009). The response rates were 56.8 per cent (n=1125) and 56.4 per cent (n=395) respectively, giving a total sample of 1520 policy workers.

Provincial and territorial data were collected from each sub-national jurisdiction in 13 separate surveys conducted in late 2008 and early 2009. Respondents were identified from job titles listed in publically available sources such as online government telephone directories, organizational charts and manuals and members of Public Service Commissions (Howlett 2009; Howlett and Newman 2010). This yielded a population of 3856 policy-based actors and 1357 responses were received for a response rate of 35.2 per cent. The total population surveyed across the federal, provincial and territorial governments was thus 6518 with an overall combined national response rate of 2877 or 44.1 per cent.

While the survey questionnaires used in these studies were very similar, they were not identical and some questions relevant to this inquiry relating to tools of analysis were not included in the federal survey. Also the range of ministries and units varies by province and territory, meaning it is difficult to arrive at an aggregate depiction of intra-governmental structure required for the analysis. As a result, the largest single provincial case, Ontario, is used as a proxy for the provincial and territorial professional policy analyst community and occasionally for the federal or national levels as well. This is reasonable since (a) Ontario has by far the largest number of respondents in the survey so the results closely approximate the overall provincial and territorial findings and (b) separate analysis of the federal and provincial cases revealed a general pattern of close similarities between analysts working in the two levels of government (Howlett and Wellstead 2012).

The second set of surveys was conducted in 2010–2011 to probe the situation with non-governmental analysts employed by think tanks and research institutes. Two surveys were conducted: (1) a government-based, 192 variable (45 questions) questionnaire, designed in part from previous capacity surveys by Howlett (2009) and Wellstead et al. (2009) and intended to capture the dynamics of NGO-government interactions; and (2) an NGO-based, 248 variable questionnaire (38 questions). Questions in both surveys addressed the nature and frequency of the tasks performed by analysts, the extent and frequency of their interactions with other policy actors, and their attitudes towards and views of various aspects of policy-making processes, as well as questions addressing their education, previous work, and on-the-job training experiences. Both also contained standard questions relating to age, gender, and socio-economic status. The survey was delivered to 2458 provincial policy analysts and 1995 analysts working in the NGO sector in the Canadian provinces of Ontario, Saskatchewan, and British Columbia. Four policy communities were selected for this survey: environment, health, immigration, and labour. The specific provinces and policy sectors dealt with in this study were chosen because they represent heterogeneous cases in terms of politics, history and economic and demographic scale.

Like the governmental studies, mailing lists for both surveys were compiled, wherever possible, from publicly available sources such as online telephone directories, using keyword searches for terms such as 'policy analyst' appearing in job titles or descriptions. In some cases, additional names were added to lists from hard-copy sources, including government organization manuals. Based on preliminary interviews with NGO representatives, it was clear that many respondents undertook a variety of non-policy related tasks in their work. As a result, the search was broadened to include those who included policy-related analysis in their work objectives. Due to the small size of both study populations, a census rather than sample was drawn from each. The unsolicited survey in January 2012 used Zoomerang®, an online commercial software service. A total of 1510 returns were collected for a final response rate of 33.99 per cent. With the exception of the NGO respondents on labour, the percentage of respondents corresponded closely with population expectations developed by the authors.

The third set of surveys was conducted in 2012–2013 to assess the activities of external consultants hired by governments. Two surveys were conducted, one of government managers involved in contracting consultants and the other of consultants themselves. Both were surveyed in order to help understand how consultants' policy advice is solicited, developed, transferred, and used in the context of the Canadian policy advisory system. The consultants' survey was administered to representatives of companies that had performed policy work for various levels of government in Canada between 2004 and 2012. The consultants were identified through sampling of over 34,000 contracts from 10,000 companies contained in the federal government's Proactive Disclosure database of procurement contracts.

The consultants' survey contained 45 questions on similar subjects as the earlier federal, provincial and NGO surveys and was administered online (SurveyMonkey®) in December 2012 to 3228 email addresses obtained for consulting firms involved in policy work. Three hundred and thirty-three complete responses and 87 partial ones were received for a total of 420 responses and a response rate of 13 per cent. Like the NGO study, the consultant survey questionnaire was designed to replicate as far as possible the exact questions asked of federal, provincial and territorial permanent policy analysts by the authors in 2009–2010 in order to allow meaningful comparisons between these actors and others in the Canadian federal policy advisory system.

FINDINGS

In what follows, some of the results of the three surveys are presented. The first set of findings is derived from the federal/provincial/territorial survey and deals with the original 'lumpiness' hypothesis concerning the expectation of analysis and analytical tools varying by venue or location within government. The second set of results addresses the situation of non-governmental policy workers.

The Distribution of Capacities within Government: Venues and Tools

In general, most studies of the use of sophisticated policy analytical tools and techniques in government have highlighted that such use requires several pre-conditions to be met. On the supply side, agencies undertaking such analyses require (a) access to high quality quantifiable data or information (Vining and Boardman 2007) and (b) the human resource and managerial capability to both demand and supply such analysis (Howlett 2009). But not all agencies meet these criteria or have not done so at all times and in all circumstances. Since existing studies have not examined each agency in detail, as pointed out above, exactly which kinds of agencies exhibit strength in which areas is uncertain and under-explored.

Furthermore, on the demand-side, not all departments have the need for the same kinds of data and information and therefore can also be expected to exhibit a different pattern of use of specific analytical tools. Thus for example, some agencies like Finance or Treasury Board typically deal with relatively easily quantifiable issues (budgets, revenues and expenditures respectively) usually with plentiful historical and contemporary data assumed to be very accurate and precise, and are well resourced and able to hire staff or consultants who are interested in and can utilize this kind of evidence. They have always employed highly technical forms of analysis and are likely to continue to do so into the future. Other agencies, however, such as those dealing with social or environmental policy deal with less quantifiable or contested data and may not be interested in or able to use the kinds of information that other agencies utilize. Still others fall in between – for example, many health or housing or transport agencies – who may have high quality data available but may only use it at some times but not others. And finally others may not have access to the data they need even if they are willing and are potentially or actually capable of using it (Howlett and Joshi-Koop 2011; Craft and Howlett 2012b).

The survey of provincial and territorial officials provides some insight into this question. The top ten policy-related analytical tools employed by policy analysts for five selected departments in the Ontario case are shown in Table 8.2. Brainstorming (91.2 per cent) is the most used and the analysts working on environmental issues tend to use this tool the most (94.8 per cent). Consultation exercises come a distant second at 76.3 per cent, with analysts working on education issues using this tool the most at 82.1 per cent. Risk analysis and checklists are ranked third and fourth respectively with health analysts (74.3 per cent) and environmental analysts (70.7 per cent) the most frequent users.

Cost–benefit analysis and scenario analysis, often thought to be fundamental tools employed in policy analysis, are in fact ranked fifth and sixth, although, not surprisingly, finance departments are the top users for both (74.3 and 63.5 per cent respectively). The next highest-ranked tool is expert judgement and elicitation, used the most by the environmental department (63.8 per cent). Finance departments also, not surprisingly,

Table 8.2   *Top ten policy-related analytical tools employed by selected departments*

Tools (Top Ten)	Education	Environment	Finance	Health	Transport	Total Responses
Brainstorming	86.3%	94.8%	86.5%	96.0%	91.3%	91.2%
Consultation Exercises	82.1%	80.2%	68.9%	77.2%	63.8%	76.3%
Risk Analysis	66.3%	65.5%	67.6%	74.3%	59.4%	66.7%
Checklists	69.5%	70.7%	58.1%	66.3%	58.0%	62.7%
Cost–Benefit Analysis (CBA)	60.0%	60.3%	74.3%	50.5%	58.0%	57.9%
Scenario Analysis	60.0%	57.8%	63.5%	53.5%	50.7%	56.2%
Expert Judgements and Elicitation	51.6%	63.8%	52.7%	51.5%	55.1%	53.1%
Financial Impact Analysis	54.7%	41.4%	73.0%	45.5%	46.4%	47.2%
Cost-effectiveness Analysis	46.3%	44.0%	58.1%	50.5%	37.7%	45.5%
Focus Groups	46.3%	34.5%	27.0%	42.6%	31.9%	38.1%

use financial impact analysis (73 per cent) and cost-effectiveness analysis (58.1 per cent) the most in their field of work. Focus groups are rarely used by such units (27 per cent) but are much more commonly employed by education analysts (46.3 per cent).

There are thus distinct differences across intra-governmental policy venues with respect to the kinds of analytical tools used. Finance is the dominant user of every 'technical' type of analysis except risk analysis and scores low on 'consultation' activity and other 'soft' tools, while transportation scores lowest on both measures. Environment scores lowest on most 'hard' tools and high on tools such as expert elicitation. Education is also low on most 'hard' tools although it is higher on financial impact analysis and health is low on most tools although high on the use of risk analysis.

This suggests, as Voyer (2007) intimated, that governmental units have their own particularities and needs. But some general conclusions can also be drawn from these figures about the nature of hard/soft tools used, based on the general nature of the tasks each unit is assigned. That is, this evidence suggests that differences in the distribution (supply and demand) for analysis can be traced back to the fundamental task or mission of each agency. This is very much along the lines Voyer (2007) initially suggested.

Table 8.3   Use of evidence-informed methods by sector

	Percentage of respondents who 'often' or 'always' feel . . .				
	evidence informs decision-making	they can access information and data relevant to their policy work	encouraged by managers to use EIM in policy work	required to use EIM in policy work	provided with support and resources to use EIM in policy work
Environment	33.0	32.6	28.0	33.0	10.2
Welfare	52.4	31.7	48.3	52.4	22.9
Health	60.0	48.2	54.0	60.0	31.7
Education	51.4	44.9	49.5	51.4	30.7
Trade	42.9	37.7	37.8	42.9	16.8
Finance	43.2	38.7	36.3	43.2	25.0

Table 8.4   Nature of issues dealt with on a weekly basis

	Percentage of respondents who *weekly* deal with issues . . .				
	for which data is not immediately available	that require coordination across regions	that require coordination with other levels of government	that lack a single, clear, simple solution	that require specialist or technical knowledge
Environment	54.1	44.0	33.7	66.7	69.0
Health	50.2	32.5	16.6	63.3	41.2
Social Development	55.8	40.0	24.9	63.0	52.1
Education	45.8	22.3	17.6	47.1	37.4
Industry and Trade	58.3	27.2	29.0	62.6	59.9
Finance	49.5	17.3	20.9	59.2	61.9
Total	**52.6**	**32.5**	**24.1**	**61.6**	**61.9**

The three tables above provide additional evidence of this supposition. Table 8.3 looks at the entire provincial and territorial dataset and finds differences in the use of tools of evidence-based or evidence-informed policy analysis among six major activity areas with more of this kind of activity found in health, the field where the idea of evidence-based policymaking originated. Table 8.4 looks at several aspects of the tasks faced by analysts in different units and finds significant variations across sectors.

Finally, Table 8.5 provides a self-assessment made by the analysts

Table 8.5   Departmental policy capacity, by sector

	Policymaking capacity rating of one's department or agency, by percentage of respondents		
Sector	Low	Moderate	High
Environment	21.4	31.0	47.7
Social Welfare	19.2	34.9	45.9
Health	25.3	45.2	29.4
Education	19.3	40.4	40.3
Trade	17.5	43.8	36.9
Finance	11.5	37.5	51.1
Total	**19.8**	**37.9**	**42.2**

themselves concerning the level of policy capacity their unit enjoys. As this table shows, despite having very different technical practices, most analysts felt their units enjoyed relatively high levels of policy analytical capacity, with only health reporting less than 30 per cent 'high' results. This implies that most analysts (outside of the health sector) were satisfied with the type, amount and range of techniques practiced in their units, their dissimilar profiles notwithstanding, and suggests that few capacity gaps exist.

The Overall Distribution of Capacity between Governmental and Non-governmental Actors

In this section we address the larger, extended, version of the Voyer thesis; that is, we extend the analysis of tools and venues for policy formulation beyond different units of government to address differences in capacity and techniques across different venues *outside* governments. Here the two key groups to be compared with professional analysts inside government are professional consultants who worked on a temporary contract basis for governments, and analysts located in the NGOs with whom government officials, and consultants, interact.

This analysis begins by comparing the backgrounds and training of the two groups of internal and external advisors. Comparing the level of formal education between analysts and consultants and NGOs, about 75 per cent of the policy consultants have a graduate or professional degree, with 23 per cent having only a lower-level university degree. This is much higher than the internal part of the professional analytical community where about 56 per cent of the policy analysts have some graduate or professional education. For those working in NGOs, the level of formal education is evenly split relative to the analysts and consultants at 51 per cent with a senior degree and 44 per cent with a lower-level one (Evans and Wellstead 2013). This suggests that the range of qualifications found in the internal and external parts of the professional analytical community differ, with policy consultants tending to be more qualified (based on graduate and professional accreditations) than policy analysts in government or those working for NGOs.

The level of formal education can influence the type of policy tools which are used in formulation. More important than general educational level, however, for our purposes, are differences in specialized training in specific subjects such as public policy and, especially, policy analysis and evaluation. Here the differences between internal and external analysts were less obvious as about 40 per cent of policy consultants and about the same number of policy analysts in government had taken three or more policy-related courses at the post-secondary level. However, only 20 per cent of the NGO policy workers surveyed had done similar courses. Almost 70 per cent of NGOs, compared with 47 per cent of policy consultants and 58 per cent of governmental policy analysts did not have any specific post-secondary courses on formal policy analysis or evaluation.

The areas of training also differ. Policy consultants tend to have a university degree in economics, business management, engineering, political science and public administration, with these five fields accounting for about 85 per cent of degrees (allowing for multiple degrees) conferred. In comparison, the five leading degree fields of internal policy analysts were political science, business management, economics, public administration and sociology, in that order. These five fields accounted for about 60 per cent of degrees (allowing for multiple degrees) conferred, while a wide range of other social science, law and humanities degrees accounted for another 40 per cent of credentials (Howlett and Newman 2010). The top five fields for NGOs, on the other hand, are general social sciences, business management, arts and humanities, political science and public administration (Evans and Wellstead 2013).

There are similarities in these fields of study, of course, as business management features highly in all three, but overall many analysts in government tend to be educated in political science and public administration, consultants in economics and analysts working for NGOs in sociology. This suggests a certain amount of self-selection by intellectual orientation among analysts employed in each area. However, it also highlights the lack of training in all venues encompassing areas such as the natural sciences, engineering and law, which are often thought to account for a sizable component of all three groups.

Further survey questions inquired into specific aspects of the

Table 8.6   Comparison of working group size between analysts,
consultants and NGOs

Working Group Size	Policy Analysts	Policy Consultants	NGOs
Groups of 1–5	30%	84%	68%
Groups of 6–10	65%	10%	15%

organization of policy work in each area. Policy consultants (84 per cent) and NGOs (68 per cent) tend to work in groups of one to five, while only 10 per cent of consultants and 15 per cent of NGOs work in groups of six to ten (Evans and Wellstead 2013). This is in contrast to policy analysts in government where almost 65 per cent work in units of fewer than ten employees and 30 per cent in units of fewer than five full-time equivalent employees (Table 8.6) (Howlett and Newman 2010). This suggests that whatever skills consultants and NGO workers have individually represents the sum of the policy formulation tools which they can bring to bear on a subject, while policy analysts in government, not surprisingly, are much better resourced as a team.

This variation in organizational capacities is reflected in the kinds of roles or tasks taken on by different group members. While this question was not asked of NGO members, policy consultants and analysts share similar types of roles but not with the same frequency. Policy consultants, for example, take on the roles of advisor (62 per cent), analyst (58 per cent), and researcher (50 per cent) in their respective consultancies, while for policy analysts the advisors make up 80 per cent, the analysts 74 per cent and the researchers only 41 per cent. The top three policy-related tasks which policy consultants undertake include research and analysis (83 per cent), providing advice (77 per cent), and providing options on issues (61 per cent). Besides policy development, however, policy consultants have to fulfill functions of project management (48 per cent), communications (41 per cent), and programme delivery (36 per cent). Policy analysts in government are more focused and very high percentages of analysts undertake research and analysis (93 per cent), provide advice (92 per cent), and prepare briefing notes or position papers (91 per cent). In comparison, NGO-based analysts most commonly consult with stakeholders (96 per cent), identify policy issues (94 per cent), and consult with decision makers (91 per cent) (Evans and Wellstead 2013) (see Table 8.7).

When it comes to their preferred analytical tools, this question was only asked of consultants and analysts in government and not of NGO respondents. From a list of 20 policy-related analytical tools, the top two employed by policy consultants are brainstorming (70 per cent) and

Table 8.7   Policy-related tasks undertaken by analysts, consultants and NGOs

Policy-related Tasks (Top Three)	Policy Analysts	Policy Consultants	NGOs
1	Research and analysis (93%)	Research and analysis (83%)	Consult with stakeholders (96%)
2	Provided advice (92%)	Provided advice (77%)	Identify policy issues (94%)
3	Prepare briefing notes or position papers (91%)	Provided options on issues (61%)	Consult with decision makers (91%)

Table 8.8   Policy-related analytical tools employed by analysts and consultants

Policy-related Analytical Tools (Top Three)	Policy Analysts	Policy Consultants
1	Brainstorming (91%)	Brainstorming (70%)
2	Consultation (75%)	Consultation Exercises (67%)
3	Risk Analysis (68%)	Focus Groups (57%)

consultation exercises (67 per cent), much the same as policy analysts. However the third choice is quite different and revealing, with focus groups (57 per cent) being the third most used tool among consultants rather than risk analysis (68 per cent) as it is for analysts (Howlett and Newman 2010) (see Table 8.8).

A fuller description of the tools used by each group of analysts and a comparison of similarities and differences is set out in Tables 8.9 and 8.10.

CONCLUSION

Until recently, only very weak, partial, dated, and usually anecdotal information existed on the situations found in different government and non-governmental venues with respect to the activities of the policy analysts found in these locations.

In the case of the US, Arnold Meltsner (1976) long ago observed that analysts undertook a number of roles in the policy-making process but emphasized their specialist training and expertise in sophisticated methods

Table 8.9   Similarities in analytical tools employed

Similarities (within 7%)	Analysts	Consultants
Specific analytical technique(s) used		
	Per cent	Per cent
High Use (>50%)		
Consultation exercises	67.5	66.7
Cost–benefit analysis	53.6	55.0
Expert judgements and elicitation	47.8	53.4
Scenario analysis	50.3	47.3
Cost-effectiveness analysis	41.7	41.7
Medium Use (>10% and <50%)		
Problem mapping	31.1	33.8
Financial impact analysis	38.3	31.8
Decision/probability trees	22.9	29.5
Environmental impact assessment	27.6	22.4
Robustness or sensitivity analysis	15.9	18.1
Low Use (< 10%)		
Preference scaling	7.0	6.4
Free-form gaming or other policy exercises	6.2	3.8
Markov chain modelling	0.8	1.8

Table 8.10   Differences in analytical tools employed

	Analysts	Consultants	Difference
Specific analytical technique(s) used			
	Per cent	Per cent	
High Use (>50%)			
Brainstorming	82.5	69.7	Analysts +12.8
Focus groups	37.8	57.3	Cons +19.5
Medium Use (>10% and <50%)			
Checklists	60.1	33.3	Analysts +26.8
Development of sophisticated techniques	11.2	26.7	Cons +15.5
Low Use (< 10%)			
Monte Carlo techniques	1.5	10.4	Cons +8.9
Process influence or social network diagrams	8.1	14.2	Cons +6.1

of policy appraisal and evaluation. Later observers of the US case, such as Beryl Radin (2000), Nancy Shulock (1999) and Sean Gailmard and John Patty (2007), however, argued that the use of such techniques was exaggerated and that many analysts engaged more often in more process-related activities.

In the United Kingdom and Germany as well, contrary to the early picture of carefully recruited analysts trained in policy schools to undertake specific types of microeconomic-inspired policy analysis presented by Meltsner (Weimer and Vining 1999), investigators such as Edward Page and Bill Jenkins (2005) and Julia Fleischer (2009) found that British and German policymaking typically featured a group of 'policy process generalists' who rarely, if ever, dealt with policy matters in the substantive areas in which they were trained and had very little training in formal policy analysis. The extent to which this average picture accurately described the situation in all venues within a country and within governments, however, has remained an open question until now.

Overall the data presented in this chapter display a picture of government, as a whole, exhibiting an uneven distribution of capacities and technical capabilities and utilization practices across different organizational and thematic venues. The data show that some departments and agencies – such as Finance – enjoy favourable circumstances which allow them to practice sophisticated analytical techniques while others may only meet these criteria from time to time depending on various factors or their task environments. Important here, for example, is the nature of the internal and external training analysts receive, their job expectations and work descriptions, the nature of the issues and tasks they commonly face in their work, and managerial demands and leadership.

Some of this unevenness within government can be offset through the use of external consultants or reliance on NGOs to provide analysis, and new data presented in this chapter suggest that the capacities and techniques of analysis practiced by analysts in government consulting and in non-government venues are indeed different from those found internally. Formal education levels, disciplinary background and policy-related training are not the same in venues outside of government as they are internally. There are some signs of a complementary relationship between internal analysts and consultants, as in general the consultants are better educated and trained relative to analysts and are able to bring a different skill set to formulation processes (Lindquist and Desveaux 2007; Lindquist 2009). The NGO sector, on the other hand, is very underdeveloped by comparison with either group and is unlikely to replace or supplement either.

The existence of such internal and external distributions of capacities and analytical practices is a situation which has significant implications for policy formulation in government and for the role played in it by advice stemming from the NGO and private sector. Although the full implications of these differences in tool use and policy work across venues remain to be spelled out, they suggest a pattern, in Canada at least: of increasing sophistication in analysis and policy work as one moves from the non-governmental sector to the governmental one, and within government from more socially involved agencies to more economically oriented ones, with policy consultants able to augment internal activities. While additional cross-national studies are needed to determine how common this pattern is, it is compatible with most of the limited work done to date examining the situation with respect to policy advice, policy formulation and the utilization of analytical techniques in countries such as the Netherlands, Australia and New Zealand, the UK and the US.[3]

NOTES

1. A subordinate hypothesis would be to expect that some aspects of non-governmental capacities could be used to bolster gaps in the governmental level, and possibly vice-versa, so that the relationship between the two components of the policy advisory system would be a complementary, synergistic one, rather than a purely duplicative or redundant one. Thus as John Halligan suggested:

    The conventional wisdom appears to be that a good advice system should consist of at least three basic elements within government: a stable and reliable in-house advisory service provided by professional public servants; political advice for the minister from a specialized political unit (generally the minister's office); and the availability of at least one third-opinion option from a specialized or central policy unit, which might be one of the main central agencies. (Halligan 1995, p. 162)

    This is a subject of another research project currently underway among the authors.
2. A Westminster-style parliamentary democracy, Canada features a very decentralized form of federalism in which ten provincial (and to a lesser extent, three territorial) governments exercise exclusive control over significant areas of governmental activity including education, urban affairs, healthcare, natural resources and many important social welfare programmes (Howlett 1999). Other important areas such as immigration, agriculture, criminal law and environmental policy are shared with the federal government. While the territorial governments and some provincial ones — such as Prince Edward Island with a population of only 140 000 — are quite small, others such as the Province of Ontario (population 13 000 000) are as large, or larger, than many national governments. Given this circumstance, data were collected from two online sets of surveys: one covering federal employees and the other covering the provincial and territorial governments.
3. See above on the US and the UK. Similar findings have been made in the cases of the Netherlands, Australia and New Zealand, by Robert Hoppe and Margarita Jeliazkova (2006), Patrick Weller and Bronwyn Stevens (1998) and Jonathan Boston and his colleagues (1996), respectively.

REFERENCES

Bernier, L. and M. Howlett (2011), 'La capacité d'analyse des politiques au gouvernement du Québec: résultats du sondage auprès de fonctionnaires Québécois', *Canadian Public Administration*, **54** (1), 143–152.

Boston, J., J. Martin, J. Pallot and P. Walsh (1996), *Public Management: The New Zealand Model*, Auckland: Oxford University Press.

Carroll, P. and A. Kellow (2011), *The OECD: A Study of Organisational Adaptation*, Cheltenham, UK and Northampton, MA, USA: Edward Elgar Publishing.

Colebatch, H.K. (2005), 'Policy analysis, policy practice and political science', *Australian Journal of Public Administration*, **64** (3), 14–23.

Colebatch, H.K. (2006), 'What work makes policy?', *Policy Sciences*, **39** (4), 309–321.

Colebatch, H.K. and B.A. Radin (2006), 'Mapping the work of policy', in H.K. Colebatch (ed.), *The Work of Policy: An International Survey*, New York: Rowman and Littlefield, pp. 217–226.

Colebatch, H.K., R. Hoppe and M. Noordegraaf (eds) (2011), *Working for Policy*, Amsterdam: Amsterdam University Press.

Connaughton, B. (2010), '"Glorified gofers, policy experts or good generalists": a classification of the roles of the Irish Ministerial Adviser', *Irish Political Studies*, **25** (3), 347–369.

Craft, J. and M. Howlett (2012a), 'Policy formulation, governance shifts and policy influence: location and content in policy advisory systems', *Journal of Public Policy*, **32** (2), 79–98.

Craft, J. and M. Howlett (2012b), 'Subsystem structures, shifting mandates and policy capacity: assessing Canada's ability to adapt to climate change', *Canadian Political Science Review*, **6** (1), 3–14.

DeLeon, P. (1992), 'Policy formulation: where ignorant armies clash by night', *Policy Studies Review*, **11** (3/4), 389–405.

Dobuzinskis, L., M. Howlett and D. Laycock (eds) (2007), *Policy Analysis in Canada: The State of the Art*, Toronto: University of Toronto Press.

Dunn, W. (2004), *Public Policy Analysis: An Introduction*, Upper Saddle River, New Jersey: Pearson/Prentice Hall.

Eichbaum, C. and R. Shaw (2007), 'Ministerial advisers and the politics of policy-making: bureaucratic permanence and popular control', *The Australian Journal of Public Administration*, **66** (4), 453–467.

Eichbaum, C. and R. Shaw (2011), 'Political staff in executive government: conceptualising and mapping roles within the core executive', *Australian Journal of Political Science*, **46** (4), 583–600.

Evans, B. and A. Wellstead (2013), 'Policy dialogue and engagement between non-government organizations and government: a survey of Canadian policy workers', *Central European Journal of Public Policy*, **7** (1), 60–87.

Fleischer, J. (2009), 'Power resources of parliamentary executives: policy advice in the UK and Germany', *West European Politics*, **32** (1), 196–214.

Gailmard, S. and J.W. Patty (2007), 'Slackers and zealots: civil service, policy discretion, and bureaucratic expertise', *American Journal of Political Science*, **51** (4), 873–889.

Gill, J.I. and L. Saunders (1992), 'Toward a definition of policy analysis', *New Directions for Institutional Research*, **76**, 5–13.

Halligan, J. (1995), 'Policy advice and the public sector', in B.G. Peters and D.T. Savoie (eds), *Governance in a Changing Environment*, Montreal: McGill-Queen's University Press, pp. 138–172.

Hertin, J., J. Turnpenny, A. Jordan, M. Nilsson, D. Russel and B. Nykvist (2009), 'Rationalising the policy mess? Ex ante policy assessment and the utilization of knowledge in the policy process', *Environment and Planning A*, **41**, 1185–1200.

Hoppe, R. and M. Jeliazkova (2006), 'How policy workers define their job: a Netherlands case study', in H.K. Colebatch (ed.), *The Work of Policy: An International Survey*, New York: Rowman and Littlefield, pp. 35–60.

Howlett, M. (1999), 'Federalism and public policy', in J. Bickerton and A. Gagnon (eds), *Canadian Politics*, 3rd edition, Peterborough: Broadview Press, pp. 523–539.

Howlett, M. (2009), 'Policy analytical capacity and evidence-based policy-making: lessons from Canada', *Canadian Public Administration*, **52** (2), 153–175.

Howlett, M. and S. Joshi-Koop (2011), 'Transnational learning, policy analytical capacity, and environmental policy convergence: survey results from Canada', *Global Environmental Change*, **21** (1), 85–92.

Howlett, M. and A. Migone (2013), 'The permanence of temporary services: the reliance of Canadian federal departments on policy and management consultants', *Canadian Public Administration*, **56** (3), 369–390.

Howlett, M. and J. Newman (2010), 'Policy analysis and policy work in federal systems: policy advice and its contribution to evidence-based policy-making in multi-level governance systems', *Policy and Society*, **29** (1), 123–136.

Howlett, M. and A. Wellstead (2011), 'Policy analysts in the bureaucracy revisited: the nature of professional policy work in contemporary government', *Politics and Policy*, **39** (4), 613–633.

Howlett, M. and A. Wellstead (2012), 'Professional policy work in federal states: institutional autonomy and Canadian policy analysis', *Canadian Public Administration*, **55** (1), 53–68.

Howlett, M., M. Ramesh and A. Perl (2009), *Studying Public Policy*, Toronto: Oxford University Press.

Linder, S.H. and B.G. Peters (1990), 'Policy formulation and the challenge of conscious design', *Evaluation and Program Planning*, **13**, 303–311.

Lindquist, E. (2009), *There's More to Policy than Alignment*, CPRN Research Report, Ottawa: Canadian Policy Research Networks.

Lindquist, E. and J. Desveaux (2007), 'Policy analysis and bureaucratic capacity: context, competencies, and strategies', in L. Dobuzinskis, M. Howlett and D. Laycock (eds), *Policy Analysis in Canada: The State of the Art*, Toronto: University of Toronto Press, pp. 116–142.

Mayer, I., P. Bots and E. van Daalen (2004), 'Perspectives on policy analysis: a framework for understanding and design', *International Journal of Technology, Policy and Management*, **4** (1), 169–191.

Meltsner, A.J. (1976), *Policy Analysts in the Bureaucracy*, Berkeley: University of California Press.

Momani, B. (2013), 'Management consultants and the United States' public sector', *Business and Politics*, **15** (3), 381–399.

Mushkin, S.J. (1977), 'Policy analysis in state and community', *Public Administration Review*, **37** (3), 245–253.

Nilsson, M., A. Jordan, J. Turnpenny, J. Hertin, B. Nykvist and D. Russel (2008), 'The use and non-use of policy appraisal tools in public policy making: an analysis of three European countries and the European Union', *Policy Sciences*, **41**, 335–355.

Noordegraaf, M. (2011), 'Academic accounts of policy experience', in H.K. Colebatch, R. Hoppe and M. Noordegraaf (eds), *Working for Policy*, Amsterdam: University of Amsterdam Press, pp. 45–67.

Page, E.C. (2010), 'Bureaucrats and expertise: elucidating a problematic relationship in three tableaux and six jurisdictions', *Sociologie Du Travail*, **52** (2), 255–273.

Page, E.C. and B. Jenkins (2005), *Policy Bureaucracy: Governing with a Cast of Thousands*, Oxford: Oxford University Press.

Perl, A. and D.J. White (2002), 'The changing role of consultants in Canadian policy analysis', *Policy and Society*, **21** (1), 49–73.

Radin, B.A. (2000), *Beyond Machiavelli: Policy Analysis Comes of Age*, Washington, DC: Georgetown University Press.

Rissi, C. and F. Sager (2013), 'Types of knowledge utilization of regulatory impact assessments: evidence from Swiss policymaking', *Regulation and Governance*, **7** (3), 348–364.

Saint-Martin, D. (1998a), 'Management consultants, the state, and the politics of administrative reform in Britain and Canada', *Administration Society*, **30** (5), 533–568.

Saint-Martin, D. (1998b), 'The new managerialism and the policy influence of consultants in government: an historical and institutionalist analysis of Britain, Canada and France', *Governance*, **11** (3), 319–356.

Saint-Martin, D. (2005), 'The politics of management consulting in public sector reform', in C. Pollitt and L. Lynn (eds), *Handbook of Public Management*, Oxford: Oxford University Press, pp. 84–106.

Shaw, R. and C. Eichbaum (2012), 'Ministers, minders and the core executive: why ministers appoint political advisers in Westminster contexts', *Parliamentary Affairs*, 1–33.

Shulock, N. (1999), 'The paradox of policy analysis: if it is not used, why do we produce so much of it?', *Journal of Policy Analysis and Management*, **18** (2), 226–244.

Sidney, M.S. (2007), 'Policy formulation: design and tools', in F. Fischer, G.J. Miller and M.S. Sidney (eds), *Handbook of Public Policy Analysis: Theory, Politics and Methods*, New Brunswick, NJ: CRC Taylor & Francis, pp. 79–87.

Speers, K. (2007), 'The invisible public service: consultants and public policy in Canada', in L. Dobuzinskis, M. Howlett and D. Laycock (eds), *Policy Analysis in Canada: The State of the Art*, Toronto: University of Toronto Press, pp. 220–231.

Sullivan, H. (2011), '"Truth" junkies: using evaluation in UK public policy', *Policy and Politics*, **39** (4), 499–512.

Tiernan, A. (2011), 'Advising Australian Federal governments: assessing the evolving capacity and role of the Australian Public Service', *Australian Journal of Public Administration*, **70** (4), 335–346.

Turnpenny, J., M. Nilsson, D. Russel, A. Jordan, J. Hertin and B. Nykvist (2008), 'Why is integrating policy assessment so hard? A comparative analysis of the institutional capacities and constraints', *Journal of Environmental Planning and Management*, **51** (6), 759–775.

Turnpenny, J., C.M. Radaelli, A. Jordan and K. Jacob (2009), 'The policy and politics of policy appraisal: emerging trends and new directions', *Journal of European Public Policy*, **16** (4), 640–653.

Vining, A.R. and A.C. Boardman (2007), 'The choice of formal policy analysis methods in Canada', in L. Dobuzinskis, M. Howlett and D. Laycock (eds), *Policy Analysis in Canada: The State of the Art*, Toronto: University of Toronto Press, pp. 48–85.

Vining, A.R. and D.L. Weimer (2010), 'Foundations of public administration: policy analysis', *Public Administration Review, Foundations of Public Administration Series*, retrieved from http://www.aspanet.org/public/ASPADocs/PAR/FPA/FPA-Policy-Article.pdf (accessed 20 January 2014).

Voyer, J-P. (2007), 'Policy analysis in the Federal government: building the forward-looking policy research capacity', in L. Dobuzinskis, M. Howlett and D. Laycock (eds), *Policy Analysis in Canada: The State of the Art*, Toronto: University of Toronto Press, pp. 123–131.

Waller, M. (1992), 'Evaluating policy advice', *Australian Journal of Public Administration*, **51** (4), 440–449.

Weimer, D.L. and A.R. Vining (1999), *Policy Analysis: Concepts and Practice*, 3rd edition, Upper Saddle River, NJ: Prentice Hall.

Weller, P. and B. Stevens (1998), 'Evaluating policy advice: the Australian experience', *Public Administration*, **76**, 579–589.

Wellstead, A. and R. Stedman (2010), 'Policy capacity and incapacity in Canada's Federal government – the intersection of policy analysis and street-level bureaucracy', *Public Management Review*, **12** (6), 893–910.

Wellstead, A.M., R.C. Stedman and E.A. Lindquist (2009), 'The nature of regional policy work in Canada's Federal Public Service', *Canadian Political Science Review*, **3** (1), 34–56.

Wildavsky, A.B. (1979), *Speaking Truth to Power: The Art and Craft of Policy Analysis*, Boston: Little, Brown.

9. The use of policy formulation tools in the venue of policy appraisal: patterns and underlying motivations

**John R. Turnpenny, Andrew J. Jordan,
Camilla Adelle, Stephan Bartke,
Thomas Bournaris, Petrus Kautto,
Hanna Kuittinen, Lars Ege Larsen,
Christina Moulogianni, Sanna-Riikka Saarela
and Sabine Weiland**

INTRODUCTION

As described in the introductory chapter, this book is concerned with the ways that actors in particular policy formulation venues gather and apply knowledge derived from using particular policy formulation tools. This chapter examines the venue of *policy appraisal*, which has received widespread attention from both policy formulation researchers and practitioners in the past two decades (Turnpenny et al. 2009; Adelle et al. 2012). As a formalized venue in which analysis is undertaken when formulating policy, it corresponds to the 'Internal-Official' type as defined in Chapter 1. Indeed, the use of policy appraisal is often required by law: by 2008, all 31 OECD countries had either adopted, or were in the process of adopting, a formal system of policy appraisal (OECD 2009). Policy appraisal systems may in turn harness a wide range of policy formulation tools to carry out the analysis (Carley 1980; De Ridder et al. 2007; Nilsson et al. 2008). All these elements mean that the study of policy appraisal can yield revealing insights into policy formulation as a whole, since it covers, often mandatorily, the key 'tasks' of policy formulation noted in Chapter 1, namely: characterization of the current situation; problem conceptualization; identification of policy options; assessment of potential policy options and recommending and/or proposing a specific policy design. This chapter uses policy appraisal as a window into policy formulation activities as a whole.

Policy appraisal functions in a multitude of different ways, sometimes for very different purposes (Radaelli 2005). In investigating exactly how it does so, it is important to distinguish between (a) the political and administrative actors who establish appraisal systems, define their purpose(s) and/or monitor their operation at a high level, and (b) those actors who routinely *perform* the actual appraisals. We will argue that it is important to examine both sets of actors, and how they function within the wider political and institutional context of appraisal.

The operation of appraisal in practice is often investigated using one of two broad approaches: those emphasizing 'quality assessment' against particular criteria (for example, Wilkinson et al. 2004; Lee and Kirkpatrick 2006; Renda 2006; Jacob et al. 2008); and those analysing the wider influences of appraisal on policy processes, especially via the political aspects of knowledge use (for example, Nilsson et al. 2008; Hertin et al. 2009b). But there is also a third and growing strand of literature which seeks to investigate exactly how 'the initial commitment of the government to carry out the [appraisal] is an incomplete contract that can be shaped by implementation actors' (Dunlop et al. 2012, p. 40). These two aspects are interdependent and there is potentially a complex interplay of different factors which affect the ways that appraisals are ultimately carried out. The emerging view is that it is vital to study both aspects (for example, De Francesco et al. 2012). The policy implementation literature (for a review see Hill and Hupe 2009) encourages us to question how much the people undertaking appraisal enjoy significant discretion over the way in which appraisals are carried out in practice.

This chapter researches the 'incomplete contract' by focusing on the patterns of use of *policy formulation tools* in appraisal, and how this compares with original aspirations for tool use and for appraisal in general. Examining tool use in this venue is particularly illuminating for two main reasons. First, using tools to collect, sift and deploy knowledge constitutes a core activity in any appraisal. One might expect that analysis of even the most perfunctory of policy appraisal reports would indicate what tools (if any) had been used, by whom and for what purposes. Since generic tools are not specifically developed for any one jurisdiction, detecting whether different types of tools are used or not provides a tangible and comparable focus for examining more precisely how particular appraisals are carried out across individual jurisdictions. It may be surprising therefore that there are but a handful of studies (such as Nilsson et al. (2008)), which examine tool use patterns in only a limited number of cases. This may be especially surprising given that significant resources have been devoted to developing new tools, not least through European Commission Framework Programme funding, and there is an oft-identified 'gap' between tools available and tools actually used within policy appraisal (Nilsson et al. 2008). The implications for where to direct resources for tool development and deployment are therefore significant.

Second, since the application of policy formulation tools is a core activity in the venue of appraisal, it might be expected that the patterns of use will provide a critical indicator of the overall attitudes towards appraisal, both in particular jurisdictions (what might be termed 'jurisdiction-level motivations') and in particular policy areas and activities (or 'policy-level motivations'), and help to illuminate the nature and workings of the 'incomplete contract'. Given that appraisal systems are now so widespread and have such extensive resources devoted to them, it is especially important to understand *why* policymakers may want to appraise policies in the course of policy formulation activities. It is known that studying the operation of a policy instrument – of which appraisal systems are arguably an excellent example (Howlett 2011) – yields important clues about the values and meanings underlying political choices (for example, Hood 1983; Schneider and Ingram 1990; Lascoumes and Le Galés 2007; Bache 2010; Halpern 2010; Jordan et al. 2012). But what actual actions should be examined? Dunlop et al. (2012), for example, analysed more than 30 variables, including evidence of the timing of appraisals, any attempts to de-legitimize the appraisal process, and resource constraints. But this approach represents a highly resource-intensive data gathering exercise which typically yields a relatively small number of cases.

In this chapter we investigate whether studying the use of policy formulation tools nested within the broader venue of policy appraisal offers a quicker and resource efficient method for revealing both jurisdiction- and policy-level motivations. Investigating the use made of tools should in theory be relatively straightforward. After all, the guidance for bureaucrats on how to carry out appraisal often includes explicit reference and/ or encouragement to use them, particularly those with quantitative and monetizing elements. The existing literature (for example, Nilsson et al. 2008; Hertin et al. 2009a) on this topic notes that cost–benefit analysis has been promoted as an example of such a tool in some jurisdictions, such as Ireland, Denmark and the UK. More specific, and in some cases highly specialized and complex, computer model-based tools such as environmental system models have been promoted in other jurisdictions, notably the European Commission (Nilsson et al. 2008).

But systematic accounts of precisely which tools are *actually* used in different appraisal systems, and an exploration of what their (non-) use reveals about underlying motivations to appraise, are nonetheless still lacking. While there has been plenty of research that seeks to develop and diffuse specific policy formulation tools, or assess how appraisal systems have performed in practice (for example, see review by Adelle et al. 2012), there has been relatively little research on the underlying political motivations for both establishing appraisal systems and conducting individual appraisals in a particular manner (but see Radaelli (2010) and Dunlop et al. (2012)). Understanding such motivations of course helps us better understand how the policy formulation process works – specifically, the question of whether thinking about policy formulation as a set of instrumental tasks constitutes an accurate description of reality. A more in-depth understanding of motivations is also important for specifying criteria to evaluate the 'success' (or otherwise) of appraisal systems, and generate operational recommendations.

This chapter contributes to these debates by drawing on and analysing specific documentary data sources: references made to certain types of tools in official appraisal guidance, and also within the reports that are produced at the end of appraisals. More specifically, it examines the types of tools used in a sample of 325 published appraisals from across eight jurisdictions, using a detailed framework which includes a seven-fold classification of tool types. The following section sets out the methods and data sources, and briefly introduces the eight appraisal systems under study. The subsequent section presents the empirical results in three parts. First, the observed patterns of tool use at the level of individual policies, based on analysis of up to 50 policy cases per jurisdiction, are presented. Second, the observed patterns of tool use are compared with how tools are referred to in the legislation establishing the eight appraisal systems, and in any official appraisal guidance. This provides one indicator of the consistency between the stated motivations to appraise and their implementation (in other words, the 'incomplete contract' noted above). Third, the jurisdiction-level motivations for appraising (as expressed in general laws and administrative guidance) are compared with the observed tool use patterns, thus presenting another way of examining the 'incomplete contract' noted above. The final section summarizes the findings and suggests potential future directions for policy formulation research.

UNDERSTANDING THE RELATIONSHIP BETWEEN POLICY FORMULATION TOOLS AND APPRAISAL MOTIVATIONS

The subsequent analysis employs three principal sources of information. First, *the legislation* (or similar) which established the policy appraisal systems and, second, *administrative guidance* for completing appraisal (where available) in the different jurisdictions were analysed for any relevant statements about (a) the overall purpose of the appraisal system, and (b) what tools, if any, were to be used in the appraisals. Third, a *documentary analysis* of a sample of appraisal reports produced by policy officials was undertaken to ascertain what tools had been used. The jurisdictions selected were: Cyprus, Denmark, the European Commission, Finland, Greece, Ireland, Poland and the United Kingdom (UK). These jurisdictions were chosen for several reasons: they represent a spread of well-studied and less well-studied places; all have reasonably accessible appraisal processes and other government documents that could be studied empirically; and they represent both 'early' and 'late' adopters of appraisal systems (Adelle et al. 2012). Brief characteristics of the eight jurisdictions and their appraisal systems are given in Table 9.1.

The sampling strategy for selecting individual appraisal reports was as follows:

- Up to 50 appraisals were sampled in each jurisdiction, to give a sufficiently large sample size both within the jurisdiction and over all eight;
- Analysts began with the most recent appraisals (as of May 2011), and worked back in time, sampling across different policy areas in proportion to the number of appraisals carried out per policy field or ministry;
- If fewer than 50 appraisals were available, all the available ones were coded.

For each appraisal in each jurisdiction, instances where tool use was reported were coded using the following categories, based on the typology of De Ridder et al. (2007):

- *Simple tools*: including checklists, questionnaires, impact tables, process steps or similar techniques for assisting expert judgement, and qualitative assessment. 'Qualitative assessment' was taken to mean some text inside a box/matrix, in other words, something more sophisticated than a paragraph of text;
- *Physical assessment tools*: including life cycle analysis, and material flow analysis;
- *Monetary assessment tools*: cost–benefit analysis (CBA), cost-effectiveness analysis, green accounting, and so on. CBA was interpreted to mean there is at least one monetized cost *or* benefit and not just that the subheadings 'costs' and 'benefits' were used for qualitative text. CBA was also taken to be indicated by some stated

Table 9.1   *Policy-level appraisal systems in eight jurisdictions: main characteristics*

Jurisdiction	History of appraisal system	What is appraised?
Cyprus	Established 2007, through a standardized questionnaire (revised 2011)	No specific legal requirements to undertake appraisal. But each bill submitted to Parliament must be accompanied by an 'Objects and Reasons' report signed by the Attorney General (UNDP 2009)
Denmark	Present form mandatory since 1993 (Circular from the Prime Minister's office No 31/1993). Current legal framework from 1998 (No 159/1998)	All government proposals to be considered in parliamentary readings must be screened, and appraisal carried out if deemed necessary (No 159/1998)
The EU (European Commission)	Framework established 2002 (CEC 2002) and introduced for 'major policy proposals' in 2003	Mandatory for most Commission initiatives, i.e. those included in its Work Programme (CEC 2010)
Finland	First obligations introduced in the 1970s (Pakarinen 2011, p. 133). Current system based on *Bill Drafting Instructions* (MoJ 2006), supplemented by *Impact Assessment in Legislative Drafting: Guidelines* (MoJ 2008)	Mandatory for all legislative proposals and, as far as possible, for subordinate regulations such as decrees (section 80 of the Constitution)
Greece	Programme for national reform of public administration (Politeia) in 2001 (Law 2880/2001); introduction of appraisal requested by Prime Minister in 2006. New law for better regulation passed by Parliament, 2012 (Law 4048/2012)	In principle, mandatory for all laws and regulations with substantial impacts
Ireland	Introduced following OECD's Peer Review report (DT 2008, p. 6). Piloting took place 2004–2005 (DT 2005). Government Decision in June 2005 extended the system to cover all government departments	Mandatory for all proposals for primary legislation that involve a change to the regulatory framework, for 'significant' Statutory Instruments, and for proposals for EU Directives and 'significant' EU Regulations. Some areas where the application of appraisal not compulsory: for example, the Finance Bill, some emergency, criminal or security legislation and some tax law/regulations (DT no date, p. 4)

Table 9.1   (continued)

Jurisdiction	History of appraisal system	What is appraised?
Poland	Introduced in 2002 (Decree No 49 of the Council of Ministers: Monitor Polski 02.13.221). Modernized guidelines introduced (2006)	Mandatory for governmental laws and decrees except for budgetary laws, governmental strategies, programmes and policies
UK	Introduced in its more modern form in 1998 under the 'better regulation' and 'modernising government' agenda (Hertin et al. 2009b)	Mandatory for all policy proposals, including primary or secondary legislation, codes of practice or guidance that impose or reduce costs on businesses/voluntary sector (BRE 2007, p. 1)

Source: Based on Jacob et al. (2008), Nilsson et al. (2008), Adelle et al. (2010).

quantitative impacts, in other words, that there are some numbers but not necessarily converted into monetized costs and benefits;

● *Modelling tools*: including economic, climate, environmental system and integrated assessment models;
● *Scenario analysis*: specifically, when a detailed scenario visioning exercise was carried out with a range of actors, rather than a simple statement of potential futures;
● *Multi-criteria analysis*: including multiple-attribute value theory;
● *Stakeholder analysis tools*: including consensus conferences, citizens' juries and focus groups. These were taken to have been used where specific analysis methods were employed to analyse the results of stakeholder consultations, rather than cases where consultations had simply happened (for example, web-based consultation);
● *Other types*: including special tests developed for specific assessment systems or policy types;
● *No tools*: cases where there is just qualitative text with no or very few numbers.

To maximize inter-coder reliability (and within the restrictions imposed by different languages), subsequent cross-checks were carried out. These particularly related to the boundaries between different tool types.

POLICY FORMULATION TOOLS AND APPRAISAL MOTIVATIONS IN PRACTICE

Tool Use in Practice

Table 9.2 summarizes the findings from the analysis of the published appraisals. For each jurisdiction it includes the number of appraisal cases studied, and the average length of the appraisal reports. Some jurisdictions, such as Poland and Cyprus, yielded fewer cases as the overall number of published appraisals available was much more limited. The variable numbers of appraisals per year in each jurisdiction meant that different time periods were required to achieve the full sample size. As there was very little reported use of scenario, multi-criteria or stakeholder analysis tools in any jurisdiction, to streamline the analysis, these three were combined into the 'other tools' category.

Some jurisdictions (for example Cyprus, Finland and Greece) appear to use hardly any tools; in the cases of Greece and Finland, more than half the appraisals sampled reported no tools. In Finland, use of a standard checklist is reported to some extent, and other methods are occasionally reported, such as partial CBA, but on average the reports are extremely brief (less than three pages). While there is an appraisal procedure in Cyprus which requires a standard form to be filled in, no specific tools were reported in any of the cases analysed. Other jurisdictions (for example, Ireland, Poland and Denmark) show a large minority of cases using no tools, but there is more evidence of use of some simple and monetary assessment tools, in around half of the cases sampled. In Ireland, 39 per cent of cases reported no tools, and the rest were mostly simple and/or monetary assessment; few examples were reported of the use of any other evaluation technique, such as multi-criteria analysis. Table 9.2 shows that only 6 per cent of the Irish cases reported use of modelling tools; these were all related to building regulations. In Denmark, the reports were very brief and mainly revealed use of monetary assessment and simple tools, with some quantification. A few cases (12 per cent) mentioned modelling tools and two mentioned physical assessment – these relating mainly to environment and tax legislation. But while a wider range of tools was reported than in some other jurisdictions, a relatively large proportion (28 per cent) of cases still reported no tools used. Poland exhibited a similar pattern to Denmark, but while both countries showed mainly use of monetary assessment and simple tools with some quantification, Poland exhibited a relatively lower prevalence of monetary assessment tools. Again, in these jurisdictions, only a few reports mentioned modelling tools and/or physical assessment, and those that did related mainly to environment and tax policy.

Table 9.2 Percentage of cases using certain types of tools over the periods examined

Jurisdiction	Number of appraisals (period covered)	Average length of report (pages)	Simple (% of cases)	PA (% of cases)	MA (% of cases)	Model (% of cases)	Other (% of cases)	No tools (% of cases)
Cyprus	20 (2009–2011)	14	0	0	0	0	0	100
Denmark	50 (2006–2011)	2.5	68	4	56	12	2	28
European Commission	50 (2008–2011)	84	96	4	44	18	8	4
Finland	50 (2009)	2.5	16	0	18	2	4	66
Greece	36 (2010–2011)	17	19	0	14	0	0	78
Ireland	49 (2004–2010)	13	33	0	45	6	0	39
Poland	20 (2008–2010)	7	60	0	40	0	5	30
UK	50 (2007–2010)	38	60	0	92	16	10	4
TOTAL	**325**							

Notes:
PA = Physical Assessment tools;
MA = Monetary Assessment tools;
Model = Modelling tools;
Other = Scenario, multi-criteria analysis, stakeholder analysis and other tools.

Conversely, the European Commission and the UK have much richer patterns of reported tool use, with only a handful of cases using no tools. In the European Commission, almost all of the cases reported use of simple tools, and just under half reported monetary assessment. There are also more cases of modelling tools being reported (about one in five cases) than in any other jurisdiction. The average length of the appraisal reports was also more than double that of any other jurisdiction. The UK, by contrast, showed greater use particularly of monetary assessment, which is mandatory in the appraisal guidelines. Analysis was mainly expressed in qualitative terms, drawing on both official and stakeholder-derived data. A few cases (16 per cent) mentioned modelling tools, and these were mainly economic models in the fields of housing, transport and pensions policy. Some such appraisals are very long (more than 200 pages) and contain much detailed analysis, but the majority are rather brief. Few appraisal reports mentioned specific tools for participatory analysis; there was often just a consultation with no additional methods employed for synthesizing the results.

Tool Use Patterns: Guidance versus Practice

We now turn to analyse the implications of the patterns shown in Table 9.2, first comparing the patterns of tool use in practice with how tools are referred to in the legislation setting up appraisal systems, and in any official guidance. As noted above, this provides one indicator of the consistency between the stated motivations behind the establishment of the appraisal system, and the implementation of appraisal.

In all the jurisdictions examined, tools were not mentioned at all in the enabling legislation. For that, one has to look at the guidance handed out to officials. For Cyprus and Greece, guidance was sparse, and limited to relatively simple tools such as a simple questionnaire (Greek Government 2009) or a procedure for consultation, and a statement of the broad aims for impact analysis of economic, social and environmental consequences (Orphanidou and Heracleous 2009). This is consistent with the minimal tool use observed in Table 9.2. Finland provides a marked contrast, since in spite of its apparently sparse use of tools in practice, its guidance mentions several different types of more sophisticated tools, such as numerical equilibrium models and econometric models, and 'expert analyses, check-lists and matrices drawing from existing data, such as statistics and longitudinal environmental studies' (MoJ 2008, p. 33), as well as societal impact assessment (MoJ 2008, p. 37). A similar discrepancy between guidance and practice can be found in Poland.

For Ireland, Poland and Denmark, monetary assessment tools are explicitly encouraged in the guidance. In Ireland, for example, a 'formal cost–benefit analysis . . . may need to be undertaken within the context of a broader multi-criteria approach' (DT 2009, p. 21). In Denmark, 'the most important examples are cost–benefit analysis and cost-effectiveness analysis' (FM 2005, p. 29), and 'it may be relevant to do an economic estimation of the distributional effects' (FM 2005, p. 8). There is also recurring advice to use short forms and lists of questions (in other words, simple tools). However, as Table 9.2 shows, monetary assessment is only reported in about half of the cases. One might deduce a rather weak commitment to using tools and/or following guidance, in these jurisdictions. In contrast, some cases are observed (if only a few) with more advanced tool use, in spite of this not being very explicitly encouraged. Ireland, for example, simply provides worked examples in the 2009 Guidelines for cases 'where the impacts may be broader than economic'.

In the case of the European Commission, a variety of tools and models for assessing impacts are presented in Annex 11 of the Commission's Guidelines (CEC 2009b, pp. 61–72), including: three checklists covering key questions on economic, social and environmental impacts; a checklist for determining unknown figures (qualitatively); problem tree/ causal models (in other words, simple tools); and a section on different types of advanced models. In the main guidelines, cost–benefit analysis, cost-effectiveness analysis, and multi-criteria analysis are all introduced in detail (CEC 2009a, pp. 45 et seq.). In practice, almost all of the cases examined used simple tools, just under half used monetary assessment, and a sizeable minority used modelling tools too. Even so, this pattern still does not fully reflect the richness of the guidance.

Finally, in the UK, cost–benefit analysis is mandatory (BRE 2010), and there is online training on the Standard Cost Model to measure the administrative burden of regulation. The mandatory policy appraisal template operates like a simple tool; other simple tools are also used but are less recognized, such as various impact matrices in Specific Impact Tests. The observed pattern of tool use shows a closer correspondence with the guidelines than for other jurisdictions, while the guidance is rather modest in its espousal of tools.

Tool Use Patterns and Jurisdiction-level Motivations for Appraising

While the way tools are referred to in appraisal guidance provides one indicator of the motivations for performing appraisals, more explicit statements are often to be found in the laws establishing an appraisal system as well as the associated guidance. Table 9.3 shows the motivations appearing in these statements.

Table 9.3   Jurisdiction-level motivations: stated

Jurisdiction	Stated motivations as described in laws and administrative guidance
Cyprus	Norm-following, better legislation, reducing administrative burden (NAP 2007)
Denmark	Better regulation (FM 2005, p. 7), evidence-informed decision making (FM 2005, p. 13)
European Commission	Better regulation (CEC 2002, p. 2) Improving regulatory quality (CEC 2002, p. 2; CEC 2009a, p. 6); efficient regulatory environment (CEC 2002, p. 2); improving consultation and communication (CEC 2002); sustainable development (CEC 2002, p. 3)
Finland	Better regulation (MoJ 2008, p. 9); improving participation in regulatory process (MoJ 2008, p. 9); improving transparency (MoJ 2008, p. 10); evidence-informed decision making (MoJ 2008, p. 9)
Greece	Better regulation, consultation, deliberation and participation (Greek Prime Minister's Office 2006); Reduction of Administrative Burden (Greek Government 2009)
Ireland	Reducing regulatory costs; evidence-based policymaking; consultation (DT 2004, p. 5; DT 2009, p. 3); better regulation (DT 2004)
Poland	Better regulation, evidence-based policymaking and reducing regulatory costs (MG 2006; 2010). Also: transparency and consultation (MG 2006, p. 4, 19 ff); norm-following (esp. EU and US) (MG 2006, p. 3)
UK	Reduce administrative burden; transparency/accountability (Regulatory Reform Act, 2001; Legislative and Regulatory Reform Act, 2006; BRE 2010; HMG 2011, p. 5); assess costs and benefits (HMG 2011, p. 5)

The 'stated' motivations are often varied, with most jurisdictions giving several different reasons simultaneously for establishing an appraisal system. All declare an aim to improve regulatory quality, and many (for example, Cyprus, the Commission, Greece, Ireland, Poland and UK) explicitly mention reducing the costs of regulation and/or administration. Many also express a desire to improve participation in policymaking (the Commission, Finland, Greece, Ireland, Poland and UK) and others (the Commission, Finland, Poland and UK) mention improving the transparency of the policy process. A desire for appraisal to help achieve more evidence-based policymaking (expressed in various ways) is also found in many jurisdictions (Denmark, the Commission, Finland, Ireland, Poland and UK).

Analysis of these 'stated' motivations alongside the pattern of observed tool use over a large number of appraisals is one useful indicator of the nature and extent of the 'incomplete contract'. The brevity of the appraisal reports and lack of reported tool use in some jurisdictions, especially Cyprus and Greece, in spite of commitments to better regulation and reducing administrative burdens, suggests a rather incomplete contract between high-level aspiration and policy practice. Similarly, Finland shows an evident contradiction between the publicly expressed aims to improve transparency and pursue evidence-informed decision making, and the brevity of appraisal descriptions in the government bills with respect to the appraisal process and tools used. A similar contradiction is observed in Poland, but here the reported tool use is greater. Indeed, in Poland, along with Ireland and Denmark, there are high-level commitments to goals such as reducing regulatory costs, evidence-informed policymaking, and/or improving transparency of the policy process, but the pattern of tool use emphasizing monetary assessment (albeit carried out rather patchily) suggests an unevenly completed contract, emphasizing reducing the costs of regulation as a key priority.

Tool use in the UK and European Commission displays a very different pattern; reports in these jurisdictions are longer and more detailed with respect to the tools used, especially those produced in the Commission. There is still a particular focus on monetary assessment, particularly in the UK, implying the importance of reducing regulatory costs. Commitment to administrative reform is also more evident than in other jurisdictions, as evidenced by the accessibility of comprehensive appraisal reports, and also more evidence of tools for eliciting wider participation beyond formal consultation, although these remain rather rare.

CONCLUSIONS AND NEW DIRECTIONS

This chapter has examined the operation of a number of policy formulation tools within one specific venue – policy appraisal. In doing so it has created something new – a systematic picture of precisely which tools are actually used in different appraisal systems. This significantly extends the existing literature, which has often focused on a limited number of cases and jurisdictions. The chapter has also provided a detailed mapping of appraisal guidance, which is used to shed new light on the 'incomplete contract' between stated aspiration and practice. It has illuminated one element of how policy formulation – a notoriously difficult process to observe – works in practice; a picture that challenges the conventional view of policy formulation as a discrete 'stage' of policymaking, encompassing an instrumental set of tasks.

A wide range of tool use patterns was observed across the eight jurisdictions studied, ranging from partial and minimal in some jurisdictions, to deeper and wider in others. This chapter has compared the tools encouraged in appraisal guidance and aggregated observed tool use patterns and investigated the extent of the consistency between guidance and practice. Several interesting patterns emerged. First, for some countries (for example, Greece and Cyprus), the guidance and the aggregated tool use patterns are rather consistent – guidance is sparse and tool use in practice appears minimal. Second, the UK and the Commission in particular revealed the opposite. In these jurisdictions, the guidance is rather detailed and prescriptive in its encouragement of different tools, and there is more evidence of such tools being used in practice than in other jurisdictions. Both these opposite cases exhibit a degree of 'completeness of contract', or consistency, between the commitment by government as expressed in guidance and the behaviour of implementation actors.

Third (and in stark contrast), other countries (such as Finland, Ireland, Poland and Denmark) show rather greater gaps between the encouragement of the guidance to use – particularly – monetary assessment tools, and a somewhat patchy use of those tools in practice. Although there may be a basic willingness to engage in appraisal activities at the highest level in these jurisdictions, for whatever reasons this is not being translated into everyday appraisal practices. This corresponds to what Dunlop et al. (2012) call 'perfunctory usage'. Several constraints have been suggested at different scales, ranging from the very micro level (such as lack of training) to the macro level (such as underlying political priorities) (Nilsson et al. 2008), including the priority given to appraisal and the results it produces, and what is seen as a proportionate analysis.

Regardless of which is important, this pattern indicates that there may be important differences between how those working at a high level in jurisdictions would like appraisal to be conducted, and the way it is performed in practice. This underlines the importance of analysing patterns *within* as well as across jurisdictions (for example, Dunlop et al. 2012); an issue which we explored when we compared the stated motivations for appraising at the jurisdiction level with the aggregated patterns of tool use in practice. Clearly, some aspirations are not appearing in practice. Furthermore, a wide range of stated motivations is evident, that is, jurisdictions are espousing tools for rather different purposes (although reducing the costs of regulation appears to be a dominant motivation in most jurisdictions).

It should not, of course, be assumed that tool use patterns alone identify the main motivations for subjecting new policy ideas to an appraisal, or that the stated motivations for appraising are necessarily the only ones. Many possible motivations have been hypothesized as to why appraisal systems have been established (Radaelli 2008; 2010). These include: increasing the rationality of the policy process to make it more evidence-based (for example, CEC 2009a; Hertin et al. 2009b); facilitating 'Better Regulation', including attempts to reduce the costs of regulation (for example, Baldwin 2005; Allio 2008; OECD 2008); enhancing political control over bureaucracies (for example, McCubbins et al. 1987; Radaelli 2008); 'modernizing' the state by introducing technocratic instruments used in other jurisdictions (for example, Radaelli 2005); improving transparency by opening up policymaking to a wider range of stakeholders (for example, Hood and Peters (2004) on the New Public Management movement; Radaelli and Meuwese 2010); and engaging in political symbolism 'to signal a political response to a perceived problem in the absence of actual policy measures' (Hertin et al. 2009b, p. 1198). Disentangling these motivations is not a trivial task, beyond simply inferring a minimal level of commitment from the fact that all OECD countries have now adopted such systems (OECD 2009), or taking at face value the stated aspirations of politicians and officials. One approach – which we have already noted – involves extensive fieldwork, including elite interviewing. Radaelli (2010), for example, undertook many interviews with political and administrative actors who established appraisal systems and/or monitored their operation at a high level in several countries. Together with an analysis of the presence or absence of enabling institutions such as quality control procedures, he presented four different 'images' of policy appraisal at the jurisdiction level: rational policymaking; political control of bureaucracy; public management reform; and symbolic politics. These were deduced using a set of indicators, including the level of decentralization of, and horizontal coordination mechanisms within, central government, and the type of political system present, as well as the implementation of guidelines and publication of appraisal reports.

To what extent do the 'stated' motivations revealed in this chapter at the jurisdiction level relate to Radaelli's analyses? And to what extent does our approach provide a simpler way of yielding similar information gathered through other studies? The answer is rather mixed. Radaelli (2008, 2010) for example, argued that Denmark has a pragmatic policymaking culture, and appraisal is rather a box-ticking exercise; political negotiation is hampered by strongly centralized control. The brevity of Danish appraisal reports indeed implies box-ticking, but there are a range of other tools used as well which indicate the potential for other motivations, such as rational analysis, at the policy level. In contrast, Radaelli argues that the UK and European Commission exhibit a stronger political control element, as shown in 'relationships between core executive and regulators, as well as the substantive trajectory of regulation' (Radaelli 2010). Nilsson et al. (2008, p. 347) also found, based on interviews in the UK, 'a striking discrepancy between the political desire for more evidence-based policy and the lack of formal analysis'. But this level of political control is not confirmed in our analysis.

To conclude, while the observed tool use patterns provide important and relatively swift insight, they do not replace the need for more detailed and patient empirical work including interviews. However, the observed tool use patterns do provide a useful way of identifying potential interviewees and cases for more in-depth study.

What conclusions may we draw from these findings about policy formulation (and its venues) more generally? Focusing on a venue such as appraisal, which is explicitly functionalist in its conception, and on tools which are often framed purely as a means to formulate 'better' policy, has shown starkly the complexity of policy formulation in practice. First, tools often do not appear in their textbook form. Classifying, for example, what counts as multi-criteria analysis, monetary assessment, a stakeholder analysis tool, or 'simple tools' in different cases proved particularly difficult. Second, the partial and context-specific patterns of tool use in appraisal across many cases and jurisdictions reveals both the political nature of policy formulation and the impact this has on the way that venues operate. So while policy formulation may be divided into a number of tasks to aid understanding, it is important to avoid the temptation to assume that different venues necessarily operate 'with the aim of informing the design, content and effects of policymaking activities' (Chapter 1, this volume), forgetting the role of symbolism or political control, for example. So alongside any efforts to 'improve' the operation of appraisal, or to promote the use of new or amended tools, it is important to better understand *why* policy formulation venues operate in the way they do, and how and why this differs from a basic, that is, functionalist, understanding of policy formulation.

With this in mind, we end by identifying several interesting avenues for future research. First, the above analysis may be complemented by studies that consider other motivations. These can include the use of an appraisal system to: help depoliticize complex political issues (related to expressed desire for more evidence-based policymaking); provide political support for particular policy priorities such as subsidized agriculture or a healthier environment; foster policy learning (Radaelli 2008); or render the behaviour of policy officials more predictable (Lascoumes and Le Galés 2007) (itself related to political control or administrative reform). Arguably such motivations are revealed in tool use. Regarding motivations at the *policy level*, actors' motivations include some of the same as those mentioned at jurisdiction level, but potentially additional ones such as 'doing a good job', 'extending personal influence', 'care about the subject', 'sticking up for the policy/department'. Our analysis has examined a relatively short period of time, but it is conceivable that over a longer time span there may be shifts in motivations at both levels. Investigation of potential shifts will reveal more about the subtlety of how the 'incomplete contract' manifests itself.

A second avenue relates to the design of future research in this area. The data in this chapter are based purely on the information publicly available in written reports, which are easily accessed and provide a consistent object of study. The patterns of reporting, such as the length and availability of reports, are in and of themselves highly revealing. However, documentary information is rather limited in some countries and appraisal reports may either not exist or be too brief. The apparent absence of tools in certain countries (for example, Denmark and Finland) could be an artefact of the reporting procedures. Very brief summary appraisal reports may omit crucial details about tools which are actually used but not reported. A mixed methods approach might be more useful to explicate the underlying causes of these patterns. Indeed, mixed research designs could be envisaged which are less heavily focused on the formal actions and institutions of policy appraisal. Methods such as historical case studies, longitudinal analysis and/or process tracing (see Owens et al. 2004) could usefully elicit the perspectives of officials and other 'users' of tools within wider appraisal activities going well beyond the formal scope of appraisal, to include technical experts, consultants, scientists and think tanks. Such investigation could reveal the full extent to which those actors are driven by the jurisdiction-level motivations, and by external pressures, influences and ideas of their own.

Finally, how might the findings of this chapter help inform research on policy formulation more generally? Analysis in this chapter, for example, has been framed in terms of variations in the operation of one venue between jurisdictions. However – and building on Lowi (1972) – it would be interesting to explore whether tool use and venue operation, both sought and in practice, vary across different policy fields. Investigating the extent to which tools and venues are specific to certain types of problems and policy cases will add another dimension to the analysis. In the case of policy appraisal, while modelling and other advanced tools appear infrequently in even the most 'analytically advanced' jurisdictions, this is not to say they are not used at all. Investigating cases where *individual* appraisals' tool use varies significantly from the 'jurisdictional average' may yield interesting insights into what factors affect underlying motivations to appraise. For example, are supposedly more complex policy problems such as climate change more intensively appraised?

Understanding why appraisal is being done, for whose benefit and with what effects are important for understanding not just how appraisal as a whole is evaluated, but how policy formulation works in practice, and why. A 'tools in practice' perspective offers a new and equally important perspective on much older debates in public policy and public administration, such as the political control of administrations, policy design and the evidence base of policymaking. This vibrant but relatively small sub-area has much to contribute to the mainstream of research, potentially allowing fruitful links to be formed between tool developers and different branches of public policy research and practice.

ACKNOWLEDGEMENTS

We would like to thank our funder, the FP7 Network of Excellence 'LIAISE', and the LIAISE Policy Advisory Board for their challenging and insightful comments on an earlier draft of this chapter.

REFERENCES

Adelle, C., A. Jordan and J. Turnpenny (2012), 'Proceeding in parallel or drifting apart? A systematic review of policy appraisal research and practices', *Environment & Planning C*, **30**, 400–414.

Adelle, C., A. Jordan, J. Turnpenny et al. (2010), *A Summary of User Needs and Expectations with Regards to Impact Assessment*, Deliverable 1.3 of the LIAISE Network of Excellence, European Commission Seventh Framework Contract no. 243826.

Allio, L. (2008), *The Emergence of Better Regulation in the European Union*. PhD Thesis: Kings College London.

Bache, I. (2010), 'Partnership as an EU policy instrument: a political history', *West European Politics*, **33**, 58–74.

Baldwin, R. (2005), 'Is better regulation smarter regulation?', *Public Law*, Autumn, 485–511.

BRE (2007), *Impact Assessment Guidance*, London: Better Regulation Executive, Department for Business, Innovation and Skills.

BRE (2010), *Impact Assessment Toolkit*, London: Department for Business, Innovation and Skills.

Carley, M. (1980), *Rational Techniques in Policy Analysis*, London: Heinemann Educational Books.

CEC (2002), *Communication from the Commission on Impact Assessment*, COM (2002) 276, Brussels: Commission of the European Communities.

CEC (2009a), *Impact Assessment Guidance*, SEC (2009) 92, Brussels: Commission of the European Communities.

CEC (2009b), *Impact Assessment Guidelines – Annexes*, Brussels: Commission of the European Communities.

CEC (2010), 'Commission initiatives requiring an impact assessment', retrieved from http://ec.europa.eu/governance/impact/which_com_init/which_com_init_en.htm (accessed 22 May 2014).

De Francesco, F., C.M. Radaelli and V.E. Troeger (2012), 'Implementing regulatory innovations in Europe: the case of impact assessment', *Journal of European Public Policy*, **19**, 491–511.

De Ridder, W., J. Turnpenny, M. Nilsson and A. Von Raggamby (2007), 'A framework for tool selection and use in integrated assessment for sustainable development', *Journal of Environmental Assessment Policy and Management*, **9**, 423–441.

DT (2004), *Regulating Better: A Government White Paper Setting out Six Principles of Better Regulation*, Dublin: Department of the Taoiseach.

DT (2005), *Report on the Introduction of Regulatory Impact Analysis*, Dublin: Department of the Taoiseach.

DT (2008), *Regulatory Impact Assessment: An Operational Review*, Dublin: Department of the Taoiseach.

DT (2009), *Revised RIA Guidelines: How to Conduct a Regulatory Impact Assessment*, Dublin: Department of the Taoiseach.

DT (no date), *Progress Report to Government by the Better Regulation Group on Regulating Better*, Dublin: Department of the Taoiseach.

Dunlop, C.A., M. Maggetti, C.M. Radaelli and D. Russel (2012), 'The many uses of regulatory impact assessment: a meta-analysis of EU and UK cases', *Regulation & Governance*, **6**, 23–45.

FM (2005), *Vejledning om konsekvensanalyser*, Copenhagen: Ministry of Finance.

Greek Government (2009), *Guidelines for RIA report*, Athens: General Secretariat of the Greek Government.

Greek Prime Minister's Office (2006), *Circular Y190* (18 July 2006).

Halpern, C. (2010), 'Governing despite its instruments? Instrumentation in EU environmental policy', *West European Politics*, **33**, 39–57.

Hertin, J., K. Jacob, U. Pesch and C. Pacchi (2009a), 'The production and use of knowledge in Regulatory Impact Assessment – an empirical analysis', *Forest Policy and Economics*, **11**, 413–421.

Hertin, J., J. Turnpenny, A. Jordan, M. Nilsson, D. Russel and B. Nykvist (2009b), 'Rationalising the policy mess? Ex ante policy assessment and the utilisation of knowledge in the policy process', *Environment and Planning A*, **41**, 1185–1200.

Hill, M. and P.L. Hupe (2009), *Implementing Public Policy*, London: Sage Publications.

HMG (2011), *Impact Assessment Guidance: When to do an Impact Assessment*, London: Her Majesty's Government.

Hood, C. (1983), *The Tools of Government*, London: Macmillan.

Hood, C. and G. Peters (2004), 'The middle aging of new public management: into the age of paradox?', *Journal of Public Administration Research and Theory*, **14**, 267–282.

Howlett, M. (2011), *Designing Public Policies: Principles and Instruments*, Abingdon: Routledge.

Jacob, K., J. Hertin, P. Hjerp et al. (2008), *Improving the Practice of Impact Assessment*, EVIA (Evaluating Integrated Impact Assessments) project, European Commission Sixth Framework Programme.

Jordan, A.J., D. Benson, R. Wurzel and A.R. Zito (2012), 'Environmental policy: governing by multiple policy instruments?', in J.J. Richardson (ed.),

Constructing a Policy State? Policy Dynamics in the EU, Oxford: Oxford University Press, pp. 104–124.

Lascoumes, P. and P. Le Galés (2007), 'Introduction: understanding public policy through its instruments – from the nature of instruments to the sociology of public policy instrumentation', *Governance*, **20**, 1–21.

Lee, N. and C. Kirkpatrick (2006), 'Evidence-based policy-making in Europe: an evaluation of European Commission integrated impact assessments', *Impact Assessment and Project Appraisal*, **24**, 23–33.

Lowi, T.J. (1972), 'Four systems of policy, politics, and choice', *Public Administration Review*, **32**, 298–310.

McCubbins, M.D., R.G. Noll and B.R. Weingast (1987), 'Administrative procedures as instruments of political control', *Journal of Law, Economics and Organization*, **3**, 243–277.

MG (2006), *Guidelines for the Regulation Impact Assessment Adopted by the Council of Ministers on 10 October 2006*, Warsaw: Polish Ministry of Economy.

MG (2010), *Regulatory Impact Assessment*, Warsaw: Polish Ministry of Economy.

MoJ (2006), *Bill Drafting Instructions*, Helsinki: Ministry of Justice, Finland.

MoJ (2008), *Impact Assessment in Legislative Drafting: Guidelines*, Helsinki: Ministry of Justice, Finland.

NAP (2007), *Cyprus National Action Plan for Better Regulation*, Nicosia: Ministries of Finance/Public Administration and Personnel.

Nilsson, M., A. Jordan, J. Turnpenny, J. Hertin, B. Nykvist and D. Russel (2008), 'The use and non-use of policy appraisal tools in public policy-making: an analysis of three European countries and the European Union', *Policy Sciences*, **41**, 335–355.

OECD (2008), *Building an Institutional Framework for Regulatory Impact Assessment: Guidance for Policy-Makers*, Paris: Organisation for Economic Co-operation and Development.

OECD (2009), *Indicators of Regulatory Management Systems*, Paris: Organisation for Economic Cooperation and Development.

Orphanidou, S. and E. Heracleous (2009), *Better Regulation in Cyprus Simply Explained*, retrieved from http://www.better-regulation.org.cy/Portals/0/Documents/presentation%20for%20BR%20in%20cyprus%20for%20KEBE%2016.3.12.pdf (accessed 24 November 2014).

Owens, S., T. Rayner and O. Bina (2004), 'New agendas for appraisal: reflections on theory, practice and research', *Environment and Planning A*, **36**, 1943–1959.

Pakarinen, A. (2011), 'Lainvalmistelun kehittämisprojektien historia ja historiattomuus [Legislative development projects in Finland – a critical reflection]', *Hallinnon Tutkimus*, **30**, 129–142.

Radaelli, C.M. (2005), 'Diffusion without convergence: how political context shapes the adoption of regulatory impact assessment', *Journal of European Public Policy*, **12**, 924–943.

Radaelli, C.M. (2008), 'Evidence-based policy and political control: what does regulatory impact assessment tell us?', European Consortium for Political Research Joint Sessions Workshop on 'The Politics of Evidence-based Policymaking', Rennes, 11–16 April.

Radaelli, C.M. (2010), 'Rationality, power, management and symbols: four images of regulatory impact assessment', *Scandinavian Political Studies*, **33**, 164–188.

Radaelli, C.M. and A.C.M. Meuwese (2010), 'Hard questions, hard solutions:

proceduralisation through impact assessment in the EU', *West European Politics*, **33**, 136–153.

Renda, A. (2006), *Impact Assessment in the EU: The State of the Art and the Art of the State*, Brussels: Centre for Policy Studies.

Schneider, A. and H. Ingram (1990), 'Behavioral assumptions of policy tools', *Journal of Politics*, **52**, 510–529.

Turnpenny, J., C.M. Radaelli, A. Jordan and K. Jacob (2009), 'The policy and politics of policy appraisal: emerging trends and new directions', *Journal of European Public Policy*, **16**, 640–653.

UNDP (2009), *Ex-ante Policy Impact Assessment in Cyprus*, UNDP.

Wilkinson, D., M. Fergusson, C. Bowyer et al. (2004), *Sustainable Development in the European Commission's Integrated Impact Assessments for 2003: final report*, London: Institute for European Environmental Policy.

10. Policy formulation tool use in emerging policy spheres: a developing country perspective

Sachin Warghade

INTRODUCTION

In many ways, policymaking in developing countries is known to be different from that in developed countries (Pye 1958; Hirschman 1975; Horowitz 1989; Corkery 1995). Apart from the fact that they lack resources and capacities in policy formulation, there is a more fundamental difference related to the political structure of developing countries. According to Pye (1958), the political sphere in the traditional societies of developing countries has remained undifferentiated from the spheres of social and personal relations. The private and group interests arising out of such relations are often the key drivers of policy formulation decisions. This hinders the development of a distinct policy sphere, thus limiting the scope for more evidence-based forms of policy formulation.

Due to this lack of a distinct policy sphere, political struggle often revolves around issues of identity and interests, themselves determined by patterns of social and personal relations, rather than the implications of alternative public policy options. In this situation, political leaders and parties enjoy political loyalty governed more by a sense of identification with a social group than by identification with a concrete policy option. This affective or expressive aspect overrides the problem-solving or public policy aspect of politics (Pye 1958). In turn, this provides space for the dominant sections of society to further their interests at the expense of the poor and marginalized.

What are the uses – both existing and potential – of policy formulation tools in such societies? Can policy formulation tools be effective in creating a space for more evidence-based policymaking and countering interest-based policymaking – as suggested in Turnpenny et al. (2009)? In other words, how does the political system in developing countries – characterized by interest-based politics embedded in social and personal relations – react to the introduction of policy formulation tools? This chapter addresses these questions by analyzing the case of India. An important question that this chapter also addresses is whether the type of policy formulation venue selected for tool use influences the prospects for using tools to counter interest-based policymaking.

The chapter begins with a short review of the emerging prospects for the introduction of tools in the context of ongoing economic reforms in India. The use of two policy formulation tools, cost–benefit analysis (CBA) and participatory assessment – each in different policy venues (in other words, institutional locations), of varying degrees of political influence – is then analyzed with a particular focus on the design, implementation and outcome. Based on this analysis the key questions are answered in the final section.

EMERGING PROSPECTS FOR TOOL USE IN DEVELOPING COUNTRIES

Developing countries like India are on a path of rapid modernization. However, the features of traditional society still have a dominating influence on policy outlooks. Policies get formulated and determined based on narrow political considerations emanating from vested interest alignments. They emerge largely from political consensus among political and industrial elites (Mathur and Mathur 2007). Many of the development failures in developing countries are attributed to ill-conceived, inadequate and poorly implemented policies (Corkery 1995). Yet in principle, policy formulation tools can still play an important role in assisting governments to undertake systematic assessment of policy options and arrive at policies based more on evidence than vested interests.

In the past, policymaking processes outside formal political venues were non-existent. Policies were not formulated based on application of scientific tools for developing and assessing policy options. This situation prevailed until non-governmental actors started questioning public policies in India. Economic reforms over the last three to four decades gave rise to a new breed of policy influencers acting outside the formal political venues. The civil society actors involved in various social movements and struggles, fighting against the ill effects of the economic reforms, created space for participatory politics. This is contributing to the development of the field of policy analysis and especially that of policy formulation tools.

To understand these changes, it is important to study developments related to large-scale infrastructure projects, such as dams and power plants, undertaken as part of the broader economic reforms being implemented in comparable developing countries. Hence, we focus our attention on water sector reforms. In this sector, infrastructure projects have been regarded as necessary for fuelling growth in the era of globalization. However, such projects have created strains in the social fabric due to the disproportionate benefits they have brought to particular stakeholders. In India, the economic reforms were intensified in 1991 under the renewed and more comprehensive policy for liberalization, privatization and globalization. These reforms have further widened the rift between winners and losers (Bardhan 2009). Acquiring land, water and other forms of resources for such projects has become a significant bone of contention. The plight of 'project-affected people' has become the rallying point for several social campaigns and movements working against large infrastructure projects (Dwivedi 2006). These movements have started questioning the unilateral, closed-door, non-transparent and politically motivated nature of the policymaking process, creating space for more rational, participatory and analysis-based policymaking through the use of policy formulation tools.

Apart from its construction, recent economic reforms have begun focusing on changing the institutional design aimed at effective management and maintenance of the infrastructure created. One of the important institutional reforms pertains to the establishment of independent regulatory agencies (IRAs). It is assumed that these independent expert bodies will be able to determine policies and regulations in a more rational way by maintaining a distance from mainstream politics, and that this will provide the credibility and consistency in policy matters required for long-term planning. Thus, the IRAs are now becoming new venues for policy formulation within the boundaries of the larger policy framework determined by the government. IRAs have been set up in India in infrastructure sectors including electricity, water and telecoms.

This new venue of policy action has its own distinctive features as compared with the conventional venues of government departments headed by political leaders. IRAs comprise members who are generally expert in the particular sector in which the agency is created. These bodies are created through special legislation and accorded powers to make decisions independent of the approval of legislators. Appointments are ideally determined by a separate selection committee and not by respective government ministries or department heads. They are often given powers equivalent to a court and act as quasi-judicial bodies. Thus, the IRAs provide a venue for policy formulation that is independent of political interventions. Establishment of IRAs is an important institutional reform recommended by international financial institutions, such as the World Bank, in many developing countries including India (Dubash and Morgan 2012).

The legitimacy of such non-majoritarian bodies hinges on 'procedural robustness' (Dubash 2008, p. 46). Participatory tools are an integral part of procedural legitimacy required by these independent bodies in formulating regulations. Being composed mainly of experts, the IRA is also seen as a technocratic form of policymaking venue. With the independent regulation model at a nascent stage in India, it is important to see what change this new venue could bring with respect to application of policy formulation tools.

India may be regarded as at a stage of evolution from formal democratic system to more meaningful and participative democracy (Mathur 2001). The erstwhile closed-door and centralized policymaking is being challenged with the demand for more open, transparent and participatory practices. In this transition phase, it is important to understand and assess the role of policy formulation tools in relation to the old and new policy venues. For this we turn to the cases of tool use in water policy formulation in two different venues: one government-led (cost–benefit analysis and participatory tool) and the other IRA-led (participatory tool).

TOOL USE BY GOVERNMENT MINISTRIES

Broader policy analysis has received less attention compared with routine public administration for reasons clearly related to the nature of policymaking in India. The public administrators, or civil service officials, provide the analytical and intellectual back-up to political leaders for developing and analyzing policy options. Public administrators are at the centre-stage of policy analysis and not experts or bodies outside the formal political venue (Sapru 2004). Thus, the policy process is coordinated by government departments manned by bureaucrats and headed by a Minister (an elected political leader). This has been the most prominent venue for policy formulation in India. The Minister heading the department has control over the appointments and transfer of public administrators. Hence, the Minister commands considerable influence on administrative procedures and outcomes. This type of venue is hereafter referred to as government-led. The following subsections discuss the cases of tool use under this particular policy venue.

Cost–Benefit Analysis in Dam Building Policy

Cost–benefit analysis (CBA) is one of the oldest and most commonly used policy formulation tools in India. Although also used for project evaluation and approval, it has a strong bearing on the overall policy related to publicly funded infrastructure projects. This experience will have a bearing on the future use of tools in policy formulation. Hence, for these reasons, it is important to review the use of CBA.

The design of CBA
Under British rule, dam projects were largely undertaken for returns in the form of revenue to the government, although a few projects were also undertaken specifically for drought mitigation (Singh 1997). The main criterion for undertaking projects was financial return, typically assessed by calculating internal rate of return (Iyer 2003; Singh 1997). This was a stringent criterion for assessing projects and helped in maintaining financial discipline in project planning and execution (Singh 1997). In the post-independence period, the Government of India followed a less stringent approach to project appraisal. Its approach was based on a simple cost–benefit analysis where the benefits are measured in terms of the net benefits of irrigation accruing to farmers and thereby to the economy. Costs represented only the direct cost for constructing the dam (Iyer 2003).

The less stringent design of CBA for dam projects was certainly beneficial for farmers who otherwise would have not benefitted from irrigation. Hence, it was referred to as a 'social CBA' (Singh 1997). But the main question was about distribution of these benefits. The social CBA was not a comprehensive socio-economic analysis. It did not include the full cost associated with resettlement of project-affected people and environmental damage. Had these costs been included in the design of the tool then many projects that exist today would have been rendered unviable. Hence, the design was only partly 'social'.

The execution of CBA
The less stringent design and narrow scope of CBA led to a shrinking of the role of evidence and created space for vested interests to penetrate the tool execution process. In the absence of the criterion of rate of return, there remains no accountability on project implementers to ensure that proposed benefits have accrued. No accounting procedures are required for monitoring the rate of return. Thus, the less stringent design of CBA adopted for dam appraisal and approval has made it liable to political manipulation or distortion (Iyer 2003), either direct or indirect.

One of the common manipulations while executing CBA is to understate the costs and overstate the benefits by exploiting the gaps and uncertainties that prevail in calculating future agricultural prices or costs. Here, calculations are not done as meticulously as they could be, so as not to render the project unviable. There have been instances where too many projects get cleared in a single meeting of the reviewers of CBAs of particular projects (Iyer 2003). There are cases in which the project costs stated during the appraisal have been revised to a very large extent after a project has been approved (Pallavi 2012). There is no system for fresh appraisal of projects after such cost escalations. This has fuelled allegations of corruption against Ministers in the Water and Resources Department (WRD).

There are pressures on government engineers to select sites for dam projects such that the political constituency of the particular political leader gets the highest benefits, irrespective of the results of the CBA. This in turn would strengthen the political domination of the leader in question. The bureaucrats and the government engineers have to yield to the pressure and select sites that are politically favourable for the leader.[1] Thus, vested interests prevail over evidence in such cases.

The design of the CBA and its execution is a closed-door process. The policy formulation venue is controlled by government bureaucrats and political leaders. There is no participation of stakeholders, nor is consideration given to alternative water management options to the dam project, such as small-scale watershed conservation and development. This has been the major concern raised by various social movements opposing dam projects on the basis of negative social and environmental impacts.

The outcomes of CBA

Making the criteria for evaluation relatively lax has made it possible for government to undertake dam projects at a very large scale. This activity has fuelled the growth in large-scale irrigated cash crops and agro-industrialization (Singh 1997), creating deep-rooted inequities between upstream and downstream communities. It became the central point of argument for various social movements demanding justice for the people who lost their lands and livelihood resources such as forests and river flows.

The second most important aspect of inequitable benefits is related to the huge capital investments made through public funds. The policy of building dams has received excessive focus from government at the cost of attention to other welfare efforts, especially those required for drought-prone regions and dry-land farmers. For example, irrigated agriculture in the plains has benefitted at the cost of lower budget allocation to development of the rain-fed and drought-prone regions. Water meant for the benefit of farmers in the plains is now being reallocated for urban-industrial growth (as discussed further below). This shows that there has been an implicit political process that has facilitated building of such dams for the benefit of only selected sections of society. In other words, the way in which CBA has been used within the government-led policy venue has played a vital role in the inequitable distribution of benefits.

The Use of Participatory Tools in Water Allocation Policy

There are several studies suggesting that public investment in dams has not led to expected returns either in terms of government revenues or farm productivity (Singh 1997; Dharmadhikary et al. 2005). However, this did not persuade the state governments to stop the policy of building dams during the first phase of economic reforms. In fact, the budgetary allocation for constructing, operationalizing and maintaining dams has kept on increasing. The revenue receipts from water charges were not adequate to support the budgetary allocation. Financial constraints were evident. This is why the process of the second phase of reforms was undertaken with technical and financial support from international financial institutions like the World Bank. The focus was now on institutional reforms, including among other things the establishment of an IRA, rationalizing of water tariffs and creation of a system of tradable water rights (World Bank 2005).

The State of Maharashtra was one of the first to begin with this type of reform process in 2002–2003. The World Bank was the 'knowledge partner' in this process. The important reforms included adoption of a State Water Policy (SWP) and establishment of the Maharashtra Water Resources Regulatory Authority (MWRRA). Formulation of this policy framework began in 2002. While the SWP was formulated and adopted by the Government in 2003, the MWRRA Act was passed in 2005. This is the point where an attempt was being made to develop a distinct policy sphere, in which decisions could be made based on evidence rather than vested interests.

Consultation with stakeholders and the public has been the *modus operandi* of World Bank-led reform processes. Hence, participatory tools were used in various policy formulation stages under a government-led venue. In this case, stakeholder consultation workshops were conducted by the Water Resources Department (WRD). Headed by a Minister, it has all the characteristics of a government-led policy venue.

Key issues in water allocation policy

India's dams are a vital source of water due to the seasonal (monsoon) pattern of rainfall. In line with the official policy of central government, water for industrial use has been accorded lower priority than domestic and agricultural use (Government of India 1987; 2002). This was in line with the policy to protect and promote agro-based livelihoods for rural prosperity and sustainability. Policies were implicitly shaped by the notion of water as a 'social good'. However, the increasing international discourse around water as an 'economic good' started having its influence on water policy in India. Thus, water for the high income-generating activities associated with urban-industrial growth came to be seen as important for realizing the greater economic value of water. Thus, the Government of Maharashtra, in contradiction of central government policy, proposed that industry should be given higher priority than agriculture for water allocation.

The World Bank prescription was to assign water rights to users in the form of 'tradable entitlements'. It was claimed that the farmers could voluntarily transfer the water entitlements to industries at an acceptable compensation determined by the market. This was seen as an 'equitable' policy for water allocation (World Bank 2005). It is interesting to see the use of tools in the formulation of these policy proposals and how it impacted the fate of these policies.

Tool design for water allocation policy
The use of participatory tools for the formulation of the SWP and MWRRA Act was not mandatory by any law. Tool design and execution were solely a matter for the WRD. In light of the radical changes that the reforms were attempting, it was expected that the participatory tool would be designed meticulously with adequate provision of transparency, accountability and effective participation. But in reality, the design of the participatory tool was not undertaken systematically.

Consultation workshops – one at the state level and three at the lower regional level – were organized. These were severely inadequate for representation let alone direct participation of the vast majority of the rural populations that would be affected by the reforms. There was no consideration given to adequate publicity for the consultation events and related documents. Nor was a mechanism decided for publishing a 'reasoned report' that would compile all the policy options suggested by the participants in the consultations and provide assessment and considerations given by government for each of the options.

Tool execution for water allocation policy
The consultation workshops were not held as public events. Only selected people from the government and non-governmental sectors were invited. It was observed that the majority of participants were government officials. These workshops were presided over by the political leaders and Ministers, including the Minister with responsibility for the WRD which was in charge of implementing the participatory tool. The people who were selected as invited speakers mostly represented government agencies.[2]

A senior social activist referred to these consultation workshops as 'stage-managed events'. The workshops were managed and dominated by the presence of Ministers and officials sitting on the stage or dais during the event. The seating arrangement on the stage made the event look like a government-led discussion with less importance given to the non-government participants. The opening speeches by the Ministers created a favourable tone for the policy proposals, which was further amplified by the invited participants. Very few critical voices were heard in the workshops. This arrangement of space and the nature of invitees provided ample opportunities to override the evidence-based arguments provided by some of the participants and instead further arguments in the interests of the dominant political stakeholders.

One such evidence-based argument was made by the representatives of the social movements in Maharashtra. Based on the facts related to the existing inequity in the state, these representatives proposed an alternative water allocation policy based on a more inclusive principle of equity. This proposal was based on the principle of distribution of equal shares of water to all in the particular river basin or sub-basin, irrespective of whether individuals were landowners or not. This would of course benefit the landless rural community which has been at the receiving end of injustices caused by the age-old 'caste system' in India that has restricted land ownership to only a few upper-caste communities. The demand for such an equitable allocation policy came from actual community-based experiments and advocacy developed over the years by a group of activists and community organizations; the water rights movement in the state is spearheaded by several grass-roots organizations including the *Shramik Mukti Dal* organization. It was expected that this demand would be seriously considered since the benefits accruing were based on evidence coming from actual ground-level experiments and advocacy efforts.

However, in their opening speeches the political leaders including the Minister of the WRD strongly supported the reforms towards giving higher priority to industry in water allocation. This argument was made on the basis of the higher economic growth in the form of jobs and personal income that industries can bring for citizens. However, no concrete evidence was put forward in favour of this argument. The dominant groups were successful in ensuring that the opponents of reforms did not get adequate space to raise their demands and arguments.

It should be noted that in the same consultation process, the government began showcasing 'equity' as the primary principle for water allocation to be adopted in the MWRRA bill. During consultations, legal provisions were promised to ensure water rights for farmers in the form of entitlements. The emphasis on 'equity' was seen as an important change in the policy proposal achieved by the activists and organizations promoting public interest. But the operational definition of equity was narrow and ensured water only to agriculture landholders. At the same time it was proposed to provide higher priority for water allocation to industries as compared with farmers. Thus, considerable confusion and obscurity was created in the allocation policy, and especially in priorities for allocation (Wagle et al. 2012).

The outcome of using tools

The confusion and obscurity in allocation policy is evident from the contradictory provisions in the related policy instruments. On the one hand a higher priority was accorded to industrial as compared with agricultural water use in the SWP (Government of Maharashtra 2003). On the other hand the MWRRA Act provided for equitable water distribution in the form of assurance of water entitlements to each farmer in the command area (the area in which the benefits are experienced) of the dam. The principle of allocating water to the landless remained unaccepted.

The MWRRA Act is legally enforceable while the SWP was just a policy statement without the force of a law. The SWP was passed by the government in 2003 and the MWRRA Act came into force in 2005. So it was expected that the Act would supersede the provisions in the SWP which accorded higher priority to industrial water use. Based on this it was expected that the farmers should get their due rights in the form of water entitlements. However, in reality these provisions in the law were bypassed by the Minister for WRD while making decisions on water reallocations after the MWRRA law had passed. The Minister continued using the pre-MWRRA mechanism of re-allocating water from irrigation to non-irrigation purposes without any public hearing or compensation to affected farmers. In total, the Ministerial committee reallocated about 2000 million cubic metres of water from 51 different dams, leading to a reduction of 313 196 ha of irrigation. Out of this reallocation, 54 per cent was for the urban and domestic sector and 46 per cent was for the industrial sector.[3] Thus, the outcome of the participatory tool – in the form of acceptance of the principle of 'equity' – was not adhered to by the political leaders who were involved in influencing the policy formulation process. Thus, tool use during formulation of these policies was not completely successful in countering the vested interests.

TOOL USE BY INDEPENDENT REGULATORY AUTHORITIES

The MWRRA Act of 2005 gave birth to a new and untested policy venue of an IRA in a highly politicized sector: water. As mentioned in the introductory section, an IRA is an autonomous venue for policy action. Use of tools for policy formulation by a quasi-judicial IRA could be expected to giver higher importance to evidence-based analysis and arguments.

The Act empowered the regulatory authority to formulate and decide regulations for determining water tariffs. The focus of the process was on determining the tariff for bulk water supply. Bulk water users were identified as domestic, industrial and agricultural. The regulator initiated the process of formulating regulations in 2008. The law mandated the regulator to apply participatory tools for formulating these regulations.

The Design of the Participatory Tool

MWRRA decided to appoint a consultant to develop an approach for tariff regulations. Terms of Reference (ToR) were prepared for deciding the scope of the consultancy assignment. Among other things, the scope consisted of designing the process of formulating regulations, including the design of the participatory tool to be adopted.

The regulator initiated the consultation process right at the stage of finalizing the ToR. The ToR were circulated for comments to a select audience comprising government officials, NGOs and experts. The key features finally accepted as the design of the participatory tool included:

1. Regional-level (below state-level) public consultation meetings to be held for adequate representation from different parts of the state;
2. Publication and dissemination of consultation documents to be made available in English as well as in the local *Marathi* language;
3. Meetings to be open for participation by all those stakeholders affected by the water tariff to be determined;
4. Meeting invitations to be publicized in widely circulated newspapers at a prominent place;
5. All comments, options and recommendations made by the participants should be submitted to the IRA in written form;
6. 'Conduct of Business Regulations' to be prepared and enforced before initiating the consultative process so that there is transparency in, and commitment to, the overall process.

However, there were several important recommendations related to tool design which were not accepted by the regulator. The participants in the consultation on the ToR suggested that the regulator should show the impacts related to increase or decrease in the tariff based on various criteria suggested for tariff determination. But the same was not accepted in the final design. Other recommendations not accepted in the final design of the participatory tool included, among others (Prayas 2009):

1. Allowing verbal comments to be video recorded and used for assessment of the policy options – necessary for illiterate and less articulate stakeholders, especially farmers.
2. Publication of a reasoned report comprising all the possible regulatory options suggested by the stakeholders. Such a report should also provide explanation of why certain policy options were accepted or rejected by the regulator in its final decision.
3. Formation of a 'stakeholder review committee' to provide inputs in the form of review of the ongoing participatory process.
4. Use of 'technical validation' as a tool to assess the validity of data to be used for determining tariffs.

The Execution of the Participatory Tool

The process of policy formulation started on a positive note due to concrete efforts put in to designing of the tool (as set out in the ToR). However, the implementation did not progress as per the provisions of the ToR. The analysis of adherence to the ToR suggested that almost 53 per cent of its provisions were not adhered to (Prayas 2009). For example, the 'Conduct of Business Regulations' were not prepared before initiating the consultation process. This important aspect of procedural commitment was ignored. The approach paper published for consultation was initially available only in English. After several objections by civil society organizations a short summary of the 300 page approach paper was prepared in the local language by the IRA. However, this summary was highly inadequate in conveying all the important aspects of the policy proposal. The civil society organizations then voluntarily prepared a small booklet on the proposal and disseminated widely among farmers and other marginalized communities.

Four stakeholder consultation meetings on the approach paper were announced by MWRRA. The policy proposed in the approach was found to be substantively inadequate by the civil society groups. A group of stakeholders comprising experts, NGOs and farmer organizations came together as a loosely held coalition of civil society actors (hereafter referred as the coalition). The coalition provided a policy option in the form of 'equity' and 'rights-based' approach to tariff determination. They emphasized criteria of 'minimum tariff for water required for life and livelihood' (so-called 'lifeline and livelihood tariff') and overall adherence to the principle of 'affordability'. Contrary to this demand for a 'social tariff' approach, the proposal prepared by the consultant was largely based on the principle of rationalizing tariffs based on economic principles such as reduction of cross-subsidy.

The methodology suggested by the consultant for assessing tariff options and determination of final tariffs was based on the task of assigning weights. A set of criteria were identified for apportioning costs between irrigation, industrial and domestic water users. Weights have to be assigned to these three water user categories under each criterion. However, the assignment of weight was based on the subjective judgement of the final decision maker. This cost-apportionment matrix was found to be highly objectionable by the coalition as it would provide a high level of discretion to the regulator to adjust the weights according to its subjective judgement, to arrive at a tariff. This type of design, based on subjectively arrived-at weightings, requires adequate procedures to seek preferences on weights from all concerned stakeholders in an open and transparent environment. There was no such procedure designed in the tool, leaving space for the vested interests to creep into its execution and influence the outcome. This was evident from the proposal for cross-subsidy reduction put forward by the consultant. The coalition considered the approach paper to be biased towards industry because it proposed a reduction of the prevailing tariff burden on industries and an increase of the same on agriculture. This was the outcome of particular weights assumed by the consultant in the cost-apportionment matrix. The influence of the industrial stakeholders was evident.

The method of subjective weights would mean that the weaker stakeholders would suffer if they do not get organized and raise their voice. The coalition of civil society actors played an important role in this regard. The coalition held a meeting with the IRA and recommended complete revision of the approach before initiating any further policy formulation process. It was also brought to the attention of the regulator that the four consultation meetings were inadequate for proper representation of the vast number of farmers across the state. The regulator was reluctant to accept the demand for complete revision in the approach paper but agreed to increase the number of consultation meetings from four to a total of nine. This provided an opportunity to the coalition and individual farmers to raise their voices and demand alternative 'equitable' and 'rights-based' options for tariff determination.

The nine consultation meetings provided an opportunity for open sharing, criticism and recommendation of alternative options. The regulator played a neutral role and avoided giving any judgements on the approach paper prepared by the consultant. There was no priority given to elected political leaders. This neutral position helped in facilitating open discussions in the consultation meetings and made it possible to raise several alternatives for determining water tariffs.

After this first round of consultation meetings the regulator initiated the process of revising the approach paper. The alternative options suggested in the consultation meetings were assessed in this process. But it was a totally closed-door process, with no opportunity for stakeholders to engage in the assessment of the options or revise the approach paper. The regulator prepared a short report on assessment of various options, including a summary of some of the main comments and suggestions received from stakeholders. Here, the regulator recorded its assessment of various comments and options suggested in consultations. It included a brief justification of why certain options were worth considering and including while others were not.

The revised approach paper came out with new criteria based on the various social considerations suggested by participants in the first round of consultations. This was a positive development for the coalition. The implicit policy of reduction of cross-subsidy adopted in the first approach paper was abandoned in the revised approach paper by altering the weights in the cost-apportionment matrix. But the methodology based on subjective assignment of weights remained untouched. Objective criteria were suggested by stakeholders but not considered in the revised approach paper. Hence, a concern was raised on the possibility of alteration of weights in the future and thereby resurfacing of the cross-subsidy reduction strategy. The proposal for an equitable and rights-based approach to tariff-setting based on criteria of 'lifeline and livelihood tariff' was not accepted.

The revised approach paper was again published for consultation. But this time the regulator decided to have only one state-level consultation meeting. This was considered inadequate by the stakeholder groups. The state-level consultation meeting was organized in the form of a panel session to be followed by open discussions. The coalition made a demand for increasing the scope of consultation on the revised approach by conducting more meetings on the revised approach paper. However, there was no response from the regulator. Seeing that the regulator was not giving any attention to their demand, the group stalled the proceedings of the panel session, bringing the meeting to a standstill for some time, until the regulator agreed to hold regional consultation meetings at six more places in the state. This enhanced the scope of the consultative process and allowed larger numbers of participants to engage and provide alternative options for tariff determination. The regulations were finalized after this round of consultations. This event throws light on the need for providing space for negotiation even within the autonomous regulatory setting.

The Policy Outcomes of Tariff Regulations

The outcome of the participatory tool can be seen by comparing the initial draft approach paper with the final regulations for tariff determination. Considerable changes were made in the final regulations based on the comments and suggestions given in the participatory process. Concessions on water tariffs were awarded to various disadvantaged sections such as tribal communities (indigenous people), small and marginal farmers, and people affected by dam projects. The rights-based approach in the form of the 'lifeline and livelihood tariff' was not accepted.

An important aspect of regulation in a utility sector like water is the 'financial regulation' of projects and services. This pertains to regulation of the capital and other costs along with its effective use in creation and maintenance of capital assets. Ineffective regulations in this area have been responsible for various malpractices, irregularities and corruption in construction works. Recommendations were made several times in this regard by the coalition but were ignored by the IRA. This shows the influence of the vested interests associated with financial aspects of projects even in an autonomous policy venue such as an IRA.

CONCLUSION

The economic reforms sweeping across developing countries are changing the social fabric of traditional societies. Reforms that were once focused on development projects and programmes (such as building of dams) are now aiming at institutional restructuring through changes in the policy and legal frameworks in different sectors. These sectoral institutional reforms are moving 'policy' centre-stage in politics. This can be seen as the beginning of the creation of a distinct political sphere, woven around issues of public policy as against the issues of identity and interests determined by social and personal relations. This will eventually facilitate the incorporation of policy formulation tools in formal policy processes. However, the legacy of interest-based politics in developing countries continues to have an influence on the design and use of such tools. Transplantation of models from industrialized countries without cognizance of this legacy leads to the capture of policy venues and of the process of tool use by the dominant sections of the society. The case of tool use in one particular government-led venue points towards such a capture.

The analysis of tool use in one government-led venue has shown that vested interests enjoy a high level of influence. A sophisticated and precise tool like CBA is easily manipulated in such a venue. Opening up the process through the use of participatory tools has provided some space for more critical analysis of policy options. It was possible to bring equity and other social considerations in the public discourse through such participatory tools. But due to the domination of political leaders and associated vested interests, the inclusion of social principles remains partial and marred by obscurity and confusion created around its operationalization. The consultation process is dominated by the political leaders through the mechanism of 'stage-managed events'. When it comes to the implementation of the policy, the obscurity created around the social principles comes as a handy tool for the political leaders to completely bypass the policy provisions related to these principles. Thus, tool use under a government-led venue remains ineffective in countering vested interests.

The model of the independent regulatory authority (IRA) has its origin in developed countries. Transplantation of this model of independent regulation to developing countries has given rise to a new venue for tool use. The focus of tool use by IRAs in developed countries has been to ensure techno-economic rationality in policy decisions. The IRA is supposed to achieve this by keeping an arm's-length distance from the political executive. In the case of developing countries, social policy considerations are so critical that an IRA cannot remain focused purely on techno-economic rationality. The case of tool use under this new policy venue shows the potential of independent regulatory processes in countering vested interests and bringing in social policy considerations.

Tool use in an IRA-led venue has shown higher potential in countering vested interests. Unlike the 'stage-managed events' in the government-led venue, the IRA was able to provide a neutral institutional location for the sharing of policy options and their assessment. This provided an important opportunity for civil society actors to form a coalition and represent the poor and marginalized sections in the policy formulation process. The autonomous nature of the venue ensured that the policy options presented by these social actors are heard and incorporated in the official policy assessment process. This provided the much needed space for presenting evidence in favour of a pro-poor approach to tariff policy. The tool use under the autonomous policy formulation venue was actually able to counter the dominant interests linked to the reduction of cross-subsidy. This is evident from the fact that the policy option of cross-subsidy reduction was abandoned and on top of this, new concessions in water tariffs were awarded to various disadvantaged sections of the society.

FUTURE PROSPECTS

There are several rationales put forward for delegating powers to non-majoritarian agencies, such as the IRA (Thatcher and Stone Sweet 2002). They largely focus on the policy outcomes in a developed country context. This chapter has suggested an important process-related rationale specifically relevant for developing countries. The process-related rationale is to provide a neutral and autonomous venue for design and implementation of policy formulation tools. Based on this rationale, the mechanism of policy formulation by autonomous agencies can be extended beyond the scope of IRA-led policymaking. An 'autonomous policy formulation venue' can be envisaged irrespective of whether the final policy decision is made by an IRA or other government agencies or Ministers. However, the cases show that there are still some barriers in this regard. Although there have been positive outcomes, the policy options related to 'rights-based' water tariffs or the option of cost regulation of water utilities were not accepted in the final policy. Hence, there are certain conditions of tool use that need to be created and maintained to achieve the objective of countering vested interests in the policy formulation process.

Considering the specific context of developing countries, we suggest four important conditions of tool use in an 'autonomous policy formulation venue'. First, there is a need to evolve systems and mechanisms for mobilization and organization of the marginalized sections so that they can effectively participate in the process of tool use. This will act to counter-balance attempts by dominant interests to capture the tool-use process. Enabling the formation of coalitions of the marginalized sections and capacity building of such groups are some of the important mechanisms that the cases in this chapter throw light on. Second, the autonomous policy venue should be backed by a robust institutional design for tool design and implementation. The design should include rules and regulations for maintaining high levels of transparency and accountability.

Third, there is a need to leave some space for enabling 'negotiations' that might be needed at different stages of tool design and implementation. Theoretically such a space for negotiation should not exist in an autonomous type of venue because of its non-majoritarian status. But the cases show that one-to-one negotiation with the IRA helped the representatives of the marginalized sections gain a stronger foothold on the design of the tool, especially in terms of increasing the intensity of the participatory consultations. Given the social-political reality of developing societies there is higher possibility that whatever system is evolved for ensuring evidence-based policy formulation, including the autonomous venue for tool use, it will eventually be captured by dominant groups.

Thus, extra efforts are needed to even out the excess advantage of the dominant sections by providing negotiation space for the marginalized. The cases presented in this chapter show how the coalition of civil society actors played an important role in negotiating a more participatory and transparent tool design in favour of the marginalized. Thus, officially recognizing the existing coalitions as representative of this section of society, or appointing special representatives for it, are some of the mechanisms that would facilitate the development of a negotiated approach within an autonomous venue.

A fourth important condition in this regard relates to the pre-existence of a framework of social principles under which policy formulation within autonomous venues can be exercised. Such a framework may be spelled out in the country's Constitution or other legal instruments. The framework will lay down the broader principles such as equity and social justice. Without such a framework, tool use under an autonomous venue will lead to de-politicization of the policy process which might be harmful for the poor and marginalized sections of the society.

These four conditions define the features of the autonomous policy formulation venue adapted to the sociopolitical reality of developing countries. Tool use in such a venue can prove to be an effective strategy in developing countries to counter the interference of undue vested interests and promote evidence-based politics that are more pro-poor. Thus, the path to reforms in developing countries cannot be merely of 'institutional transplantation' of developed country models. Instead there is a need to undertake a fresh 'institutional design' approach to accommodate and address the problems specific to developing countries.

NOTES

1. Based on interviews with senior social activists working on rehabilitation of project-affected people.
2. Based on interviews with social activists who participated in the consultation process.
3. Based on government data collected by Right to Information Act by the NGO PRAYAS.

REFERENCES

Bardhan, P. (2009), 'Notes on the political economy of India's tortuous transition', *Economic & Political Weekly*, 5 December, **44** (49), 31–36.
Corkery, J., A. Land and J. Bossuyt (1995), 'The process of policy formulation: institutional path or institutional maze? Study based on the introduction of

cost-sharing for education in three African countries', Policy Management Report 3, Maastricht: European Centre for Development Policy Management.

Dharmadhikary, S., S. Sheshadri and Rehmat (2005), *Unravelling Bhakra: Assessing the Temple of Resurgent India: Report of a Study of the Bhakra Nangal Project*, Badwani (MP): Manthan Adhyayan Kendra.

Dubash, N. (2008), 'Independent regulatory agencies: a theoretical review with reference to electricity and water in India', *Economic & Political Weekly*, **43** (40), 46–54.

Dubash, N. and B. Morgan (2012), 'Understanding the rise of the regulatory state of the South', *Regulation & Governance*, **6** (3), 261–281.

Dwivedi, R. (2006), *Conflict and Collective Action: The Sardar Sarovar Project in India*, Routledge: New Delhi.

Government of India (1987), *National Water Policy*, New Delhi: Government of India, Ministry of Water Resources.

Government of India (2002), *National Water Policy*, New Delhi: Government of India, Ministry of Water Resources.

Government of Maharashtra (2003), *Maharashtra State Water Policy 2003*, Mumbai: Government of Maharashtra, India.

Hirschman, A.O. (1975), 'Policymaking and policy analysis in Latin America – a return journey', *Policy Sciences*, **6**, 385–402.

Horowitz, D.L. (1989), 'Is there a Third-World policy process?', *Policy Sciences*, **22** (3/4), 197–212.

Iyer, R. (2003), *Water: Perspectives, Issues, Concerns*, Sage: New Delhi.

Mathur, K. (2001), 'Governance and alternative sources of policy advice: the case of India', in K. Weaver and P.B. Stares (eds), *Guidance for Governance. Comparing Alternative Sources of Public Advice*, Tokyo and Washington, DC: Japan Centre for International Exchange and Brookings Institute, pp. 207–230.

Mathur, N. and K. Mathur (2007), 'Policy analysis in India: research bases and discursive practices', in F. Fischer, G.J. Miller and M.S. Sidney (eds), *Handbook of Public Policy Analysis: Theory, Politics, and Methods*, Boca Raton, New York, and Oxford: CRC Press Taylor & Francis Group, Chapter 39.

Pallavi, A. (2012), 'Maharashtra's white paper on irrigation projects fails to answer key questions', *Down To Earth* (3 December 2012), retrieved from http://www.downtoearth.org.in/content/maharashtras-white-paper-irrigation-scam-fails-answer-key-questions (accessed 31 November 2013).

Prayas (2009), *Independent Water Regulatory Authorities in India: Analysis and Intervention, Compendium of Analytical Work by PRAYAS (2006–09)*, Pune, India: Prayas.

Pye, L.W. (1958), 'The non-Western political process', *The Journal of Politics*, **20** (3), 468–486.

Sapru, R. (2004), *Public Policy: Formulation, Implementation and Evaluation*, New Delhi, India: Sterling Publishers.

Singh, S. (1997), *Taming the Waters: The Political Economy of Large Dams in India*, Oxford: Oxford University Press.

Thatcher, M. and A. Stone Sweet (2002), 'Theory and practice of delegation to non-majoritarian institutions', *West European Politics*, **25** (1), 1–2.

Turnpenny, J., C.M. Radaelli, A. Jordan and K. Jacob (2009), 'The policy and politics of policy appraisal: emerging trends and new directions', *Journal of European Public Policy*, **16** (4), 640–653.

Wagle, S., S. Warghade and M. Sathe (2012), 'Exploiting policy obscurity for legalising water grabbing in the era of economic reform: the case of Maharashtra, India', *Water Alternatives*, **5** (2), 412–430.

World Bank (2005), 'India's water economy: bracing for a turbulent future', Washington, DC: World Bank.

11. The effects of targets and indicators on policy formulation: narrowing down, crowding out and locking in

Christina Boswell, Steve Yearley, Colin Fleming, Eugénia Rodrigues and Graham Spinardi

INTRODUCTION

Targets have become an increasingly important component of governance and public sector management in the last two decades, especially across OECD countries. Such targets often involve the use of performance indicators, a policy tool introduced to measure and vouchsafe how far specific targets have been met. Indeed, the possibility of reliably measuring the achievement of targets through performance indicators (PIs) is generally a precondition for the selection of targets (Bevan and Hood 2006; Audit Commission 2000a). The two policy instruments are thus closely interconnected.

The received wisdom among policymakers is that PIs and targets are management tools, adopted to improve the quality and value-for-money of public services. By introducing clear and transparent targets, and subjecting these to regular monitoring through measuring them against PIs, governments incentivize improvements in the performance of those involved in service delivery, and increase public accountability (HM Treasury 1998; Audit Commission 2000a; 2000b). Ostensibly, then, targets and related PIs might be best characterized as instruments for ensuring the effective delivery, or implementation, of policies and programmes that have already been adopted.

However, we argue in this chapter that targets and PIs can also have an important role in policy formulation. They serve to shape and delimit the range of options open to policymakers. As scholars of public administration have noted, targets and PIs can have a number of unintended effects, encouraging forms of gaming or creating perverse incentive structures

(Smith 1990; 1995; James 2004; Pidd 2005; Bevan and Hood 2006). Building on these contributions, we identify three main ways in which targets and PIs might potentially constrain policy formulation. First, in order to be deployable as targets, policy goals need to meet a number of managerial, political and technical criteria. This implies that only a subset of policy objectives may end up being codified as targets, narrowing down the range of policy options or objectives that receive the target treatment. This 'narrowing down' effect may be exacerbated by a second effect, which we call the 'crowding out' effect. Once adopted, targets can become the (sometimes exclusive) focus of political discussion and organizational action. This can 'crowd out' other objectives and considerations in policy formulation processes, with the target in some cases even supplanting the original underlying objective. What was initially a means becomes an end in itself. Third, targets and PIs may also have a 'locking in' effect over time. Once adopted, they can commit governments – and their critics – to overly specified courses of action, which are not responsive to changing conditions. Taken together, these three effects imply that the introduction of targets and PIs can have a significant effect on policy formulation, and not always in ways intended by those originally introducing them.

This chapter explores how far these three constraining effects have influenced policy formulation in the case of targets and PIs developed as part of the Public Service Agreements (PSAs) rolled out by the UK government between 2000 and 2010. We compare three different policy areas: immigration control, climate change and defence procurement. These cases offer scope for comparing policy areas with quite distinct 'audiences'. Immigration is a highly politicized area, which is the object of ongoing media and political attention, and there is strong pressure on incumbents to demonstrate their capacity to manage the problem. Climate change is a more technocratic area, relatively protected from popular media and political attention, but subject to more specialized scrutiny from NGOs and bound by international treaty obligations. Defence procurement remains largely sequestered from popular, political or media attention, despite continued problems of overspend and poor performance – its main form of scrutiny is through parliamentary committees, the National Audit Office (NAO), and the controller of its purse strings, the Treasury. We expect these variations in audience to produce different types of pressures in selecting targets and PIs, in turn generating different patterns of constraint in policy formulation.

The chapter starts by setting out the main features of the PSAs introduced by the post-1997 Labour administration. It suggests the ways in which PSA targets and PIs may have had a constraining effect on policy formulation through processes of narrowing down, crowding out and locking in. In part two, we explore to what extent these effects operated in our three cases. In conclusion, we suggest the need for targets and PIs to build in procedures of scrutiny that help avoid the narrowing down and crowding out effects we observe. Our analysis draws on a range of policy documents: departmental annual reports and annual performance reviews; NAO reports on performance; and scrutiny of targets and PIs by relevant parliamentary committees.

TARGETS AND PERFORMANCE INDICATORS UNDER NEW LABOUR, 2000–2010

UK governments have been enamoured of targets and indicators since the early 1980s, when the Thatcher administration rolled out a series of performance targets across sectors (Smith 1990). This approach was reinforced under the Labour administrations of 1997–2010. In 1998, the government conducted a Comprehensive Spending Review, which introduced performance requirements across government. Each department was instructed to undertake a series of improvements to the way they delivered their services, in order to justify funding allocations. These targets were updated in 2000 with a more comprehensive set of PSAs. The new PSAs set out for each major government department 'its aim, objectives and the targets against which success will be measured' (HM Treasury 2000). A key component was the measurement and monitoring of delivery of these targets, through annual departmental reports. Each objective was required to have at least one target which was 'SMART': specific, measurable, achievable, relevant and timed. PSAs were accompanied by Service Delivery Agreements (SDAs), concluded between the Treasury and each department, which set out more specific, lower-level targets and milestones to support delivery of the PSA targets.

While government rhetoric on targets and PIs focused on performance and delivery, implying that they were a tool for implementing policy, in many cases the selection of targets could be better characterized as an instrument of policy formulation. The selection of targets involved translating broad policy aims and objectives into specific and practically achievable goals. It therefore implied a process of identifying and assessing different options for addressing policy problems – akin to Howlett's definition of policy formulation (Howlett 2011, p. 30; see also Chapter 1, this volume). This raises important questions about the process for, and rationale behind, selecting targets. For example, what sorts of consideration underpinned the selection of targets?

From the outset, it was clear that targets and PIs had a dual function.

The Treasury characterized the PSAs as 'a major agenda to deliver *and demonstrate* change in the commissioning, management and delivery of public services' (HM Treasury 2002a, p. 13; emphasis added). 'Departments were given a real incentive to drive up standards in public services and the public was given the opportunity to judge their performance' (ibid, p. 12).

This dual purpose of steering performance while also demonstrating improvement conforms to insights which suggest that targets and indicators function as 'boundary objects' (Turnhout 2009, p. 405; see also Chapters 4 and 12, this volume). On the one hand, targets and PIs are adopted to enhance public sector performance, through what might be termed their 'disciplining' function: they provide incentives for actors involved in formulating and implementing policy to improve their performance and ensure 'value for money'. But at the same time, targets and PIs clearly have a range of other, more political, functions. They may be developed for symbolic reasons, to signal commitment to, and underscore achievement of, a range of political or organizational goals. Targets and PIs thus need to operate as management tools, providing relevant and practical guidance for steering policy; but at the same time, they need to resonate with – and often mitigate – public concerns about public service performance; and in some cases, they also need to signal to other audiences such as lobby groups, foreign governments or international organizations that the government is committed to a particular course of action (Boswell 2014).

Aside from this dual function of delivering and demonstrating improved public services, there were a number of formal and technical criteria that guided the selection of targets. First, targets needed to be monitored, and thus linked to indicators. The potential to measure and monitor targets through PIs was built into the very definition of targets. Second, targets increasingly became focused on outcomes. The House of Commons Treasury Select Committee, which monitors Treasury policy, calculated in 2000 that most of the targets under the 1998 PSA had been 'process' (51 per cent) or 'output' (27 per cent), with only 11 per cent comprising outcome targets (House of Commons Treasury Select Committee 2000). It recommended that the new PSAs established in 2000 focus more on outcomes; and indeed the National Audit Office classified 68 per cent of the targets adopted in 2000 as outcome targets (NAO 2001, p. 1).

In short, the selection of targets and PIs was guided by three sets of considerations: the managerial goal of disciplining behaviour to improve performance; the political goal of signalling to key audiences that key objectives were being met; and formal requirements linked to measurement, with a focus on outcomes.

What sorts of constraining effects did PSAs have on policy formulation?

For a start, we can expect that the various managerial, political and technical requirements for selecting targets might have the effect of narrowing down the range of policy objectives that were to be considered. It was certainly a tall order for targets to meet all of the formal and substantive criteria set out. PSAs are therefore likely to have fostered a reliance on a narrow set of indicators as proxies for meeting a set of broader organizational and policy objectives. They represent what Bevan and Hood (2006, p. 521) have identified as a form of synecdoche: treating a part to stand for the whole.

Second, and related to this, we might expect targets and PIs to have a crowding out effect, re-orienting both political debate and organizational action to focus on performance against the selected targets. There is limited scope in this chapter for examining how far PSAs influenced political debate on policy objectives. However, we can identify processes of crowding out by examining the type of scrutiny exercised by peer organizations. Notably, the NAO and parliamentary select committees had a formal role in monitoring performance, and assessing the effectiveness of PSAs across policy sectors. Thus one important indicator of crowding out is to explore how far these bodies bought into, or challenged, the selection and scope of targets and PIs.

Third, PSAs might be predicted to have a locking-in effect, tying government departments to a particular course of action, even in the event of a change in circumstances or policy priorities. Indeed, from early on, targets and PIs were criticized for being overly rigid and centralized, and allowing insufficient flexibility for local government and other actors involved in service delivery (NAO 2001; House of Commons Public Administration Select Committee 2003). The 2004 PSAs responded to these criticisms by claiming to reduce the number of targets, allowing more flexibility. Many targets also became more 'directional', with performance measured in terms of improvement or deterioration, rather than meeting a specific numerical target. Yet clearly the scope for such adjustments was constrained by the setting of earlier commitments and the fact that such commitments were transparent and had a built-in system of monitoring and scrutiny.

In order to investigate these constraining effects, we examine three areas: immigration control, climate change and defence procurement. One of our expectations is that these dynamics will vary depending on the audience being targeted by policymakers. Are policymakers involved in the selection of targets trying to meet the expectations of public opinion/ the media, parliamentary or other organizations involved in oversight, or the specialized policy community (practitioners, NGOs, researchers)? We expect this to have an influence on which targets and indicators they select;

and, as a result, how pronounced the three effects on policy formulation are. For each case, we therefore start by examining the rationale for the selection of targets. We then explore how far this selection was associated with a crowding out effect. And finally, we analyse how far policymakers became locked in to a given course of action in the face of changed circumstances.

CASES OF POLICY FORMULATION

Immigration Control

Immigration control covers a range of measures to control the entry, residence and employment of immigrants and refugees. It has long been part of the remit of the Home Office, and more specifically its Border Agency. The UK Border Agency (UKBA – originally named the Border and Immigration Agency) was set up in 2007, as successor to the Immigration and Nationality Directorate.

A striking feature of the targets adopted on immigration control in the 2000s was the gap between very broad strategic objectives, and the very narrow scope of the targets adopted. The 2000 PSA and the 2002 Service Delivery Agreement both set out a broad objective for the Home Office in this area, covering the areas of meeting economic and skills requirements through work permits/entry policies, facilitating international travel, more efficient asylum systems, and – in the case of the 2002 SDA – effective programmes for dealing with citizenship and long-term immigration applications. Yet the targets set under this objective all related to asylum applications, removals and detention. Thus the 2000 targets were (1) to ensure that by 2004, 75 per cent of asylum applications are decided within two months, and (2) to remove a greater proportion of failed asylum seekers. The 2002 SDA further refined these two targets, and added a third target of increasing detention capacity. So despite a very broad set of objectives, the targets adopted focused on one very narrow area. What explains this disparity?

One possible explanation is technical: many areas of performance relevant to the broader objectives would be difficult to measure. There is a high degree of uncertainty in measuring, for example, the successful integration of refugees, or the social and economic impact of immigration, or the scale of irregular migration. By contrast, asylum statistics are regular, reliable and based on a well-established registration system (Boswell 2012). Yet the same would apply to other aspects of the target – such as work permits, or citizenship applications and acquisition. It would also have been quite feasible to measure performance on, for example, the quality of first decisions on asylum applications. So while technical criteria may have partly explained the focus on asylum, it certainly was not the only aspect of policy meeting these conditions.

A far more plausible explanation is the political saliency of asylum at that time. Asylum applications had been rising in recent years, and there was intense mass media coverage of the issue. So while asylum is just one aspect of immigration policy – and arguably not as critical for socio-economic welfare as others, such as the impact of immigration on Britain's economy or society – it was the most politicized, and the one on which the government was receiving most criticism from the media. In the case of the Home Office's immigration targets, then, the criterion of selection seems to have been very much geared to meeting political objectives, notably addressing public concerns as articulated in mass media reporting.

The importance of public opinion becomes even clearer if we consider the audiences that were *not* being addressed through this selection of targets. It was certainly not responding to concerns about administrative inefficiency within the Home Office, which had been articulated in parliamentary debate and mass media reporting. Nor was there a concern to address the business/employers audience, who would be more concerned about ensuring an efficient and swift process for processing permits, and a flexible approach to policy on entry. The focus on removals and detention, as well as the emphasis on speeding up asylum decision making (rather than improving its quality) was also likely to be the object of criticism by NGOs and human rights groups. Indeed, given that the Labour government's immigration policy was in many ways emerging as quite liberal and progressive – at least in the area of labour migration – it is striking that they should have adopted a set of targets exclusively emphasizing the restrictive and potentially human-rights-violating aspects of Home Office policy. It represents a very pronounced case of narrowing down.

The highly politicized nature of the asylum-related targets was illustrated by Prime Minister Tony Blair's appearance on the BBC's flagship television current affairs programme, *Newsnight*, in early 2003. Blair unexpectedly pledged to halve asylum seeker numbers within a year, although this had not been part of either the 2000 or 2002 targets, and was not the object of prior consultation with the Home Office (Boswell 2009, p. 140). A target reflecting this new pledge was introduced in the Home Office Departmental Report, 2004–2005, and thereafter the goal of reducing the number of new asylum applications became one of the targets (incorporated into the PSAs covering 2004 and 2007).

If targets had a narrowing down effect, how far did they crowd out a focus on other policy objectives? The focus on asylum targets, and especially Blair's high profile announcement on *Newsnight*, was the object of wide media coverage. The target also became one of the top priorities for the Prime Minister's influential Delivery Unit, implying intense scrutiny and pressure from No. 10. This crowding out effect was reinforced by the system for monitoring performance. In principle, one might expect the bodies responsible for scrutinizing PSAs to have questioned the selection of targets as being overly narrow. Yet the bodies most closely involved in monitoring Home Office PSAs – the National Audit Office, and the House of Commons Home Affairs and Public Administration Select Committees – largely bought into the selection of targets. NAO reports on Home Office targets and PIs over this period focused almost exclusively on technical aspects of the PSAs. The Home Affairs Committee did raise some issues around the selection and potential effects of targets. Yet their focus was on problems of feasibility, whether they were sufficiently ambitious and whether there were too many targets. Rather than challenging the narrowing down and crowding out effects, these bodies arguably contributed to them by urging a focus on even narrower and more ambitious 'stretch' targets.

Finally, how far did these targets have a lock-in effect, restricting the flexibility of the Home Office in responding to changing circumstances? Here the evidence suggests that the lock-in effect was relatively limited. The Home Office was able to shift its targets and objectives several times, in response either to challenges in meeting the targets, or changed political objectives. For example, the target on removals saw a number of shifts over the decade. The first shift was towards a more precise target. While the 2000 PSA simply talked of 'removing a greater proportion of failed asylum seekers', the 2002 SDA aimed to increase the number of removals to 30,000 by March 2003. The Home Office was subsequently forced to admit this target was too ambitious. In a scathing critique, the House of Commons Home Affairs Select Committee (2003, p. 23) noted that:

> We are at a loss to understand the basis for the belief that a target of 30,000 removals a year was achievable, and ministerial pronouncements on the subject are obscure. It is surely not too much to expect that, if it is thought necessary to set targets for removals, they should be rational and achievable.

In the new 2004 PSA, this target was adjusted from a specific numerical target back to a 'directional' target, that is, to remove a greater proportion of failed asylum seekers in 2005–2006 compared with 2002–2003. This represents a clear case of 'gaming' through an attempt to manage the presentation of performance (James 2004, p. 409). Even this more modest target was not achieved. Despite criticism by the Home Affairs Select Committee, the Home Office retained its directional target.

The Home Office was also able to adjust its substantive targets over the decade. By the time of the 2007 PSA, the Home Office's objective for immigration had become more narrowly focused on control: 'Securing our borders, preventing abuse of our immigration laws and managing migration to boost the UK' (Home Office 2007, p. 54). With declining numbers of asylum applicants, the focus was also shifting to border control. In line with the government's approach of reducing the number of targets, the Home Office claimed to have just one target: reduce the time taken to process asylum applications.

To summarize, the setting of targets in the area of immigration policy appears to have been strongly driven by political considerations, notably the perceived need to signal to the public that the government was acting to reduce asylum applications and detain or deport those who were not considered to be genuine refugees. This led to a significant narrowing down of policy priorities, and a focus on scrutinizing performance against those targets. However, the Home Office found ways to avoid being locked in to these targets when they appeared either unfeasible, or no longer relevant to its core strategic objectives.

Climate Change

Before 2001, environmental commitments including climate change were dealt with by a large, portmanteau Department of the Environment, Transport and the Regions (DETR). From June 2001, the DETR was reorganized with the principal environmental responsibilities shifting to DEFRA (the Department for Environment, Food and Rural Affairs), resulting in the objectives and targets for climate change being located in a more conventionally environmental framework. Then, as a consequence of the new climate policy architecture defined by the 2008 Climate Change Act, in October of that year a new Ministry was established – the Department of Energy and Climate Change (DECC). While DEFRA retained some responsibilities for climate change, these were essentially restricted to adaptation to impacts – it was clear that climate change was now being framed as an energy (and thus industrial) issue as much as an environmental one (see Yearley 2002, p. 277–279). Thus, within a decade the political and organizational location – and, to some degree, the framing – of the climate issue moved around a good deal and this in itself impacted the context for relevant PSAs.

Policies for and action around climate change have featured as objectives in all three sets of PSAs and the government's plans and obligations in this area have consistently occupied a prominent position among the PSAs, being typically included high up in the list of environmental topics.

Though the 1998 Comprehensive Spending Review made no mention of climate change nor the greenhouse effect in its targets for DETR – the only possible link was to the overall aim of promoting sustainable development (HM Treasury 1998, p. 13) – by the time DEFRA's PSAs were spelled out in 2002, performance target 2 was to '[i]mprove the environment and the sustainable use of natural resources, including through the use of energy saving technologies, to help reduce greenhouse gas emissions by 12.5% from 1990 levels and moving towards a 20% reduction in carbon dioxide emissions by 2010' (HM Treasury 2002b, p. 27). The specific target here was precisely that adopted in the Kyoto Protocol of the United Nations Framework Convention on Climate Change (agreed in outline in 1997), to which the UK and the EU were signatories.

The Kyoto Protocol stipulated that signatory countries had to reduce emissions of six greenhouse gasses by set amounts. The UK commitment was to achieve a 12.5 per cent reduction by 2008–2012. As is clear in the quote above, in the 2002 PSA, this goal was supplemented by the more vaguely expressed idea of 'moving towards' a bigger reduction in CO_2 alone, though it was unclear whether the idea was to achieve this larger cut by 2010 or merely to be moving towards it by that date. The Treasury's document (2002b, p. 28) noted that the Secretary of State for Trade and Industry was jointly responsible for delivering these goals, though no mechanism was identified for ensuring joint action (see the subsequent probing comments in the Fourth Report of the House of Commons Select Committee on Environment, Food and Rural Affairs [2005, section 5, para 35]). In its Autumn Performance Report 2002, DEFRA (2002, p. 33) gave more detail in separate chapters on the Spending Review 2000, the 1998 Comprehensive Spending Review, and the Spending Review 2002: *PSA and the Future*, noting in each case a commitment to meeting the Kyoto targets and noting explicitly that DEFRA took on the environmental PSAs that formerly related to DETR. It also looked forward to the PSA for 2003–2006, for which it expressed the greenhouse gas target in exactly the same manner.

When DEFRA published its 2004 PSAs for the Comprehensive Spending Review, the same target 2 was in place, this time with the international treaty dimension made even clearer:

> To reduce greenhouse gas emissions to 12.5% below 1990 levels in line with our Kyoto commitment and move towards a 20% reduction in carbon dioxide emissions below 1990 levels by 2010, through measures including energy efficiency and renewables. Joint with the Department of Trade and Industry and the Department for Transport. (HM Treasury 2004a, p. 33)

This target was still in place at the time of the Autumn Performance Report 2006 (see p. 22ff) though in this document much greater detail was given about trends in performance of emissions and about new initiatives such as the Office of Climate Change (OCC) which was created 'to work across Government to provide a shared resource for analysis and development of climate change policy and strategy' (DEFRA 2006, p. 25). Details of how emissions are gauged were also available in the Technical Note to the PSAs (HM Treasury 2004b). In a summary table (DEFRA 2006, p. 73) listing 'progress against 2004 Spending Review Public Service Agreement targets', the climate action was said to be 'on course'.

The alignment of targets with international treaty obligations is in marked contrast to the immigration control case, where the selection of targets was dominated by more populist domestic political considerations. It suggests a quite different rationale for PSAs on climate change: that of seeking to meet international obligations through disciplining the behaviour of organizations and actors involved in delivering emissions reductions. The choice of such a transparent and public tool for setting out this target is also likely to have had a symbolic function, designed to signal to the specialized climate change community that the government was fully committed to meeting its obligations – a signal backed up in the detail of the Technical Note.

However, as with the immigration case, the focus on a very restricted range of targets is interesting in itself. In this policy area the focus on reductions in aggregate greenhouse gas emissions and in total releases of CO_2, at least for the first two rounds of PSAs, did serve to narrow down the question of what climate policies are fundamentally about. The focus fell exclusively on emissions ascribed to the UK according to the conventions of Kyoto and thus, for example, reporting did not address emissions from the (then fast-growing) airline business. Equally, though it is clear that the British Government was keen to have a 'stretch' target for CO_2 beyond mere compliance with Kyoto, there was also a narrowing down in that the PSA targets highlighted emissions reductions, as opposed to adaptation to impacts for example. The concentration on the Kyoto targets narrowed down the scope for questioning whether those targets were adequate or rapid enough and, like the whole Kyoto process, tended to emphasize territorial emissions made directly from the UK rather than consumption-based ones embedded in products imported to the UK.

Such narrowing down was also accompanied by crowding out. As mentioned above, the rapid rise in emissions from innovative (often low-cost) airlines was not factored in. Also crowded out was the question of whether emissions reductions are being achieved simply through de-industrialization or switching to less polluting energy sources such as gas. On this latter point, it is noteworthy that the goods and services that British people consume could continue to have a rising 'carbon footprint' even while the UK's officially attributable emissions fell. There is at least one further crowding out effect which is that attention – even within the broad environmental gaze of DEFRA – was focused on emissions and much less on adapting to the unfolding impacts of climate change.

There is less evidence of a strong locking-in effect. If the 2002 and 2004 targets closely matched Kyoto commitments, the 2007 commitment adopted more ambitious goals, as adumbrated by the Royal Commission on Environmental Pollution (HM Treasury 2004b, para 2.6). The new *PSA Delivery Agreement 27* of October 2007 proclaimed in its title the objective of leading the 'global effort to avoid dangerous climate change' (HM Treasury 2007). This was to be assessed through six 'key indicators' ranging from the UK's own emissions to international emissions trends, a proxy measure used to assess climate impacts (access to sustainable water abstraction) and an assessment of the size of the world carbon market (HM Treasury 2007, p. 5–6). This document also referred to the draft Climate Change Bill and its aim of setting CO_2 emissions for 2050 at least 60 per cent lower than the reference year, 1990.

This PSA was distinctive in several ways. For one thing, it introduced dramatically more demanding emissions-reductions targets for the UK. Second, it introduced a specific discussion of the issue of adaptation to climate change. It promised to set out an integrated adaptation framework, dealing with issues such as flooding arising from changing rainfall patterns, and potential impacts on biodiversity and agriculture. Finally, it had a focus on the UK's role not just in combating climate-changing emissions at home but in 'leading' the global effort and, in particular, 'demonstrating to other parties the practical, economic, environmental and social benefits that tackling climate change in a cost-effective way can deliver' (HM Treasury 2007, p. 3). Recognizing that climate problems cannot be addressed by any one country in isolation – and indeed that a country that is a lone pioneer could incur costs and accrue few benefits – the objectives shifted. The UK set itself a very demanding headline target but also put an emphasis on promoting international action; at the same time it has a clear notion of the shape that the international action should take: it should be a solution based on carbon markets.

This more ambitious goal reflected a changing political context in which no successor to the Kyoto agreement was in sight and where China and other fast-developing economies were highly significant CO_2 emitters but not required to take any action under the Kyoto Protocol. The government's domestic achievements could be seen to have been in vain if no steps were taken to address these aspects of climate change. In this sense, the signalling function was important. In its 2009 report, the National Audit Office picked up on this sensitivity, noting that:

> Under the HM Treasury performance rating system, the Department could have assessed its performance as 'strong progress' because more than half of the indicators were demonstrating improvement or meeting the success requirement. However, given that forecasts of global CO_2 emissions in 2050 have continued to rise, the Department considers that it has made only 'some progress' in 2008–09. (NAO 2009, p. 21)

In its Annual Report (DECC, Annual Report and Resource Accounts 2008–2009, p. 51, cited in NAO 2009), DECC scored itself lower than it could have in order to signal that the key ambition of helping to contain global emissions had not been attained. It was apparently keen to forestall criticism through humble demeanour.

Defence Procurement

Defence procurement covers the commissioning and purchase of equipment for the British armed forces, and falls under the remit of the Ministry of Defence (MoD). A series of organizational changes and initiatives took place over the post-1997 period, including the establishment of the Defence Procurement Agency (DPA) and the Defence Logistics Organisation (DLO) in April 1999, a new Smart Procurement Agency in 2000, and eventually reorganization of the DPA and DLO into Defence Equipment & Support (DE&S) in 2007. As with DECC in the last section, these changes shaped the evolution of the MoD's PSA targets over the period 2000–2010.

The overall objective stated for equipment in the first Ministry of Defence PSA was 'to procure equipment which most cost-effectively meets agreed military requirements' (HM Treasury 1998, p. 69). The focus was on two key defence procurement concerns: cost and schedule overruns. There were three specific performance targets for procurement: 'on average, no in-year increase in major project costs'; 'on average, in-year slippage of In-Service Date of new major projects of less than 10 days'; and 'on average, in-year slippage of In-Service Date of existing major projects of less than 4 weeks' (HM Treasury 1998, p. 72). The targets for 2003–2006 included a further PI: '97% of customers' key requirements attained and maintained through the PSA period' (MoD 2004, p. 12), but did not detail how this was to be measured (MoD 2002, p. 58).

The focus on issues of cost and overrun is not surprising given long-standing concerns about efficiency and value-for-money in defence procurement practices. Defence procurement in the UK, as elsewhere, has long suffered from difficulties with delivering suitable equipment on time and on budget (Gansler 1980; Page 2006). In 2009 an authoritative independent report carried out for the Ministry of Defence noted that on average equipment programmes 'cost 40% more than they were originally expected to, and are delivered 80% later than first estimates predicted' (Gray 2009, p. 16). A series of critical reports and attempts at reform over many decades has done little to improve what is an intractable problem.

By their nature, state-of-the-art weapons systems are likely to be expensive and take longer than planned. In this sense, the development of targets and PIs focused on these procedural aspects of procurement may not in themselves have narrowed down the MoD's focus: rather, they were an accurate reflection of organizational priorities over this period. Yet the preoccupation with procedural aspects of procurement, as codified in the targets, had the effect of decoupling narrow performance goals from considerations about the effectiveness of equipment. In this sense, the targets appear to have reinforced a crowding out tendency within the MoD. This can be illustrated most clearly by the gap between MoD claims about meeting PSA targets on the one hand, and real-world military performance on the other.

Between 1998 and 2010, the MoD consistently claimed to be meeting the targets and PIs set out in the PSAs. The MoD's 1998–1999 Performance Report, for example, claimed that 'cost and technical performance targets were met' (though the latter was not a target specified in the PSA), and provided combined data for project slippage dates for both new and existing projects which exceeded the target of four weeks by about 50 per cent (MoD 1999, para 38). The following year, the MoD's 1999–2000 Performance Report (MoD 2000, p. 11) matched performance data more explicitly to the targets, with the cost target reported as achieved, the in-service slippage of existing projects reported as achieved for a revised interim target and date, and the in-service slippage of existing projects not achieved, again for an interim target. This report also claimed that there were no projects with 'unsatisfactory technical performance' (MoD 2000, p. 34) (though technical performance was still not a PSA target at the time). The cost target was again met the following year, but slippage of in-service dates exceeded the targets, with the verdict that performance was 'on course' rather than 'met' (MoD 2001, p. 10). Subsequent years showed similar performance, with cost again met in 2001–2002, but schedule targets not met. Over the rest of the decade some targets would be met and some not, typically with apparently small slippages in schedule more common than cost overruns.

From 2002 onwards, however, it was becoming increasingly apparent that these PSA reports' messages that 'key requirements' were being attained contrasted strongly with real-world military performance. With

British forces involved in Afghanistan and Iraq after 2002, deficiencies in defence procurement processes were becoming increasingly apparent. Providing combat troops with suitable equipment in a timely fashion 'relied on a separate stream of fast-tracked acquisition to meet "urgent operational requirements" (UORs)' (Gray 2009, p. 22). As the House of Commons Defence Select Committee noted (2009, p. 18) 'the extent of UORs represents at least a partial failure by the MoD to equip adequately its forces for expeditionary operations'.

This gap between PSA targets and operational performance was largely overlooked by bodies scrutinizing MoD performance, such as the Select Committee and the NAO, which retained a focus on problems of over-spend and over-run. Neither body fundamentally questioned whether the procurement PSAs were fulfilling their supposed purpose. Taking one example, in its report, 'Defence Procurement 2006' (House of Commons Defence Select Committee 2006, para 17), the Select Committee cautioned that 'while cost growth on defence equipment projects in 2005–2006 was below target, we have concerns that the main reason for this was reduction in the quantity of equipment ordered'. Despite highlighting its concern that '[m]eeting key targets should not be given priority over meeting the requirements of our Armed Forces' (ibid, para 17), there is no discussion of whether targets are appropriate or relate to the wider strategic objectives of the department. Indeed, suggestive of a crowding out effect, the same report underscores its desire that the MoD 'continue to monitor its performance at procuring equipment to time, cost and quality . . . Otherwise, there is a risk that poor procurement performance could be buried in long-term project management data' (House of Commons Defence Select Committee 2006, para 26).

The overall judgement of UK defence procurement at the end of the 2000s can be seen in the critical report by Gray (2009, p. 28), which notes that every year the procurement agency would begin 'with plans to conduct activity some 10 per cent greater than the available, and known, budget for that year', and this shortfall could only be resolved by 're-profiling' – in effect delaying programmes to delay their costs, but at the expense of schedule slippage, greater eventual costs, and 'projects more likely to experience problems'. For example, in 2008 the National Audit Office criticized the MoD for 'failing to forecast aggregate costs', resulting in an 'additional 96 month slippage rate' despite the exclusion of the Typhoon aircraft project on the grounds that it was 'commercially sensitive' (NAO 2008, summary paragraph 1). One target (cost) is prioritized because it is the most pressing as regards MoD budgets, but both schedule and performance thus suffer. Arguably, this crowding out was already endemic within the MoD, a response to long-standing pressures on the organization to focus on narrow procedural aspects of performance. But the codification of these goals within PSAs, and the reporting and scrutiny processes put in place as part of the PSAs, undoubtedly reinforced this tendency. The targets and PIs developed failed to provide an adequate measure of operational performance, with the result that this most important feature of performance was under-emphasized.

As with the two other cases, the defence procurement PSA is unlikely to have had a strong locking-in effect, except in the superficial sense of creating a reporting requirement. The MoD's annual Performance Reports during the decade bear witness to a tendency to pay lip service to targets, while the minor failures to meet some targets in some years led to a cumulative 'black hole' in the procurement budget. The consequences of trying to squeeze too much procurement into a constrained annual budget meant that UK defence procurement was certainly locked in to a vicious cycle, but the PSA targets were not the cause of this.

CONCLUSION

This chapter has explored the ways in which targets and PIs can influence policy formulation, focusing on three types of constraining effect: narrowing down the range of policy options considered; crowding out attention to broader policy objectives; and locking policymakers into a particular course of action regardless of changing conditions. We also examined how far these effects varied across policy areas characterized by rather different sets of pressures: immigration control; climate change; and defence procurement.

Our analysis suggested that variations in the organizations' audiences did indeed influence how targets and PIs were selected and deployed. In the case of the Home Office, the selection of targets appeared to be geared towards mollifying public opinion and the media, through focusing on a very limited set of goals associated with populist approaches to immigration. The focus on reducing asylum applications and increasing removals suggested that targets had a strong signalling function, implying a symbolic, rather than disciplining, function. In the case of climate change, DECC and its predecessors' choice of targets was oriented towards meeting international treaty obligations, again leading to a significant narrowing down of broader objectives to a very specific goal of reducing emissions. The selection of targets and PIs can be interpreted as having a dual function of disciplining those actors responsible for delivering emission reductions and signalling commitment to Kyoto. The subsequent shift to more ambitious targets was also designed to signal UK leadership in the international process of reducing greenhouse gas emissions. In the case of defence procurement, the MoD's selection of targets was again very narrowly focused, this time on addressing problems of poor management and financial oversight. The focus on these aspects of organizational practice suggests that the choice of indicators was a response to pressure exerted by organizations such as the Treasury, the NAO and the Commons Defence Committee.

In all three cases, then, we saw a significant narrowing down of policy objectives, though for different reasons. And in all three cases, the implication was that targets and PIs covered only a small part of the broader strategic objectives identified by the respective department. We also showed that in each of the three cases, the structures put in place to monitor targets and PIs appeared to reinforce this narrowing down effect. In the terminology developed in this paper, they contributed to a crowding out of other types of objectives. In the case of immigration control, the NAO and Parliamentary Committee scrutiny of targets and PIs focused disproportionately on technical questions, as well as demands for more ambitious and specific targets. Questions of whether the targets were the right ones to select, whether they adequately balanced different priorities, or whether they did justice to the broader strategic objectives of the Home Office, were not raised. Similarly, in the case of targets on climate change, the narrowing down of goals to focus on emissions reduction was not a major object of scrutiny, with oversight instead focusing on more technical questions of distance to target. In the case of defence procurement, the focus of targets and PIs on narrow managerial criteria implied that these tools became decoupled from broader objectives related to the performance of equipment in contemporary conflict situations. Paradoxically, then, a set of tools designed to shift the political focus onto outcomes was deployed in a way that resulted in a preoccupation with process.

Our cases showed less evidence of lock-in effects. To be sure, problems of lock-in to inflexible, centralized objectives were an object of general concern in discussion of PSAs from the early 1990s onwards. But the fact that the organizations we examined could and frequently did adjust, reinterpret, evade, demote or abandon targets implied a high degree of flexibility in implementing targets and PIs. The three organizations all found ways of circumventing the limitations imposed by targets. In the case of immigration control, targets were watered down when they proved unfeasible (removals) or demoted when they were no longer a political priority (asylum numbers). In the case of climate change, by contrast, targets were made more ambitious (emissions reduction). And in the case of defence procurement, targets were added to (customer satisfaction) but also repeatedly unmet. So in line with the literature, our analysis suggests that the disciplining function of targets may be less effective than their authors might claim (Bevan and Hood 2006; Smith 1990).

Our analysis has important implications for the design of systems to monitor targets and PIs. The NAO and House of Commons committees tended to focus on technical features of these tools. This is not surprising in the case of the NAO, whose very existence is premised on the ethical and managerial virtues of accountability and audit. These bodies are committed to the idea that good practice in targets and PIs necessarily increases transparency, accountability and performance. It is perhaps less obvious that parliamentary scrutiny would focus on a rather narrow set of criticisms. Once in place, targets and PIs may well provide a useful short-cut for assessing performance in some areas, relieving overloaded committees of the task of defining which aspects of organizational performance to scrutinize, or on what basis to do so. This may create a temptation either to judge departments based on the targets and PIs they have created, or – where the targets and PIs themselves are criticized – to question them on the basis of whether they are sufficiently ambitious, precise, and so on. There appears to be very limited or no provision for pointing out flaws related to narrowing down and crowding out effects. Once these bodies have bought into the notion of accountability and performance monitoring – principles which are difficult to reject per se – then it may become difficult to find a basis for a broader critique of the targets selected.

Yet given the influence of such targets and PIs on policy formulation, and the potential for narrowing down and crowding out effects, we suggest it would be useful to find a mid-level critique: one that does not reject the value of monitoring per se; but one which at the same time does not focus too narrowly on technicalities. Such scrutiny should involve deliberation on how far the selection and implementation of targets and PIs does justice to broader policy objectives. In effect, then, this implies a process of deliberation that recognizes and constantly scrutinizes the link between monitoring and policy formulation.

REFERENCES

Audit Commission (2000a), *Aiming to Improve: The Principles of Performance Measurement*, London: Audit Commission.
Audit Commission (2000b), *On Target: The Practice of Performance Indicators*, London: Audit Commission.
Bevan, G. and C. Hood (2006), 'What's measured is what matters: targets and gaming in the English public health care system', *Public Administration*, **84** (3), 517–538.

Boswell, C. (2012), 'How information scarcity affects the policy agenda: evidence from immigration policy', *Governance*, **25** (3): 367–389.

Boswell, C. (2014), 'The double life of targets in public administration: Disciplining and Signaling in UK Asylum Policy', *Public Administration* (early online, October 2014).

DEFRA (2002), *Autumn Performance Report*, retrieved from www.official-documents.gov.uk/document/cm56/5698/5698.pdf (accessed 2 October 2013).

DEFRA (2006), *Autumn Performance Report*, retrieved from archive.defra.gov.uk/corporate/about/reports/documents/apr2006.pdf (accessed 2 October 2013).

Gansler, J. (1980), *The Defense Industry*, Cambridge, MA: The MIT Press.

Gray, B. (2009), *Review of Acquisition for the Secretary of State for Defence*, London: Ministry of Defence.

HM Treasury (1998), *Public Services for the Future: Modernisation, Reform, Accountability*, Comprehensive Spending Review: Public Service Agreements 1999–2002, (December), Cm 4181, London: HM Treasury.

HM Treasury (2000), *Spending Review: Public Service Agreements*, Cm 4808 (July), London: HM Treasury.

HM Treasury (2002a), *Outcome Focused Management in the United Kingdom*, General Expenditure Policy, HM Treasury (November), retrieved from www.oecd.org/unitedkingdom/43513955.pdf (accessed 23 September 2013).

HM Treasury (2002b), *2002 Spending Review: Public Service Agreements White Paper*, retrieved from webarchive.nationalarchives.gov uk/20071204130111/http://hm-treasury.gov.uk/media/A/3/psa02_ch13.pdf (accessed 20 September 2013).

HM Treasury (2004a), *2004 Spending Review: Public Service Agreements 2005–2008*, retrieved from http://webarchive.nationalarchives.gov.uk/20100407164511/http://www.hm-treasury.gov.uk/spend_sr04_psaindex.htm (accessed 20 September 2013).

HM Treasury (2004b), *2004 Spending Review Supporting Documents – Department for Environment, Food and Rural Affairs Technical Note*, retrieved from http://webarchive.nationalarchives.gov.uk/20100407164511/http://www.hm-treasury.gov.uk/psp_supporting_docs.htm (accessed 20 September 2013).

HM Treasury (2007), *2007 Pre-Budget Report and Comprehensive Spending Review – PSAs 'A more secure, fair and environmentally sustainable world'*, retrieved from http://webarchive.nationalarchives.gov.uk/20100407164511/http://www.hm-treasury.gov.uk/pbr_csr07_psaenvironment.htm (accessed 20 September 2013).

Home Office (2007), *Departmental Report 2007*, Cm 7096, London: Home Office.

House of Commons Defence Select Committee (2006), *Defence Procurement 2006. First Report of Session 2006–07*, HC 56, Incorporating HC 1339 i and ii, Session 2005–06, London: House of Commons.

House of Commons Defence Select Committee (2009), *Defence Equipment. Third Report of Session 2008–09*, HC 107, 26 February, London: House of Commons.

House of Commons Home Affairs Select Committee (2003), *Asylum Removals, Fourth Report of Session 2002–03*, HC 654-I, 8 May, London: The Stationery Office.

House of Commons Public Administration Select Committee (2003), *On Target? Government by Measurement*, Fifth Report of Session 2002–03, Volume 1, HC 62–1, London: House of Commons.

House of Commons Select Committee on Environment, Food and Rural Affairs

(2005), *Fourth Report*, retrieved from www.publications.parliament.uk/pa/cm200506/cmselect/cmenvfru/693/69308.htm (accessed 10 October 2013).

House of Commons Treasury Select Committee (2000), *Ninth Report, Spending Review 2000*, HC 489, August, retrieved from www.publications.parliament.uk/pa/cm199900/cmselect/cmtreasy/485/48502.htm (accessed 23 September 2013).

Howlett, M. (2011), *Designing Public Policies: Principles and Instruments*, Oxford: Routledge.

James, O. (2004), 'The UK core executive's use of Public Service Agreements as a tool of governance', *Public Administration*, **82** (2), 397–419.

MoD (Ministry of Defence) (1999), *Performance Report 1998–1999*, (December). This and other MoD Performance Reports at: http://webarchive.nationalarchives.gov.uk/20051219093945/http://mod.uk/publications/mod_reports.htm http://webarchive.nationalarchives.gov.uk/20051219093945/http://mod.uk/publications/mod_reports.htm (accessed 9 October 2013).

MoD (2000), *Performance Report 1999–2000* (December), Cm 5000, London: The Stationery Office.

MoD (2001), *Performance Report 2000–2001* (November), London: The Stationery Office.

MoD (2002), *Performance Report 2001–2002* (November), London: The Stationery Office.

MoD (2004), *Annual Report and Accounts 2003–2004*, HC 1080, London: The Stationery Office.

NAO (National Audit Office) (2001), *Measuring the Performance of Government Departments*, Report by the Comptroller and Auditor General (March), HC 301, London: National Audit Office.

NAO (2008), *Ministry of Defence Major Projects Report 2008*, London: National Audit Office.

NAO (2009), *Performance of the Department of Energy and Climate Change, 2008–2009* (Briefing for the House of Commons Energy and Climate Change Committee, October 2009), retrieved from www.nao.org.uk/wpcontent/uploads/2012/10/DECC_Performance_briefing_2008-2009.pdf (accessed 10 October 2013).

Page, L. (2006), *Lions, Donkeys and Dinosaurs: Waste and Blundering in the Military*, London: Arrow Books.

Pidd, M. (2005), 'Perversity in public service performance measurement', *International Journal of Productivity and Performance Management*, **54** (5/6), 482–493.

Smith, P. (1990), 'The use of performance indicators in the public sector', *Journal of the Royal Statistical Society*, Series A, **153** (1), 53–72.

Smith, P. (1995), 'On the unintended consequences of publishing performance data in the public sector', *International Journal of Public Administration*, **18**(2/3), 277–310.

Turnhout, E. (2009), 'The effectiveness of boundary objects: the case of ecological indicators', *Science and Public Policy*, **36**(5), 403–412.

Yearley, S. (2002), 'The social construction of environmental problems: a theoretical review and some not-very-Herculean labors' in R.E. Dunlap, F.H. Buttel, P. Dickens and A. Gijswijt (eds), *Sociological Theory and the Environment*, Oxford: Rowman and Littlefield, 274–285.

12. The use of computerized models in different policy formulation venues: the MARKAL energy model

Paul Upham, Peter Taylor, David Christopherson and Will McDowall

INTRODUCTION

At a particular point in time, a policy formulation tool may provide real opportunities for learning or serve to rationalize pre-existing decisions (Hertin et al. 2009). This chapter examines the varying uses to which a particular energy system model – MARKAL – has been put in the UK. We define the scope of policy venues to include all policy-salient institutions using the model: academic-consulting research groups, government departments and non-departmental government bodies. We view MARKAL as a boundary object (Star and Griesemer 1989) that has served the differing but intersecting needs of academic, consulting and policy communities over a sustained period of time, helping both to inform and justify major and innovative climate and energy policy commitments. We suggest that the model has functioned to bind mutually supportive epistemic communities across academic and policy worlds, helping to develop and maintain, both materially and cognitively, a networked and influential community with shared assumptions and goals in which economic and technical models are privileged.

We reflect on how the model has both been advantaged by changing understandings (images) (Baumgartner and Jones 2002) of the energy policy problem, as climate objectives have increased in salience, while also playing a role in policy path creation, that is by supporting significant new climate policy commitments. In seeking to explain the above, we connect literatures on boundary objects in policy formulation and on the way in which changing images of a policy problem can allow new analytic and policy options to enter political and policy spaces. We observe how MARKAL has played a transformative role in this context, while itself also being transformed, as the modelling process has become more target-oriented, as the objectives of UK policy venues have evolved in response to changing political objectives and as new policy formulation venues have emerged.

In the remainder of this chapter, we begin by describing how the use of MARKAL in the UK has evolved from a focus on informing research and development (R&D) priorities in a public research organization to a much more prominent role in justifying major strategic energy policy choices. In examining the use of MARKAL across UK policy venues and over time, we suggest that it is an example of how a scientific model and its output may function as a boundary object that persists despite and because of the changing images of a particular policy problem. Finally, we comment on both the apparent hegemony and limits of technical energy policy modelling, in the light of possible future policy developments.

Our analysis of the ways in which the MARKAL model has been used across different policy venues draws on an examination of some 70 policy documents and presentations, of which 21 items were selected for closer inspection using qualitative analysis software. The selection of themes was guided by the theoretical considerations summarized below and the personal experience of the author team. The grey literature examined includes government policy documents, Parliamentary committee documents and also expert critiques of MARKAL. Changing use over time was evidenced and tracked; evidence for the changing policy image of the energy problem is inferred from the change in policy objectives, which are external to (though supported by) the model. Inference of the functioning of MARKAL as a boundary object is primarily based on observation of: (a) its value to the small academic-consultancy modelling community based at AEA Technology (now Ricardo-AEA) and originally at the Policy Studies Institute, then Kings College London and currently University College London; (b) its use in support of key energy-climate policy documents; and (c) its use in support of recommendations by the UK Committee on Climate Change regarding greenhouse gas (GHG) emissions budgets (sectoral and temporal).

THE CHANGING USE OF MARKAL IN UK POLICY DEVELOPMENT

During the late 1970s, the UK took part in the early development of MARKAL through the involvement of scientists from the UK Atomic Energy Authority (UK AEA) (Finnis 1980). Much of the early MARKAL modelling used scenarios that considered the trade-off between price (measured as the total cost of the energy system) and security of supply (represented by the quantity of imported oil) under different assumptions about the availability and rate of deployment of a range of new energy technologies (Altdorfer et al. 1979). Despite the early participation of the UK in its development and application, it would appear that there was little further use of the model to inform UK policymaking over the subsequent decade, perhaps reflecting the UK government's withdrawal from direct involvement in the energy sector and reliance on a market framework (Department of Energy 1982).

In the early 1990s, the MARKAL model was completely reconfigured and updated, and used to underpin an appraisal of energy technologies and the implications for associated R&D programmes (ETSU 1994a; 1994b). Nonetheless, the model remained at the periphery of mainstream energy policymaking at this point. Indeed, between 1998 and 2001, the UK government suspended active participation in the Energy Technology Systems Analysis Programme, which licences the use of the model generator that underpins all MARKAL models, retaining only an official observer status. Only in 2001, after several years without any substantial MARKAL-related analysis for the government, but with climate change shooting up the political agenda, was AEA Technology plc commissioned by the Department of Trade and Industry (DTI) to undertake its first project using the model specifically to examine energy-related CO_2 emissions. The aim of the work was 'to develop a range of bottom-up estimates of carbon dioxide emissions from the UK energy sector up to 2050, and to identify the technical possibilities and costs for the abatement of these emissions' (DTI 2003b). This work was featured in the Energy White Paper of 2003, in which MARKAL was used to estimate the costs of reaching deep emissions reduction targets.

The above notwithstanding, until 2005, the use of MARKAL in the UK was confined to government agencies or consultancies working under contract for government, rather than academia. This changed with the advent of the UK Energy Research Centre (UKERC), funded by the UK Research Councils' Energy Programme. During the early 2000s, it was clear that the UK's capacity to undertake energy research had become very limited. Overall research funding had fallen in response to two major trends: liberalization of energy markets and privatization of state-owned energy companies, which led to a decline in in-house R&D undertaken by energy companies, while low oil prices during the 1990s and the UK's status as an oil and gas exporter had ensured that energy was not a policy priority for R&D spending. As concern over the long-term security of supply rose, and climate change emerged as a pressing policy problem for future energy systems, UKERC was established as a cross-research council initiative. A key priority, identified early on, was the need to enhance the UK's ability to conduct analyses of the UK energy system as a whole, through an energy system modelling capacity (Strachan 2011). UKERC negotiated access to the UK MARKAL model with the DTI and funded the capacity to conduct a significant revision of it.

Following the major overhaul of the model beginning in 2005, led by the Policy Studies Institute, MARKAL took a prominent role in the analytic work underpinning the 2007 Energy White Paper (Strachan et al. 2009). It was subsequently used to inform the impact assessment for the Climate Change Bill, the 2008 White Paper on nuclear power, and the Committee on Climate Change's work on carbon budgets. In recent years, MARKAL's monopoly as an analytic tool for thinking about long-term (2050) energy system evolution has begun to be challenged by the emergence of other models. The Energy Technology Institute has developed the ESME model, a similar bottom-up, technologically explicit, cost-optimization framework for examining 2050 energy futures. The Department of Energy and Climate Change (DECC) itself developed an in-house tool, the 2050 Calculator, another technologically detailed, bottom-up framework that enables users to examine the implications of different choices in a number of abatement options.

These newer frameworks – which required considerable resources to develop – are very similar to the MARKAL paradigm. Like MARKAL, they focus on the detailed technology pathways to achieve 2050 emissions targets. There is a relative absence in policy processes of other types of tool for thinking about long-term energy systems change, such as highly disaggregated general equilibrium models, or various types of hybrid model. This suggests that the paradigm underpinning MARKAL (defined by technologically explicit whole-systems approaches focused on supplying energy at acceptable or least cost to meet carbon targets) has become so dominant in energy policy discourse that alternative frameworks struggle to achieve policy influence.

THEORETICAL PERSPECTIVES

In this section, we connect the idea of scientific models and their output as boundary objects to the theory of changing policy images as a facilitator of policy change. External pressures give issues greater political and policy salience, enabling policy change (Baumgartner and Jones 2002). We also see the punctuated equilibrium theory of policy change as being particularly relevant. This perspective views policy change occurring as a result of the interaction between policymakers and society (Baumgartner and Jones 1993; 2002; Princen 2000), with this change taking the form of relatively long periods of stasis being 'punctuated' by shorter periods of change (ibid; van Egmond and Zeiss 2010), also reminiscent of Kingdon's 'policy window' (Kingdon 1995) concept. Policy stasis is explained by the dominance of closed groups of policy experts, but can be interrupted by a changing image or idea of the nature of the policy problem. Driving these changes are competitive processes, both between government departments and in wider society, in which actors seek to achieve policy change that is consistent with their agendas (van Egmond and Zeiss 2010).

Our argument is, first, that MARKAL's changing use through the period circa 1990–2011 reflects a change in the prevalent image of the energy policy problem, from one in which the government saw its primary role as structuring and facilitating the market to provide for future energy demand, to a policy image of a climate-constrained world in which radical changes to the energy system would be required, with the attendant need for the government to identify how this transition could be achieved and which technologies might require support. MARKAL has been well positioned to allow consideration of new goals and configurations for the energy system. Second, we argue that this changing use has been strongly supported by the way in which MARKAL and its outputs have success-fully functioned as a boundary object, connecting needs in different policy communities.

As van Egmond and Zeiss (2010) observe, the concept of a boundary object has proved useful in explaining the hybrid nature of scientific models used in policy – that is, the way in which such models are not only based on mathematical representations of the world, but are also shaped by, and play a role in shaping, the social world in which they are embedded (MacKenzie and Millo 2003). Scholars have previously studied the rela-tionship between modelling practices and policy practices (for example, van Daalen et al. 2002; Evans 2000; Mattila 2005; Shackley and Wynne 1995), in general observing that models play a role in co-ordinating policy practice, specifically by providing 'discursive spaces' in which shared understandings are created between modellers and policymakers (Evans 2000). Previous understandings (in other words, shared perspectives) are made tangible in the form of numbers and their implications. Depending on their mode of use, models can define the terms in which policy questions are posed and answers given. Through the process of their use, the different parties involved retain their own norms and natures but are connected by the model, which satisfies needs in both (Star and Griesemer 1989).

In summary, we can see that scientific models may support, through their role as boundary objects, the entry of new ideas and perspectives into policy discourse, facilitating and reinforcing new policy images and hence policy change.

VARIATION AND CHANGE IN THE USE OF MARKAL

Changing images of the energy policy problem have enabled MARKAL to shift from an initial role in technology assessment, driven by concerns about oil import dependency; to a new context of liberalized energy markets in which different technologies competed to meet demand; to a key role in target-oriented climate policy, as the need to reduce greenhouse gas emissions increased in policy salience through the 2000s. This shift involved a change from using the model to focus on the relative prospects of specific technologies in order to inform R&D priorities, towards a focus on the costs and possible evolution of the entire energy system to meet carbon targets. Even more particularly, it came to involve the use of MARKAL to envisage radical changes in that system: MARKAL as a quantitative visioning, scenario generation tool. Throughout these changes, the model continued to play a valuable role for the key parties involved.

Use by Academic Policy Modellers

For UK academic policy modellers, MARKAL provides a means for examining a series of issues in energy system evolution and, in the case of some model variants, for exploring a (limited) set of interactions between these developments and the wider economy. The development of a UK version of the MARKAL–MACRO model in 2007 was a major experimental test of the importance of macroeconomic feedbacks on energy system development (Strachan et al. 2009). Subsequent model experiments have examined the importance of spatially constrained infrastructures by linking MARKAL to a geographical information system (Strachan et al. 2009), enabling representation of demand responses to price rises through the use of MARKAL–ED (Ekins et al. 2011), examining regional representation (Anandarajah and McDowall 2012), testing the importance of uncertainty and assumptions about foresight with Stochastic–MARKAL (Usher and Strachan 2010), and in ongoing work, testing the importance of consumption-based emissions accounting through linking MARKAL to a multi-region input–output model.

Use by UK Government Departments

During the 1990s, UK energy policy was supported by quantitative analysis from econometric models used by the Department of Energy and later the Department of Trade and Industry. These models principally relied on the historical analysis of drivers and trends in energy markets to provide insights about how they may evolve in the future and the implications for CO_2 emissions (DTI 1992; 1995; 2000). Policymakers were mostly interested in understanding how future energy supply and demand would evolve, rather than asking questions about how it could or should develop. Econometric models are well suited to analysing relatively stable energy markets, such as those seen in the late 1980s and early 1990s, when past trends and relationships could reasonably be expected to continue. They are not, however, suitable for envisaging large, long-term transitions in the technological make-up of an energy system, such as the kind that would be needed to seriously tackle the problem of climate change.

Since 2000, the environmental goals of energy policy, particularly in relation to climate change, have come to prominence in UK energy policy discourse. Policymakers have looked to the energy systems modelling community to provide answers to two major types of questions. First, they have asked 'what are the expected costs of meeting a given emissions reduction target?' Only a small number of model types are suitable for asking this question (particularly bottom-up energy systems models like MARKAL, and so called 'top-down' macroeconomic and general equilibrium models). Second, policymakers have asked 'what technologies are necessary for meeting the targets?' MARKAL-type models are uniquely well suited to providing an answer to the latter question. MARKAL thus provides a platform for meeting two basic government needs. First, it provides a way of justifying action in the face of climate change in terms acceptable to the bureaucratic norms embodied in the Treasury Green Book (HM Treasury 2011), that is, those of cost-effectiveness.[1] Second, it provides a way to imagine, understand and explore the dynamics of the complexity of the energy system and to identify potential technological pathways to meeting targets.

Use in the 2003 Energy White Paper

It was the publication of the 2003 Energy White Paper, *Our Energy Future,* that marked a clear transformation in the way that energy issues were approached in UK policy. The document noted that: '[e]nergy can no longer be thought of as a short-term domestic issue' (DTI 2003a, p. 3) and went on to state that: '[i]t will be clear from this white paper that we believe we need to prepare for an energy system that is likely to be quite different from today' (DTI 2003a, p. 16). The driving force behind this change was a growing awareness of the threat of climate change. The 22nd report of the Royal Commission on Environmental Pollution, *Energy – The Changing Climate*, published in 2000, played a highly influential role in this process, urging the government to 'adopt a strategy which puts the UK on a path to reducing carbon dioxide emissions by some 60% from [2000] levels by about 2050' (RCEP 2000, p. 28).

While our argument is that the changing image of the policy problem provided an opportunity for MARKAL's use (in other words, for MARKAL modellers), at this relatively early stage in the development of interlinked UK climate and energy policy, the extent to which MARKAL was used to support the 2003 White Paper is unclear. The White Paper states that it 'is based on a large amount of analysis and modelling' (DTI 2003a, p. 20). However, the only MARKAL results cited in the White Paper itself relate to the economic costs of the transition, including its impact on future levels of GDP and the costs of carbon abatement per tonne. It is worth noting that the figures for GDP loss were not a direct output from the model (the version of MARKAL used at this point simply reported total energy system cost, with no representation of the rest of the economy). Rather, they were calculated 'off-model' using MARKAL output and other simple assumptions and are noted by the modellers in the supporting material (DTI 2003b, p. 76) as being a 'ball park estimate'.

Furthermore, a memo published by DTI on the use of MARKAL modelling for the 2003 White Paper noted that 'there is great uncertainty about the forecasts which [MARKAL] provides' and that 'this type of approach is better suited to consideration of long-run impacts than transitional costs' (DTI, no date, p. 5). The fact that these GDP figures are given such prominence reflects the extent to which the economic cost of emissions reductions was central to the policy debate. Indeed, in an evaluation of the RCEP report, the Institute for European Environmental Policy (IEEP 2005, p. 51) explains that:

> DTI carried out a parallel modelling exercise using the MARKAL model, and concluded from this that the technology required could be installed at a relatively modest cost . . . .. It is understood that this exercise overcame a key barrier to acceptance of the 60 per cent target, and appears greatly to have helped develop a positive attitude to carbon reductions in government.

The findings of the White Paper, and the role played therein by MARKAL, were not without their critics – although some of these perhaps credited MARKAL with more influence than it actually had. For example, during a House of Lords Select Committee hearing, Dr Dieter Helm noted:

> It is very important in this context to bear in mind that one of the advantages of MARKAL is to show you that if you pick certain assumptions you get particular answers. It turns out the government was deeply interested in a solution to the climate change problem which was largely based on wind and energy

efficiency and not much else, particularly not nuclear power ... *I am not at all clear in the policy process that the people making decisions fully understood how dependent they were on the nature of the assumptions that were going into the answer.* (House of Lords Select Committee on Economic Affairs 2005b, Q264–279, emphasis added)

Helm's evidence and that of other critics of the model led to the House of Lords concluding that '[w]e are concerned that UK energy and climate policy appears to rest on a very debatable model of the energy-economic system and on dubious assumptions about the costs of meeting the long-run 60% target' (House of Lords Select Committee on Economic Affairs 2005a, para 94). Despite this and, we would suggest, drawing strength from the increasing policy salience of climate change and the dearth of alternative models, MARKAL continued to play an important analytical role as the government further developed its more pro-active energy policy.

Use in the 2007 Energy White Paper

In 2007, MARKAL was used to support the government's subsequent White Paper *Meeting the Energy Challenge* (DTI 2007a). The Stern Review (Stern 2007) also added to a growing body of literature that underscored the urgency of reacting promptly to climate change. In addition to this, however, rapid rises in gas and oil prices which had occurred led to the issue of energy security joining carbon mitigation as a priority for energy policy (Pearson and Watson 2012). Following the Stern Review, the likely costs and benefits of a low-carbon transition continued to be an important element of the policy debate. In response, *Meeting the Energy Challenge* made use of the newer version (MARKAL–MACRO), which links MARKAL to a simple macroeconomic model. Unlike the standard version, MARKAL–MACRO can directly estimate the impacts on GDP of emissions reduction. However, use of this new model did not dramatically change the estimates of GDP impacts and many of the limitations associated with the 2003 MARKAL version, such as the omission of transition and behavioural costs, were still relevant.

Perhaps as a result of the earlier criticism, the 2007 White Paper discusses in some detail the cost estimates and their limitations, making clear how and why MARKAL results can 'be expected to produce lower-bound estimates of the costs of carbon abatement' (DTI 2007a, p.292). Additionally, the 2007 document compensates for some of the weaknesses of MARKAL by also drawing on the results of other models. Yet the use of MARKAL to support the 2007 White Paper went far beyond calculating GDP impacts. *Meeting the Energy Challenge* explains its use of MARKAL–MACRO in the following terms: 'for the period to 2050, we have used a model of the entire UK energy system (UK MARKAL–Macro model) to explore the changes to the amount and use of energy required if we are to deliver our goal of reducing carbon emissions by 60% by 2050 at least cost' (DTI 2007a, p. 194).

MARKAL was also used to support a subtle change in government attitudes to what was at the time one of the most controversial of the technology options, nuclear power. The 2003 White Paper had concluded that 'its current economics make [nuclear] an unattractive option for new, carbon-free generating capacity' (DTI 2003a, p. 12), despite it making a significant contribution in many of the MARKAL scenarios developed as part of the supporting analysis. However, in the 2007 White Paper the technological results from MARKAL are given greater prominence, including sensitivity analyses of key parameters such as future fuel prices and innovation rates and runs to examine the impact of excluding certain technologies. These led to the conclusion that 'excluding nuclear is a more expensive route to achieving our carbon goal even though in our modelling, the costs of alternative technologies are assumed to fall over time as they mature' (DTI 2007a, p. 194).

This change in the government's stance on nuclear power was likely for a wide variety of reasons, including (but not limited to) the increased importance of security of supply, improvements in nuclear waste storage prospects and rising fossil fuel prices (DTI 2007a, pp. 180–216). However, the ability of MARKAL to clearly demonstrate the economic value of nuclear power appears to have been an important element in justifying nuclear as a low carbon option.

Use in Relation to the Climate Change Act

Following the 2007 Energy White Paper, the government published a draft Climate Change Bill, which became an Act of Parliament in 2008. This put in place a new legislative framework of five-year carbon budgets and established an independent Committee on Climate Change to advise government on the level of these budgets. As of mid-2013, the most recent use of MARKAL within this context has been in *The Carbon Plan*, published by the Department of Energy and Climate Change in 2011 (HMG 2011), which sets out proposals and policies for meeting the first four carbon budgets (covering the period to 2027). This report continued to rely substantially on quantitative modelling results to envisage how best to achieve the emission reduction targets (AEA 2011). The *Carbon Plan* states that: 'in line with our principle of seeking the most cost effective technology mix, our starting point for this has been to take the outputs of the "core" run of the cost-optimizing model, MARKAL' and that this core run 'illustrat[es] the technologies likely to contribute to reducing emissions, and the most cost effective timing for their deployment' (HMG 2011, p. 16). It should be noted that MARKAL is not the only model used to inform the *Carbon Plan*, which also draws on results from ESME (developed by the Energy Technologies Institute) and DECC's own Carbon Calculator. The *Carbon Plan* made use of MARKAL–'Elastic Demand', or MED, another variant on the standard version of the MARKAL model, in which the level of demand for energy services varies according to the costs of meeting them, based on a set of user-specified price elasticities. This is framed in the published reports as providing some insight into how changes in consumer behaviour (for example, lifestyle changes) could influence reductions in carbon emissions.

Use by the UK Committee on Climate Change

The Committee on Climate Change (CCC) has itself arisen as an institutional innovation from the changing energy-climate policy conception (other such innovations include the Low Carbon Innovation Co-ordination Group, which has also used results from MARKAL among other models). While the CCC shares the need of central government to analyse costs and technology pathways, it is not in the position of having to justify specific legislative proposals in the impact assessment format specified by the Treasury. While government departments have a strong need for tools that provide closure around specific options, the CCC is able to take a more reflective and advisory approach – including more explicit acknowledgement of the many uncertainties.

The Committee's first carbon budget report (CCC 2008) was the first policy venue to use the MARKAL–Elastic Demand (MED) model to examine the economic and technological implications for reducing carbon emissions by 80 or 90 per cent by 2050 (AEA 2008a; 2008b). The CCC appears to differ from other venues in the way in which it approaches assumptions and limitations of the modelling process. A frequently referenced limitation of the MARKAL model is its assumption of perfect foresight, meaning that the model is unable to capture the impact of uncertainty associated with factors such as technological innovation rates or fuel prices. While this limitation of modelling results is acknowledged and discussed in publications from government departments, modelling in support of the CCC's fourth carbon budget goes much further to overcome these limitations. Work for the CCC's fourth carbon budget (Usher and Strachan 2010), reported also in the fourth carbon budget report

(CCC 2011) deepens the focus on uncertainties by making use of the stochastic formulation of MARKAL.

Other Policy Venues

The Technology Innovation Needs Assessment (TINA) led by the Low
Carbon Innovation Co-ordination Group (made up of government departments and other stakeholders) has used MARKAL and ESME outputs
in identifying technology and innovation needs. Apart from its use within
government departments and by the CCC, MARKAL has also been used
in an NGO policy venue context, by the Institute for Public Policy Research
in collaboration with the World Wildlife Fund (WWF) and Royal Society
for the Protection of Birds in a report on reducing national carbon emission by 80 per cent by 2050 (IPPR et al. 2007). The goal of this work was
to demonstrate how an 80 per cent target was within reach, both economically and technically, whilst excluding new nuclear build, placing limits on
the use of both wind and biofuels and including emissions from international aviation in the analysis. In comparison with the 60 per cent target
held in government policy at the time of publication, this study explores
a far more ambitious future, 'effectively establish[ing] an upper bound on
technological feasibility and costs' (IPPR et al. 2007, p. 6). The model used
in the analysis is based largely on the MARKAL–MACRO model used in
the 2007 Energy White Paper (Strachan et al. 2009). Although the report
states that it uses the same underlying assumptions as the government and
the Stern Review (IPPR et al. 2007, p. 4), the modification of just a few
key parameters in MARKAL can have a substantial influence upon the
results.

MARKAL AS A BOUNDARY OBJECT

In our view, a changing consensus on the policy image of the energy-
climate policy nexus or problem has supported changing but sustained, if
differentiated, use of MARKAL by several different but intersecting policy
communities. From information flow and systems perspectives, Fong et al.
(2007, pp. 16–17) observe that the value of a boundary object depends
primarily on how well it can 'decontextualize knowledge on one side of a
boundary and recontextualize it on the other side'. MARKAL is far from
readily comprehensible by all, but we would suggest that its technological focus has made it valuable to a number of influential constituencies,
particularly those with private or public interests in advancing the R&D
required for energy system transformation.

The model also has further, interrelated attributes that lend themselves to playing a boundary object role. As an optimization model, MARKAL sets in the foreground the more knowable and more analytically tractable elements of a pathway to meeting targets, while putting in the background issues such as the politics and cultural and behavioural dimensions and (largely) the interaction with the macro-economy. As such, it facilitates the (perhaps tacit) belief that it is possible to 'plan' (more or less) an explicitly 'optimal' transition to a low-carbon energy system, in cost terms. Other modelling paradigms, such as a macroeconomic model with some form of endogenous technological change, could be considered just as valid an approach to thinking through some of the same issues. These would not, though, provide the policy image of a clear, technology-based roadmap, nor the sense of control over the structure and evolution of the energy system. Indeed, part of MARKAL's appeal is that it is not confined by historical relationships and hence allows users to envisage new energy systems; conversely, however, its recommendations risk being divorced from institutional and behavioural realities, often conceived of as 'barriers'. This capacity for facilitating new visions and new scenarios seems to help in gaining consensus across influential communities. One could even say that there is an affective role to scenario tools such as MARKAL, in that they give *hope* that different energy futures are possible. In a sense such tools are socially progressive, capable of supporting the imagining of radically different futures, freed from the constraints of some of the more difficult realities. Others, too, have commented on the role of technological imaginaries in aspects of UK energy policy (Levidow and Papaioannou 2013). To date, little has been said about the role of models in this regard, which we would suggest in the case of MARKAL has been highly influential.

Yet, the aspects of the future that MARKAL envisages are limited and largely technical. MARKAL enables one to examine radical change within the energy system but the model is not designed to capture directly those dimensions of change that are more emergent, uncertain, ungovernable and harder to quantify. These include aspects of political, social, corporate and other understandings of, and responses to, attempts to manage a transition. These in turn relate to, for example, perceptions of the distribution of costs and benefits to different parts of society; issues of market structure, vigorously debated during the Electricity Market Reform process in the UK; the institutional and policy arrangements required to enact change as rapidly as that depicted in MARKAL scenario results; and the culturally and socially embedded nature and determinants of consumer energy demand. In short, MARKAL is forced to meet particular targets but questions about their political feasibility, and the institutional arrangements and political strategies necessary to meet them, are unaddressed. Arguably, the reduction of these and other issues to indirect representation via demand elasticities (a feature also typical of other models), helps to connect elite communities by the act of elision: controversy is avoided or reduced by the reductionist shift to technical parameters.

In the use of MARKAL, we see mutually supportive connections between interests. Some aspects of the dispositional variant of the advocacy model referred to by Hoppe (2005) are evident, in which science and technology advisors and policy actors are seen as jointly shaping political discourse around a central story line (Hajer 1995), problem definition (van der Sluys 1997), or rhetorical style (Hood 1998), in a way that connects different epistemic and interest communities and government agencies, to form interlocking networks of knowledge and power or discourse coalitions (Wittrock 1991, p. 333). However, advocacy would be too strong a description of the actuality in this case, at least on the academic-consultancy side. Rather there is co-production of knowledge and understanding, and some degree of policy shaping by those within and outside formal government organizations. Moreover, as suggested above, the nature of MARKAL itself determines what can and cannot be modelled and further shapes policy through its own authority and the legitimacy given to its output, particularly through the privileging of techno-economic and numerical information.

In the latter, we see something of the potentially *exclusive* aspect of a boundary object: it binds communities with overlapping interests but this may also confer a certain political power and the ability to resist attack or critique by those with different agendas or views. MARKAL is unlikely to be replaced in its particular role until the policy image of the climate-energy problem changes once again, or until alternative models are perceived to perform the same role in a better or preferable way. In this respect, UK energy modelling has been described as in need of a broader range of analytical tools (Strachan 2011) and perhaps a likely scenario is that MARKAL becomes supplemented by a number of tools suited for related but different purposes: as and when the energy policy problem becomes perceived as more differentiated and multifaceted, so the opportunity for policy entry by additional and/or alternative tools will arise. If these are to succeed, it is important that they, too, are capable of delivering output capable of being rendered (translated) by and for multiple influential constituencies and, moreover, of supporting the interests of those communities.

Moreover, the mode of use of a policy-relevant tool is likely to vary by institutional context and MARKAL is no exception in this regard. Drawing on a large body of policy literature, Hertin et al. (2009) identify three main types of knowledge use: conceptual learning, when knowledge gradually allows new information, ideas and perspectives to enter the policy system; instrumental learning, when knowledge directly informs concrete decisions; and political use, when knowledge is used to attain political objectives, including justification of decisions already taken. Looking across policy venues, use of MARKAL would seem to fall into each of these categories, though definitive claims are generally difficult to make in these contexts.

CONCLUSIONS

In this chapter, we have described the way in which a particular model, namely the MARKAL least-cost energy system model and its variants, has achieved considerable influence in UK energy and climate policy, being deployed in several key policy venues and over a considerable period of time. We have accounted for this influence in terms of the various outputs of MARKAL being transferable across contexts, to support alternative, long-term technological visions in a timely and flexible manner. MARKAL's target-oriented capabilities and technological focus arguably reduce the opportunity for controversy and political friction, while serving the needs of private as well as public sector constituencies with an interest in the major research, innovation and deployment needs of energy system transformation. Despite the relative opacity of the MARKAL model and the limitations of numerical models in terms of capturing important qualitative aspects of energy system change, for the time being it continues to function as a successful boundary object, capable of being deployed in response to changing images of the climate-energy policy problem in the UK. Of course, it is thoroughly dependent on the existence of related policy priorities and it would certainly be instructive to compare the use of models in other national contexts, particularly where climate policy is afforded a lesser priority.

In terms of future research directions, a key issue is how the policy use of this particularly long-standing model (and its successor, the closely related TIMES model) will develop (a) in relation to other modelling tools suited to similar purposes and (b) in relation to the increasing understanding that energy system models typically have limited capacity to engage with the social factors that are critical in socio-technical transitions. In the context of climate change, despite social, institutional and policy innovation arguably being more urgent than technological innovation (Upham et al. 2013), the primary focus of innovation funding and discourse remains technological (ibid). Energy policy modelling remains likewise largely technology-focused. There are many reasons for this, not the least of which is that technology development has a broad, supportive constituency arising from its economic value to particular actors, whereas behavioural and social changes tend to have more diffused, social benefits (often relating to a reduction in various social costs rather than an increase in income) (ibid), tend to be more controversial, difficult to steer and anticipate and hence more difficult to model. If we were to take one key message from the social and behavioural change literature (Whitmarsh et al. 2011), it would be that most people view energy as thoroughly embedded in their daily lives, which of course it is. Yet this means that energy policy is de facto inseparable from other policy arenas and it means that when individual and organizational decision makers make energy-related choices, consciously or unconsciously, cost-based decision rules are unlikely to capture the range of possible or likely outcomes. Given this, it may well be that those macro energy policy modelling tools that are best able to make use of other types of data, be this gained through qualitative or quantitative techniques, will function as the most successful boundary spanners, bringing together the various constituencies of energy transitions.

Finally, it should be noted that there is an historical contingency to policy model use, even if this use may be relatively sustained. The period that we have documented has witnessed a political consensus emerge in the UK about the need for decarbonization. This consensus appears less secure at the time of this writing than it did in the late 2000s. As the image of the policy problem continues to shift, the alignment between policymaker focus and model paradigm may no longer hold, creating space for alternative tools – perhaps tools that engage better with affordability and equity, social innovation or smart grid systems – to compete with MARKAL.

ACKNOWLEDGEMENTS

David Christopherson acknowledges support from the EPSRC Future Leaders Research Internship Scheme.

This chapter draws on the related paper: Taylor, P. G., P. Upham, W. McDowall, and D. Christopherson (2014), 'Energy model, boundary object and societal lens: 35 years of the MARKAL model in the UK', *Energy Research and Social Science*, **4**, 32–41.

NOTE

1. While the wider case for action in this form was made through the Stern Review, MARKAL enables assessment of particular options for taking that action.

REFERENCES

AEA (2008a), *MARKAL-MED Model Runs of Long-Term Carbon Reduction Targets in the UK. Phase 1*, Didcot: AEA, retrieved from http://www.theccc.org.uk/publication/building-a-low-carbon-economy-the-uks-contribution-to-tackling-climate-change-2/ (accessed 31 October 2013).

AEA (2008b), *MARKAL–MED Model Runs of Long Term Carbon Reduction Targets in the UK. Phase 2*, Didcot: AEA, retrieved from http://www.theccc.org.uk/publication/building-a-low-carbon-economy-the-uks-contribution-to-tackling-climate-change-2/ (accessed 31 October 2013).

AEA (2011), *Pathways to 2050 – Detailed Analyses. MARKAL Model Review and Scenarios for DECC's 4th Carbon Budget Evidence Base*, Didcot: AEA, retrieved from https://www.gov.uk/government/uploads/system/uploads/attachment_data/file/48073/2270-pathways-to-2050-detailed-analyses.pdf (accessed 31 October 2013).

Altdorfer, F., M. Blasco, G. Egberts et al. (1979), 'Energy modelling as an instrument for an international strategy for energy research, development and demonstration', *International Conference on Energy Systems Analysis*, Dublin: D. Reidel Publishing Company, pp. 140–157.

Anandarajah, G. and W. McDowall (2012), 'What are the costs of Scotland's climate and renewable policies?', *Energy Policy*, **50**, 773–783.

Baumgartner, F.R. and B.D. Jones (1993), *Agendas and Instability in American Politics*, Chicago, London: The University of Chicago Press.

Baumgartner, F.R. and B.D. Jones (eds) (2002), *Policy Dynamics*, Chicago, London: The University of Chicago Press.

CCC (2008), *Building a Low-Carbon Economy – The UK's Contribution to Tackling Climate Change*, London: Committee on Climate Change, retrieved from http://www.theccc.org.uk/publication/building-a-low-carbon-economy-the-uks-contribution-to-tackling-climate-change-2/ (accessed 31 October 2013).

CCC (2011), The Fourth Carbon Budget Reducing emissions through the 2020s, London: Committee on Climate Change, retrieved from http://www.theccc.org.uk/publication/the-fourth-carbon-budget-reducing-emissions-through-the-2020s-2/ (accessed 31 October 2013).

Department of Energy (1982), Speech on energy policy: given by the Rt Hon Nigel Lawson MP, Secretary of State for Energy, to the International Association of Energy Economists on 28 June 1982, London: Her Majesty's Stationery Office. Also cited in P. Pearson and J. Watson (2012), *UK Energy Policy 1980–2010. A History and Lessons to be Learned*, London: The Parliamentary Group for Energy Studies, retrieved from http://www.theiet.org/factfiles/energy/uk-energy-policy-page.cfm (accessed 31 October 2013).

DTI (Department of Trade and Industry) (1992), *Energy-Related Carbon Emissions in Possible Future Scenarios for the United Kingdom*, London: HMSO.

DTI (1995), *Energy Projections for the UK: Energy Use and Energy-Related Emissions of Carbon Dioxide in the UK, 1995–2020*, London: HMSO.

DTI (2000), *Energy Projections for the UK: Energy Use and Energy-Related Emissions of Carbon Dioxide in the UK, 2000–2020*, London: The Stationery Office.

DTI (2003a), *Our Energy Future – Creating a Low Carbon Economy*, London: DTI.

DTI (2003b), *Options for a Low Carbon Future*, DTI Economics, Paper No. 4, London: DTI.

DTI (2007a), *Meeting the Energy Challenge*, London: DTI.

DTI (no date), *White Paper Modelling – Use of the MARKAL Energy Model*, retrieved from https://www.gov.uk/government/uploads/system/uploads/attachment_data/file/48122/file21348.pdf (accessed 31 October 2013).

Ekins, P., G. Anandarajah and N. Strachan (2011), 'Towards a low-carbon economy: scenarios and policies for the UK', *Climate Policy*, **11**, 865–882.

ETSU (1994a), *An Appraisal of UK Energy Research, Development, Demonstration and Dissemination*, London: HMSO.

ETSU (1994b), *An Assessment of Renewable Energy for the UK*, London: HMSO.

Evans, R. (2000), 'Economic models and economic policy: what economic forecasters can do for government', in F.A.G. den Butter and M.S. Morgan (eds), *Empirical Models and Policy-Making*, London, New York: Routledge, pp. 206–228.

Finnis, M.W. (1980), *Phase II Final Report of MARKAL Studies for the United Kingdom*, Jülich, Germany, Kernforschungsanlage Jülich.

Fong, A., R. Valerdi and J. Srinivasan (2007), 'Boundary objects as a framework to understand the role of systems integrators', *Systems Research Forum*, **2**, 11–18.

Hajer, M. (1995), *The Politics of Environmental Discourse: Ecological Modernisation and the Policy Process*, Oxford: Clarendon Press.

Hertin, J., J. Turnpenny, A. Jordan, M. Nilsson, D. Russel and B. Nykvist (2009), 'Rationalising the policy mess? Ex ante policy assessment and the utilisation of knowledge in the policy process', *Environment and Planning A*, **41** (5), 1185–1200.

HM Treasury (2011), *The Green Book*, London: TSO.

HMG (2011), *The Carbon Plan: Delivering our Low Carbon Future*, London: Department of Energy and Climate Change.

Hood, C. (1998), *The Art of the State. Culture, Rhetoric and Public Management*, Oxford: Clarendon Press.

Hoppe, R. (2005), 'Rethinking the science–policy nexus: from knowledge utilization and science technology studies to types of boundary arrangements', *Poiesis and Praxis: International Journal of Technology Assessment and Ethics of Science*, **3** (3), 199–215.

House of Lords Select Committee on Economic Affairs (2005a), *The Economics of Climate Change. Volume I: Report. HL (2005–06, 12–I)*, London: House of Lords.

House of Lords Select Committee on Economic Affairs (2005b), *The Economics of Climate Change. Volume II: Evidence. HL (2005–06, 12–II)*, London: House of Lords.

IEEP (2005), *Evaluation of the 22nd Report of the Royal Commission on Environmental Pollution 'Energy: the Changing Climate'. Final report*, London: IEEP, retrieved from http://tinyurl.com/pvkulet (accessed 16 July 2014).

IPPR, WWF and RSPB (2007), *80% Challenge – Delivering a Low Carbon UK*, London: IPPR, retrieved from www.ippr.org/publications/80-challenge-delivering-a-low-carbon-uk (accessed 21 February 2015).

Kingdon, J.W. (1995), *Agendas, Alternatives and Public Policies*, London: Longman.

Levidow, L. and T. Papaioannou (2013), 'State imaginaries of the public good: shaping UK innovation priorities for bioenergy', *Environmental Science & Policy*, **30**, 36–49.

MacKenzie, D. and Y. Millo (2003), 'Constructing a market, performing theory: the historical sociology of a financial exchange', *American Journal of Sociology*, **109** (1), 107–145.

Mattila, E. (2005), '"Interdisciplinarity" in the making: modeling infectious diseases', *Perspectives on Science*, **3** (4), 531–554.

Pearson, P. and J. Watson (2012), *UK Energy Policy 1980–2010: A History and Lessons to be Learned*, London: Institution for Engineering Technology and Parliamentary Group for Energy Studies.

Princen, S. (2000), *Agenda-Setting in the European Union*, Basingstoke: Palgrave.

RCEP (Royal Commission on Environmental Pollution) (2000), *Energy – The Changing Climate*, 22nd Report, London: The Stationery Office.

Shackley, S. and B. Wynne (1995), 'Global climate change: the mutual construction of an emergent science–policy domain', *Science and Public Policy*, **22** (4), 218–230.

Star, S.L. and J.R. Griesemer (1989), 'Institutional ecology, "translations" and boundary objects: amateurs and professionals in Berkeley's Museum of Vertebrate Zoology, 1907–39', *Social Studies of Science*, **19**, 387–420.

Stern, N. (2007), *The Economics of Climate Change: The Stern Review*, Cambridge: Cambridge University Press.

Strachan, N. (2011), 'UK energy policy ambition and UK energy modelling – fit for purpose?', *Energy Policy*, **39**, 1037–1040.

Strachan, N., S. Pye and R. Kannan (2009), 'The iterative contribution and relevance of modelling to UK energy policy', *Energy Policy*, **37** (3), 850–860.

Upham, P., P. Kivimaa and V. Virkamäki (2013), 'Path dependency in transportation system policy: a comparison of Finland and the UK', *Journal of Transport Geography*, **32**, 12–22.

Usher, W. and N. Strachan (2010), *UK MARKAL Modelling – Examining Decarbonisation Pathways in the 2020s on the Way to Meeting the 2050 Emissions Target. Final Report for the Committee on Climate Change*, London: University College London.

van Daalen, C.E., L. van Dresen and M.A. Janssen (2002), 'The roles of computer models in the environmental policy life cycle', *Environmental Science and Policy*, **5**, 221–231.

van der Sluys, J. (1997), *Anchoring Amid Uncertainty. On the Management of Uncertainties in Risk Assessment of Anthropogenic Climate Change*, Leiden: Mosterd en van Onderen.

van Egmond, S. and R. Zeiss (2010), 'Modeling for policy: science-based models as performative boundary objects for Dutch policy making', *Science Studies*, **23** (1), 58–78.

Whitmarsh, L., P. Upham, W. Poortinga et al. (2011), *Public Attitudes to and Engagement with Low-Carbon Energy: A Selective Review of Academic and Non-academic Literatures. Report for RCUK Energy Programme*, London: Research Councils UK.

Wittrock, B. (1991), 'Social knowledge and public policy: eight models of interaction', in P. Wagner, C.H. Weiss, B. Wittrock and H. Wollman (eds), *Social Sciences and Modern States, National Experiences and Theoretical Crossroads*, Cambridge: Cambridge University Press, pp. 333–353.

PART IV

Conclusions and new directions

13. The tools of policy formulation: new perspectives and new challenges

Andrew J. Jordan, John R. Turnpenny and Tim Rayner

INTRODUCTION

It is generally accepted that policy tools and instruments exist at all stages of the policy process (Howlett 2011, p. 22). But as was pointed out in Chapter 1, only some tools and instruments, operating at certain policy stages, have garnered the sustained analytical attention of policy researchers. Policy formulation – a very important but imperfectly understood stage – has certainly been targeted by developers of new tools, ranging from foresight and scenario tools that seek to open up problem framings and conceptualizations, through to tools like cost–benefit analysis (CBA) that seek to recommend preferred policy solutions. Tool developers and policy analysts have also made many normative recommendations on how these and other policy formulation tools *should* be used (Vining and Weimer 2010; Dunn 2004). But as was made clear in Chapter 1, mainstream policy researchers have largely ignored policy formulation tools, meaning that a lot less is known about how they have actually been utilized in practice. As Howlett et al. (Chapter 8) suggest, policy researchers have long suspected that they probably play some role in structuring policymaking activity, but what that function is remains a largely unexplored research topic.

The general aim of this book is to investigate – for the first time – what can be gained by bringing the study of policy formulation tools back into the mainstream of public policy research. We say 'back into' because having been a central concern of policy analysis in the 1950s and 1960s, it gradually fell out of fashion and, as Chapter 1 explained, policy researchers turned their attention to the fine detail of a small sub-set of the policy implementation instruments, namely regulation and taxation. The aim of our final chapter is to draw upon the findings of the empirical chapters to identify some initial conclusions and pinpoint a number of promising new avenues for research on policy formulation tools. Conscious that this has the look and feel of a sub-field 'in the making', in the second section we begin by critically reflecting on the typology and definition of tools proposed in Chapter 1. Given the current state of knowledge, we believe it is especially important to engage in basic, foundational activities such as these, otherwise the sub-field will not consolidate quickly enough to support future endeavours. We then analyse all the chapters (2–12) from the perspective of the analytical framework for understanding policy formulation tools, covering *actors, venues, capacities* and *effects*.

In the third section, we seek to make sense of this rich empirical detail by drawing on relevant policy theories. In our view, it would be a mistake to develop a dedicated theory of policy formulation tools as this would perpetuate the isolation of the sub-field. A more productive strategy is, as many scholars of policy instruments have finally come to recognize (Jordan et al. 2013), to build upon and where possible enrich more general policy theoretical frameworks. Unlike tool theories that mostly operate at the micro level, these frameworks allow analysts to move beyond definitions and typologies, towards more conditional explanations of tool choices, capacities and uses. To that end, the third section explains why and how three particular bodies of theory are especially well suited to this task. We show that potentially one of the most valuable functions performed by the theories is to problematize the underlying motive for using the tools in the first place (and hence task(s) to be accomplished). Recall from Chapter 1 that when the tools first began to emerge in the 1950s, they were mainly perceived as a means to harvest information to help decision makers address the substantive aspects of policy problems (Radin 2013, p. 23). Consequently, we start with theories which broadly correspond to this fairly rationalistic and linear conceptualization of policy formulation, before moving onto other, rather different motives and/or tasks. Finally, the last section reflects on what a more systematic approach to examining the tools may add to our collective understanding of – in turn – the tools themselves, policy formulation and policymaking more generally, politics, and finally, the field of policy analysis. Throughout, we pinpoint some critical challenges that are likely to emerge as a new sub-field of policy research of tools coalesces and matures.

THE TOOLS OF POLICY FORMULATION

Definitions and Typologies

In Chapter 1, we argued that policy formulation tools constitute a particular category of policy tools, which is analytically distinct from the implementing instruments exhaustively catalogued by Salamon (2002) and the procedural instruments identified by Howlett (2000). We defined a policy formulation tool as:

> a technique, scheme, device or operation (including – but not limited to – those developed in the fields of economics, mathematics, statistics, computing, operations research and systems dynamics), which can be used to collect, condense and make sense of different kinds of policy relevant knowledge to perform some or all of the various inter-linked tasks of policy formulation.

On reflection, we believe that this definition is sufficiently broad to capture all the relevant tools, including, crucially, those developed within both positivist and post-positivist traditions. Below, we dwell a little more on what is meant by the tasks of policy formulation. But for now, it is sufficient to note that a broad definition allows the full range of tools explored in this book to be brought out of the 'back room' and studied in a more politically attuned and comparable fashion.

A broad definition also allowed us to propose a comprehensive typology of the main tool types (see Table 1.1), which maps onto – to quote our definition – 'the interlinked tasks of policy formulation'. Crucially, it relates the tool functions as they are often presented – in other words, according to idealized, 'textbook' functions – to the policy formulation tasks that they have potential to be harnessed to in practice. The typology does this by deliberately not, as has often been done in the past, drawing on the 'idealized' policy appraisal steps or the internal specifications of particular tools, both of which assume that the tools are centre-stage. Rather, it attempts to situate tools within an appreciation of what actually goes on in policy formulation.

At the broadest level (and drawing on Chapters 2–7), the various tools do seek to address different policy formulation tasks. For example, scenarios were originally created to explore different visions and objectives, as opposed to recommending a particular policy response, a task for which CBA was designed and appears much better suited. In addition, to the extent that their main task is to collect, condense and make sense of policy-relevant information, there appears to be no significant overlap between policy formulation tools and the main implementing instruments. In fact, they are different entities: policy formulation tools can and are used to assess the impacts of different implementing instruments.

However, when confronted by the rich empirical detail contained in Chapters 2–7, we can appreciate that Table 1.1 misses some important nuances. First, many of the main tool types contain many more subtypes than we originally expected. For example, there are prospective, explorative and descriptive types of scenarios; descriptive, performance and composite types of indicators; and multi-attribute, outranking and interactive forms of MCA. And one of the striking findings of Chapter 2 was that participatory tools are in fact an agglomeration of many different tools and methods. Nonetheless, speaking in favour of Table 1.1, there does not appear to be a significant degree of overlap between the main subtypes.

Second, in spite of this variety, many tools do not simply stand alone as separate and clearly specified entities. Some appear to defy the assumption that their application is necessarily an exclusive, expert-led affair; for instance, scenario tools, CBA and MCA can all be applied in a more or a less participatory fashion. Third, and relating to how tools may – in theory – be applied in practice, some of the more technical, substantive and content-related tools (such as CBA) seem to have relatively 'hard' boundaries, which in turn encourage score cards and other measures of the quality of application. By contrast, the more process-based tools such as scenarios and participatory tools have relatively fuzzy boundaries, with much less agreement on purposes and methods of quality evaluation. For these, the quality of application is even more value-laden a judgement. This could be why some chapters (for example, Chapter 2) have the word 'tools' in the title whereas others (for example, Chapter 7) refer to 'a tool'.

Finally, tools do not necessarily map neatly onto policy formulation tasks; they may be appropriate for different tasks in different ways. To take two examples, the same tools may be used for options assessment and to assist with selecting a policy design, and scenarios can be used to characterize problems as well as clarify objectives. This should not be too surprising: in Chapter 1 we noted that the policy formulation tasks are often interlinked in practice and do not necessarily follow a linear progression. Expecting anything different would be to conflate policy *formulation* with an idealized conception of policy *assessment*.

Therefore, on closer inspection, creating a usable typology of formulation tools is not as straightforward as one might imagine. In fact, this difficulty might explain why so many tool developers and users have invested so much (perhaps far too much?) time and effort in debating typologies and toolkits (Chapter 1) of decision support tools. Simply listing the policy formulation tools (as is done in Table 8.2, for example) is not a typology; similarly the distinction between simple, formal and advanced tools (see Chapter 1) does not appear to suffice either (for example, depending on the venue of use, CBA can be practised in all three forms). If used flexibly, therefore – an assumption which we open up a little more below – we believe that Table 1.1 offers a sufficiently sharp analytical device for organizing and making sense of the main (sub)types, and flagging how they are intended to work in principle. It provides a better way to organize the formulation tools than the broader typologies that have been created to encompass all tools and instruments (such as Hood (1983)). And, crucially, when used alongside the more finely grained typologies that have been developed for the implementing (Salamon 2002) and procedural instruments (Howlett 2000), it draws the observer's attention to some significant differences that have not attracted sufficient discussion in the instruments literature until now.

So far the discussion of Table 1.1 has been about policy formulation tools as they are designed and could theoretically be deployed. In the following subsections we explore – via our analytical framework – how these tasks (or uses) work out in practice.

Actors

The first element of the analytical framework concerns the *actors* who develop and/or promote particular policy formulation tools. As well as highlighting the critical importance of agency in tool selection and deployment, this element speaks to a broader debate, raised in Chapter 1, about the status and behaviour of the various policy formulators. Across the 11 empirical chapters, three main types of actor appear to have actively promoted and/or developed policy formulation tools: *decision makers; knowledge producers* and/or *providers*; and *knowledge brokers* (Howlett 2011, pp. 31–33).

Decision makers at state and international levels have been assiduous promoters of policy formulation tools, almost since the dawn of policy analysis (Dunn 2004, p. 40). Chapter 7 confirms that states were an early and influential promoter of CBA as the 'cornerstone of modern policy analysis' (Mintrom and Williams 2013, p. 5). CBA was initially developed in the 1930s to take the political heat (and conflict) out of state-planned and funded infrastructure projects such as dams – a role, incidentally, now being reprised in the developing world (Chapter 10). Nowadays, national finance ministries and core executives continue to support the application of indicators and CBA through the publication of rules, statutes and best practice guides (Chapters 7 and 9), under different rhetorical banners including better regulation, administrative modernization and evidence-based policymaking. Governmental actors also work within international organizations such as the OECD and scientific bodies like the Intergovernmental Panel on Climate Change to share best practices on many tools, including scenarios (Chapter 3), indicators (Chapter 4) and CBA (Chapter 7). The research arm of the European Commission has directly funded many complex computer models (Nilsson et al. 2008) and taken active steps to ensure they are more heavily utilized in formalized systems of policy-level appraisal (Chapter 9). Chapter 9 identifies the policy officials in line ministries that undertake such appraisal as both potential users and promoters of the tools. We explore their motives for doing these things below.

Under the category of *knowledge producers* and/or *providers*, the chapters identify a myriad of actors, in state and non-state settings, who variously:

- Invent tools and numerous variants thereof (for example, academics and technical officials in state bureaucracies);
- Refine and update them (for example, scenario developers);
- Provide the policy-relevant knowledge that is fed into policy formulation activities (for example, statisticians, policy specialists and special advisers).

Academics have constituted a notable source of support for tools. Initially it was economists with strong technical skills (Mintrom and Williams 2013, p.4) who were in the vanguard, but then other disciplines fed a growing supply of tools such as indicators, MCA and computer modelling. Participatory approaches have emerged, very much out of the post-positivist critique of the policy sciences (Chapter 2). Tools, therefore, have both pragmatic (*how* to formulate policy) and normative (how policy *should* be formulated) underpinnings. Industry too has made notable contributions to the development of forecasting, simulation gaming (Chapter 2) and scenario tools (Chapter 3). Consultants and think tanks have also created complex modelling tools such as the influential MARKAL energy model (Chapter 12) as well as scenarios (Chapter 3), and been active disseminators of other tools across government (Chapter 8).

Finally, in some of the chapters, knowledge (or policy) brokers are identified as playing critically important roles. In theory, knowledge brokers are supposed to adopt a more or less neutral role between science and policy. In practice, there are many different subtypes and some chapters emphasize the potentially important role they play in matching tools to policy problems (for example, models to scenarios in processes of integrated assessment – see Chapter 5).

Crucially, all these actors are analytically distinct from the suppliers of policy-relevant knowledge (Radaelli 1995). The tools provide a means to turn knowledge to different policy purposes, that is, a translation function. The growth in policy formulation tools is a tangible manifestation of the broadening and deepening of the policy analysis and advisory community from one dominated by generalist bureaucrats and 'econocrats' (Mintrom and Williams 2013, p.9), to one comprising a multitude of actors within a more open and plural policy advisory system. Instead of 'speaking truth to power' as Wildavsky (1979) would have it, putting policy formulation tools alongside the actors that utilize them provides a sharper picture of how modern policy analysts seek to 'share the truth with many actors of influence' (Craft and Howlett 2012, p.85). Adopting a tools perspective on policy formulation – that is, following a particular tool as it is picked up and deployed in different policy formulation venues – arguably offers a new and potentially fruitful way to 'open up the black box' of policy formulation, supplementing the standard methods of following issues or focusing on policy advisory systems.

Venues

The second element of our analytical framework relates to the suggestion that policymakers apply tools in policy formulation venues, defined on the basis of their *location* (internal and external to government) and the *sources of knowledge* that they draw upon (official versus unofficial). In Chapter 1, we sought to open up two lines of potentially productive inquiry. First, by whom, for what purposes and in what form are tools used in particular policy formulation venues? By 'use' we mean that a particular tool has been specifically deployed to inform the formulation of policy, or its contribution has somehow been referenced or otherwise credited in a particular set of policy formulation activities. Second, what factors shape the selection and deployment of particular policy formulation tools?

Venues of use: by whom, for what purposes and in what form are tools used?
By *whom* have different policy formulation tools been used? In the past, the standard assumption in policy analysis was that it was the state and its constituent organizations that mainly selected and deployed the tools, with a particularly strong preference (according to Meltsner (1976) at least) for the more substantive-technical variants such as models and CBA (see also Chapter 1). In other words, tool use was mainly clustered in the internal-official quadrant of Figure 1.1. Much later Radin (2013) and others (Nilsson et al. 2008) argued that even in this quadrant, the use of such tools was greatly exaggerated; process-related tools such as checklists and participatory tools were at least as common (see Chapter 8), and in the other three quadrants of Figure 1.1 were likely to be relatively more common.

Chapters 2–12 show that these standard assumptions should indeed now be questioned. Evidently, there are many different actors involved in the policy formulation process, drawing upon and deploying a broad range of tools (in other words, tools are much more widely spread across the four quadrants in Figure 1.1). Nonetheless, the pattern of use across the venues is even more uneven (or 'lumpy') than Meltsner (1976) and Radin (2013) suggested. Chapters 8 and 9 offer a much more detailed insight into the differentiated patterns of uptake. Chapter 8 suggests that in Canada, more substantive-technical tools are more likely to be used in the governmental (as opposed to the NGO) sector, and in the more economically (as opposed to socially and environmentally) focused sectors. That said, even amongst government officials, Radin's suspicion does seem to hold true: government officials are more likely to use tools such as brainstorming, consultation exercises and checklists than more formalized tools such as CBA (see Table 8.2). Chapter 9 examines tool use in the relatively new and formalized venue of impact assessment (in other words, squarely in the top right quadrant of Figure 1.1) and finds a strong variation between countries where tools are hardly used at all, and others where their use is much more the norm. In other words, specific tools do not completely dominate specific venues.

A more general point emerges from many chapters: in practice it can be difficult to determine when a tool has been 'used' because it may not necessarily appear in its 'textbook' form, or be formally documented in a way that researchers can study empirically. The distinction between textbook and 'actual' forms stands out for tools such as CBA, which prescribe clear steps and procedures which are often not followed in practice (Chapter 7). For the less standardized tools, variable use is not simply difficult to measure but is often seen as a virtue – think of the 'contextualization' of modelling tools for example (Chapter 5) or the more exploratory types of participatory tool.

The chapters suggest too that the *purposes* to which the tools are put in the various policy formulation venues also exhibit a great deal of variation. Purposes can be thought of in at least two distinct senses: *vis-à-vis* the well-known *stages* or *steps of policy formulation* (as in Chapter 1); and in relation to the pre-existing 'design space' (Howlett 2011, p. 141), that is, does it seek a radical or a more incremental departure from the status quo? As regards the former, certain tools appear to be far better suited (and be more heavily used in relation) to certain policy formulation tasks than others. In Chapter 1, the first step was presented as being one of *problem characterization* (in other words, what is the nature of 'the problem'?). For this, scenarios and public participatory techniques seem to be uniquely well suited. Nevertheless, the more projective forms of modelling and even indicators can be used to – and, according to the chapter authors do – shape problem perceptions. The second step (*problem evaluation*) is something that scenarios and indicators appear to be better suited to. By contrast the final step (*policy design* – recommending a mix of policy interventions) is something that CBA and MCA were specifically designed to address, although participatory tools may also play a part in ensuring that the design process remains transparent and/or legitimate. Indicators may be less likely to recommend one single option, but they can be (and indeed are – Chapter 10) used to justify the option that is selected and help to monitor performance over time.

The other way to consider the purposes to which a tool is put is relate it to the pre-existing 'design space'. In other words, does it seek to implement the existing policy regime (comprising an internally consistent set of policy objectives, goals and instruments) (Howlett 2011, p.142), in a more efficient or cost-effective fashion, or does it seek to stretch the existing design space by incorporating new problem formulations or radically different policy approaches? In many tool-related literatures this is directly comparable to the distinction between policy analysis that 'opens up' debate and that which 'closes it down' (Stirling 2008). Here we come across the normative divide between tool developers whose goal is to 'open up' (see for example the debate in the participatory tools literature – Chapter 2) and those for whom 'selecting the best option' is the overriding priority (economists in particular seem to be the obvious exemplar). In Chapters 2–7, this fundamental difference was repeatedly stated; indeed in the chapter on participation (Chapter 2), the difference between so-called 'differentiation' and 'unification' divides the literature in two. Similarly, politicians may initially be attracted to tools such as indicators to 'open up' debate, but by adopting them may unwittingly end up 'closing down' political debate in a way that 'locks in' extant policy designs (Chapter 11).

Venues of use: what factors shape the selection and deployment of particular tools?

Originally, in the policy instruments literature the choice between tools was regarded as mainly determined by ideological factors (Doern and Phidd 1992). However, this assumption was quickly dropped and researchers set about exploring more specific/conditional factors. These are generally divided into the characteristics of the instruments themselves (whether they open up or close down; whether they match the steps in formulation – see above) and various external factors (actor constellation; situational/contextual conditions such as prevailing institutions; and international factors) (Bähr 2010, p.3; Peters 2002; Eliadis et al. 2007, p.40).

The literature on policy formulation tools is still too immature to test these explanations, although the authors of the chapters in Part III were asked to select different tool–venue relationships and explore them from their preferred theoretical vantage points. Nevertheless, taken together the 11 chapters hint at some possible explanations which could, in future, be more systematically tested. A number of attributes characteristic of the tools are cited in several of the chapters. For example, is a tool capable of (or salient to) the main policy formulation tasks to be addressed? A computer model, for example, must be capable of manipulating certain key variables to be deemed worthy of consideration. Similarly, indicators that are measurable, simple and adaptable appear more likely to be taken up than others. The idea, commonplace in the policy instruments literature, that policy tools are in principle substitutable (Hill 2009, p. 178), does not seem as applicable to policy formulation tools.

Regarding factors external to the tools, international factors are noted in several of the chapters, including the perceived need to follow EU requirements (Chapter 9) or align to OECD best practices (Chapter 7) – or, in the case of participatory tools (Chapter 2), the relatively weak compulsion to apply them expressed in some international legal agreements. Legalization as a potential driver of tool use is also noted in a number of chapters (including 6 and 7). In the UK and Canada, Chapters 7 and 8 respectively suggest that pressure from ministries of finance lies behind the relative popularity of CBA. By contrast, the use of MCA, indicators and most participatory tools is less likely to be mandatory (Chapters 2 and 6). Consequently, there is a live debate on what can be gained (and also conceded – see Chapter 2) by legislating to force tool use. Finally, the fit between a tool and its external environment (including the policy design space) appears to be a critical determinant of the extent to which they are used in policy formulation. The fit can, of course, be manipulated by any of the actors discussed above.

To conclude, there do appear to be clear and discernible patterns in the way that policy formulation tools are used. Whether one starts with the tools and looks across to the venues (in other words, Chapters 2–7) or explores different combinations of tools in and across particular venues (in other words, Chapters 8–12), the patterns seem to recur and hence in principle seem worthy of further exploration. Indeed, one especially intriguing possibility is that the most significant differentiating factor may eventually be policy type, not venue, something which was not fully captured in Figure 1.1. A number of chapters (including 4, 6, 8 and 9) reveal that certain types of tools are more commonly deployed in relation to particular policy areas and problems (for example, the correlation between modelling/scenarios and areas of scientific uncertainty such as climate change), but there may be others, as the authors of Chapter 9 imply.

The two questions posed at the beginning of this section on 'venues' may appear rather straightforward. They are of course basically congruent with the two questions that Salamon (1989, p. 265) originally posed, namely: what influences the choice of tools? And what policy consequences ('or effects') does this choice have? Indeed, the first of these – the selection of tools – is to a large extent *the* issue of policy formulation in a nutshell (Howlett – in Hill 2009, p. 176). But they are unlikely to be easy questions to answer; after all, Salamon's intervention has pretty much defined the research agenda in the instruments sub-field for the last 25 years. In a later section, we suggest that the most preferable way to relate these questions to policy formulation tools is to start from a set of sound theoretical bases.

Capacities

Chapter 1 conceived of the relationship between policy capacity and policy formulation tools in three main ways. First, there are the policy-analytic capacities that inhere within each tool; capacities that have already been partially discussed under the subheading of 'venues' above. Thinking more broadly about the main tasks of policy analysis in government – analysing problems, recommending responses, clarifying value choices and under-lying assumptions, democratizing and legitimizing (Mayer et al. 2004, section 7) – it is obvious that each one is associated with different policy formulation tools. The more tools that a policymaker can draw upon, then *ipso facto* the greater her potential policy capacity. In principle, therefore, the presence and availability of policy formulation tools help to expand policy capacities, although we should not automatically assume that the relationship is immediate or unidirectional, as the previous sections have revealed.

Second, the chapters also raise the question of what policy capacities are in turn required by policymakers in order to employ – and perhaps more fundamentally to *select* – certain policy formulation tools. For example, the more rigidly procedural tools such as MCA and CBA are associ-ated with demands for specialist staff, systems of training and oversight. Where these associated capacities are weak or not present, the utilization of the tool may be less effective than expected (see Chapters 8 and 9 for example). Chapter 7 suggests that one – and only one – of the reasons why benefits are more likely to be omitted in CBA calculations is because of the technical difficulty of accounting for them in situations of concentrated costs and dispersed benefits (a typical situation in many regulatory design situations) (Lowi 1972). Less overtly procedural tools such as scenarios and foresight exercises seem to require the presence of somewhat different capacities. For example, in many countries the application of such tools was institutionalized in central planning bureaus from the 1960s and 1970s (Chapter 3). Similarly, one of the prime movers in the dissemination of indicators has been the very national statistical offices that subsequently produce and report on their implementation. Finally (and as noted above), it may be important that national finance ministries and international organizations such as the World Bank and the OECD appear to have been the most enthusiastic adopters and advocates of CBA. Chapter 1 hints at the presence of a self-replicating logic: these ministries first push for the application of such tools and then use evidence of their patchy performance to justify the need for new capacities, such as training, more staff, and/or more oversight functions. The presence of strong associations between certain existing capacities and the selection of new tool capacities may not, therefore, be necessarily unidirectional (in other words, actors select tools) or open (in other words, there may be some inherent bias towards certain types of tools). We return to this point below. Staying for a moment longer at the more generic level, what a focus on these associated capacities may eventually provide is, for example, a means to understand the effects of deploying particular tools, how they might fit into or seek to stretch the existing 'design space' and so on.

Finally, several chapters open up the potentially very broad (but nonetheless important) question of what factors might conceivably enable or constrain the availability of the capacities associated with particular policy formulation tasks. The fact that critical supporting capacities may not automatically be available in all policy systems is raised in several chapters, but especially 8 and 9. For example, the authors of Chapter 8 on policy capacities in Canada demonstrate that the toolkit used is much larger than that summarized in Chapters 2–7. Moreover, they identify a pattern of increasing sophistication in policy analysis as one moves from the non-governmental sector to the governmental one, and from the less 'economic' units of government to the more economically oriented ones. Chapter 9 paints a similar picture of differentiated use across the EU.

To conclude (and as noted in Chapter 1), the term 'policy capacity' has been in good currency in public administration and institutional analysis for many decades (for a summary, see Weaver and Rockman 1993), but is now enjoying renewed interest in the context of the re-discovery of the state as a powerful agent of governing and a site of policy formulation (Howlett et al. 2014, p. 4; Matthews 2012; Jenkins and Patashnik 2012). What the chapters of this book offer is a different way to think about policy capacities, as well as a source of fresh insights into how patterns of capacity availability affect, and are affected by, the availability and use of certain tools. These relationships appear in a rather different form in developing countries and in complex, multi-level governance situations such as the EU, where capacities are inchoate and/or in a particularly strong state of flux (Jordan and Schout 2006; Hertin et al. 2009). In developing countries with weakly developed policy spheres, policy formulation tools such as CBA are promoted as a means of overcoming long legacies of political clientalism. However, those seeking to transplant policy formulation models unmodified from the OECD to such settings should be aware of the need for them to be underpinned by sufficiently strong capacities. Chapter 10 revealed that these tools were much more likely to be available when independent agencies are given control than when this task is allocated to government.

Effects

Finally, Chapters 2–12 examined what effects, both intended and actual, the policy formulation tools produce when they are employed. The policy instruments literature has been struggling to answer this question, at least for implementation instruments, ever since Salamon (2002, p. 2) noted that each instrument imparts its own unique spin or 'twist' on policy. Not surprisingly, the less mature sub-field of policy formulation tools has much work to do in relation to 'effects'. Indeed, one of the striking findings from the tool-focused literatures summarized in Chapters 2–7 is how few of them have even identified it as a priority research topic. Some literatures (around CBA and computer models for example) have made more progress than others, but in general, the level of critical engagement has been low. More often than not, certain effects have simply been presumed to flow from the selection of particular tools (for example, that using CBA results in the identification of the pareto optimal policy solution).

As noted in Chapter 1, this collective failure probably has much to do with the disciplinary background of the contributors, but it also reflects an entirely understandable desire to stay anchored in the relatively clear-cut world of textbooks and typologies. Nonetheless, the chapters do suggest some potentially useful categorizations that could form the basis of future work. For example (and drawing on Turnpenny et al. (2009, p. 648)), a broad distinction can be drawn between 'substantive' effects (the extent to which tools generate change – or work to ensure continuity – in a given policy field) and 'process-based' effects (in other words, system-wide effects which arise from the use of particular tools). A wide array of *substantive* effects are flagged up in the chapters, ranging from learning around new means to achieve policy goals (predominant amongst tools such as CBA, but also computer modelling) to heuristic-conceptual effects on problem understandings (see for example Chapters 2 and 5). Large-scale, system-wide energy models may play an important role in facilitating adjustments to new 'policy images', through the development of new policy paradigms and policy objectives (Chapter 12). More fundamentally, some tools (for example, participatory backcasting) have been developed with the avowed aim of facilitating 'out of the box thinking', that restructures actor preferences in a profound way. Meanwhile, the *procedural effects* are potentially also very wide ranging. For example, Chapter 11 argues that indicators help to channel political attention – especially among overloaded oversight bodies – such that a 'broader critique' of the policy status quo becomes less and less likely. In addition, some participatory tools such as the devil's advocate technique and participatory backcasting have the aim of generating new understandings and uncovering extant political power relationships.

A second important distinction relates to the difference between intended and unintended effects. We have already noted the difference between the 'imagined' effects that the advocates of tools aspire to provide (to use the terminology employed by Atkinson in Chapter 7) and their 'actual use'. In some of the chapters, the unintended effects are presented positively (as new problem framings – see Chapters 2 and 4 for example) whereas in others, they are presented much more negatively (for example 'gaming the system', 'closing down' debate, and nurturing 'reductionist' thinking are all noted in Chapter 4). To a large extent, the difference is one of prior expectations, purposes and ultimately values. Thus, by their very nature, the more procedurally inflexible tools such as CBA appear more prone to performance deficits. But more open, participatory tools can also produce unexpected effects; for example, Chapter 2 recounts how backcasting approaches all too easily entrench political differences and forms of participation. Consequently, the new sub-field of policy formulation research should be careful to pose more probing questions (for example, unexpected by whom and why?) rather than assume that everything which is unexpected is necessarily bad (or the opposite!). Finally, some effects may be extremely difficult to categorize. For example, Chapter 11 tells the story of how, paradoxically, in the case of indicators, 'a set of tools designed to shift the political focus onto outcomes was deployed in a way that resulted in a preoccupation with process'.

To conclude, understanding effects arguably constitutes the biggest analytical challenge of all, but one which the nascent sub-field of policy formulation is beginning to engage with. Chapters 2–12 already suggest that it will require very careful and patient diachronic forms of analysis (cf. Owens et al. 2004), sensitive to the multiple rationalities that motivate actors to use particular tools in the first place. At present, there remains a definitive 'pro-use' bias in the tools literatures (indeed Chapters 5 and 6 explicitly focus on known examples of use). Indeed, the authors of Chapter 2 argue that political elites may be reluctant to explore the potential of more open participatory tools and methods that typically aim at opening up current problem framing and thus imperil their control. Yet experts in policy formulation tools may also be unwittingly sustaining this blind spot, especially if (as seems to be the case for participatory tools and to a lesser extent for indicators) they cannot agree on what their purpose should be, hence the prevalence of very open evaluation criteria that are extremely difficult to apply.

THEORIZING POLICY FORMULATION TOOLS: RE-ASSEMBLING THE PIECES

In this section we explore some of the issues raised above through three different theoretical lenses, with the aim of both grounding the findings within established theoretical traditions, and using the findings to highlight particular gaps in each theory. Both approaches lead to a range of promising new research questions.

If all tools embody an 'implicit political theory' which provides both a *raison d'être* for policy analysis and a causal account of how it should proceed (Weale 2001, p. 378), then the theory informing many studies and practices of policy formulation is a rational–instrumental one: '[t]he idea is one of a linear process in which a problem exists, information is lacking, [tools] produce information, and the decision maker can eventually decide' (Radaelli 2004, p. 743). Rational theories have constituted such a significant theme of policy analysis since the 1950s that they represent an obvious stepping off point for those wishing to think afresh about policy formulation (Howlett et al. 2014) and other aspects of the 'new' policy design (Howlett and Lejano 2013). In what follows, we therefore start with this theoretical lens before moving onto two very different ones.

Policy Formulation as Rationality

Although policy analysts long ago dispensed with the notion that policymakers are rational in the sense of having very clear and stable views of means and ends, a sense of rationality lives on in many contemporary frameworks such as policy learning, knowledge utilization, evidence-based policymaking and policy instrument selection and use. Selecting tools in a more or less rational fashion to achieve policy formulation goals and tasks clearly corresponds to what Weiss (1979, p. 427) identified as a 'problem-solving model' of knowledge utilization.

Scholars who wish to study policy formulation tools from a more or less rational standpoint will find a number of reasons to do so. First of all, it offers an intuitively straightforward basis on which to typologize tools. Our proposed typology is, after all, inherently rationalistic in its conception of the intersection of means and ends. Although it offers an incomplete guide to tool choices in practice, it may be regarded as a good starting point all the same.

Second (and related to the above), more rational theories offer a means to engage in normative policy analysis (in other words, 'analysis for' policy). To varying degrees of explicitness, rational assumptions pervade the thoughts of those who produce tool handbooks, supply (in other words, develop) tools and/or 'compliance test' their performance (for example, de Ridder et al. 2007, pp. 430–431). In fact, the original purpose of tools was to base decisions on rational arguments and evidence, instead of bargaining and political interests (Chapter 1; see also Turnpenny et al. (2009, p. 644)). Even if this normative ideal is rarely observed, it behoves of policy analysts to explain the divergence. And there is also the question of why rationalism appears to appeal so strongly to politicians and (perhaps in a somewhat different way) to scholars of policy design, on which more below.

Third, the rationality or otherwise of policy formulation also encourages scholars to think about tool choices in and across different venues. Were rationality dominant, we would expect policy formulators to select tools to match problem types and policy formulation tasks, rather than repeatedly rely upon the same tool (Linder and Peters 1989, p. 37). Different actors may prioritize different kinds of knowledge depending on, among other things, their core preferences and whether they are in the public, private or third sectors. Furthermore, actors operating in venues at different levels of governance might be expected to seek out different types of knowledge. For example, actors at EU and UK levels of decision making appear to seek out a more strategic overview of drivers and impacts (Turnpenny et al. 2014), whereas those charged with implementing policy at the 'street' level tend to be more heavily influenced by their client groups (Haines-Young and Potschin 2014).

Of course politics repeatedly intrudes into the operation of all tools – even the most explicitly 'rational' ones such as CBA. One of the most active debates in the CBA literature (see Chapters 7 and 10), is around the apparent asymmetry between cost and benefit predictions *ex ante* versus *ex post*. Is this genuinely the product of 'appraisal optimism' amongst policy analysts (Chapter 7), or because of special interests crying wolf over cost estimates? Although specific examples of policy formulation may not follow a rational–instrumental form, many of the chapters in Part II nonetheless reveal a surprisingly strong element of purposiveness in the selection and use of policy tools in general. Many detect a rather limited use of more sophisticated modelling-based tools, which suggests that some actors may be following the (rational) principle of proportionality, that is, using tools only where and when significant impacts and/or high levels of uncertainty are expected.

Fourth, if the main purpose of policy appraisal is to 'make institutions think differently' (Radaelli 2007, p. 3), then policy formulation tools are an obvious means to extend their collective 'regulatory imagination' (Dunlop 2014, p. 215). Rationalism thus encourages analysts to consider what types of tools generate what types of learning in particular venues (Turnpenny et al. 2009, p. 648). There are many types and degrees of policy learning (Dunlop 2014, pp. 210–211), and potentially many different research designs that could be employed to probe them. One approach is to follow Chapter 12 and trace out the use of a single tool across different policy venues. Chapter 12 found that the MARKAL energy model has provided opportunities for (conceptual) learning and helped to rationalize pre-existing policy decisions (in other words, more political uses of knowledge). Causality is, of course, very difficult to pin down in such studies, particularly as regards the more conceptual forms of use which regularly extend over long periods of time. Policy formulators may themselves also unwittingly compound this problem by refusing to reveal sources, especially in relation to the more symbolic and political categories of use. Nonetheless, these analytical challenges – which are well known to scholars of learning and knowledge utilization – will have to be confronted if scholars of policy formulation tools are to move beyond broad brush explanations of selection and adoption couched in Cash et al.'s (2002) terms of 'credibility, salience and legitimacy' (see Chapters 3 and 4).

Policy Formulation as Control

A rather different lens through which to study the interaction of actors, venues, capacities and effects is that of executive oversight and/or political control over non-majoritarian agencies (Turnpenny et al. 2009, p. 645). This idea was originally elaborated with the USA in mind, and has since been tested on the UK by Froud et al. (1998) and on the EU by Radaelli and Meuwese (2010). According to an extensive literature (for a summary, see Thatcher and Stone Sweet (2002)), elected politicians actively promote the use of certain policy formulation tools in order to:

- Provide information on whether departments and agencies, or supranational bodies such as the European Commission, are operating in venues and in ways which damage important political constituencies;
- Prevent these bodies from being captured by vested interests, engaging in overzealous implementation and/or presenting their political masters with a policy *fait accompli*;

- Build delay into the policy system, thereby permitting greater oversight and ensuring political legitimacy. (Radaelli and de Francesco
  2010, p. 284)

Several chapters in this book draw on the terminology of political control
to highlight certain tool-related tasks and thus explain the development
and utilization of certain kinds of tool. The classic example is of course
CBA, the use of which is legally prescribed in many countries. Other
than indicators (Chapters 4 and 11) and certain types of risk analysis, no
other policy formulation tool consistently enjoys such high-level political
backing. A focus on political control can, however, also help to explain
the emergence of more process-based tools such as forms of participatory assessment. According to Chapter 2, some were originally developed
(and are now widely deployed) to deal with 'an angry public'. Indeed focus
groups, consensus conferences and forms of brainstorming are used much
later in the policy process too, chiefly to secure sufficient public support for
the policy option which is eventually selected at the end of the formulation
stage.

There are, however, many important questions still to be addressed by
those seeking to move the new sub-field in this theoretical direction. First
of all, while political control may be the means through which certain
tools are imposed on agencies, theories of control do not fully account for
why politicians learn about, and over time become committed to, them
in the first place. Both the chapters on indicators (Chapter 4) and CBA
(Chapter 7) imply that diffusion partly occurs via softer channels of influence, such as guidelines, best practice examples and academic networks
(Benson and Jordan 2011). Related to that (and building on the findings
of Chapter 9), it is important to explain why only certain countries, policy
sectors and/or policy venues are so heavily populated with tools of control
such as CBA, whereas in others their use is virtually absent. It should
therefore be possible to start with theories of comparative politics such as
political control of bureaucracies, and use policy formulation tools as a
case study (Turnpenny et al. 2009, p. 647). It will be especially intriguing to
try to explain how far the adoption of tools that 'open up' debate and challenge the status quo can be explained using theories of political control.

Second, just because agencies and departments are required to employ
formulation tools does not necessarily mean that they will faithfully use
them. Chapter 9 suggests that tools constitute 'an incomplete contract'
between principals and agents that can be actively shaped by the latter.
The notion of 'perfunctory' forms of usage invites further work, perhaps
linked to the idea that some agents might be following rituals of verifica-
tion (Radaelli and de Francesco 2010, p. 282), as manifest in the tendency

for some tools to be used in a manner that departs significantly from the guidance in the handbooks and textbooks. One possible explanation is that bureaucrats in the agencies actively resist political control. Another is that they might like to use tools, but lack the policy capacities to do so (Russel and Jordan 2009). Finally, it might be that all policy formulation tools are prone to suffer some unintended consequences, no matter how much political backing or force they enjoy. This observation is certainly one of the explanations offered by Boswell et al. to account for the use of indicators in the UK (Chapter 11).

Finally, there are opportunities to build links between the rationality and control perspectives in order to explain how policy formulators resist the imposition of political control. Do they, for example, employ the tool (for example, CBA) as required, but in a manner that utilizes knowledge in a politically advantageous way? One of the emerging debates within the CBA community (Chapter 7) is how and why policy knowledge is fed into assessments in a form that suits particular actors (for example, target groups seeking laxer regulation, or eligible regions bidding for greater state spending).

Policy Formulation Tools as Institutions

A third perspective views policy formulation tools as institutions in themselves that over time generate enduring policy feedback effects. In comparison with theories emphasizing control and rationality, this perspective challenges the sense of linearity apparent in many tool literatures and of course our own tool typology. From this perspective, as they are used, tools gradually take on a life of their own. Tools do, as noted above, seem to incorporate a particular logic or view of the world. Those employing them will, therefore, tend to conceive of problems in a way that perpetuates their use. Over time, tools tend to develop 'tool constituencies' that have invested time and resources in furthering their use; a pattern that only becomes fully apparent when their long-term 'careers' are studied over time (Lascoumes and Le Galés 2007, p. 17). To the extent that tools are not politically neutral, this body of theory suggests that they deserve to be treated as causal factors in their own right (Kassim and Le Galés 2010, p. 5; Radaelli and Meuwese 2010). For example, in terms of the choice between tools, technical effectiveness considerations will not necessarily be the dominant criteria; sometimes instruments may determine preferences (not the other way around).

In some respects, this approach corresponds to the self-sustaining logic that appears to have been at work in the way that certain tools have created a need for more policy specialists in government – think, for example, of how the need for skills in CBA has grown (at least relatively) in the last 10 years, as government in general has shrunk (Mintrom and Williams 2013, p. 7). Indeed in several chapters, references are explicitly made to tool constituencies (Voss and Simons 2014) (for example, the 'indicator industry' – Chapter 4), which have a stake in the development of a particular policy formulation approach, as distinct to their commitment to a particular policy objective or level of governance. In Chapter 2 the claim was made that certain participatory tools evolve slowly over time, pushed by particular advocates. Schick (1977, p. 261) was one of the first to raise this point when he argued that the policy analysis community had fragmented into different tool-focused sections that engage in 'tireless tinkering' (Schick 1977, p. 261) with 'their' preferred tools and methods. At the time, he claimed that their main effect was to bewilder policymakers. In fact, the effects may be more complex; they may, for example, open the door to policy influence. Dunlop (2014, p. 212), for example, has noted how certain tools confer legitimacy on (or 'certify') particular knowledge claims made by particular actors. CBA, for example, is well known amongst environmentalists for having a much greater ability to 'clinch' policy debates than other tools (Owens and Cowell 2002). This may explain why some environmentalists actively seek out opportunities to employ such tools to ensure their own knowledge claims are equally valid and hence usable (Dunlop 2014, p. 213).

In Chapter 2, however, a slightly different set of claims was made in relation to tool-specific constituencies. For example, over time participatory conferences and conflict avoidance tools, as well as certain computerized models (see Chapter 12), might develop such a strong set of political backers that they gradually morph into new policy venues. Or advocates of different tools compete for political attention and funding, or even engage in a much deeper ideological battle with one another (see Chapter 2). The manner in which newer tools such as MCA and scenarios have gradually emerged as a reaction to the more mainstream tools such as CBA and models, could conceivably be explained in much the same way.

In comparison to the other two, this perspective has rather mixed theoretical roots, drawing on political sociology (Lascoumes and Le Galés 2007; Voss and Simons 2014), systems thinking (Jordan and Matt 2014), historical institutionalism (Wurzel et al. 2013) and social constructivism (Hajer 1995). Future work might therefore profitably explore the relationship between actors, venues, capacities and effects in a more precise and systematic fashion. For example, in some situations politicians are assumed to select certain tools to conceal their true motives, whereas in others they appear to do so in order to reveal them (Kassim and Le Galés 2010, p. 10). This suggests that actors may have different and to an extent unique tool preferences – a matter which we considered in section 2 above.

Following the careers of particular tools is unlikely to uncover the specific tool choices at work; but analysing the choice between tools may do (an approach, for example, adopted in Chapters 8 and 9).

Second, and related to that, there do appear to be discernible patterns in the selection and use of tools that seem a lot more functional than this theoretical perspective seems able fully to account for. Indeed, it struggles to account for the appearance of entirely new tools; if self-replication were entirely dominant, the scope for tool innovation would be minuscule. The impression given, however, is that new tools emerge in the wake of crisis events.

CONCLUSIONS, NEW PERSPECTIVES AND NEW CHALLENGES

Over thirty years after Hood (1983) published his landmark book on policy tools, political and academic interest in them remains as high as ever. Many definitions, taxonomies and explanatory theories have been developed. However, public policy researchers have somehow managed collectively to overlook an entire class of policy-relevant tools. To policy *instruments* and *procedural* tools, we should now add the 'new' sub-category of *policy formulation* tools. In the 1970s and 1980s, certain types of policy formulation tool fell out of academic and political fashion and many observers assumed – understandably – that they were no longer relevant or could even be quietly forgotten.

Having looked – as we have done for the first time in this book – across the main types of policy formulation tool, we can confidently conclude that they are not in decline and nor have they been consigned to the dusty shelves of Self's (1981) backroom. On the contrary, they have expanded in number and their use has multiplied across many different venues. Recalling Salamon's argument that there has been a 'massive proliferation' in the tools of government, policy researchers should appreciate that the revolution in tool use was actually even more 'remarkable' than he claimed (Salamon 2002, p. 609). Why? Because he neglected to add the tools of policy formulation to his stock take.

Nevertheless, the existing literatures on policy formulation tools remain fragmented, not only across the main tool types but also different disciplines. For policy analysts, the divide between those tool experts seeking to pursue research 'on policy' and those preferring to undertake analyses 'for policy' seems even more pronounced than in other comparable sub-areas of policy analysis such as policy instruments. Indeed, the chapters of this book have more fully revealed that the debate amongst the policy analysts about tools can, on occasions, be as heated as that relating to policy goals and objectives (Mintrom and Williams 2013, p. 13), relating to both technical matters such as definitions and typologies, but also extending to more fundamental ontological and normative matters.

The tools summarized in the chapters of this book are very different to the ones that emerged in earlier eras, reinforcing the need for a fresh look. Indeed many have emerged out of, and been actively informed by, the critique emerging from the democratic theorists and the post-positivists. This book seeks to reinvigorate our understanding by drawing them back into the mainstream. For this, analysts require common concepts, parsimonious definitions and usable taxonomies. In this and the opening chapter we have sought to supply and then critically reflect on all three. We now invite readers to apply, test and critique them, perhaps using the theoretical perspectives outlined above; perspectives that we feel should, in time, be more fully integrated into broader theories of the policy process. Of course at the level of specific tools, debate about definitions, typologies and purposes will doubtless continue. We see that as a healthy sign, but believe that agreement at the broader level is now needed to generate a common and hopefully more fruitful research agenda, perhaps organized around our framework of actors, venues, capacities and effects.

What stands to be gained by embarking on a more systematic approach to the study of policy formulation tools? In Chapter 1 we suggested that there is potentially much more to add to our collective understanding of the tools themselves which, as repeatedly noted throughout this book, have often been studied in a rather isolated, static and descriptive manner. At the time of this writing it is very difficult to answer questions about tool choices and effects that Salamon challenged scholars of policy instruments to address many decades ago. It is also very difficult to work out how policy formulation tools interact with other tools and instruments (Howlett 2011, p. 27). Thinking more generally about forms of analyses for policy, the policy formulation tools literature has much ground to make up in relation to prescriptive advice on the selection and mixing of tools. At present there are no maxims (Howlett et al. 2014) of the type found in the policy instruments literature (for example, escalate slowly up the pyramid of intervention) or meta-tools to inform the design of tool packages. Clearly, inconsistencies between some tool pairings are more obvious than between others. MCA and participatory approaches do seem to mix more freely with one another than, for example, CBA and scenarios. But there is plenty of fresh work to be done on whether and indeed why this might be the case.

Second, in Chapter 1 we argued that a renewed focus on policy formulation tools can add to our collective understanding not only of policy formulation but public policy more generally. Of all the stages of the policy processes, policy formulation is arguably the one we know the least about. It is often complex, fluid and usually much less accessible to public scrutiny than other stages. Looking through the prism of tools is methodologically advantageous in the sense that, drawing on Hood (1983, pp. 115–131), it reduces complexity and permits comparisons to be made more easily across time, and between different policy areas and political systems. The chapters in this book have, we think, shown the potential of a 'tools approach' to shed new light on these issues. They confirm that the tools play a significant role in structuring policymaking activity and in determining the content of policy outputs and thus policy outcomes. The chapters also suggest that the tools are vital aspects not only of policy design, but also the nascent debate about policy capacities (Howlett 2011, p. 146).

Third, we have suggested that studying policy formulation tools more intensively may – paradoxically – add something to our collective understanding of politics; 'paradoxically' because the tools were originally conceived as a means to take the political heat *out* of policymaking. The chapters of this book have confirmed that the politics around policy formulation tools are, by their nature, often more subtle than those emerging around policy instruments, but they are no less important for it. Moreover, the chapters have shown that even if tool choices seldom make political headlines, over time they can have profound effects on the way problems are conceptualized and policy recommendations made to decision makers. They have also more fully revealed how they are used to control line agencies and depoliticize areas of policymaking. Policy formulation is the point in the policy process when the political commitment to 'do something' expressed during agenda setting runs into the constraints and the opportunities of the status quo. Long ago, Dahl and Lindblom (1953, pp. 16–18) argued that instruments lie at the very heart of the public policy process. Rather than debating in terms of grand ideologies such as capitalism and socialism, policy actors communicate in the more technical language of regulations, taxes and so on. A tools perspective offers insights into governing beyond formal rules, administrative systems and constitutions. Academics, scientists, policy consultants and think tanks were shown to play a determinative role. Matters of policy formulation are often not publicly debated, but the tools used and the effects they eventually generate undeniably involve questions of political power and the distribution of social values, and as such deserve to be a subject of analysis in their own right.

Finally, the chapters have suggested that bringing the tools into the mainstream of policy research may also help us to learn more about ourselves and our multidisciplinary field of policy analysis. To tell the story of policy formulation tools is to tell of the emergence and professionalization of policy analysis. From their origins in the 1940s, the popularity of the tools waxed and waned. They were originally developed by economists, statisticians and systems analysts to 'speak the truth to power' (Goodin et al. 2006, p. 7). As we pointed out in Chapter 1, their designers and advocates fell short in delivering upon their undoubted promise and they were conveniently forgotten about by many public policy scholars. When and why this happened is a story that deserves to be told as part of the broader 'turn back' to policy formulation tools.

REFERENCES

Bähr, H. (2010), *The Politics of Means and Ends*, Farnham: Ashgate.

Benson, D. and A.J. Jordan (2011), 'What have we learned from policy transfer research? Dolowitz and Marsh revisited', *Political Studies Review*, **9** (3), 366–378.

Cash, D., W. Clark, F. Alcock, N. Dickson, N. Eckley and J. Jäger (2002), *Salience, Credibility, Legitimacy and Boundaries: Linking Research, Assessment and Decision Making*. Faculty Research Working Papers Series RWP02-046, Harvard: John F. Kennedy School of Government.

Craft, J. and M. Howlett (2012), 'Policy formulation, governance shifts and policy influence: location and content in policy advisory systems', *Journal of Public Policy*, **32** (2), 79–98.

Dahl, R. and C. Lindblom (1953), *Politics, Economics and Welfare*, New York: Harpers.

de Ridder, W., J. Turnpenny, M. Nilsson and A. von Raggamby (2007), 'A framework for tool selection and use in integrated assessment for sustainable development', *Journal of Environmental Assessment Policy and Management*, **9**, 423–441.

Doern, B. and R. Phidd (1992), *Canadian Public Policy: Ideas, Structure, Process*, Toronto, ON: Nelson.

Dunlop, C. (2014), 'The possible experts: how epistemic communities negotiate barriers to knowledge use in ecosystems services policy', *Environment and Planning C*, **32** (2), 208–228.

Dunn, W. (2004), *Public Policy Analysis: An Introduction*, Upper Saddle River, NJ: Pearson/Prentice Hall.

Eliadis, P., M. Hill and M. Howlett (2007), 'Introduction', in P. Eliadis, M. Hill and M. Howlett (eds), *Designing Government: From Instruments to Governance*, Montreal: McGill Queens University Press, pp. 3–20.

Froud, J., R. Boden, A. Ogus and P. Stubbs (1998), *Controlling the Regulators*, Basingstoke: Macmillan.

Goodin, R., M. Moran and M. Rein (2006), 'The public and its policies', in M. Moran, M. Rein and R. Goodin (eds), *The Oxford Handbook of Public Policy*, Oxford: Oxford University Press, pp. 3–35.

Haines-Young, R. and M. Potschin (2014), 'The ecosystems approach as a framework for understanding knowledge utilisation', *Environment and Planning C*, **32** (2), 301–319.

Hajer, M. (1995), *The Politics of Environmental Discourse*, Oxford: Oxford University Press.

Hertin, J., J. Turnpenny, M. Jordan, A. Nilsson, B. Nykvist and D. Russel (2009), 'Rationalising the policy mess? The role of ex ante policy assessment and the utilization of knowledge in the policy process', *Environment and Planning A*, **41** (5), 1185–1200.

Hill, M. (2009), *The Public Policy Process*, 5th edition, Abingdon: Routledge.

Hood, C. (1983), *The Tools of Government*, London: Macmillan.

Howlett, M. (2000), 'Managing the hollow state. Procedural policy instruments and modern governance', *Canadian Public Administration*, **43** (4), 412–431.

Howlett, M. (2011), *Designing Public Policies: Principles and Instruments*, Abingdon: Routledge.

Howlett, M. and R. Lejano (2013), 'Tales from the crypt: the rise and fall (and rebirth?) of policy design', *Administration and Society*, **45** (3), 357–381.

Howlett, M., J.J. Woo and I. Mukherjee (2014), 'From tools to toolkits in policy design studies: the new design orientation towards policy formulation research', *Policy and Politics*, **42**, http://dx.doi.org/10.1332/147084414X13992869118596.

Jenkins, J. and E. Patashnik (eds) (2012), *Living Legislation*, Chicago: University of Chicago Press.

Jordan, A. and E. Matt (2014), 'Designing policies that intentionally stick: policy feedback in a changing climate', *Policy Sciences*, **47** (3), 227–247.

Jordan, A. and A. Schout (2006), *The Coordination of the European Union*, Oxford: Oxford University Press.

Jordan, A., R. Wurzel and A. Zito (2013), 'Still the century of "new" environmental policy instruments? Exploring patterns of innovation and continuity', *Environmental Politics*, **22** (1), 155–173.

Kassim, H. and P. Le Galés (2010), 'Exploring governance in a multi-level polity', *West European Politics*, **33** (1), 1–22.

Lascoumes, P. and P. Le Galés (2007), 'Introduction: understanding public policy through its instruments', *Governance*, **20** (1), 1–22.

Linder, S. and B.G. Peters (1989), 'Instruments of government', *Journal of Public Policy*, **9** (1), 35–58.

Lowi, T. (1972), 'Four systems of policy, politics and choice', *Public Administration Review*, **32** (4), 298–310.

Matthews, F. (2012), 'Governance and state capacity', in D. Levi-Faur (ed.), *The Oxford Handbook of Governance*, Oxford: Oxford University Press, pp. 281–293.

Mayer, I.S., C.E. van Daalen and P.W.G. Bots (2004), 'Perspectives on policy analyses', *International Journal of Policy and Management*, **4** (2), 169–191.

Meltsner, A.J. (1976), *Policy Analysts in the Bureaucracy*, Berkeley: University of California Press.

Mintrom, M. and C. Williams (2013), 'Public policy debate and the rise of policy analysis', in E. Araral, S. Fritzen, M. Howlett, M. Ramesh and X. Wu (eds), *Routledge Handbook of Public Policy*, London: Routledge, pp. 3–16.

Nilsson, M., A. Jordan, J. Turnpenny, J. Hertin, B. Nykvist and D. Russel (2008), 'The use and non-use of policy appraisal tools in public policy making', *Policy Sciences*, **41** (4), 335–355.

Owens, S. and R. Cowell (2002), *Land and Limits: Interpreting Sustainability in the Planning Process*, London and New York: Routledge.

Owens, S., T. Rayner and O. Bina (2004), 'New agendas for appraisal: reflections on theory, practice and research', *Environment and Planning A*, **36**, 1943–1959.

Peters, B.G. (2002), 'The politics of choice', in L. Salamon (ed.), *Tools of Government*, Oxford: Oxford University Press, pp. 552–564.

Radaelli, C. (1995), 'The role of knowledge in the policy process', *Journal of European Public Policy*, **2**, 159–183.

Radaelli, C. (2004), 'The diffusion of regulatory impact analysis: best practice or lesson-drawing?', *European Journal of Political Research*, **43**, 723–747.

Radaelli, C. (2007), 'Whither better regulation for the Lisbon Agenda?', *Journal of European Public Policy*, **14**, 190–207.

Radaelli, C. and F. de Francesco (2010), 'Regulatory impact assessment', in R. Baldwin, M. Cave and M. Lodge (eds), *Oxford Handbook of Regulation*, Oxford: OUP, pp. 279–301.

Radaelli, C. and A. Meuwese (2010), 'Hard questions, hard solutions: proceduralisation through impact assessment', *West European Politics*, **33** (1), 136–153.

Radin, B. (2013), *Beyond Machiavelli*, Washington DC: Georgetown University Press.

Russel, D. and A. Jordan (2009), 'Joining up or pulling apart? The use of appraisal to coordinate policy making for sustainable development', *Environment and Planning A*, **41** (5), 1201–1216.

Salamon, L. (1989), *Beyond Privatisation*, Washington: Urban Institute Press.

Salamon, L. (2002), 'The new governance and the tools of public action: an introduction', in L. Salamon (ed.), *Tools of Government*, Oxford: Oxford University Press, pp. 1–47.

Schick, A. (1977), 'Beyond analysis', *Public Administration Review*, **37** (3), 258–263.

Self, P. (1981), 'Planning: rational or political?', in P. Baehr and B. Wittrock (eds), *Policy Analysis and Policy Innovation*, London: Sage, pp. 221–236.

Stirling, A. (2008), '"Opening up" and "closing down" power, participation, and pluralism in the social appraisal of technology', *Science, Technology, and Human Values*, **33** (2), 262–294.

Thatcher, M. and A. Stone Sweet (eds) (2002), *The Politics of Delegation*, London: Routledge.

Turnpenny, J., D. Russel and A.J. Jordan (2014), 'The challenge of embedding an ecosystems approach: patterns of knowledge utilisation in public policy appraisal', *Environment and Planning C*, **32** (2), 247–262.

Turnpenny, J., C.M. Radaelli, A. Jordan and K. Jacob (2009), 'The policy and politics of policy appraisal: emerging trends and new directions', *Journal of European Public Policy*, **16** (4), 640–653.

Vining, A.R. and D.L. Weimer (2010), 'Foundations of public administration: policy analysis', *Public Administration Review, Foundations of Public Administration Series*, retrieved from http://www.aspanet.org/public/ASPADocs/PAR/FPA/FPA-Policy-Article.pdf (accessed 20 January 2014).

Voss, J-P. and A. Simons (2014), 'Instrument constituencies and the supply side of policy innovation', *Environmental Politics*, **23** (5), 735–754.

Weale, A. (2001), 'Science advice, democratic responsiveness and public policy', *Science and Public Policy*, **28**, 413–421.

Weaver, R.K. and B. Rockman (1993), *Do Institutions Matter?*, Washington: The Brooking Institute.

Weiss, C. (1979), 'The many meanings of research utilization', *Public Administration Review*, **39**, 426–431.

Wildavsky, A. (1979), *Speaking Truth to Power: The Art and Craft of Policy Analysis*, Boston: Little, Brown.
Wurzel, R.K.W., A.R. Zito and A.J. Jordan (2013), *Environmental Governance in Europe: A Comparative Analysis of New Environmental Policy Instruments*, Cheltenham, UK and Northampton, MA, USA: Edward Elgar Publishing.

Index